MacArthur's Jungle War

MODERN WAR STUDIES

Theodore A. Wilson
General Editor

Raymond A. Callahan
J. Garry Clifford
Jacob W. Kipp
Jay Luvaas
Allan R. Millett
Dennis Showalter
Series Editors

MacARTHUR'S JUNGLE WAR

The 1944 New Guinea Campaign

Stephen R. Taaffe

University Press of Kansas

Published by the University Press of Kansas (Lawrence, Kansas 66049),
which was organized by the Kansas Board of Regents and is operated and
funded by Emporia State University, Fort Hays State University, Kansas State
University, Pittsburg State University, the University of Kansas, and
Wichita State University

Library of Congress Cataloging-in-Publication Data

Taaffe, Stephen.
    MacArthur's jungle war : the 1944 New Guinea campaign / Stephen
Taaffe.
        p.   cm. — (Modern war studies)
    Includes bibliographical references and index.
    ISBN 0-7006-0870-2 (alk. paper)
    1. World War, 1939–1945—Campaigns—New Guinea.   2. MacArthur,
Douglas, 1880–1964.   I. Title.   II. Series.
    D767.95.T316   1997
    940.54'26—dc21   97-25228

British Library Cataloguing in Publication Data is available.

Printed in the United States of America

10   9   8   7   6   5   4   3   2   1

The paper used in this publication meets the minimum requirements of the
American National Standard for Permanence of Paper for Printed Library
Materials Z39.48-1984.

CONTENTS

ACKNOWLEDGMENTS

Although authors should always take sole responsibility for their work, research and writing are rarely solo endeavors. In writing this book I had the help and advice of many talented people. It started as a dissertation under the tutelage of Dr. Marvin Fletcher, whose good humor and sage guidance counterbalanced his often blunt criticism. Ryan Johnson, Ron Paulson, Scott Kaufman, Dr. Donald Jordan, Dr. Katherine Jellison, Dr. Sung Kim, Dr. William Leary, Dr. Eric Bergerud, and Dr. Chester Pach also read through the work and offered sound advice. I am especially grateful to Dr. Pach for his help in the publication process. Ohio University's Contemporary History Institute paid for some of my research trips, and the archivists at United States Army Military History Institute, United States Military Academy, Duke University, Washington National Records Center, and the Douglas MacArthur Memorial Archives provided invaluable aid and information. In addition, I am thankful for the patience and kindness of my editor, Michael Briggs, and the folks at the University Press of Kansas.

I also want to thank my wife, Cynthia, for being there when things were difficult, and my parents for starting me down the educational road. I inherited my love of history from my dad, and to him this work is dedicated.

ABBREVIATIONS

A-20	Small two-man light bomber
AAF	Army Air Forces
APD	High-Speed Transport (Destroyer)
AWOL	absent without leave
B-24	American heavy bomber
B-25	American light bomber
B-29	American long-range heavy bomber
BAR	Browning automatic rifle
C-47	American DC-3 cargo plane
C-54	American DC-4 cargo plane
CCS	Combined Chiefs of Staff
CNO	Chief of Naval Operations
EBSR	Engineer Boat and Shore Regiment
ESB	Engineer Special Brigade
G-1	Personnel
G-2	Intelligence
G-3	Planning
G-4	Logistics and supply
GHQ	General Headquarters
JCS	Joint Chiefs of Staff
JMTC	Joint Military Transportation Committee
JPS	Joint Staff Planners
JSSC	Joint Strategic Survey Committee
JWPC	Joint War Plans Committee
LCI	Landing craft, infantry
LCM	Landing craft, mechanized
LCVP	Landing craft, vehicle, personnel
LST	Landing ship, tank
LVT	Landing vehicle, tracked
MP	Military Police
P-38	American single-seat fighter
P-39	American single-seat fighter
P-40	American and Australian single-seat fighter

POA	Pacific Ocean Areas
PT boat	Patrol torpedo boat
RAAF	Royal Australian Air Force
RCT	Regimental Combat Team
SOPAC	South Pacific Area Command
SWPA	Southwest Pacific Area
TF	Task Force
WAC	Women's Auxiliary Corps

CHRONOLOGY

JANUARY 1944

27   Pearl Harbor conference begins

FEBRUARY

1   POA troops storm Kwajalein in the Marshall Islands
18   Marines land at Eniwetok in the Marshall Islands
24   MacArthur orders Krueger to invade Los Negros with
      reconnaissance-in-force by the end of February
29   Chase's 5th Cav lands at Hyane Harbor

MARCH

4   Big Japanese assault on the Los Negros beachhead
12   JCS decides on a dual drive offensive toward the China-Formosa-
      Luzon area
15   7th and 8th Cavs land at Lugos on Manus Island
25   MacArthur and Nimitz meet in Brisbane to discuss the POA role in
      the Hollandia operation
27   Rossum falls to the 1st Cavalry Division
30   Kenney launches the first surprise air attack against Hollandia
      airdromes

APRIL

18   Pacific Shipping Conference begins in Washington
22   Hollandia-Aitape landings
26   Hollandia's airdromes fall

MAY

17   163rd RCT lands at Toem
18   Wakde Island assaulted
21   158th RCT arrives at Toem
22   Nyaparake evacuated by the 127th RCT
23   158th RCT begins its advance on Lone Tree Hill

27   162nd and 186th RCTs land at Biak
28   158th RCT withdraws from Lone Tree Hill
      162nd RCT ambushed on its way to Mokmer airdrome
29   162nd RCT evacuated by sea back to Bosnek
31   Most of 163rd RCT arrives at Biak to reinforce Fuller

JUNE

1   Fuller begins new offensive toward Mokmer airdrome
2   Japanese initiate Kon 1
3   Japanese cancel Kon 1
5   6th Division begins to arrive at Toem
6   D-Day in Europe
7   186th RCT takes Mokmer airdrome but is ambushed
      Kon 2 begins
8   Patrick begins second effort to take Lone Tree Hill
9   Fuller attempts to storm Mokmer ridges
10   Japanese initiate Kon 3
13   Japanese cancel Kon 3
14   Krueger orders Eichelberger to Biak
15   POA invasion of Saipan in the Marianas
18   34th RCT arrives at Biak
19   Battle of the Philippine Sea begins
      Eichelberger launches his assault against Mokmer ridges
20   6th Division attacks toward Lone Tree Hill
22   Elements of 20th RCT trapped on Lone Tree Hill
24   20th RCT breaks Japanese hold on Lone Tree Hill
27   Hall's XI Corps arrives at Aitape
28   Eichelberger leaves Biak
      112th RCT begins disembarking at Aitape

JULY

2   Patrick's 158th RCT lands at Noemfoor
3   First 503rd Parachute Infantry Regiment parachute drop on
      Noemfoor
      124th RCT begins disembarking at Aitape
4   Second 503rd Parachute Infantry Regiment parachute drop on
      Noemfoor
5   Unsuccessful Japanese assault on Hill 201 on Noemfoor
10   Reconnaissances-in-force crosses the Driniumor
      Japanese breakthrough along the Driniumor

13 XI Corps counterattacks to the Driniumor
14 Marines invade Tinian Island in the Marianas
16 Gap between North and South forces along Driniumor closed
18 112th RCT attacked around Afua
21 Marines invade Guam in the Marianas
26 MacArthur meets with President Roosevelt and Nimitz at Pearl Harbor
30 6th Division lands at Sansapor-Mar
31 Ted Force crosses Driniumor for its counterattack

AUGUST

8   Ted Force reaches the Driniumor
10 Ted Force expedition ends
15 Invasion of southern France

SEPTEMBER

15 POA invasion of Palaus
    XI Corps lands at Morotai
    JCS decides to invade Leyte

OCTOBER

20 6th Army lands at Leyte

INTRODUCTION

On 28 May 1944, the day after American troops waded ashore onto the Japanese-held island of Biak, just off New Guinea's north coast, CBS war correspondent William Dunn broadcast that

> the Biak landings climaxed the most outstanding five months in the history of the war in the southwest Pacific. . . . One of the most remarkable features of the campaign has been the unbelievable economy of life. By superb planning and execution, by consistent success in hitting the enemy where he is, this campaign has been brought to a decisive and final goal with no waste of life. It's a record that will go down in history.[1]

To be sure, Dunn's observations were not entirely accurate, but his optimism reflected that of Southwest Pacific Area (SWPA) headquarters. In an official communiqué, SWPA commander General Douglas MacArthur stated that his offensive across the New Guinea littoral "more than fulfilled my most optimistic expectations."[2] Later in the year, one SWPA official noted that "along the [New Guinea] axis General MacArthur conducted a series of brilliant amphibious maneuvers. All intermediate seizures were a part of this central theme carried out by ground, air and navy components welded into a practically integrated machine."[3] Moreover, lest anyone forget who was responsible for this dazzling success, the official went on to add: "Against a background of brilliant central strategic themes, the factor of personal leadership is outstanding. General MacArthur has personally accompanied each important operation, generally landing with a shore echelon, thereby adding that psychological touch which has inspired soldiers through history to give their last ounce of energy to the Commander who accompanied them."[4]

Such frothy adulation was hardly unusual in MacArthur's camp, where promoting the general was synonymous with preserving Western civilization, but praise came from non-SWPA sources as well, including Australian Prime Minister John Curtin.[5] Nor was this approbation solely for public consumption. Chief of Staff General George C. Marshall, for example, wrote to MacArthur shortly after the Biak landing that "the succession of surprises effected and the small losses suffered, the great extent of territory

I

conquered and the casualties inflicted on the enemy, together with the large Japanese forces which have been isolated, all combine to make your operations of the past one and a half months models of strategical and tactical maneuvers."[6]

After the war, when the initial flush of victory had faded, MacArthur and his subordinates continued to extol their New Guinea campaign. Dissecting the offensive in their memoirs, they attributed SWPA's triumph to MacArthur's superior generalship, sound tactics, effective interservice cooperation, and creative planning. They emphasized the speed of SWPA operations, minimal American losses, heavy Japanese casualties, and the lack of support from Washington. All this, they insisted, was in stark contrast to the Navy's bloody concurrent drive across the central Pacific.[7]

Indeed, many scholars echo this laudatory view. Like MacArthur and his adherents, they stress the huge discrepancy in American and Japanese losses, the vast distances covered in a relatively short time, and MacArthur's lack of resources.[8] Other historians who look more closely at the campaign, however, are more cautious in their praise. They note that SWPA benefited more from American materiel superiority, Japanese strategic confusion, and excellent intelligence-gathering techniques than from MacArthur's supposed military genius.[9] Others state that the American offensive, while undoubtedly successful, would have yielded greater strategic benefits had all Pacific War resources been concentrated under one command, instead of split between SWPA and the Navy.[10] Even so, on the whole, the New Guinea campaign has gone down in history as one of MacArthur's shining successes.

The American strategy to win the war against Japan was based on a dual drive offensive across the Pacific toward the triangular China-Formosa-Luzon area. One prong, under Navy command, attacked across the central Pacific, while the other prong, led by MacArthur and the Army, drove through New Guinea. After isolating the big enemy stronghold at Rabaul on New Britain island, in early 1944 MacArthur confronted a series of Japanese bases along New Guinea's north coast. Rather than assault them all head on, MacArthur used his superior forces to leapfrog selectively along the coast, bypassing and neutralizing many of these immobile enemy garrisons through a series of amphibious landings on the Admiralty Islands, Hollandia-Aitape, Wakde-Sarmi, Biak, Noemfoor, Sansapor-Mar, and Morotai. By September 1944, MacArthur had reached beyond the northwestern tip of the big island to Morotai, smashing or isolating all Japanese resistance and placing him in position to assault the Philippines.

Although the New Guinea campaign played a vital role in the Pacific War, few historians have looked at it in any depth, perhaps because the more glamorous concurrent Marine operations in the central Pacific and the subsequent Philippines liberation campaign have overshadowed it.[11] The New Guinea offensive, however, was no small or insignificant affair. By the end of the campaign, MacArthur commanded some 1,377,000 American, Australian, and Dutch troops. Eight American divisions, three independent Regimental Combat Teams (RCTs), three Engineer Special Brigades (ESBs), an entire fleet, and two Army Air Forces saw action. Some 11,300 Americans were killed or wounded in the process. By comparison, the Army committed only five divisions to the better-known Sicily campaign and suffered 3800 fewer casualties.[12]

Numbers, however, tell only a small part of the story; the New Guinea campaign was important for other reasons as well. For one thing, it exemplified the strategic differences that plagued the Pacific War effort. MacArthur's view of the offensive was frequently at odds with those of many other military planners. To MacArthur, New Guinea served first and foremost as a road to the Philippines, whose liberation he pursued with an almost fanatical devotion.[13] Apart from oil deposits under the Vogelkop peninsula, the island was valueless in and of itself, except to the extent it served to advance future operations toward the China-Formosa-Luzon area.[14] New Guinea contained few natural resources vital for the war effort, and by early 1944 its role as a strategic shield for Australia had long since waned. Whereas part of the rationale for the central Pacific offensive was to draw the Japanese Navy into a decisive Mahanian battle,[15] this was not a consideration in SWPA. Even wearing down the Japanese was not a major factor; MacArthur wanted to get around enemy forces as quickly as possible, not grind them down, although this was sometimes an inadvertent result of his actions. Finally, some SWPA commanders saw the campaign as an opportunity to bloody inexperienced American troops, but even this was in preparation for bigger and more important battles to come.[16] From MacArthur's perspective, the New Guinea offensive was merely a means to a much more glorious end, the shortest line between two points.

Not all American military planners, however, saw the offensive in this MacArthur-generated light. No one ever discouraged MacArthur from conquering New Guinea, but the motivating rationale behind the campaign was different for many, especially high-ranking naval officers and airmen, who viewed the New Guinea offensive mainly as a diversion, a way to pin down large numbers of Japanese troops while the Navy and Army Air

Forces (AAF) delivered the main blows in the central Pacific. Although the Joint Chiefs of Staff (JCS)[17] ultimately decided to underwrite both a central Pacific and a SWPA offensive, differences of opinion as to the ultimate goal—Luzon or Formosa—continued to haunt American strategists. Because MacArthur's views ultimately prevailed, his conception of the New Guinea offensive is the one history remembers.

Not only does the New Guinea campaign enable scholars to better understand American Pacific War strategy, but, as one of the highlights of MacArthur's military career, it also serves as a tool with which to evaluate the SWPA chief as a commander. Although MacArthur's military skills played a large part in the offensive's ultimate success, the general made several errors that he would repeat, on a larger and more tragic scale, later on in Korea. Indeed, many of his strategic inadequacies appeared long before his New Guinea offensive and in fact formed an integral and consistent part of his makeup. In his desire to reach the Philippines quickly, MacArthur frequently downplayed or overlooked the difficulties inherent in a New Guinea campaign. Because he viewed the offensive from a broad strategic perspective, MacArthur was often unwilling or unable to understand the immediate operational or tactical situation. This discrepancy between the general's strategic ambitions and battlefield realities occasionally caused SWPA personnel considerable grief.

Moreover, although MacArthur emphasized that his New Guinea campaign strategy was based on bypassing and neutralizing strong Japanese garrisons,[18] he sometimes attacked immobile enemy troops for questionable reasons, causing American forces to suffer needless casualties for little commensurate gain. The SWPA chief at times failed to recognize that these static and otherwise isolated Japanese garrisons still had the power to disrupt his strategic timetable by frustrating American forces at the tactical level. In addition, MacArthur repeatedly dispersed his troops and equipment along the New Guinea coast, leaving them vulnerable to attack by mobile Japanese forces inserted from outside his theater. Fortunately for MacArthur, as well as the soldiers, airmen, and sailors under his command, American materiel and technological supremacy, superior mobility and intelligence-gathering techniques, the dual drive offensive he so derided, and enemy strategic confusion prevented the Japanese from taking advantage of the general's shortcomings.

Because he was such a controversial figure, historians have tended to worship or demonize MacArthur. Despite some strategic lapses, and whatever his personal or political failings, most of his World War II associates, including those who disliked him, attested to his strategic abilities.[19] Indeed, throughout the New Guinea campaign MacArthur proved to be a forceful and courageous general willing to take strategic and logistical risks most American commanders would have shunned. He successfully fought the New Guinea offensive on a logistical shoestring, stretching his resources to the limit to sustain the campaign's fast pace. He stressed celerity over caution, partly because he was at heart an offensive commander, but also for selfish reasons. To maintain his New Guinea offensive, MacArthur often used tired and inexperienced troops to maintain momentum rather than waste time and resources bringing fresher and better-trained forces forward. To achieve his strategic objectives, MacArthur was flexible enough to adjust his plans according to ever-changing circumstances. In doing so, MacArthur helped ensure that the New Guinea campaign was fought and won *his* way, which, at least from his point of view, guaranteed the most cost-effective means to victory over Japan.

One high-ranking SWPA commander, reflecting in his memoirs, noted that "like everyone else in the Southwest Pacific, I soon found myself falling into the habit of referring to 'MacArthur's troops,' 'MacArthur's planes,' and 'MacArthur's ships.' The habit was widespread."[20] So widespread, in fact, that many historians have adopted it.[21] Because of MacArthur's dominating personality, as well as deliberate efforts on his part to portray SWPA as a one-man show, MacArthur's subordinates are far less well known than, say, Eisenhower's lieutenants.[22] Nevertheless, these men played an important role in winning the New Guinea campaign. While MacArthur limited their access to the press, he gave his field commanders considerable leeway to plan and conduct tactical operations, as long as their actions did not interfere with his rigid strategic timetable.[23] As SWPA's naval commander, Vice Admiral Thomas C. Kinkaid, later put it, "[MacArthur] would organize an expedition, and give someone command, and then he did not interfere."[24] The New Guinea campaign demonstrated that the behavior of his subordinates sometimes affected operational outcomes in ways their SWPA commander had not anticipated, proving that they were not MacArthur automatons but rather independent-minded men waging war under difficult circumstances.[25]

Finally, New Guinea's remote and hostile terrain challenged an American military establishment that emphasized firepower, technology, simplicity, mobility, and materiel superiority. In order to win the campaign, MacArthur had to overcome not only the Japanese but also the big island's horrendous topography and climate. Fortunately, SWPA successfully modified American military doctrine so as to accommodate and work within the limits of New Guinea's adverse environment, enabling MacArthur to wage war against the Japanese on his terms.

During World War II, the American military was confronted with a multitude of logistical, strategic, political, social, personnel, and geographic challenges. In New Guinea, a multinational and interservice force waged war under one of the Army's most controversial commanders. Despite innumerable difficulties, however, SWPA was able to prevail through strategic and technical innovation, effective coordination and planning, materiel supremacy, and strategic opportunism. By examining the Pacific War's strategic background, military components, and individual operations, it is possible to discern the interaction among American military planning, interservice politics, MacArthur's generalship, his field commanders, combined operations, and the American way of war. From this perspective, then, the New Guinea offensive was not a backwater affair but an important part of World War II.

ONE

STRATEGIC BACKGROUND

As if the seventeen-hour flight from Ceylon to Australia, undertaken without navigational aids across the vast and trackless Indian Ocean, were not nerve-wracking enough, the C-54's pilot was also burdened with the knowledge that he was responsible for the safety of perhaps the most precious cargo in the American arsenal. Not war materiel, at least not exactly, but rather a man: General George C. Marshall, the American Army's stern and austere chief of staff, and, as much as any one person could claim the title, the leading architect of the United States' gargantuan war effort.

In December 1943, after attending the Teheran conference, Marshall decided to return to the United States via the Pacific. After two years of war, he had not yet visited SWPA, despite the area's strategic importance. Twice before he had made plans to do so, but each time he had been diverted by more pressing business. Not only did the chief of staff want a firsthand view of one of the Army's most remote theaters, he also wanted to reassure the ever prickly MacArthur that Washington had not slighted or forgotten him.[1] So, without informing President Roosevelt, Marshall and several high-ranking service representatives flew eastward.[2]

The chief of staff might have had second thoughts had he known what awaited him across the globe. MacArthur had never thought much of Marshall; indeed, years earlier he had stated flatly, "George Catlett Marshall is the most overrated officer in the United States Army. He'll never be a general officer as long as I am Chief of Staff."[3] That had been true enough, but the Army continued to churn out promotions after MacArthur's tenure ended. Now, in a twist of fate, the man he once denigrated was his superior, with the power to bring his campaign, if not his career, to a halt. MacArthur considered avoiding a potentially embarrassing meeting with Marshall by accompanying the impending Cape Gloucester operation in New Britain, but he ultimately decided to stay and greet that "most overrated officer."[4]

On 15 December 1943, Marshall arrived to Goodenough Island, off New Guinea's east coast, where MacArthur was conferring with Lieutenant

7

General Walter Krueger, his ground commander. Observers thought that Marshall looked tired, which was hardly surprising considering his immense responsibilities and the distance he had traveled.[5] On the surface at least, the meeting went well; Marshall and MacArthur were impeccably polite, addressing one another by first names. Marshall reviewed the global military situation for MacArthur and his subordinates and encouraged them to use what tools they had effectively, but he said nothing about future plans. MacArthur, for his part, urged the chief of staff to adopt his strategic conceptions and pressured him for more resources. Marshall promised to do what he could in the latter area, especially to bolster SWPA's air power.[6] After inspecting troops with the gruff Krueger in the pouring rain, Marshall departed the next day.[7] On the plane ride home, Brigadier General Thomas H. Handy, who accompanied Marshall on this globe-encompassing journey, wondered what the chief of staff thought of his first meeting with MacArthur in eight years. Marshall, however, remained close-mouthed and passed the time reading a book as the plane headed eastward into the sun.[8]

Interservice Rivalries and an Ad Hoc Strategy

On the surface at least, Marshall's visit seemed to accomplish little beyond exposing him to one of New Guinea's torrential downpours and MacArthur's equally inundating rhetoric. MacArthur's pleas, however, indicated that even after two years of conflict, American Pacific War strategy remained in a state of flux.

It was not supposed to be that way. American strategists had spent a generation preparing for war with the Japanese. According to the Navy's long-established War Plan Orange, conflict with Japan called for American forces in the Philippines to fight a holding action against the anticipated Japanese assault while the Navy steamed westward to relieve the beleaguered archipelago. Along the way, the fleet expected to destroy its Japanese counterpart in a decisive Mahanian battle that would open the way for a naval blockade of Japan itself. As time went on, however, and the more complex interservice Rainbow plans for conflict with Japan superseded Plan Orange, American war strategy grew ambiguous. Most American strategists acknowledged that the Philippines could not hold out long enough for the Navy to come to the rescue, especially since war in Europe would have first priority; nonetheless this remained the formula.[9]

As it was, all this preparation proved academic. The Japanese attack on Pearl Harbor crippled the American fleet before it could reach the

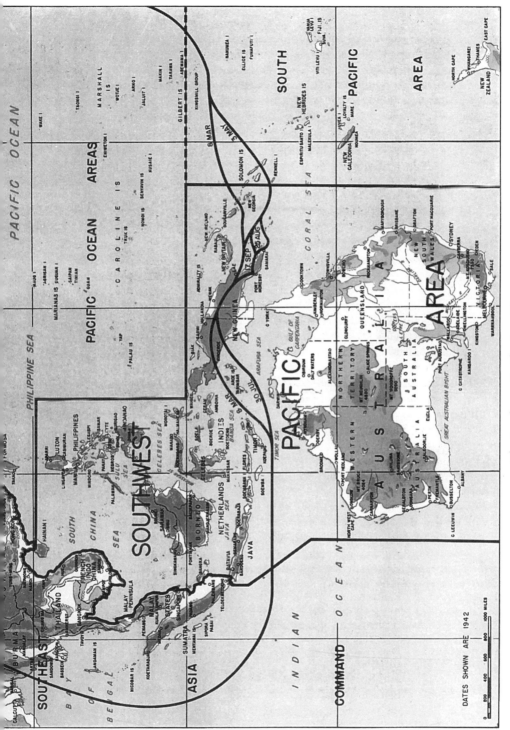

The Southwest Pacific Area Theater

Philippines, before, indeed, it received its marching orders to do so. Pre-war planning, however, did establish the notion that the American Navy would call the shots in any conflict with the Japanese, and even after it became obvious that the Pacific War could not be waged without significant Army support, naval officers continued to behave as if it were *their* war.[10]

Even before entering World War II, American policymakers decided that in the event of hostilities the United States would concentrate on beating Nazi Germany first, a position reaffirmed immediately after Pearl Harbor at the Arcadia conference in Washington. Despite this commitment, in the first year after Pearl Harbor nearly half of the United States' resources flowed westward to the Pacific. This was partly because the Navy wanted it that way but more so as a result of the pressures of war. Stopping the Japanese amphibious juggernaut proved no easy task, and after the United States seized the strategic initiative at Midway and Guadalcanal—or, more accurately, stumbled upon it—the JCS was loathe to give it up and permit the American Pacific War effort to stagnate. This view was sanctioned at the Casablanca conference in January 1943, when the British and American Combined Chiefs of Staff (CCS) endorsed a limited counteroffensive against the Japanese.[11]

Approving such a counteroffensive was one thing; undertaking it was something else again. The JCS—the Pacific War was primarily an American affair, so the JCS determined its strategy on behalf of the CCS—had to determine how, when, where, and with what to carry out this counterattack. Initially, the prevailing military situation made the decision for them, focusing their efforts on the southwest Pacific, where American and Australian forces were fighting in the Solomons and New Guinea to protect Australia and its supply line to the United States. Since significant American and Australian resources were already in the area, and since the biggest immediate threat was there as well, the JCS took aim at the big Japanese base at Rabaul in New Britain. Indeed, the region seemed to suck up American, Australian, and Japanese resources as fast as they were committed, resulting in the steady attrition of troops, ships, and planes on both sides. To occupy Rabaul and eliminate the Japanese threat to Australia's lifeline, in early July 1942 American military planners designed Operation Cartwheel, a two-pronged attack up the Solomons and through Papua New Guinea under MacArthur's general command but with considerable Navy autonomy in the former area.[12]

Simply getting to Rabaul turned out to be harder than anyone anticipated. No sooner had American planners agreed on their strategy than the Japanese war machine sputtered into motion in an effort to secure all of

New Guinea. After landing 13,000 soldiers at Buna-Gona on Papua's north coast in July 1942, Japanese troops crossed the all but impenetrable Owen Stanley Mountains and headed for Port Moresby, the nexus of Allied operations on the island. Only a handful of Australian forces were initially arrayed against the advancing Japanese, but they proved every bit as troublesome as the horrendous terrain, tenuous supply lines, and debilitating diseases, which took an increasingly heavy toll on the emperor's soldiers. By mid-September, however, the Japanese were within forty miles of Port Moresby. Reinforcing American and Australian troops had equipment and manpower shortages of their own, as well as quarrelsome commanders and coordination problems, but in the end they held. In late September, after a diversionary attack on Milne Bay on New Guinea's southeastern tip failed, Imperial Headquarters ordered a retreat to Buna-Gona.

Before MacArthur could undertake his role in reducing Rabaul, he needed a foothold on Papua's north coast, and Buna-Gona seemed as suited for this as anyplace else. Unfortunately, attempts to take the area starting in November 1942 rapidly degenerated into a military nightmare. MacArthur and his staff underestimated both the logistical problems of fighting in New Guinea and the number of Japanese in the vicinity. Green American troops floundered in the swampy jungle against an unseen foe at Buna while their more experienced Australian allies also ran head on into heavy Japanese opposition at nearby Gona and Sanananda. Not until mid-January 1943—several weeks, incidentally, after MacArthur claimed that the operation was over and only minor mopping up remained to be done—did the Allies eliminate the last die-hard Japanese defenders. Storming Buna, Gona, and Sanananda cost the Australians and Americans more than 8000 casualties.

While MacArthur's forces fought and died back and forth across the Owen Stanleys, the Navy's South Pacific Area Command (SOPAC) faced problems every bit as difficult and trying as their SWPA brethren in carrying out their part of Cartwheel's two-pronged offensive toward Rabaul. The Marines easily seized the Japanese airfield on Guadalcanal in August 1942, but soon SOPAC found itself locked in a brutal six-month war of attrition for the island against the cream of the Japanese Army and Navy. After heavy losses all around, American materiel superiority told in the end, and the Japanese evacuated what was left of their starving and disease-ridden troops in February 1943. SOPAC spent the next year slowly and painfully working its way up the Solomon Islands chain, conquering New Georgia, Vella Lavella, and finally Bougainville.

While SOPAC climbed the Solomons ladder, MacArthur's forces advanced toward Rabaul from New Guinea. American and Australian troops

gradually pushed the Japanese out of their strongholds on the Huon peninsula, so that by the end of the year Lae, Salamaua, and Finschhafen were
in Allied hands. For all the valor of his Australian and American infantry,
MacArthur's success was due in no small part to the skillful use of air-
power. At the Battle of Bismarck Sea in March 1943, the AAF terminated
large-scale Japanese efforts to reinforce the Huon peninsula by sinking a
convoy carrying some 6000 troops. Later that year, in August, a surprise
AAF attack on Japan's Wewak airbase, west of the Huon peninsula, wiped
out the bulk of the enemy's remaining air forces in the area. By early 1944,
MacArthur's offensive had worn down Rabaul's air and naval defenses,
pushed the Japanese as far west as Saidor, and placed American troops on
New Britain itself.

Whatever Rabaul's importance, conquering it—or, as events turned out,
bypassing and neutralizing it—would not win the war, and throughout
1943 American strategists concentrated on the best way to mount a counteroffensive that would crush the Japanese. Planning this offensive, however, involved several touchy and interrelated issues that continually
plagued the American Pacific War effort: overall command, strategy, and
resource allocation. Indeed, these problems popped up repeatedly, pitting
the Army and the Navy against one another. A series of jury-rigged compromises resolved immediate disputes, but the basic issue of which service
would dominate the war continued until the end of the conflict. Although
Army and Navy officers frequently sided with one another over the secondary issues of strategy and resource allocation, they almost always returned to the fold when the ultimate question of overall Pacific authority
was raised. General Handy, who witnessed the power struggle, later noted,
"I felt that the discussion really wasn't basically concerned about the best
way to [win the war]. It was who was going to do it, and who was going
to be in command, and who was going to be involved."[13] Like everything
else in the Pacific War, the New Guinea campaign was a pawn in that interservice power struggle.

Discussion of an overall Pacific command got nowhere. In June 1943,
for instance, Admiral Ernest J. King, the Navy's hard-driving and
MacArthur-hating chief of naval operations (CNO), declared to the JCS that
future Pacific operations should be more tightly controlled. The problem,
said King, was that frequent overseas conferences made it difficult for the
JCS to exercise such control. To remedy this situation, he suggested that
the JCS delegate to Admiral Chester Nimitz, commander of MacArthur's
rival Pacific Ocean Areas (POA) and all naval units thereabouts, the authority to coordinate the timing of Pacific operations.[14] Not surprisingly,

King's staff subordinates backed him up, stating that Nimitz needed such power to move his fleet as quickly as possible to combat any Japanese naval threat. MacArthur's SWPA operations, on the other hand, required no such flexibility.[15]

King's proposal fooled no one. Marshall said that operational timing was and should remain a JCS prerogative, though he added that the JCS should of course take into account the views of their field commanders. Admiral William D. Leahy, Roosevelt's chief of staff and chairman of the JCS, dryly concluded that King's proposal would, in effect, make Nimitz overall commander in the Pacific, something that MacArthur should be consulted on first.[16] King, stabbed in the back, as it were, by one of his own, quickly retreated and suggested that they defer action for now, and Marshall, Army Air Forces commander General Henry H. Arnold, and Leahy agreed.[17]

In this case, "for now" meant a long time, and in fact the Pacific War never achieved a truly unified command structure. Even so, failure to resolve the Pacific command issue did not prevent the JCS from tackling Pacific strategy throughout 1943. Everyone agreed that the United States should not surrender the strategic initiative, but consensus broke down over exactly where and how to apply the pressure. There were two possible Pacific routes to Japan. The first, from Hawaii through the Japanese Mandate islands—the Marshalls, Marianas, Carolines, and Palaus, which Japan had seized from the Germans during World War I—was Nimitz and the Navy's sphere of responsibility. The second route, through the southwest Pacific from Australia to New Guinea to the Philippines, was under MacArthur's SWPA command.

Despite an American military doctrine that emphasized concentration of force, American strategists at the Casablanca conference in January 1943 decided to underwrite offenses by both MacArthur and Nimitz. Significant American resources were already concentrated in MacArthur's southwest Pacific theater, but King demanded an independent naval role and got the JCS to go along. Casablanca committed the United States to a limited, albeit scattershot, counteroffensive against the Japanese in the Marshalls, Carolines, Solomons, Aleutians, and New Guinea. From these points the JCS hoped eventually to launch a full-scale attack that would bring Japan to its knees. This basic outline was confirmed and clarified at other CCS conferences that year in Washington (Trident), Quebec (Quadrant), and Cairo (Sextant).

Having glossed over the issue of overall Pacific command, and having decided upon a dual drive against the Japanese, the JCS turned to allocat-

ing resources for these offenses. Here, unlike the other two issues, New
Guinea played a role in determining JCS thinking.

The JCS's early conception of a New Guinea campaign was a far cry
from the final product. In May 1943, the Joint War Plans Committee
(JWPC)[18] stated, "The capture of NEW GUINEA will facilitate the opening of
a line of communications to the CELEBES SEA and contribute to the defense
of AUSTRALIA."[19] The key to victory in New Guinea, according to JCS staff
planners, was the Vogelkop peninsula in the island's northwest. Not only
was the Vogelkop the gateway to the Celebes and a possible linkup with
British forces in the Indian Ocean, but it also possessed undeveloped oilfields at Sorong. There was, however, little thought about using New
Guinea as a springboard for a full-scale assault on the Philippines.[20]

JCS staff planners believed that reaching the Vogelkop would require simultaneous advances along both of New Guinea's coasts, which would not
be easy. On the positive side, New Guinea's north coast had suitable anchorages and airfield sites for an offensive, and forces moving along the
south coast would be safe from the Truk-based Japanese fleet, possess secure lines of communication, and have convenient air support in nearby
Australia. Moreover, many of the necessary forces were already on hand,
fighting in the Papua and Northeast New Guinea as part of Operation
Cartwheel.[21]

The ledger's other side, however, contained some formidable entries of
its own. Not only would such an offensive necessitate two independent
forces advancing along each coast, but the attack would be in the face of
large numbers of Japanese deployed in depth and within easy reach of their
logistical support. This would require lots of troops, and there was the rub.
The JCS estimated that such a campaign would call for 2 airborne and 16
infantry divisions, including 5 trained in amphibious warfare, 57 air groups
of 3048 planes, and all the equipment and logistical support necessary to
conduct such complex and distant operations. Moreover, this total did not
even take into account additional requirements for operations planned in
the nearby Bismarcks. All this was beyond American resources; by January
1944, the United States would still be short 5 divisions in the region.[22]

There were other disadvantages as well. Malaria-ridden New Guinea
was inadequately charted and full of coral reefs and bars that could knock
out landing craft before they even came under fire. Attacking across this
poorly developed area would be a logistical nightmare, despite its proximity to Australia. Even if the offensive were successful, it would still place
American forces far away from Japan, although it would cut off Japanese
oil resources in the Netherlands East Indies.[23] Despite these significant

drawbacks, however, JCS staff planners liked the *idea* of a limited New Guinea offensive; it could advance the Pacific War effort by pinning down and wearing out large numbers of Japanese forces, with the subsequent strain on Japan's limited shipping resources.[24]

On the other hand, JCS staffers believed that an offensive across the central Pacific would enable an increasingly powerful American Navy to attack the tiny and isolated Mandate islands from three sides, once the Bismarcks fell, negating the Japanese advantage of interior lines. Unlike the situation in New Guinea, Japanese forces in the Mandates were not deployed in depth, so a relatively small number of Americans could theoretically take them with few casualties. To be sure, a central Pacific offensive would lack land-based air support, but the proper use of carrier aircraft would make up that deficiency. Not only would the offensive permit American forces to cut Japan off from its Netherlands East Indies oil resources, but, unlike a SWPA campaign, it would place American forces within easy striking distance of Japan. Finally, and most importantly, a POA advance toward the big Japanese naval base of Truk in the Carolines would lure the Japanese fleet out into the open for a decisive battle. A SWPA advance, on the other hand, would enable an unhindered Japanese Navy to harass American forces from the north, forcing its American counterpart to disperse its ships to combat this widespread threat. JCS planners recognized that a central Pacific offensive, like one in SWPA, would require a huge logistical effort, but they believed it provided the fastest and most cost-effective way to win the war.[25]

Looking over these and other reports, King saw them as more evidence that the Navy dominated central Pacific route was the way to go. He believed that the current slow progress of Cartwheel operations was not going to win the war; indeed, they were originally initiated to protect Australia's threatened lines of communications, not win the war. Moreover, King felt that a SWPA offensive would lead American forces into the tangled mess of the Netherlands East Indies, vulnerable to a host of Japanese airbases and land forces. A central Pacific campaign under the aegis of the growing American fleet against small Japanese islands, on the other hand, could gain fast results, especially if the Japanese fleet were destroyed along the way. Leahy tended to agree, as did Arnold, who saw a central Pacific advance as the best way to get the bases his new long-range B-29 bombers needed to hit Japan. At the Sextant conference in Cairo, the three men persuaded a reluctant Marshall to go along. Although they agreed to a New Guinea offensive, there was no mention of using it as a springboard to the Philippines, and Nimitz's forces would get a preponderance of resources. A

CCS document stated: "Due weight should be accorded to the fact that operations in the CP [central Pacific] promise at this time a more rapid advance toward Japan and her vital lines of communication; the earlier acquisition of strategic air bases closer to the Japanese homeland; and, of greatest importance, are more likely to precipitate a decisive engagement with the Japanese fleet."[26]

Thus, despite the failure of the JCS to delegate an overall Pacific commander, by the end of 1943 they had decided that Nimitz and the Navy should spearhead the Pacific counteroffensive. The JCS, however, had not reckoned with General Douglas MacArthur.

Major General Richard K. Sutherland was among the officers, civilian policymakers, advisors, and hangers-on at the Sextant conference in Cairo in November 1943. As MacArthur's chief of staff, his role was not only to represent his boss on Pacific War issues but also to keep MacArthur informed. MacArthur believed that his superiors were every bit as dangerous to his plans as the Japanese, if not more so; the Japanese could only kill him, whereas the JCS could send him into ignominy. To be sure, the brusque and hard-nosed Sutherland lacked a spy's subtlety, but he more than made up for it in loyalty to the cause—meaning MacArthur. The Sextant conference decision relegating SWPA to a secondary role alarmed Sutherland, and he relayed his concern to MacArthur soon after he accompanied Marshall to Australia.

To MacArthur, the Pacific War was about more than just grinding the Japanese into powder; it was also about personal honor. The loss of the Philippines, with his humiliating departure from Corregidor, haunted him, and he pursued the archipelago's liberation with a determination bordering on fanaticism. MacArthur saw the Pacific War through this lens and geared his strategy to that end.[27] He once said that he intended to free the islands even if he was "down to one canoe paddled by Douglas MacArthur and supported by one Taylor cub [plane]."[28] Naval dominance of the Pacific War, as well as a central Pacific offensive that bypassed the Philippines, both threatened his plans.

Moreover, MacArthur combined this obsession with a deep-rooted paranoia that outside forces—not the Japanese, who at least had the decency to face him like men—were conspiring against him. These dark forces included the British, the White House, and especially the Navy, which, as his chief Pacific War competitor, was in the best position to thwart his ambitions. MacArthur believed that the Navy wanted to limit his offensive to New Guinea, pinching him off at the Vogelkop while they bypassed the Philippines and swept forward to finish the war by themselves.[29] Indeed, MacArthur blamed the Navy's voracious logistical appetite in the central Pacific for his own lack of resources, claiming that he was "always the underdog, and always fighting with destruction just around the corner."[30]

To be sure, there were some grounds for his suspicions of the Navy. Many naval officers, including King, despised MacArthur and wanted to limit his role in the Pacific War.[31] One Army general said, "It was quite obvious that [the Navy] resented General MacArthur having any chance of leading them on into Japan."[32] The Navy, like MacArthur, saw the Pacific War as a redemptive crusade, only in this case Pearl Harbor, not Bataan, was the wrong to be righted.[33] Marshall was well aware of MacArthur's paranoia, and he generally sympathized with his SWPA commander's strategic plans, but he had to treat the Navy as an equal, so he tried to steer a middle course between his egocentric field commander and the volatile King.[34]

MacArthur was naturally dismayed by the Sextant conference directive giving the Navy's central Pacific offensive priority over his own. Although the JCS had not yet made any decision on the Philippines, events in Cairo were not a good omen. All hope was not yet lost, however, if he could persuade the JCS to rethink their decision. To that end, in late 1943 and early 1944, MacArthur brought into play every weapon in his personal arsenal, including his heart-to-heart with Marshall at Goodenough, as well as the advantages of a New Guinea campaign.

The first thing MacArthur could do—he had, indeed, been doing it all along—was to argue against a central Pacific offensive on purely military grounds. MacArthur believed that an attack from Hawaii was just plain bad strategy. As he saw it, the Japanese were in the Mandates in strength, and prying them out would require costly frontal assaults. Due to the vast distances involved, American forces would have to return to Hawaii after each operation, with a subsequent loss of strategic momentum as the Japanese rushed reinforcements to the region while the Navy took a logistics-imposed breather. Moreover, these Japanese reinforcements would not be hindered by the AAF because the Mandates were beyond American land-based air support. MacArthur believed that the Navy was too wedded to the old Plan Orange scenario and was not taking into account a military reality that extended far beyond prewar expectations.[35]

A SWPA counteroffensive, on the other hand, was strategically sound. MacArthur felt that the hard-fought Cartwheel campaign had severely mauled the Japanese in the region, presenting him with a golden opportunity to exploit the enemy's weaknesses and drive rapidly toward the Philippines. Indeed, MacArthur, not surprisingly, saw the Philippines as the key to the entire Pacific War. Not only would its reconquest cut the Japanese off from their vital oil resources in the Netherlands East Indies, but it would provide an ideal base from which to grind down Japanese merchant shipping and attack Japan itself with those big long-range bombers Arnold was so gung-ho about. Repossession of the Philippines would also expose the Chinese coast to American attack and, he believed, provoke the Japanese fleet into the decisive battle the Navy craved. Moreover, MacArthur had the advantage of using nearby Australia as a staging base for deploying and supplying his land, air, and sea power to bypass and isolate Japanese bases en route to the Philippines. Besides, there were already plenty of American troops in the area. Finally, MacArthur believed that the United States had a moral obligation to free its Philippine colony from the Japanese yoke.[36]

To persuade the JCS that the reconquest of the Philippines was indeed the way to go, MacArthur had to convince them that the New Guinea road to the archipelago would not be too rocky. To that end, MacArthur's staff developed a series of plans for a New Guinea campaign code-named Reno. The most influential were Reno III, submitted to the JCS in October 1943, and Reno IV, which the JCS saw the following March.

By mid-1943, the JCS wanted to increase the tempo of the Pacific War, but they continued to recognize that only limited resources could be committed to the conflict with Japan.[37] Reno III was designed to appeal to both these inclinations. Its five-phase program called for temporarily bypassing and neutralizing Rabaul by seizing nearby Kavieng on New Ireland, the Admiralty Islands, and the big Japanese base at Hansa Bay in February and March 1944 with seven divisions, two parachute regiments, and fifty-nine air groups. From there, MacArthur hoped to devote June to attacking Hollandia, as well as conducting operations in the Arafura Sea, south of the island. Then he would move on to Geelvink Bay in August, the Vogelkop in October, and Halmahera Island in December. Having accomplished all this in record time—record time, that is, in comparison with the slow progress of Operation Cartwheel—SWPA would be in position to leap to the southern Philippine island of Mindanao in February 1945.[38]

To carry out Reno III, MacArthur wanted all American forces in the Pacific placed under a single commander for a single drive to the Philippines.[39] To MacArthur, the dual drive concept decided upon at Casablanca was folly; it dispersed American forces and weakened the war effort.[40]

What he wanted most from the Navy, however, was carrier support for his advance across New Guinea.[41]

Indeed, throughout the New Guinea campaign, and despite effective service from SWPA's naval officers, MacArthur was frustrated by King's refusal to provide SWPA with aircraft carriers. As he later put it: "The presence of carriers with their inherent mobility would have immeasurably increased the scope and speed of our operations. I know of no other area and no other theater where they could have been used to such advantage."[42] MacArthur believed, quite correctly, that the mobile short-range air support carriers provided would have enabled SWPA to take bigger jumps up the New Guinea coast, accelerating his campaign and reducing casualties. MacArthur pressured the JCS for the carriers, and even had Australian Prime Minister John Curtin try to wheedle some out of the British, but to no avail.[43] King believed that Nimitz needed every carrier he had for the impending showdown with the Japanese fleet, and anyway he disliked the thought of placing his big ships under MacArthur's command in the southwest Pacific's congested waters. During the New Guinea campaign, therefore, MacArthur's amphibious range was usually restricted by the radius of ground-based fighter planes in his rear.

MacArthur did benefit directly, however, from another aspect of the Navy's crusade. Although initially plagued by faulty torpedoes, haphazard strategy, and overly cautious captains, by the end of 1943 the Navy's submarine campaign against the Japanese was beginning to yield impressive results. That year, submarines operating from Pearl Harbor and the southeastern Australian port of Fremantle sank 335 Japanese ships, or 1.5 million tons.[44] This was just a curtain raiser; the following year the submariners wiped Japanese shipping off the high seas for all practical purposes by sinking 2.7 million tons of shipping.[45] Japanese shipbuilding simply could not keep up with the losses. The submariners' success stemmed primarily from using Ultra intelligence to zero-in on Japan's vulnerable merchant marine. Indeed, the submarine war gradually paralyzed the flow of raw materials to and reinforcements from the home islands, immobilizing the Japanese war effort. Without adequate shipping, the Japanese found it increasingly difficult to supply and fortify its overseas possessions, which included New Guinea.

The JCS was not completely satisfied with Reno III. The service chiefs had no objections to conquering New Guinea, though they had not yet made any decision on objectives beyond that, but they did not think that MacArthur would have enough assault shipping and naval forces for such an ambitious undertaking. They suggested that MacArthur eliminate operations in the Arafura Sea, coordinate his plans with Nimitz's forces to the north, and resubmit his plan.[46] If nothing else, however, the JCS's limited endorsement of Reno III showed that the service chiefs were willing to commit to operations that would place SWPA within range of Luzon, the political and psychological heart of the Philippines and MacArthur's ultimate goal.

If this rational appeal on military grounds failed to dissuade the JCS from its unwise emphasis on a central Pacific offensive, MacArthur was prepared to resort to nonmilitary, emotional means to attain his goal. As part of the American war effort, propagandists used MacArthur's "I shall return [to the Philippines]" pledge to rally the public.[47] To MacArthur, such a strategy had its place, not only in raising civilian morale but also in pressuring the JCS to endorse a Philippines campaign. It would hardly do to bypass the islands after so much public emphasis had been placed on their liberation. MacArthur played upon this, repeatedly stressing publicly his self-proclaimed mission to liberate the archipelago, even though the JCS had yet to endorse such an idea.[48] For instance, at a Canberra banquet hosted by the Australian Parliament and Prime Minister Curtin to celebrate the second anniversary of his arrival on Australian soil, after the New Guinea campaign got under way, but before the JCS decided to liberate the Philippines, MacArthur said, "Two years ago when I landed on your soil I said to the people of the Philippines whence I came 'I shall return.' Tonight I repeat these words, 'I shall return.' Nothing is more certain than our ultimate reconquest and liberation from the enemy of those and adjacent islands. One of the great offenses of the war will at the appropriate time be launched for that purpose."[49] This was not quite true; the JCS had authorized no such offensive, but promising one might compel an embarrassed JCS to order MacArthur to underwrite one. Such public pressure might or might not have an impact on the JCS, but it probably would on Roosevelt, who, if or when push came to shove, would be the ultimate arbiter of American Pacific War strategy.[50]

MacArthur also attempted to influence the decision through his erstwhile colleagues in the POA. If he could not directly persuade the JCS to forgo a central Pacific offensive, he would attempt to subvert them from below, so to speak, by swaying their Pacific field commanders to his way of thinking. A late January 1944 Pearl Harbor conference among SWPA, POA, and SOPAC officers to discuss naval support for upcoming operations against Kavieng, the Admiralties, and Hansa Bay provided the opportunity to convert the nonbelievers. MacArthur himself did not go but instead relied on his subordinates—in this case Sutherland, chief planner Major General Stephen Chamberlin, and SWPA air and naval commanders Lieutenant General George C. Kenney and Vice Admiral Thomas C. Kinkaid—to proselytize on his behalf.

Their task was made much easier by inner doubts among King's subordinates, especially Nimitz, about the Sextant conference decisions. Heavy Marine losses at Tarawa in the Gilbert Islands in November had shaken Nimitz's faith in the vulnerability of the Mandates to American attack. The POA commander believed that Japan could only be defeated from bases on the China coast, and as he saw it, the fastest way to get there was through the Philippines. To reach the archipelago, Nimitz wanted to bypass Truk, attack the Marianas in June, and then cover SWPA's New Guinea offensive flank by hitting the Palaus. Others doubted the value of the Marianas, believing the islands were too far from Japan to be of much use for Arnold's long-range bombers, which could be better employed in SWPA. The consensus among both Army and Navy representatives, therefore, was that, contrary to Sextant conference decisions, more emphasis should be placed on a SWPA offensive through New Guinea to the Philippines.[51]

Returning to Brisbane, Kenney gleefully informed MacArthur that the Pacific field commanders agreed on a SWPA-dominated advance along the New Guinea–Philippines axis. MacArthur was pleased but cautious, noting that the consensus meant nothing without the JCS stamp of approval, which was by no means certain.[52] To that end, MacArthur took another whack at Marshall, informing the chief of staff that both Army and Navy commanders in the Pacific had determined that:

1. SWPA should get Arnold's precious B-29 bombers, with all their logistical support, for attacks on Japanese oil installations in the Netherlands East Indies.
2. The Admiralties, when conquered, should be developed into a naval base that would support the Pacific fleet's efforts to cover SWPA's right flank as MacArthur moved across New Guinea toward the Philippines.
3. The Arafura Sea operations, which the JCS disliked so much, were necessary to support operations against the Vogelkop.
4. Any British naval units deployed against the Japanese should be put under SWPA command.
5. SWPA should receive all SOPAC forces after Operation Cartwheel.
6. Once the Marshall Islands were taken, all Pacific forces should be concentrated on the New Guinea offensive toward the Philippines.

7. MacArthur should command the land, air, and naval forces directly involved in this advance to the Philippines.

In closing, MacArthur added that he was sending Sutherland to Washington to explain and clarify his suggestions.[53]

Admiral King was hardly an even-tempered man, so his reaction to the Pearl Harbor conference was anything but calm. Not only had MacArthur done an end run around the JCS, but he had accomplished it through his long-range powers of persuasion over King's apparently weak-willed naval subordinates. Field commanders had no business making grand strategy anyway; that was a JCS prerogative. Besides, as King saw it, MacArthur had not yet submitted any detailed plan for a New Guinea–Philippines offensive, whereas recent central Pacific victories in the Gilberts showed that the POA campaign was already yielding results. Finally, there was no way King would consent to placing significant naval units under MacArthur's command, no matter what his field subordinates wanted.[54] In a stern letter to Nimitz he wrote: "I have read your conference notes with much interest, and I must add with indignant dismay. . . . The idea of rolling up the Japanese along the New Guinea coast . . . and up through the Philippines to Luzon, as our major strategic concept, to the exclusion of clearing our Central Pacific line of communications to the Philippines, is to me absurd. Further, it is not in accordance with the decisions of the Joint Chiefs of Staff."[55]

King's rage, however, was a small price for MacArthur to pay to compel the JCS to review its Sextant conference decision. Marshall, who had doubts about a central Pacific offensive anyway, suggested that the JCS staff planners take another look at Pacific strategy, and King agreed.[56]

Showdown in Washington

The elder military statesmen who made up the Joint Strategic Survey Committee (JSSC) and advised the JCS on grand strategy could be forgiven if they were exasperated in February 1944. The previous year they had warned the JCS to clarify Pacific strategy, lest it degenerate into the fly-by-night procedure that characterized the European War, where British and American strategic disputes were resolved by compromises that satisfied no one and seemed to settle very little. The Sextant conference had supposedly rectified this problem by allotting the bulk of available resources to the Navy's central Pacific offensive, but the issue had risen again, phoenix-like, when touched by MacArthur's magical rhetoric.

Nevertheless, orders were orders, and the JSSC dutifully reexamined the issue, reaching the same conclusions as before. As they saw it, the objective was to force the Japanese back to their Japan-Korea-Manchuria citadel, and effecting a lodgment in the China coast was the best way to do that. To get to China, however, the United States needed Formosa, and the quickest, most cost-effective way there was through the Mandates. Moreover, a central Pacific offensive would take best advantage of growing American naval and air power, preserve the momentum gained by the recent victory in the Gilberts, cut the Japanese off from SWPA, provide bases for Arnold's B-29 long-range bombers against Japan, and provoke a showdown battle with the Japanese fleet.

A SWPA-dominated offensive, on the other hand, would require an extensive land campaign against large Japanese forces close to their supply lines, and even if MacArthur did succeed in reaching Mindanao, then what? Mindanao was nowhere, at least nowhere that would hurt the Japanese war effort. In short, the JSSC continued to believe that Nimitz's offensive should have primary emphasis and SWPA should get what was left over.[57] The JWPC report more or less endorsed this position.[58]

To complete the sweep, the Joint Staff Planners (JPS) weighed in against MacArthur as well. In their thinking, the key to the Pacific War was not the Philippines, as MacArthur claimed, but Formosa, whose capture, unlike either Luzon or the China coast, would enable American forces both to cut off Japan from the Netherlands East Indies and to provide staging positions for a blockade of Japan itself. Getting to the Philippines would take too long, and anyway the archipelago's port facilities were too underdeveloped for the operations the JPS had in mind. To reach Formosa, the JPS, like the JSSC and JWPC, advocated—or, more accurately, re-advocated—a central Pacific offensive.[59]

Not that the JPS believed that MacArthur should be taken out of the game altogether, especially with the Japanese reinforcing New Guinea. The island should be conquered and used to support the central Pacific offensive. To that end, the JPS recommended that SWPA bypass Kavieng and strike Hollandia on New Guinea's north coast. From there, MacArthur could exploit Hollandia's airbases to neutralize western New Guinea and aid the Navy's operations against the Palaus. Indeed, the JPS believed that SWPA could jump directly from Hollandia to Mindanao, bypassing the Vogelkop, Halmahera, and the Arafura Sea islands. This would place MacArthur within range of the China-Formosa-Luzon area, although the JCS had not yet decided which of those three targets would be invaded.[60]

These reports by and large confirmed King's long-established views and gave the CNO plenty of ammunition against Sutherland when MacArthur's chief of staff came within range. King, however, was prepared to go even further to discomfort the SWPA commander. As King saw it, MacArthur was more interested in personally liberating the Philippines than in winning the war.[61] King, however, believed that Luzon should be bypassed altogether in favor of Formosa, although he continued to favor a New Guinea offensive to Mindanao.[62]

AAF chief Arnold, for his part, questioned Mindanao's value. If Formosa was the goal in the China-Formosa-Luzon area, then Mindanao's airfields were too far away to support a landing there. Like King, he saw Formosa as the key, but he was not as sure how to get there. He was certain, though, that now was the time to decide and put the issue to rest.[63]

Marshall also had doubts. He agreed with King, Arnold, and Leahy that the immediate objective was the China-Formosa-Luzon area, but he questioned the JSSC report, which left some unanswered questions in his mind about amphibious craft allocation, the role of land and naval air power, and the timing of POA and SWPA offenses. In addition, he wanted more information about the big Japanese naval base on Truk before determining whether it should be bypassed.[64] Moreover, unlike the rest of the JCS, Marshall had to deal directly with MacArthur, and he could not have been happy with what he was hearing from his SWPA commander. MacArthur sent Sutherland to Washington armed with two weapons— three, if you count the bare-knuckled Sutherland himself—to fight the long-odds battle over Pacific strategy.

The first, Reno IV, was legitimate enough; in fact, the JCS had asked for it when they rejected its predecessor. Reno IV, submitted on 5 March 1944, after MacArthur's sudden victory in the Admiralties, called for an acceleration in New Guinea operations. MacArthur still wanted to take Kavieng and conduct operations in the Arafura Sea, but he favored bypassing Hansa Bay in favor of Hollandia, up the coast. From there, SWPA forces could take Geelvink Bay and Halmahera, and then assault Mindanao not in February 1945 but in mid-November. Mindanao could be used as a springboard for Formosa if necessary, although MacArthur was really aiming at Luzon in January 1945.[65] To MacArthur, the Philippines remained the key to the Pacific War, and at issue was the control and timing of that campaign.[66]

If this did not do the trick, MacArthur was prepared to resort to a more underhanded tactic: coercion. MacArthur told Sutherland to relay to Marshall that any decrease in his forces or responsibilities would reflect negatively on him and his subordinates as well as undermine Australian confidence in the war effort, especially now that success was in sight in his theater. However, he conceded that he did not need to be placed in overall Pacific command since he believed he and Nimitz could cooperate effectively.[67] To make sure Marshall got the point, MacArthur instructed Sutherland to warn the chief of staff that if the Sextant conference decisions were carried out, "my professional integrity, indeed my personal honor would be so involved that if otherwise I request that I be given early opportunity to personally present the case to the Secretary of War and the President before finally determining my own personal action in the matter."[68]

MacArthur's threat to disrupt the Pacific War effort undoubtedly weighed on Marshall's mind on 11 March 1944, when the JCS met to resolve Pacific strategy once and for all. They did not meet alone, at least not yet. Sutherland, representing MacArthur, was there, as were JCS staffers defending their papers and Nimitz and chief POA planner Rear Admiral Forrest Sherman, both brought in to reinforce King's—and pretty much everyone else's—position that a central Pacific offensive was the way to go.

Despite the odds, or perhaps because such desperate straits required desperate tactics, Sutherland, here and in his written statement, assumed the offensive by attacking the JCS staff position papers. He called the JSSC report "a biased argument to support a predetermined decision" that disregarded "the views of both responsible commanders in the Pacific."[69] As for the JPS study, it was full of erroneous assumptions, such as its assertion that a central Pacific offensive could succeed without ground-based air support. Even under the best of circumstances, a Mandates campaign would consume an entire year, with few strategic benefits. If and when the Navy ever did get around to attacking Formosa, it had underestimated the amount of air support such an operation entailed.

Moreover, the JPS also did not understand SWPA, and they underestimated what MacArthur could do with his limited forces—assuming, of course, that he could do it his way. To work his strategic magic, however, MacArthur needed intermediate bases between Hollandia and Mindanao; Hollandia did not have the proper facilities to support an assault on Mindanao, so SWPA would have to stage out of faraway Milne Bay. Before MacArthur even got to Hollandia, however, he had to have Kavieng and its airfields. Due to the poor terrain, the Admiralties alone would not do, especially if SWPA had to share the place with the Navy. Moreover, who knew what those 60,000 Japanese in and around Rabaul would do if SWPA could not seal them off by taking Kavieng? Besides, a Kavieng assault against its

7000-man Japanese garrison was feasible, even if the Hollandia operation was scheduled only two weeks later. King snorted and said that the Kavieng garrison should starve and SWPA simply could build more airfields in the Admiralties.[70]

Stung by Sutherland's criticisms, the JPS planners defended their study. Any campaign on the Asian littoral would require extensive logistical support from the American mainland, so the Mandates had to be taken to provide and protect the direct lines of communications to the Far East. As for SWPA, JPS still believed that seizing Kavieng was both unfeasible and unwise; one staffer called it a "serious error." If the Admiralties did not provide SWPA with enough airfields, then MacArthur could take lightly defended Emirau to the north. The JPS staffers still thought that Hollandia-based air power could neutralize western New Guinea but acknowledged that a SWPA offensive might continue west along the coast.[71]

Sutherland had not come merely to criticize, though. He had a plan, and he presented the specifics of Reno IV. By way of overview, he emphasized that there were not enough resources in the Pacific for both a POA and SWPA offensive and that there was no need for an overall Pacific commander because MacArthur and Nimitz could cooperate effectively, though some naval forces should be placed under SWPA command. Nimitz's responsibilities, however, should be limited to protecting MacArthur's offensive up the New Guinea coast to Mindanao and then Luzon. In response to a question from Marshall, Sutherland stated that although the Vogelkop's oil demanded its seizure, other points along the New Guinea coast could be bypassed if the situation developed properly. He emphasized, however, that a decision had to made soon so that SWPA could get to Mindanao before the rainy season.[72]

Nimitz and Sherman had their say as well. Under King's baleful eyes, Nimitz, encouraged by the Navy's recent easy successes in the Marshalls, said that he concurred with the JPS report. He emphasized that any Pacific plan required the seizure of the Mandates to protect lines of communications with the United States; ground-based planes from New Guinea could not do the job. Nimitz also disliked the idea of attacking Mindanao; Japanese air strength in the Celebes Sea was uncertain, and such an offensive probably would not lead to a decisive naval battle. King added that the area was anyway too crowded for the American fleet to maneuver in, making it vulnerable to Japanese submarines and aircraft. The Formosa region, on the other hand, was very roomy, and the island was important enough to provoke the Japanese fleet into action. As for the Mandates, King went on to say that "the importance of the Palaus cannot be overestimated. Ultimately the Mariannas [sic], Carolines, and Palaus must be cleared. It is to our advantage to do this as early as possible. . . . Since [the islands] must be cleared sooner or later, it should be done now."[73] Sherman essentially agreed and added that the Japanese could reinforce the Marianas fast, which prompted Leahy to say that if this was true, then the islands better be taken soon.[74]

The Big Decision

On the morning of 12 March 1944, the day after Sutherland and the Navy shot it out in the Pentagon, the JCS met in closed session to, they hoped, settle Pacific strategy once and for all.[75] It was not to be; emerging later that day, they presented MacArthur and Nimitz with yet another compromise that resolved the immediate strategic issue but little beyond that. Their decision, however, had an enormous impact on the conduct of MacArthur's New Guinea campaign that summer.

On the surface at least, the JCS decision looked like just another reaffirmation of the decisions made at Casablanca and Cairo. The Joint Chiefs ordered both SWPA and the POA to conduct offenses across the Pacific toward the China-Formosa-Luzon area, but they placed the emphasis on Nimitz's forces. As the JCS saw it, the "most feasible route to Formosa-Luzon-China area is by way of Marianas-Carolines-Palaus-Mindanao area." To get there, Nimitz was ordered to bypass Truk from the north—recent carrier operations showed that the Japanese naval citadel was not that strong after all—take the Marianas for bases for Arnold's B-29s, and hit the Palaus in September.

MacArthur's job was to support this northern offensive by overrunning New Guinea and occupying Mindanao. Speed and economy being all important, the service chiefs told him to bypass Kavieng and seize Emirau instead.[76] Emirau, along with the Admiralties, would provide enough airfields to seal off Rabaul and support operations further west. Believing that Hollandia was the key to New Guinea, the JCS ordered MacArthur to take it and use its airbases to assist naval operations in the Palaus and to neutralize western New Guinea. After that, SWPA, "with available forces [will] conduct operations along the New Guinea coast and such other operations as may be feasible in preparations in support of the Palau operation and the assault on Mindanao." The Mindanao attack was slated for 15 November; however, the objective was not to liberate the Philippines, but rather, "the establishment of air forces to reduce and contain Japanese forces in the Philippines preparatory to a further advance to Formosa either directly or"—and surely this caught MacArthur's eye—"via Luzon."[77]

At first glance, MacArthur had not won the interservice battle over Pacific dominance, but neither, a second hard look showed, had he lost it. To be sure, the JCS placed most of its hopes on the central Pacific campaign, but MacArthur had not lost his seat at the Pacific War table. The JCS directive permitted him an offensive toward the Philippines and held out the possibility of a Luzon campaign. MacArthur and the service chiefs differed on Luzon's role in Pacific strategy, but the JCS directive was broad enough to accommodate both conceptions—for now anyway. MacArthur, in short, could still liberate the Philippines, provided that his SWPA offensive placed him in a good enough position to resurrect the debate in earnest when he and Nimitz approached the China-Formosa-Luzon area.[78]

The New Guinea campaign came into play here. To reopen the strategic debate in favor of Luzon, MacArthur had to prove that SWPA could outperform the POA offensive by getting to the China-Formosa-Luzon area before his Navy comrades. A speedy and cost-effective drive across the New Guinea coast would do just that. New Guinea, in short, was now more than just a road to the Philippines; it was a racetrack as well, with the Navy running hard on a parallel lane to the north. MacArthur gambled that the victor's prize would be enough enhanced influence over Pacific strategy to persuade the JCS to underwrite a triumphal Philippines liberation campaign. This emphasis on haste played a major role in the manner MacArthur conducted the New Guinea campaign.

Why the JCS constructed yet another jury-rigged strategy is not hard to discern. At heart was interservice politics. Both routes had merit, as seen by Nimitz's recent victories in the Gilberts and Marshalls and MacArthur's sudden occupation of the Admiralties, but adopting one at the cost of abolishing the other was politically impossible. King was unwilling to have the Navy play a subordinate role to MacArthur, and MacArthur made it equally clear that he would not participate in an offensive under naval command that overlooked the Philippines. By permitting both offenses toward the vaguely defined China-Formosa-Luzon area, the JCS appeased the Navy and held out to MacArthur the carrot of liberating the Philippines somewhere down the line if he cooperated now. The basic issue of Pacific War dominance remained, but it would have to be resolved at a future date.

The irony is that despite an American military doctrine that advocated concentration of force and an industrial infrastructure that enabled the United States to apply overwhelming power at any point of its choosing, the JCS used these tools not to wage war with maximum effectiveness but to placate bureaucratic rivalries, even though, arguably, harmonious inter-service relations did constitute an achievement that best advanced the war effort. As it turned out, the American military could afford even this costly tendency. Despite the dispersion of Pacific resources, the United States still had enough power to overwhelm the outgunned Japanese.

Scholars have often criticized the dual drive decision.[79] Two offenses scattered scarce Pacific resources and increased pressure on a logistical net-work already stretched to the limit by the far-flung Pacific War. Moreover, two weaker drives presented opportunities to the Japanese to use their in-terior lines to concentrate their dwindling resources on either prong in the hopes of defeating the Americans in detail. King's refusal to give SWPA sig-nificant naval forces exacerbated this possibility, making MacArthur's of-fensive especially vulnerable to a sudden attack by the Japanese fleet. For-tunately for the Americans, the Japanese Navy, itself entranced by Mahanian visions of a decisive sea battle, never took full advantage of this opportunity. Using both Nimitz's and MacArthur's routes doubled the number of islands the Americans had to pry loose from their die-hard Japanese defenders, with a proportional decline in the number of men that could be applied to each operation and, presumably, a commensurate in-crease in the time and casualties it took to reach the Japanese mainland.

Such criticisms, however, downplay or discount the seriousness of the interservice rivalry. Of course, the consensus-bound JCS, unable to resolve their Pacific strategy differences, might have petitioned the president, but none of the service chiefs wanted to abdicate their strategic responsibilities to the unpredictable Roosevelt, who had already shown a positive genius for disrupting American grand strategy.[80] The JCS, in other words, was gambling that their flawed dual drive strategy would cause less damage to the American war effort than any plan FDR might come up with should they appeal to him.

Besides, as things turned out, there were some advantages to the dual drive offensive. JCS predictions that the two offenses would be mutually supporting came true.[81] The central Pacific campaign drained off most Japanese naval and air power in SWPA, reducing their mobility and limiting their strategic options in the region, thus contributing to MacArthur's swift advance across New Guinea. Similarly, the SWPA offensive tied down large numbers of ground troops, which the Japanese might otherwise have stuffed into the Marianas and Palaus, whose capture in June and Septem-ber 1944 proved difficult enough as it was.

Moreover, resource dispersal cut both ways. The dual drive diluted American military power in the Pacific, but it did the same to the Japanese, who could far less afford it. Japan's defensive role forced them to scatter their forces among innumerable potential objectives, unlike the Americans, who possessed the strategic initiative and therefore determined which potential targets became real ones. Two offenses against the eastern half of their far-flung defense perimeter made it more difficult for the Japanese to figure out where the next blow would fall, keeping them off balance. MacArthur and Nimitz were thus able to concentrate their resources against relatively weak and isolated positions. By the time the Japanese rushed reinforcements to the threatened point—if they tried at all—it was too late. Later in the war, however, as the Japanese perimeter shrank and it became more obvious where the closing-in American forces would attack, American casualties increased dramatically in bloody slugging matches against well-prepared Japanese positions on Iwo Jima and Okinawa.

To be sure, the dual drive was logistically difficult, but a single offensive, despite a proportionate increase in support personnel, would not necessarily have eased the burden. As it was, the underdeveloped and far-flung SWPA and POA theaters, both of which lacked the infrastructure modern war demanded, could support only so many troops. Throughout much of 1944, only a few of the available combat units were actually fighting. The balance were resting or training in swamp-ridden pestholes, but they still had to be fed, clothed, and otherwise supplied. A single thrust offensive might not have found timely employment for all these idle units. Doubling MacArthur's or Nimitz's resources, in short, did not guarantee a commensurate increase in tempo. Nor is it likely that the JCS could have simply diverted superfluous units to Europe. By the time the JCS made its decision, all but five of the divisions that ultimately saw combat in the Pacific were already there. Of the remaining five, two were Marine divisions that would probably have been deployed in the Pacific no matter what. During the war, MacArthur and Nimitz tried hard to hold on to what units they had, and gave them up only in exchange for something of commensurate value. This, along with prevailing shipping constraints and King's commitment to the Pacific War made any major redeployment unlikely.

Either way, for good or ill, the JCS 12 March directive set the stage for MacArthur's New Guinea offensive. Now the SWPA commander could focus his attention—for the moment, anyway—on that other enemy: the Japanese.

MACARTHUR GEARS UP

After thumbing through an Army-issued guidebook about New Guinea as his troopship steamed toward the big island, Private Sy Kahn noted in his diary, "New Guinea did not sound particularly inviting."[1] That turned out to be an understatement of monumental proportions, but Kahn guessed otherwise when the New Guinea coast came into view. His first impression was of "a vast mountainous country, bathed in mist, and luxuriously green" with a shore that "looked inviting, and like the typical tropical islands that one has seen pictures of, read about, or imagined."[2] As Kahn subsequently discovered, the Army, with more than a year of bitter experience under its belt, was considerably closer to the mark. Later, after taking it all in, Kahn referred to New Guinea as possessing "the most unreceptive terrain imaginable."[3] Another visitor, seeing misery beyond just the island's landscape, called the place "a military nightmare."[4]

A nightmare indeed, and in more than one way. Behind New Guinea's beautiful green-carpeted mountains, placid coastline, and bright blue ocean lurked countless hazards that threatened a GI's life and limb as much as Japanese bullets, which were numerous enough. The mountains were jagged and impassable, the coast a swamp- and jungle-ridden expanse full of razor-sharp kunai grass up to seven feet high, and uncharted coral reefs skulked offshore, waiting to rip open landing craft bottoms like so many tin cans.

The wildlife complemented the terrain. The man-eating crocodiles, three-foot-long lizards, birds of paradise, big black flightless cassowaries, huge bats, tree kangaroos, parrots, and poisonous snakes were scary enough but rarely life-threatening or even visible. More irritating were the insects—mosquitoes, wasps, scorpions, centipedes, cockroaches, fleas, chiggers, leeches, ants, and flies—that swarmed everywhere, as if receiving orders directly from Tokyo. Most dangerous of all, however, were the microorganisms that thrived on the island, transmitting malaria, dengue and blackwater fevers, amebic and bacillary dysentery, tropical ulcers, scrub typhus, yaws, and innumerable other exotic diseases that had little in common beyond point of origin and misery inflicted.

Mother nature took her toll in other ways as well, mostly, but not exclusively, through continual torrential downpours that rotted everything from clothes to skin and rusted guns and other implements of war. Some areas received more than 100 inches of rain annually, and deluges continued almost daily even through the May–October "dry season." The rain caused sluggish streams and rivers to rise with dirty, debris-ridden water that inundated camps, turning them into foul-smelling bogs of mud for GIs to slog through. When it was not raining, the scorching sun and humidity made life just as wretched. Indeed, the clouds reminded one suffering soldier of hot steam rising.[5] Night brought some relief, but eerie animal sounds, cracking rotting wood, crawling insects, and condensed moisture dripping from trees punctuated the inky darkness, convincing more than one lonely sentry that all the Japanese in the world were just a few feet away. One journalist later remarked, "We who experienced New Guinea thought it was the ultimate nightmare country."[6]

The nightmare was pretty big, too. New Guinea, the planet's second largest island, extends 1300 miles east to west, covering a total of 312,329 square miles, more than Texas. Put another way, a United States map superimposed over SWPA (as shown in Figure 1), with Bougainville at New York City, would show Milne Bay at Charleston, Darwin at El Paso, Borneo at Seattle, Sourabaya at San Francisco, and the Japanese bases on New Guinea's north coast scattered across the Great Lakes and upper Midwest. MacArthur's Brisbane General Headquarters (GHQ) would be located in Miami. From another geographic perspective, the distance from Milne Bay to Manila—the road MacArthur planned to travel—was equal to that from the Black Sea to Iceland.[7]

Size complicates military operations in all sorts of logistical and operational ways, but the problem posed by New Guinea's vast expanse was exacerbated by a primitiveness bordering on prehistoric. With almost no roads, port facilities, or airfields, staging and supplying a modern army there was more complex and difficult than fighting it, which was hard enough. Unable to move very far or fast along the jungle-ridden coast, the Army took to the sea, using the long northern coastline as a transportation artery for troops, equipment, and supplies. As such, the New Guinea campaign resembled Nimitz's central Pacific offensive; both advanced from point to point by water. The Army brought its civilization along—if not in behavior then at least in technological terms—as it moved up the coast, clearing the jungle to construct the wharves, dockyards, warehouses, depots, dumps, airdromes, hospitals, highways, and recreational facilities a modern American army required to function in its primary task of destroying its opponent.

Strategy is the creature of geography, and the New Guinea campaign was no exception. MacArthur saw the island as a road to the Philippines,

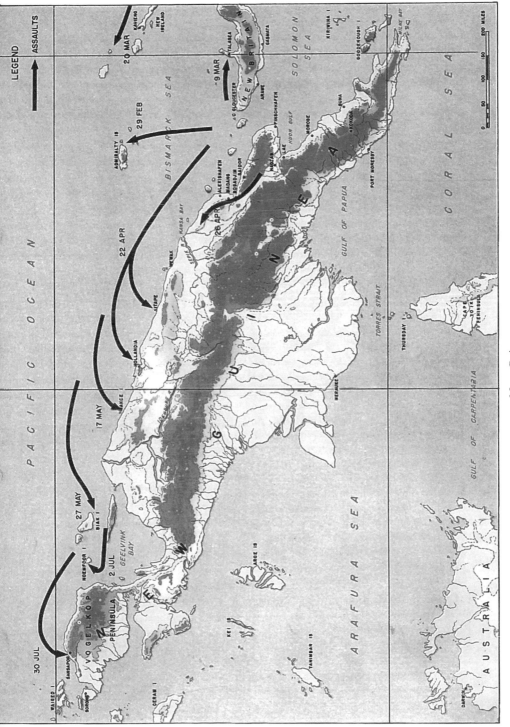

New Guinea

but it was a road fraught with peril, not so much from the south, where the impassable Central Range screened the advancing Americans from any Japanese attacks from the Arafura Sea region, but from the more dangerous north. There Japanese fortresses lurked not only up and down the long New Guinea coastline but also on the vulnerable right flank of MacArthur's advance, providing island bases for sudden Japanese naval sorties, a threat made worse by the Navy's refusal to donate many ships to SWPA.[8] On the other hand, Nimitz's offensive provided some protection, although it was not foolproof. Poor logistical facilities, as well as the campaign's fast tempo, frequently scattered SWPA forces along the coast and exposed them to Japanese attack. American air power only somewhat offset this problem.[9]

Not only did New Guinea's geographic position cause SWPA difficulties, but so did the big island itself. The Army was unaccustomed to waging war in a jungle far from its logistical network. Poor visibility, inadequate maps, a dearth of landmarks, and superb Japanese camouflage techniques forced the Army to fight squad-, platoon-, and company-sized actions, not at all the big conventional European slugging match military thinkers contemplated in their serene prewar days.[10] Nor had they given much thought to the interservice coordination a New Guinea campaign entailed. The Army adjusted, but it never quite learned to accept this alien environment. According to a perhaps apocryphal story, one educated native, asked about American fighting abilities, noted that the GIs were not very good jungle warriors, but that was irrelevant; they simply brought in their heavy equipment, cut down the trees and underbrush, and fought on what was left.[11] It was war, American style.

Lieutenant Colonel Bruce Palmer, Jr., was one of a group of 6th Division staff officers introduced to MacArthur at his Brisbane headquarters in 1944. Addressing the men in dramatic terms, MacArthur told them, "Don't ever surrender because the enemy will not treat you properly. Don't ever back up an inch. Don't give them an inch." Like most men subjected to MacArthur's stirring oration, Palmer was moved and inspired enough to recall the event years later.[12] Indeed, MacArthur always seemed to speak beyond the immediate audience to posterity, as if trying to rally future generations to his posthumous banner.[13]

MacArthur had that effect on people, here and throughout his illustrious life. His abilities, moreover, extended far beyond the rhetorical. He impressed men with his charisma, force of personality, keen intellect—one observer compared his mind to "a beautiful piece of almost perfect machinery"[14]—purposefulness, and courage. Explaining to a subordinate why he never wore his helmet while under fire, MacArthur said, "Well, I wear this cap with all the braid. I feel in a way that I have to. It's my trademark . . . a trademark that many of our soldiers know by now, so I'll keep on wearing it."[15] This, combined with the natural leadership skills of a gentleman aristocrat and an absolute certainty of the justice of whatever cause he advocated, went a long way in explaining his brilliant career.

So far so good, but MacArthur possessed a dark side that made him, as one scholar noted, one of the "most exasperatingly complex men ever produced by the American military, a blend of Caesar and Caligula, skittering along the thin line between brilliance and eccentricity."[16] The fact that his undoubted physical courage bordered on the suicidal, once realized, put a completely different face on the notion of following him into battle. Similarly, his total commitment to his causes often degenerated into self-righteousness, pomposity, self-deception, and egomania. To achieve his goals— which he all too often confused with the nation's—MacArthur lied to and manipulated those around him.[17] Lieutenant Colonel Gerald Wilkinson, Britain's liaison officer to SWPA, probably described MacArthur best: "He is shrewd, proud, remote, highly strung and vastly vain. He has imagination, self-confidence, physical courage and charm, but no humor about himself, no regard for truth, and is unaware of these defects. He mistakes his emotions and ambitions for principles. With moral depth he would be a great man; as it is he is a near miss which may be worse than a mile."[18]

In time, MacArthur—and, more tragically, the men under his command—would pay for these less noble characteristics, but not yet. During the New Guinea campaign, MacArthur's GHQ skillfully protected and advanced its chief's reputation. Informally known as the "Bataan Gang" because many of them had shared the SWPA commander's Philippines ordeal, this exclusive clique helped plan the New Guinea campaign and perpetuated the MacArthur mystique. Like any turbulent household, they frequently quarreled among themselves. Indeed, the only thing they had in common was their association with and devotion to General Douglas MacArthur.[19]

Most of them agreed, however, on their hatred of Sutherland, MacArthur's heavy-handed chief of staff and, as such, the second most powerful figure in SWPA. Brusque, tough, decisive, hard-working, remote, and smart, Sutherland ably served as MacArthur's hatchet man and was capable of dressing down or relieving a subordinate without sympathy or tact. Well aware of the enmity he generated, he resigned himself to it, saying, "Somebody around here has got to be the s.o.b. General MacArthur is not going to be . . . so I guess I'm it."[20] And he was good at it. In doing so, however, he paid a price both personally and professionally. The job stress aggravated his already chronically high blood pressure, and his service to MacArthur ultimately destroyed his career.

For now, though, Sutherland possessed considerable power by maintaining MacArthur's confidence and support. He ran MacArthur's GHQ well enough. Even a rival, SWPA intelligence chief Major General Charles A. Willoughby, acknowledged, "He was almost an ideal chief of staff with a combination of ability and executive vigor."[21] MacArthur was not much of a detail man, so one of Sutherland's tasks was to translate his chief's big ideas into reality. He did this in part by serving as MacArthur's sounding board, someone the SWPA commander could bounce ideas off and get honest responses. Even so, he and MacArthur were never intimates; their relationship was strictly business.

MacArthur paid a price for Sutherland's efficiency. More than one person questioned Sutherland's loyalty to his chief.[22] It was difficult for these doubters to get access to MacArthur, however; Sutherland built a wall around his commander by intimidating his staff and isolating him from outsiders.[23] In fact, Sutherland was intensely ambitious, and this, combined with a cold-blooded willingness to claw his way to the top, did not endear him to SWPA field commanders, who were well aware that his advancement might be at their expense.[24] Without a field command of his own, however, Sutherland's power was completely dependent on his relationship with MacArthur, and as the New Guinea campaign progressed, this relationship was undermined not only by his ambition and tactlessness but also by his relationship with a married Australian woman.

Across the Coral Sea at his Goodenough Island headquarters, Lieutenant General Walter Krueger, MacArthur's New Guinea ground commander, no doubt would have contemplated with pleasure any indication of Sutherland's eventual discomfiture.[25] He had small use for officers anyway, as a class, and he had certainly slain bigger dragons than MacArthur's glass-jawed chief of staff to secure his current position as head of the American 6th Army.[26] Indeed, Krueger had come up the hard way, enlisting as a private for the Spanish-American War, then working his way through the ranks. Under normal circumstances the sixty-three-year-old Krueger should have spent the war stateside training troops—Marshall disliked giving field command to anyone over sixty—but MacArthur, searching for an officer senior enough to outrank all Australians who might otherwise command American troops, but low-key enough to keep out of his limelight, asked

Marshall for the German-born general, and Krueger went overseas in February 1943.[27]

Krueger fit MacArthur's bill perfectly, both in rank and personality. Taciturn, careful, disdainful of publicity, and no-nonsense, he reminded more than one person of a tough Prussian officer.[28] His grumpy disposition prompted one high-ranking SWPA officer to observe that he was better than he looked.[29] Another compared him to "a long-suffering high school principal."[30] A former enlisted man himself—he once said, "I want every corporal to understand he's running an army. The only difference between us is I have a bigger army"[31]—Krueger took great interest in the average GI. He emphasized that officers should above all look after their men and claimed, "Weapons are no good unless there are guts at both ends of the bayonet."[32] Beneath the gruff exterior, however, Krueger was something of a military intellectual; he taught at Leavenworth, read widely, and possessed a sound and thorough mind. Still another observer, seeing a duality in Krueger's makeup that escaped most SWPA personnel, called Krueger the meanest man alive with a heart of gold.[33]

That may be, and such a combination had its uses, particularly in surviving the court intrigue that constantly swirled around SWPA GHQ. Fortunately for Krueger, he and MacArthur went way back. Krueger served under Army Chief of Staff MacArthur in the War Department as head of the General Staff's War Plans Division. They got along well enough, and Krueger's nuts-and-bolts conception of war complemented MacArthur's emphasis on the military big picture. Krueger usually kept his peace when he disagreed with his chief, but he often found other ways to get what he wanted.[34] During the New Guinea campaign, MacArthur's desire for speed often conflicted with Krueger's meticulousness, to their mutual frustration. Krueger referred to GHQ pressure as the "needle from behind,"[35] and MacArthur frequently complained about Krueger's lack of dash.[36] To carry out MacArthur's orders, Krueger rode his field commanders hard, pressuring them to take actions they sometimes thought were unwarranted. He was also responsible for developing SWPA's operational plans and coordinating them with the AAF and Navy, and he displayed a surprising amount of tact in doing so. Krueger, in short, served as MacArthur's fullback, running with the ball his chief handed off to him.

The New Guinea campaign, as MacArthur liked to remind people, called for triphibious operations on land, on sea, and in the air.[37] Krueger handled the first area, and Lieutenant General George C. Kenney was responsible for the last arena. Cocky and innovative, Kenney took over SWPA's demoralized 5th Army Air Force in July 1942 and turned it into a

formidable operation that contributed greatly to SWPA's New Guinea victories—and, incidentally, converted MacArthur into an air power enthusiast in the process. To Kenney, war *was* air power; no other dimension interested him.[38] At the same time, however, he did not think that his planes
could win the conflict on their own; instead, he saw his AAF as the tip of
SWPA's triphibious sword. Extremely popular among his men because of his
energy and informal style, he was equally respected by his fellow officers,
one of whom said, "He was a little, rotund, excellent buccaneer. He was
the 'go-get-'em' and 'to-Hell-with-how-we-do-it' type. But he got it done.
He had a great ability to raise morale and give [the men] something to fight
for."[39] Kenney possessed one more attribute. He was one of the few people
willing to tell it to MacArthur straight. "General, you're crazy!" was his favorite form of delivery.[40]

Vice Admiral Thomas C. Kinkaid was the last member of this triphibious triumvirate—together with Kenney and Krueger, the three were called
"MacArthur's KKK," which may or may not have said something about
the SWPA chief's stance on race relations—and the least enviable. Shipped
down to SWPA in late 1943 to command SWPA's small 7th Fleet because he
had got along so well with his Army colleagues while stationed in the Aleutians, Kinkaid had the unpleasant task of serving both MacArthur and his
arch enemy, King.[41] Caught, as it were, between the SWPA devil and King's
deep blue sea, Kinkaid worked hard to gain and maintain MacArthur's
confidence without betraying King's respect.[42] He was smart, professional,
and usually pleasant enough, although sometimes indecisive. As it was, his
chief subordinate, Rear Admiral Daniel Barbey, the forceful, ambitious,
and irreverent commander of the VII Amphibious Force—and respectfully
nicknamed "Dan Dan the Amphibious Man"—provided the Navy's punch
in the New Guinea campaign by commanding SWPA's amphibious forces.[43]

Despite MacArthur's efforts to portray the New Guinea offensive as a
one-man show, his subordinates both at GHQ and in the field played a vital
and independent role in determining the course, tempo, and outcome of the
campaign. They did not always get along with one another, and they were
frequently hindered by insufficient resources, but, in the end, they got the
job done.

Tools of the Trade

New Guinea was not the ideal place for the technology-bound and firepower-loving American Army to wage war. Taking on the Japanese any-

time anywhere was bad enough, but horrible terrain, poor logistical facilities, and long communications lines made it difficult for the Army to function according to standard operating procedure. Fortunately, both the Army and Navy displayed a surprising amount of innovation in developing, enhancing, and applying the tools of war they needed to successfully overcome both New Guinea and the Japanese entrenched along its coast.

There was nothing all that new about intelligence collection; it had been part of warfare since time immemorial. Although SWPA did not have well-placed agents in the enemy's ranks to gather information, it found other ways to uncover Japanese military secrets.

Aerial photographic reconnaissance of Japanese positions provided one mechanism for gathering strategic, operational, and tactical intelligence. Acquiring such intelligence, however, was not easy. Until 1944, only one overworked air photo recon squadron was available for these dangerous and difficult missions. The new year brought reinforcements but no better performance. In January 1944, for instance, only half the photo recon missions flown were successful, and there was not much change in the following months.[44] This prompted an angrier-than-usual Sutherland to complain to Kenney, "In no instance has photography been submitted as originally requested. It has been necessary to constantly revise the priority dates to accommodate the failure to meet the original schedules."[45] By the time GHQ got the photos it requested, it was too late; operational plans had progressed too far to change them much.

These problems were due to a number of factors. The targeted areas were often beyond the recon planes' effective range, and bad weather, inexperienced crews, a lack of landmarks in the dense New Guinea jungle, and lurking Japanese fighter planes did not help matters. Moreover, as the tempo of New Guinea operations increased, and as MacArthur became increasingly flexible in his planning and targets, air photo recons were hard put to keep up.[46] Not that Kenney did not try, and performance improved with better weather and crews, but such information was too late to help GHQ plan the early stages of the campaign, and it often did not satisfy the troops on the ground.[47] Later, although aerial reconnaissance provided SWPA with some good data, interpreters and planners often misinterpreted the photos by underestimating topographical obstacles for amphibious operations.

There were other equally dangerous ways to find out what went on behind Japanese lines, such as ground reconnaissance. Sometimes SWPA trained natives to infiltrate Japanese positions, and although they had little trouble doing so, they lacked the ability to sufficiently explain what they saw. Papuan and pidgin English simply did not have suitable words to describe the host of military equipment in the Japanese arsenal.[48] SWPA also employed civilized white Americans, presumably with bigger vocabularies—usually, but not always, elite Alamo Scouts—to reconnoiter beaches for possible amphibious assault sites. These teams, inserted by plane or submarine, measured tides, beach gradients, shore widths, soil composition, and coral reefs. Unfortunately, they often underestimated the difficulties of getting amphibious men and equipment ashore. Moreover, planning these missions took time, and often the fast-moving and ever-changing New Guinea offensive outran the beach reconnaissance teams.[49] Even when there was enough time, Krueger was often reluctant to use them; if detected, they might tip off the Japanese as to the next American target, depriving SWPA of the element of surprise.

Captured prisoners and documents were also useful, provided they could be attained. The Japanese were notoriously difficult to take alive—although they were surprisingly loose-lipped once interrogated—and the GIS' reluctance to spare those few who did surrender did not help matters, despite SWPA's admonitions to the contrary.[50] Moreover, the typical Japanese soldier rarely had access to any important secrets, although captured officers' diaries occasionally provided valuable material.

Aerial and ground reconnaissance was all well and good, but by 1944 SWPA had a weapon that trumped every other intelligence-gathering mechanism. In January 1944, an Australian engineer unearthed an abandoned Japanese steel trunk at Sio, on the north coast of Northeast New Guinea. After drying the wet paper inside, SWPA intelligence officers discovered that they possessed the main Japanese Army cipher.[51] As it was, SWPA and other Allied codebreaking organizations were already reading other Japanese codes, including, for instance, their water transport system messages—such intelligence was largely responsible for American victories at the Battle of the Bismarck Sea and in the skies over eastern New Guinea—but breaking the Imperial Army's encryption system was SWPA's biggest signal intelligence triumph yet. Collectively known as "Ultra" intelligence, this top secret decryption of Japanese wireless military codes became the most destructive weapon in SWPA's intelligence arsenal.[52] By reading enemy messages, SWPA could determine with relative accuracy Japanese strategy, positions, strengths, ship and troop movements, and supply status.[53]

Since its declassification, some enthusiasts have heralded Ultra as *the* weapon in winning the war, but this is inaccurate. To be sure, Ultra was an immensely valuable tool, but it was not foolproof. It was effective at discerning Japanese activity and plans at the strategic level, but it was less useful operationally and tactically, where local commanders communicated with their subordinates over landlines or via short-range low-powered radio. This disconnect caused problems during the New Guinea campaign. Ultra informed MacArthur when the Japanese Imperial Headquarters wrote off outnumbered, isolated, and outgunned Japanese in New Guinea, who were therefore presumably easy strategic targets. However, American troops at the ground level, taking heavy punishment from their supposedly impotent enemy, saw the situation somewhat differently. Neither GHQ nor its field commanders were wrong, strictly speaking; each simply viewed the situation from different perspectives.

Another problem with SWPA's Ultra was Major General Charles A. Willoughby, MacArthur's German-born intelligence chief and the man responsible for developing the intelligence reports distributed to the theater's field commanders. Willoughby was disliked almost as much as Sutherland, which was saying a lot. Pompous, overbearing, arrogant, big and strong, he was sneeringly called "Sir Charles" behind his back. His appearance and bearing reminded one observer of Hollywood's worst version of a stereotypical Prussian martinet.[54] The real problem, however, was that Willoughby frequently colored his analyses with unsupported opinions, contradictions, and idle speculation. One field commander later said sarcastically, "I was always impressed with the intelligence from GHQ, headed by General Willoughby. He was always very positive in his views . . . and usually wrong."[55] Others, however were more generous: "He was not as bad an intelligence officer as a lot of people will tell you. He was really not too bad. But they used to laugh at some of his estimates of enemy strength. . . . After we collected all the evidence and found out how many were buried, how many got away, and how many were killed in previous bombardments, counting one thing or another, it would add up pretty close to his estimate."[56] That was true enough, in hindsight, but during the New Guinea campaign Willoughby's inconsistent reports, whatever his gold-plated sources, sometimes hindered the successful prosecution of operations. On the whole, however, SWPA's intelligence, especially Ultra, gave MacArthur a huge advantage over the Japanese, much like that of a poker player who can read an opponent's hand without his knowledge. Such information contributed immensely to several of MacArthur's greatest New Guinea victories.

Intelligence—even Willoughby's—was of course important, but it meant nothing unless MacArthur's forces could come to grips with the enemy. To sustain itself on the primitive island, the American Army had to turn New Guinea into a proper war-waging playing field, complete with port facilities, roads, and airfields. Building all this was the Army engineers' responsibility, and a difficult one at that. Despite their obvious importance to SWPA operations, during the New Guinea campaign the engineers were constantly hindered by shortages resulting from the long distance to the American mainland, the difficulty in getting requisitions filled, and GHQ's tendency to give combat commands first priority.

One major problem SWPA engineers faced in 1944 was that there simply were not enough of them. Turning New Guinea into a proper American-oriented battlefield took huge numbers of construction, port, and aviation engineer battalions, as well as depot companies, base equipment companies, dump truck companies, parts supply companies, forestry companies, and a host of other obscure but important units. Even though SWPA had some 85,000 engineers in early 1944, GHQ still estimated that it needed 51,000 more, which would bring the total to 20 percent of all SWPA ground forces.[57] By April, including Australian engineers and the Navy's Construction Battalions (Seabees), SWPA was still short 15,000 engineers, not counting those en route, who raised the total to 33,000.[58] Such shortages took a toll, not only on military operations, but also on the men themselves, whose morale was eaten away by overwork in isolated areas, slow promotions, no opportunity for leave, and broken-down equipment.

The Army tried to bring engineer strength up to par. Reinforcements eventually arrived, but not until after the campaign was nearly over. In the meantime, SWPA reorganized superfluous units like camouflage companies into construction battalions, put aviation engineer units to work on non-AAF projects, and even transferred in lucky infantrymen and artillerymen.[59] All this helped, but the engineers always had more jobs than men and equipment to complete them.

Indeed, frequently enough one of these jobs was combat. Engineers often worked at the front clearing mines, building roads and bridges, unloading supplies and equipment, and undertaking a multitude of other dangerous tasks that exposed them to enemy fire. The infantry called upon the engineers' demolition skills to help them flush hard-to-reach Japanese from pillboxes, bunkers, and caves, an extremely hazardous job under the best of circumstances. Moreover, Japanese infiltrators threatened engineers even behind the front lines, forcing them to go about their jobs armed and on edge. Such extracurricular duties won even Krueger's praise.[60]

Krueger demanded that the engineers keep their machines running around the clock.[61] This was hard to do, however, when the equipment lacked spare parts, which was pretty much all the time.[62] There were constant shortages of electrical supplies, welding materials, bolted steel tanks, lubricators, bulldozers, semitrailers, motorized shop sets, and innumerable other seemingly insignificant components that engineers needed to complete their tasks. It got so bad that an engineer officer was sent back to the States specifically to speed up the requisition process. The problem was not, however, so much inefficiency—although there was a good deal of it— as geography and infrastructure. Distance, the inevitable lag between the submission and fulfilling of requests, and New Guinea's lack of port facilities, warehouse space, and shipping all contributed to these chronic shortages.[63] Here too, matters gradually improved, especially with the arrival of a spare parts company to organize and distribute the thousands of pieces that made machines run, but during the New Guinea campaign, engineer units never had all their equipment in working order.

To make an already bad situation even worse, the engineers themselves often did not understand their jobs. Before Pearl Harbor no one gave much thought to war on a tropical island thousands of miles from nowhere, so the engineers were not well trained for such a contingency. In 1942 and 1943 they had to learn on the job, and often under fire. One report noted that the engineers did not know much about planning and laying out buildings, drainage, earth moving, soil compaction, and equipment operation.[64] It was difficult enough to get the materials necessary for building projects, but the engineers could not even use what they had. As more engineers arrived and war pressures eased in 1944, the Army responded by setting up engineering schools in Australia and Port Moresby, but high-quality workmanship was never a New Guinea hallmark.

Despite these shortcomings—or, more critically, because America's prodigious output of war materiel compensated for these glaring deficiencies—the engineers were in the end able to give MacArthur a huge advantage over the Japanese. Labor-saving American heavy equipment such as bulldozers, angledozers, cranes, rollers, graders, crushers, drilling equipment, and power shovels enabled SWPA to build airfields and ports quickly from scratch.[65] This permitted MacArthur to bypass heavily defended, but, thanks to these newly constructed American airfields and ports, strategically useless, Japanese bases, thus minimizing casualties and maximizing the speed of his advance.

In addition to applying its engineering resources to New Guinea, the Army, in conjunction with the Navy, developed innovative vehicles to transport men and materiel over water to hostile and primitive shores.[66] Among this slew of new, oddly-assorted amphibious craft, one of the most valuable was the oceangoing 328-foot Landing Ship, Tank (LST), which could carry 20 medium tanks, 2000 tons of equipment, or 1000 men directly onto a

beach and unload them via its ramp door. Nicknamed "Large Slow Target"
by its passengers because of its speed—or lack thereof—and its annoying
tendency to attract every Japanese plane in the immediate neighborhood,
LSTs were SWPA's workhorse, carrying men and supplies up and down the
New Guinea coast and participating in amphibious operations.

LSTs were not the only landing craft that transported troops and equipment long distances. The dual-ramped Landing Craft, Infantry (LCI) could
carry 188 troops apiece, almost as many as old converted destroyers, or
APDs. Neither of these could land under fire, so the Army for this purpose
initially used the Landing Craft, Vehicle, Personnel (LCVP), a 36-foot armor-
plated wooden vessel that carried 36 men or 8100 pounds of cargo. In fact,
LCVPs were so important that SWPA set up assembly plants for them in Australia and New Guinea. Later, LCVPs were gradually phased out in favor of
the more effective 50-foot all-steel Landing Craft, Mechanized (LCM) craft,
which carried 60,000 pounds of cargo or 60 troops. To supplement LCVPs
and LCMs, the Army used DUKWs, which, with their watertight hull and
wheels, served as amphibious trucks that shuttled men and supplies ashore.

Amphibious operations involved more than just hitting the beach. The
assaulting infantry had to move inland, and the Army built amphibious vehicles to accompany them. With its steel hull, low silhouette, and cleated
tracks, Landing Vehicles, Tracked (LVTs), or, as they were nicknamed, "Alligators," could travel over water and reefs, scale beaches whatever their
gradient, and move inland with ammunition and materiel. Armed LVTs,
called "Buffaloes," were even more dangerous to the Japanese. They possessed enough firepower to cover advancing infantry, transport heavy
weapons, evacuate wounded under fire, and neutralize hostile bunkers.
One officer stated: "[The Buffalo's] ability to cross coral reefs, to reach dry
land without regard to the slope of the beach and to advance inland, cou-
pled with the low silhouette target presented while they are in the water,
and the fire power with which they can cover their own advance, combine
to make them an essential part of Amphibious Forces."[67]

Bulldozers were equally helpful in securing beaches by clearing fields of
fire, burying Japanese positions, and opening beach exits and trails for
tanks. Said one report: "It is believed that this tactical combination of bulldozer and tank to overcome stubborn enemy resistance from fortified positions is unique in modern warfare. . . . [T]he combined action of bulldozer and tank was one of the most effective means yet discovered to cope
with the problem."[68]

Amphibious vehicles, however, were no better than the soldiers who
crewed them, and in SWPA these men were members of the Army's Engineer

Special Brigades (ESBs). Created by the Army in 1942—the Navy did not have the manpower or resources to do the job—the ESBs were designed specifically to transport and land men and equipment by water over short distances onto a hostile shore, move them off the beach, assist in supplying them, and provide perimeter defense. For this task the Army scoured the east coast for yachtsmen, fishermen, small boat operators, renegade sailors, engineer mechanics, and anyone else with a seagoing background. Fully equipped, each ESB—three of which served in New Guinea—consisted of 7300 men manning some 600 LCVPs and 150 LCMs. They performed beyond everyone's expectations, except perhaps MacArthur's, who was an early enthusiast and snagged them whenever they were offered.[69] ESBs were divided into three Engineer Boat and Shore Regiments (EBSRs), each of which was assigned to a division during amphibious operations. Despite their acknowledged value, the ESBs often had trouble getting proper equipment and spare parts. Only the Navy could provide the bolts, rope, anchors, propellers, and other seagoing necessities, but it did not always have enough of them to go around.

A big problem with amphibious operations was that the landing craft were especially vulnerable to Japanese fire once the preliminary naval and air bombardments had lifted but before the vehicles hit the shore. To fill this gap, the ESBs developed fire support batteries of LCMs and Buffaloes fitted with rockets and machine guns that accompanied the assault waves to the beach. They worked very well; so well, in fact, that by mid-1944 each ESB possessed 1800 machine guns and 1000 rocket tubes, in addition to a host of antiaircraft weapons. By comparison, an infantry division, with twice as many men, had only 435 machine guns.[70] The support batteries gave the ESBs a tremendous wallop and contributed enormously to the success of many amphibious landings on the New Guinea coast. One officer who watched round after round of ESB rockets scream toward a Japanese-held beach wrote afterward:

> In my opinion rockets are the solution to a successful landing on enemy shores. The more boats we equip to fire rockets and the more rockets we fire the greater success we'll have on the shore. . . . They have a devastating effect on the enemy, both from casualties and from the morale standpoint. They have a great value during the time interval between naval or air bombardment and the assault waves hitting the beach. . . . The more we use them the fewer casualties we are going to have.[71]

Without these developments in intelligence, amphibious craft, and engineering, it is doubtful that the New Guinea campaign would have been nearly so successful. These tools gave MacArthur a flexibility, mobility, and firepower that helped compensate for the resources Nimitz's POA offensive siphoned off.

Logistics, Logistics, Logistics

More than 140 ships at a time—oilers, LSTs, Liberty and Laker cargo ships, troop transports, and various other vessels—crowded Milne Bay harbor in January 1944, a sight that undoubtedly warmed the hearts of more than one soldier contemplating the difficult campaign to come. In this case, unfortunately, numbers indicated not logistical efficiency but inertia and mismanagement. Of the scores of ships in Milne Bay, and at the other American-held New Guinea ports of Port Moresby, Oro Bay, and Finschhafen, only a handful were unloaded at any given time. The rest rode at anchor, killing time as seagoing warehouses, as far removed from their designed task as if Japanese torpedoes had sent them to the bottom of the ocean.[72]

A closer look did little to inspire confidence. Some of these cargo ships contained the equipment needed to improve the primitive port facilities and offload more vessels, but supplying combat units up the coast had higher priority, so the gear remained in the shipholds, unused. Even when such vessels managed to dock, the vital but heavy and unwieldy cranes, bulldozers, and earth-moving machines were usually the last items unloaded.[73] This, of course, assumed that the gear got there in one piece; all too often equipment was scattered among several ships and delivered to more than one port. One person reported, "A concrete plant was delivered at ports ranging from Melbourne to Oro Bay. Booms for cranes arrived on different ships at different ports from the main part of the crane."[74]

Unfortunately, getting a ship into dock did not ensure proper and timely delivery of its goods. Port battalions and combat troops pressed into unloading duty ruthlessly pilfered holds of their more valuable goods.[75] Even more mundane commodities were not safe. In 1943, one discouraged observer estimated that 40 percent of SWPA's rations were spoiled or otherwise inedible, the result of poor or prolonged storage that rendered cargo vulnerable to rust, mold, and vermin.[76] At Oro Bay, some 1st Cavalry Division men, unloading a ship, knocked a jeep overboard into the shallow water by the dock. When a chain-laden trooper descended into the Solomon Sea to haul the sunken vehicle out, he discovered eight to ten others.[77] Such wastage might not count for much in other, better-endowed theaters, but it mattered in SWPA, where getting every piece of equipment to the front lines was an ordeal.

All this was merely the tip of the logistical iceberg.[78] Carelessness and avaricious soldiers operating in New Guinea's primeval environment certainly contributed to SWPA's logistical woes, but there was more to it than that. SWPA was at the far end of an incredibly far-flung supply line; San Francisco, the main port of embarkation for ships supplying the theater, was some 6200 miles from Brisbane and 5800 miles from New Guinea.[79] Moreover, the Army had never fought an island-based war like this one. Army procedures were geared toward supplying a host of soldiers fighting on a continuous front, but SWPA troops were scattered up and down the New Guinea and Australian coasts in some seventy different locations, making it hard to systematize the flow of supplies.[80] To make matters worse, there were never enough port and quartermaster units to do the job, so untrained combat troops were often drafted to unload ships, a hard, dangerous, and repetitive task that many not only considered beneath their dignity but also took time away from combat training.[81]

The appearance of all those ships marking time in Milne Bay harbor was deceptive in other ways. Throughout the New Guinea campaign, SWPA never had enough vessels to transport the men, supplies, and equipment GHQ believed necessary to keep the war going properly. Not that MacArthur did not try; once a merchant ship entered SWPA's logistical network, GHQ attempted to keep it there and resisted all efforts to pry it loose.[82]

But it was never enough. In March 1944, an alarmed Joint Military Transportation Committee (JMTC) informed the JCS that there would be a chronic shipping crisis in the Pacific that year amounting to a 15 percent deficit. The impending assaults on Normandy and southern France that spring meant that the JCS could not tap into the Atlantic shipping pool to close the gap. Worse yet, the greatest shortfalls, by about a third, would be in May and June, just when both MacArthur's New Guinea and Nimitz's Marianas campaigns were to get into full swing. The JMTC recommended that the Pacific theaters try to unload their vessels faster and decrease turnaround time, review requirements to see what could be postponed, and meet with them for a Pacific shipping conference.[83]

MacArthur did not like this at all. Having gained the JCS's permission to run a race with the POA to the China-Formosa-Luzon area with the trophy, in his mind anyway, being the right to liberate the Philippines, he was not about to be deterred by logistical problems that denied him his running shoes, so to speak. His GHQ estimated that SWPA required not only all the vessels already in the theater but some seventy-one more Liberties not yet authorized.[84] Even so, his staffers believed that a New Guinea campaign was still possible if the shipping cutbacks were evenly distributed throughout the Pacific.[85] The Washington Pacific Shipping Conference, held on 18–25 April 1944, solved little. The JMTC members presented their recommendations, but skeptical POA and SWPA representatives claimed that they were already doing these things.[86]

In the end, although there were shipping deficits, SWPA was able to carry out its New Guinea campaign, in part because the JCS simply spread out the pain among the SWPA, POA, and China–Burma–India theaters, cutting back each's shipping. MacArthur's surprisingly easy success at Hollandia also eased SWPA's shipping burden.[87] Events in Europe, however, played an even more important role. The postponement of the invasion of southern France until August released some 208 vessels for Pacific duty, and this is what really enabled the New Guinea campaign to progress as smoothly— logistically speaking, that is—as it did.[88]

Ships carried the vast majority of SWPA equipment and supplies, but Kenney's AAF also played a vital logistical role in the New Guinea campaign. AAF transport planes—especially C-47s, a military version of the civilian DC-3, capable of carrying twenty-seven men or five tons of cargo— not only played a valuable role in evacuating the wounded but frequently bridged the gap between amphibious landings and the establishment of supply services on the beach. AAF airdrops succored advancing infantry as it moved off the beaches to attack Japanese-held airfields inland. Without these airdrops, the undersupplied infantry would have had to wait for engineers to get the beaches and trails in good enough shape for supply-laden trucks to reach them. The delay would have provided the usually surprised Japanese with valuable time to recoup and prepare their defenses, hindering MacArthur's plans for a fast advance across New Guinea. Instead, the C-47s kept the infantry moving toward its objectives, regardless of what was happening back at the congested beachheads. In addition, the AAF airdropped supplies to surrounded SWPA forces, enabling them to maintain their positions even when cut off from base.[89] Doing so, however, was not easy for anyone involved. The damp jungle frequently restricted radio communications, and it was difficult to find suitable drop zones amid the tangled undergrowth.[90] The C-47s flew in low, circled the drop zone twice to make sure they were on target, and kicked supplies and equipment out the cargo door, tactics that often exposed them to withering antiaircraft fire. To make matters worse, the descending cargo occasionally landed on unwary soldiers, killing them.[91] Despite these difficulties, air supply gave SWPA a valuable, albeit imperfect, weapon the Japanese lacked.

MacArthur frequently decried his materiel poverty, but he had a logistical ace up his sleeve: Australia. During the New Guinea campaign, the island nation contributed significantly to SWPA not only in terms of troops but also with supplies and equipment. Despite its inadequate infrastructure—at one point the northeastern city of Townsville had 185 ships in its 9-dock port[92]—Australia provided MacArthur's forces with a host of mundane goods a modern army needed: cement, pipe, tar, culverts, paints, sheet metal, wire rope, explosives, and agricultural equipment like plows, mowers, and cultivators that aviation engineers used to construct airstrips.[93] Even Lend Lease to Australia benefited SWPA: "Thus, the expansion of Australian industries, aided and accelerated by Lend Lease materials, has enabled the Australian Government to furnish under Reverse Lend Lease many vital supplies which lessen the strain upon our own production and upon the overburdened shipping resources of the Pacific."[94] Later that year GHQ itself admitted, "General MacArthur was able to supplement his supplies by drawing heavily on local production."[95]

This fact, among others, convinced some in Washington that MacArthur's constant harping about his lack of resources was not wholly justified.[96] Marshall, for one, thought that a big part of the problem was inadequate supply and administration procedures, so in September 1943 he sent Lieutenant General Brehon Somervell, the Army's chief supply officer, to SWPA to look things over and make suggestions.[97] Somervell came and went and noted that although a lack of service troops and railways, as well as the theater's distance from the United States, plagued SWPA, the real difficulty was that GHQ put itself in a logistical box. SWPA needed service troops to support combat operations, but the service troops could not function effectively until they had adequate port facilities, which would not become available until MacArthur gave the matter greater priority.[98]

Doing this, however, would mean slowing down combat operations, which could cause MacArthur to lose his race with Nimitz to the China-Formosa-Luzon region. GHQ preferred to keep shipments moving to and through underdeveloped and congested areas to make sure that combat units had the men, equipment, and supplies they needed to advance quickly along the New Guinea racetrack.[99] In the meantime, soldiers were plagued by a faulty distribution system that hindered them from getting any of the things that made war a little easier: perishable foods, movies, leave, even mail.[100] This was the price MacArthur—or, more accurately, his troops—paid to place SWPA in a position to liberate the Philippines, although such a strategy arguably speeded up the war and, in the long run, saved lives.

The Japanese Position

For the Japanese, the war had not gone entirely according to plan. At first, Japan's initial onslaught, which in six short months netted them a sizable chunk of the globe against the unprepared and bewildered Allies, exceeded their most optimistic predictions. By mid-1942, the Japanese had added the Aleutians, Gilberts, Netherlands East Indies, Burma, Malaysia and Singapore, New Britain and the Solomons, Hong Kong, Guam, Wake Island, and the Philippines to an already extensive empire that extended from the Home Islands to Manchuria, much of China, Indochina, and Formosa. After that, however, things went terribly wrong. Military defeats at Coral Sea and Midway and in New Guinea and the Solomons were bad enough, but they were symptomatic of a far more serious problem than the loss of another island or carrier. The Japanese had assumed that their shattering string of victories would demoralize and paralyze an American public unwilling to pay the bloody price required to wrest away Japan's newly won empire. Instead, a vengeful United States was organizing a military machine that was beginning to show every indication of grinding the Japanese into dust as it rolled westward across the Pacific.

Indeed, for all its initial military successes, Japan was in almost all respects incapable of waging a protracted conflict against an industrial giant like the United States, a fact many Japanese military leaders recognized from the onset.[101] Despite Japanese doubts about American industrial capacity and moral fiber, taking on the United States was a daunting task for an island empire with glaring military and economic weaknesses. By attacking the Western powers in December 1941, the Japanese committed themselves to a multifront war that stretched their resources to, and quickly beyond, the breaking point. In addition to fending off the increasingly ominous American counteroffensive across the Pacific, Tokyo had to confront an Anglo-Indian army on the Burma border, garrison an empire that comprised one fourth of the earth's total surface, keep an eye on the Soviets, and, worst of all, cope with a never-ending war in China that seemed to swallow up without a trace—or anyhow without much in the way of conclusive results—significant Japanese resources. In fact, before Pearl Harbor, Japan had to place thirty-six of its fifty-one divisions—more than a million and a half men—in China and Manchuria, reducing the forces available for its initial offensive to a mere eleven divisions. Finally, Japan had to wage this extensive air, land, and sea war with an inadequate command structure in which the Army and Navy often distrusted one another and shared plans and information only as a last resort.

All this was bad enough, but unlike the United States, the Japanese could not count on abundant materiel to compensate for shortcomings in other areas of war-making. The war in China had overstrained the Japanese economy even before Pearl Harbor, causing Tokyo to introduce rationing and to cut back on nonmilitary production. Although the purpose of the Japanese attack on the Western powers had been to gain the raw materials—especially oil—necessary to achieve economic autarchy, the end result pushed the economy toward critical mass. As an island empire, Japan was dependent upon its merchant marine, but by 1943 one in six merchantmen was out of commission,[102] and American submarines in particular were beginning to take a terrible toll on the remaining vessels, especially the all-important oil tankers. Japanese merchant fleet tonnage declined from 5.8 million at the end of 1942 to 2.7 million by December 1944.[103] Similar shortages and inefficiencies plagued the rest of the war economy from aircraft carrier to fighter plane to aluminum to truck production, particularly as it became more difficult to get raw materials to the homeland. These pressures were apparent even before the American counteroffensive got rolling.

In January 1943, recognizing that they had lost the strategic initiative, the Japanese established a defensive perimeter from the southern Netherlands East Indies through New Guinea and Rabaul, then north through the Gilberts, Wake, and finally the Aleutians. From bases scattered across this interlocking defense network, Tokyo hoped to use its interior lines to wear down any American assault, using Japanese blood to buy time for the American public to tire of the conflict and negotiate a peace favorable to Tokyo. To be sure, plenty of Japanese—as well as American and Australian—blood was shed that year as MacArthur and Nimitz painfully pushed the Japanese out of Papua and Northeastern New Guinea, the southern and central Solomons, the Gilberts, and the Aleutians, but the United States showed no signs of giving in. That September, in response to Operation Cartwheel's success, the Japanese tightened their defensive perimeter further, surrendering Rabaul to its fate, and even, in February 1944, moving their fleet from its Truk stronghold in the Carolines to safer positions westward.[104] Behind these island walls, Tokyo hoped to rebuild its forces for a decisive battle at a later date.

The Americans' methods were even more disturbing than their hitherto limited success in applying them. The Japanese garrisons on Attu and Tarawa—in, respectively, the Aleutians and the Gilberts—were not driven out but rather, in almost the blink of an eye, totally obliterated by an American military machine that applied overwhelming firepower and materiel superiority. The American assaults did not exhibit much finesse at the tactical level, but it was hard to argue with their success; not that there were many Japanese left after each operation to try. Moreover, as the Japanese would soon learn, the American amphibious steamroller seemed impervious to the laws of entropy; as it advanced it gathered momentum, violence, and fury.

To make matters worse, the Americans were already displaying an alarming tendency to strike the Japanese where they were weakest, cutting off and isolating their strong points and in effect transforming them into vast jungle prison camps. Ground down by the previous year's setbacks, and already feeling the pinch of the American Navy's increasingly relentless submarine campaign, the Japanese could not begin to match an American strategic mobility that neutralized the effect of their possession of interior lines.[105] Said one Japanese intelligence staff officer after the war:

> This was the type of strategy we hated most. The Americans, with minimum losses, attacked and seized a relatively weak area, constructed airfields and then proceeded to cut the supply lines to troops in that area. Without engaging in a large-scale operation, our strongpoints were gradually starved out. . . . [T]he Americans flowed into our weaker points and submerged us, just as water seeks the weakest entry to sink a ship.[106]

It was easy to pity those surrounded Japanese, who were quickly reduced to a squalid, disease-ridden, hand-to-mouth existence, but their fate was preferable to their comrades who found themselves in the direct path of an American juggernaut that concentrated enough firepower on its target to reduce the immediate locale to a bleak moonscape.

Not that the Japanese were giving up the fight; far from it. Tokyo saw MacArthur's offensive as the greatest threat, since its loss would expose the strategically vital China-Formosa-Luzon choke-point to attack, so Imperial Headquarters ordered in reinforcements.[107] To organize them, the Japanese created the 2nd Area Army, under General Korechika Anami, to command the 19th Army in the Netherlands East Indies and Lieutenant General Fusataro Teshima's new 2nd Army in western New Guinea. Both Anami and Teshima were headquartered in Manokwari.[108]

Ordering reinforcements to New Guinea was one thing, but actually moving and deploying them there was something else. The 36th division arrived in the Sarmi area in December 1943, and began digging in after sending a regiment to nearby Biak. Unfortunately, much of the 32nd and 35th Divisions were lost to American submarines, and pressing business in China, as well as lack of shipping, kept the 3rd Division there. To fill the gap, Imperial Headquarters assigned the 14th Division to New Guinea.

Nimitz's invasion of the Marshall Islands in February 1944, however, convinced the Japanese that the Americans planned to hit the Mandates next, so they diverted the unit to the Palaus. Moreover, moving the division siphoned off shipping to New Guinea, forcing the Japanese on the island to postpone airdrome and other construction projects.[109] Despite these problems, the 2nd Army, with the 36th Division and submarine-ravaged elements from the newly arrived 32nd and 35th divisions at Halmahera Island in the Netherlands East Indies, had some 50,000 men entrenched in western New Guinea by April 1944.[110]

Lieutenant General Hatazo Adachi's 18th Army was already in eastern New Guinea, recuperating in the Hansa Bay-Wewak area.[111] Badly mauled by MacArthur's 1943 Cartwheel operations, Adachi's three battered divisions—the 20th, 41st, and 51st—contained some 55,000 men. After the Japanese gave up on Rabaul, Tokyo transferred the 18th Army to the 2nd Area Army, which ordered Adachi westward to Hollandia. Adachi, however, convinced that Hansa Bay was next on SWPA's hit list, stalled and remained where he was.[112]

Nor did the Japanese neglect air power. The 4th Air Army and 6th Air Division were transferred from surrounded Rabaul to Hollandia, but by this time both units were shadows of their former selves. More substantial was the newly arrived 7th Air Division, although only in comparison. As for naval support, there was none, except for a motley collection of service troops, antiaircraft gunners, and shore defense units and a handful of sub chasers, armed barges, mine layers, and landing craft. Like its American counterpart, the Navy was preparing for a decisive battle up north and had little to spare for New Guinea.[113]

In short, despite the gathering American-generated clouds, the Japanese were not out of the war yet by a long shot. In November 1943 there were only nine divisions and a few aircraft east of Java, but by early the next year that number had increased to seventeen divisions scattered throughout the Netherlands East Indies, Palaus, Marianas, and New Guinea, as well as more than 300 aircraft.[114] In SWPA itself, counting the 50,000 Japanese surrounded in the Bismarcks, there were 240,000 dug-in Japanese.[115] If MacArthur wanted New Guinea, he would have to fight for it.

Australian Allies

In his crusade against the Japanese, MacArthur was aided not only by Australia's logistical apparatus but also by Australian soldiers, sailors, and airmen. Indeed, throughout 1942 and 1943, the Australians bore the brunt of SWPA's war.[116] Australian troops, rushed back home from North Africa or hastily deployed from Down Under, blunted the initial Japanese thrust at Port Moresby in 1942, and the following year they spearheaded MacArthur's drive through Papua and the Huon peninsula.

MacArthur willingly employed Australian soldiers as part of the Cartwheel campaign while he waited for American forces to arrive in strength, but he was less eager to share power with them. To be sure, he cultivated a relationship with Australian Prime Minister Curtin, but he saw this mostly as a political alliance against his enemies.[117] Although he publicly approved of Australian General Sir Thomas Blamey's appointment as SWPA's ground commander, he subverted Blamey's power by placing all American combat units under Krueger's 6th Army, deceptively termed the "Alamo Force," leaving Blamey with authority only over Australian troops.[118] During the New Guinea campaign, MacArthur relegated Australian ground units to mopping up duties, ordering them to clear out the Japanese troops the Americans swept around on their way to the China-Formosa-Luzon area. In fact, MacArthur's campaign could not have proceeded as it did without all those Australian soldiers garrisoning static rear areas.

Australian officers recognized that MacArthur was downgrading their role in SWPA's offensive, but there was little they could do about it.[119] Not only was MacArthur protected by Curtin, but by 1944 Australia's military star was waning. Australia had been at war for more than four years—Australians played a prominent and distinguished role in Britain's campaigns in North Africa, Greece, Crete, and the Middle East—and had committed so many men overseas that it had crippled its own economy. In response, in 1944 the Australian government began demobilizing many of its soldiers so they could till the fields and work the factories. By September, there were only 372,000 of them still in uniform, down from a wartime peak of some 640,000.[120] The remaining soldiers spent the rest of the conflict fighting isolated Japanese garrisons in New Guinea, the Solomons, and Borneo. MacArthur recognized that this task was strategically purposeless,[121] but the Australian government supported the idea, reasoning that such operations would keep otherwise idle and demoralized troops busy, and it might provide them with a postwar claim to Japanese territory.[122] This did not happen, and for the remainder of the war Australian soldiers fought and died in remote areas far away from home for no sufficient reason.

The Stage Is Set

As 1944 began, MacArthur prepared to resume the offensive. If he was to win his race to the China-Formosa-Luzon area, he had to move much faster than he had the previous year, when American and Australian troops advanced only 280 grim miles up the New Guinea coast. Fortunately, for the first time since SWPA assumed the offensive back in late 1942, MacArthur had the resources to undertake operations on a really big scale. Although many of the Australian troops were returning home, newly arrived American ground units more than made up the deficit. Kenney's AAF also received reinforcements to contest its Japanese counterparts in the New Guinea skies. Most important of all, perhaps, was that after a year of often frustrating trial and error, GHQ and its subordinate commands finally understood the complexities of amphibious operations along the rugged New Guinea coast. Talking to one of Krueger's staffers, MacArthur said, "I'm going to bypass the main Japanese strongholds until I get to the Philippines. Then I'm going to meet the enemy head on and destroy him."[123] Thus armed, MacArthur and SWPA were ready to act, and the New Guinea campaign was about to begin.

THREE

THE ADMIRALTIES:
AN UNNECESSARY RISK?

On 23 February 1944, after more than a week of rain and heavy cloud cover, the skies finally cleared over the Admiralty Islands, 200 miles north of New Guinea. Taking advantage of this welcome break in the weather, three photo reconnaissance B-25s scoured the two main islands of Manus and Los Negros, cameras clicking, looking for Japanese activity. They found none; no trucks, planes, ammunition dumps, smoke, gun emplacements, or even people, just two dilapidated airfields. Descending to less than 200 feet, they drew no enemy fire. Returning to base, they related their findings, or lack thereof: "3 crews all claim Manus & Los Negros Is. have been evacuated. Nil signs of enemy activity. Grass growing thickly on Momote and Lorengau airstrips. Strips u/s [unserviceable] and badly pitted. Planes spent 1 hour & a half in area circling islands. . . . [They received] nil AA [antiaircraft fire] even at low altitude."[1]

SWPA AAF commander Kenney read the report later that day in his Brisbane headquarters. Although his forces had hit the islands hard in the weeks before the weather soured—including, on 13 February, an attack by eighty-four B-25s that dropped some eighty-seven tons of bombs—he was puzzled by the complete absence of Japanese.[2] So was his chief deputy, Major General Ennis Whitehead, who recommended that ground reconnaissance corroborate these new data.[3]

Kenney liked that idea, though more as a means to exploit rather than confirm the information at hand. As he saw it, the Admiralties were the key to the immediate strategic situation, dominating as they did both the route westward and Rabaul's last communications line to far-off Tokyo.[4] Taking the islands now, when there were apparently few Japanese around, would save SWPA considerable time and energy. Besides, the following day he got all the proof he thought he needed; another aerial reconnaissance of the islands verified the previous mission's findings, convincing him that the Japanese had indeed pulled out of Los Negros, probably to nearby Manus.[5]

That was evidence enough for Kenney, so he walked upstairs to MacArthur's office to pitch his idea. There he urged his chief to seize the islands now with a few hundred troops and engineers from the "crack" 1st Cavalry Division, transported in some of Kinkaid's fast destroyers and protected by Kenney's own ever-proficient 5th AAF. If anything went wrong, the force could always be withdrawn and the whole adventure labeled—or mislabeled—a reconnaissance. Success, on the other hand, would yield significant strategic dividends. MacArthur paced as he listened, then stopped and gave his approval for an assault by the end of February, saying, "That will put the cork in the bottle."[6]

As it was, SWPA had been planning for some time to stuff the Admiralties cork into an American-made bottle. Targeted as Operation Cartwheel's finale, the JCS had originally slated the Admiralties for invasion on 20 April but had recently advanced the date to 1 April. Since the big and dangerous Japanese bases on Kavieng, Rabaul, and Hansa Bay were nearby, the JCS had ordered Nimitz to provide carrier-based air support for the operation.

To be sure, taking the Admiralties would finally isolate Rabaul, a longtime SWPA goal, but MacArthur was mostly looking forward, not back. Perched as they were north of New Guinea, the Admiralties under American control would cover MacArthur's vulnerable right flank as his troops advanced along the big island's north coast. Moreover, the Admiralties could serve as a spear as well as a shield by providing the airfields Kenney's bombers needed to reach and soften up Japanese bases along the New Guinea littoral before SWPA ground troops assaulted or bypassed them. As MacArthur saw it, Cartwheel's punishing blows had dazed and confused the Japanese, so now was the time to strike.[7]

Not surprisingly, MacArthur also viewed the Admiralties, like the New Guinea campaign as a whole, through a Philippines-bound lens. When Kenney proposed his plan, Sutherland was already in Washington lobbying the JCS for a SWPA offensive to the Japanese-held archipelago. Taking the Admiralties on the fly, as it were, would accelerate MacArthur's operations and ultimately save American lives. It would also provide his chief of staff with more ammunition in his long-odds battle with the Navy over Pacific strategy for the JCS's collective heart and mind by demonstrating what SWPA could accomplish. Finally, such a victory would counterbalance Nimitz's recent successes in the Marshalls, enabling SWPA to get back into the quickly developing race to the China-Formosa-Luzon area. Since there was no time to call on Nimitz for carrier-based air support, he could use those Navy resources later for other important operations, much like a frugal investor postponing acceptance of a line of credit. Besides, a surprise assault appealed to MacArthur's sense of the dramatic.[8]

MacArthur, like Kenney, thought the operation was a good idea for a number of reasons, but was it practicable? MacArthur believed so. Nimitz's forces had recently carried out a series of devastating air strikes against the big Japanese naval base on Truk, eliminating any chance of enemy interference from that quarter. A 22–23 February destroyer sweep through the Bismarck Sea had shown no Japanese surface elements in the immediate area either.[9] Since Kenney had already annihilated all Japanese air opposition around the islands, it appeared that MacArthur had a clear shot at the apparently lightly defended Admiralties, assuming he could get his men there quickly.

Or so it seemed. But there was a fly in the Admiralties ointment at GHQ, one with a German accent and lots of intelligence data to give it weight: Willoughby. Kenney and his cocky pilots might think that the Admiralties were lightly held, but not Willoughby, who had been keeping tabs on its all too real Japanese garrison for some time. Indeed, two weeks earlier he had warned: "To date, there has been a paucity of ground information from this sector. All indications, however, point to increased activity, especially on Los Negros where the enemy has a good road net which gives him a flexible defense."[10]

Willoughby believed that the Admiralties were too strategically important for the Japanese to give them up without a fight, no matter what the odds. He calculated that there were 3250 of them on the islands, considerably more than Kenney's glamorous flyboys had seen.[11] Later, the day Kenney received his confirming evidence, Willoughby moved in the opposite direction, revising his estimates of Japanese strength upward to 4000 and noting that "no enemy activity is apparent. This too is regarded as a case of passive antiaircraft defense necessitated by dwindling reserve ammunition. Other intelligence indicates that the enemy plans to defend the Admiralties with the forces at present located there."[12] As Willoughby saw it, the Japanese were just lying low, possumlike, waiting for some fool expedition like the one Kenney proposed to stumble ashore before they sprang to life, guns blazing. It was not unheard of; the Japanese had used the same tactic in last December's Cape Gloucester operation. He refused to be stampeded by the AAF recon accounts: "Cumulative evidence does not support air observer reports that the islands have been evacuated."[13] However, in one of those maddening inconsistencies that characterized his intelligence summaries, he later added that barge sightings on Los Negros *might* indicate that the Japanese had evacuated the place.[14]

Despite this cautionary note—if it did more to muddy than clarify the situation for operation planners, it also provided bureaucratic cover should

Kenney prove to be right after all—Willoughby was still pretty sure that the Japanese were there in strength, and he had a great deal of Ultra intercept evidence to back him up, including the identity of the garrison's individual units.[15] MacArthur knew all this but authorized the reconnaissance-in-force anyway. After all, Kenney's and Willoughby's positions were not necessarily irreconcilable. There could indeed be 4000 Japanese on the islands, but they might also be widely scattered and demoralized, vulnerable to just such an American attack.[16] Later, en route to the islands, MacArthur explained his reasoning further: "[It is] a gamble in which I have everything to win, little to lose. I bet ten to win a million, if I hit the jackpot."[17] To him, the possible gains outweighed the potential losses.

True enough, unless you were one of the soldiers whose life was on the line. Krueger, with his empathy for the average GI, saw it that way. He did not like this reconnaissance-in-force idea at all, even when MacArthur's operations officer, Major General Stephen Chamberlin, showed up at his new Cape Cretin headquarters with some of Kenney's AAF recon photos.[18] Krueger's intelligence officers by and large agreed with Willoughby, estimating that there were some 4500 Japanese on the islands, more than enough to stomp out an American reconnaissance-in-force before help arrived.[19] Orders were orders though, and Krueger readied the 5th Cavalry Regiment's 2nd Squadron for a 29 February assault, the last possible day in MacArthur's timetable.

Orders might be orders, but their interpretation, like beauty, was in the eye of the beholder, especially since MacArthur gave his subordinates considerable latitude in implementing his directives. Krueger used this privilege to reduce the risks, as he saw it, involved in this unwise operation. GHQ estimated that the reconnaissance-in-force required some 800 men, but Krueger upped the total to over 1000 and would have added more if Barbey had possessed the shipping to transport them.[20] Even so, this was still a good deal short of the 2200 men 1st Cavalry Division commander Major General Innis P. Swift thought necessary.[21] Clearly the key to victory was the timely arrival of reinforcements, so Krueger made sure that the Navy had enough ships for the followup force, which was scheduled to arrive on 2 March.[22] Despite these actions, Krueger remained pessimistic and disgruntled, even when he met MacArthur several days later on the deck of the light cruiser *Phoenix*. Sensing his gloom, MacArthur asked, "What's the matter, Walter?" and received such a hostile glare from his normally obedient subordinate that he took his ground commander into the ship's cabin for a private chat.[23]

To Krueger, the key question was whether or not there were any Japanese in the Admiralties. Despite Kenney's and Willoughby's assertions, no one—no American, that is—had been on the Admiralties for a firsthand look. To rectify that, on 25 February Krueger ordered in the elite Alamo Scouts. Created by Krueger a few months before for just such missions, this team of skilled volunteers was trained to operate independently in the jungle for long periods of time.[24] In fact, a six-man team had been slated to scout Manus in preparation for the original 1 April assault, so Krueger altered their mission and sent them to Los Negros instead. After a day-long rain delay, the team left Finschhafen on the morning of 27 February, and a Catalina seaplane put them ashore on the island's southeastern tip under cover of an AAF raid. Although the Japanese saw them land—apparently Kenney's attacks had become all too routine to be much of a distraction—they managed to survive the next harrowing twenty-four hours, dodging parties of seemingly healthy-looking enemy patrols as they tried to reach Porharmenamen Creek for a good look at Momote airstrip. Picked up next morning without losing a man, the day before the scheduled assault, they reported tersely via radio, "Could not get to river—lousy with Japs."[25]

That seemed a clear enough refutation of Kenney's position, at least on the surface, but what exactly did it mean? Kenney, confronted with unwelcome evidence that his idea might be destined to crash and burn, went into denial and speculated that in the dark jungle the Scouts would think any number of Japanese was a lot.[26] Krueger, on the hand, took the report at face value, confirming as it did his greatest fears. Not that he could do much about it by now; MacArthur's mind was made up, and the invasion convoy was by then already under way. He could, however, at least warn Brigadier General William C. Chase, the reconnaissance-in-force commander, of what to expect—further warn, actually; he had already expressed his concerns to the cavalry general before the expedition set sail[27]—so he sent the Scout team leader to Chase's destroyer to prepare him for the desperate fight Krueger foresaw.[28]

Krueger had his woes, but so did Barbey, who not only disapproved of this operation but was responsible for transporting the reconnaissance-in-force to the Admiralties.[29] This was easier said than done. MacArthur and Kenney could call the expedition whatever they wanted, but it was still a complex amphibious landing that properly required more than five short days of preparation. Incorrectly assuming that MacArthur would adhere to his original 1 April invasion timetable, Barbey had taken advantage of this expected month-long break to refurbish his ships and crews. When GHQ's call for action came, many of his sailors were on leave, and most of his vessels were either under repair or shuttling supplies from Australia. Barbey, however, was nothing if not industrious, and he quickly scraped together three APDs to carry 510 men and rounded out the total by stashing another 500 or so more on board nine destroyers pressed into temporary transport duty. He had some LSTs and LCIs, but they could not keep up with the APDs and destroyers, so he held them back for the followup force of 1500 more troopers, 1200 Navy Seabees and engineers, and 2500 tons of stores and equipment. These would leave on 29 February and arrive two days later, assuming, of course, that the reconnaissance-in-force was still around to be reinforced.[30]

This was cause for concern, not only if, as Krueger and Willoughby—as well as the six Alamo Scouts, now recovering from their recent ordeal—suspected, there were indeed more than 4000 Japanese awaiting Chase's 1000 troopers in and around Los Negros, but also because of the troopers themselves.[31] Although the 1st Cavalry Division had impressed almost everyone since it arrived in SWPA the previous June, it had not yet seen action.[32] Shipped to Oro Bay for the original Admiralties operation, the reconnaissance-in-force was tapped by MacArthur because it was handy. Now, however, Chase's men would have to go in without the usual American advantages of numbers, materiel, logistics, and firepower—at least not at first. Of all of MacArthur's risks in this operation, this use of inexperienced men was perhaps the greatest.

The 1st Cavalry was the Army's last remaining square division, with some 13,600 men in its two brigades of two regiments apiece, each with two squadrons. Many of its officers and men were old-time regulars, and it was considered a spit-and-polish outfit, with high morale. GHQ rated them as excellent, and if SWPA had to use an unbloodied division, it could not do better than the 1st Cav.[33] Although stripped of its horses before it shipped overseas, the division retained its great tradition. MacArthur thought so, and when an aide expressed concern over the 5th Cavalry Regiment's lack of experience, he replied,

> I have known this 5th Cavalry for almost 60 years. When I was a little boy of four my father was a captain in the 13th Infantry at Fort Selden, in the Indian frontier country of New Mexico. Geronimo, the Apache scourge, was loose, and our small infantry garrison was to guard the middle fords of the Rio Grande. A troop of this same 5th Cavalry . . . rode through to help us. I can still remember how I felt when I watched them clatter into the little post, their tired horses gray with desert dust. . . . They'd fight then—and they'll fight now. Don't worry about them.[34]

That remained to be seen, but whatever faith MacArthur placed in tradition, he was not about to rely on it completely. In fact, this operation was so important and dangerous that he trusted no one's judgment but his own, so he decided to accompany the invasion convoy personally to make sure that all went well.[35] An indignant and concerned Krueger protested, but MacArthur simply replied, "I have to."[36] Nor was MacArthur the only high-ranking commander going along. Kinkaid was, too, and he brought two light cruisers to add more punch to the convoy, which left Oro Bay on 28 February, camouflaged by a drizzling rain as it moved at flank speed through the Vitiaz Strait toward the Admiralties.

Close Call at the Los Negros Beachhead

Hyane Harbor, on Los Negros's east coast just north of the Alamo Scouts' recent twenty-four-hour free-for-all, was not a very good landing site. It was not really a harbor at all, just a gap in a barrier reef that exposed an 800-foot-long, tree-lined beach. Kinkaid chose it, however, not only because Momote airfield was less than 200 yards away but also because the Japanese were unlikely to suspect an invasion from that quarter.[37] He was right about that. The local garrison commander, Colonel Yoshio Ezaki, reckoned that since the Americans always did things in a big way, they would try to bludgeon their way ashore at large and obvious Seeadler Harbor, on the other side of Los Negros, so he concentrated his forces there.[38] Ezaki was correct in that Seeadler was the target of the original 1 April assault, but MacArthur's change of plans caught him looking the wrong way.

The continuing drizzle and overcast throughout the night of 28–29 February hid the invasion convoy from Japanese detection, but it also prevented the AAF from supporting the landing much. Whenever weather permitted, Kenney had bombed the islands hard ever since MacArthur had approved his plan,[39] but on D-Day morning only three of forty B-24s got through the cloud cover to soften up the beach. Star shells from the convoy attracted nine B-25s, which strafed the landing area, but on the whole the preliminary air bombardment fizzled.

Fortunately, the Navy, with thirteen destroyers and two cruisers on hand, more than made up the difference by knocking out most of the Japanese machine-gun positions, as well as a five-inch battery on the landing zone flank. Perhaps to impress MacArthur, Kinkaid ordered his vessels as close to shore as possible, stated that he would accept responsibility if any went aground, and permitted his subordinates to exceed their ammunition allowance. MacArthur, standing with Kinkaid on the bridge of the *Phoenix* with cotton in his ears to protect against the deafening roar of the naval guns, was indeed impressed by this display of 7th Fleet firepower, so much so that thereafter Kinkaid had to argue the limitations, not capabilities, of preliminary naval bombardment.[40] MacArthur was not the only observer stirred by the heavy guns pounding the shore; one correspondent called the scene frightening, awe-inspiring, and unearthly.[41]

The green troopers of the 5th Cav's 2nd Squadron, readying themselves for their baptism by fire, could take comfort in this, as well as in the Navy's traditional "battle breakfast" of steak and eggs, potatoes, hotcakes with jam and butter, and coffee—at least those of them who could force the feast into their jittery stomachs. The sight of only twelve LCVPs for the trip to shore, however, was less encouraging. Even so, at 0830 the men descended into the assault craft and headed for the beach. The first three waves received little fire; those Japanese not too busy dodging naval gunfire were hindered by the continuing rain, which obscured their view. By the time the fourth wave moved toward the shore, however, the Japanese—those who survived everything the Navy threw at them, at any rate—had readjusted their aim. Enemy fire raked the LCVPs, knocking out a third of them and decapitating a coxswain with a 20mm shell in the process. These troopers, who perhaps had prematurely counted themselves lucky for not belonging to the supposedly more vulnerable first waves, got little naval gunfire support; communications broke down with the landing forces, and Kinkaid did not want to risk hitting the men already ashore.[42]

Despite the fourth wave's harrowing experience, on land all went well. The 5th Cav met little opposition when it swarmed ashore, and the troopers took Momote by 0950. The airstrip did not seem like much of a prize though. One person described it as "a bombpocked mess of puddles, weeds, rusting fuselages, a truck and a sorry-looking Jap bulldozer."[43] But it was American territory now, and all for the bargain price, on land and sea, of four killed and six wounded.

Taking the airfield was one thing, but holding it was something else again, especially since evacuating the troopers if anything went wrong was next to impossible now that only eight LCVPs remained. Defense was foremost on Chase's mind when he came ashore and looked the situation over. As he saw it, he did not have enough men to hold the entire airstrip, which in any case could not be used until the looming battle's outcome was decided.[44] To that end, he recalled his charging troopers, tightened his new perimeter, and dug in. This last, however, was not easy; not only did the hard coral surface make spade work a considerable chore, but there was no barbed wire, so Chase had to bunch his men still further. Still under sporadic fire, the troopers entrenched, hauled up their limited supplies, and speculated on what would happen next.[45] "I feel just like a June bride," quipped one soldier. "I know just what's going to happen but I don't know how it'll feel."[46]

MacArthur, who had lost his combat virginity long before the expectant trooper was born, saw the situation from a somewhat different perspective. Standing erect and exposed on a landing craft—and thereby compelling his companions, who included his aides, Kinkaid, and a gaggle of correspondents, to do the same—he came ashore that afternoon dressed in his famous gold-braided scrambled eggs cap, khaki pants, and gray trenchcoat.[47] He reminded one correspondent of Washington crossing the Delaware River.[48] On the beach he decorated the first officer ashore, inspected the perimeter, measured shellholes, and watched the troopers haul coconut tree logs into place for machine-gun nests. Coming upon a Japanese corpse, he said, "That's the way I like to see them."[49] He agreed with Chase that the perimeter should be tightened, but he also indicated that once the 5th Cav was dug in the operation was won, provided that the troopers could hold out till help arrived in two days. "You have performed marvelously," he said. "Hold what you have taken, no matter what the odds. You have your teeth in him now—don't let go."[50]

Returning to the *Phoenix* in good humor, the convoy—except for two destroyers left behind by Kinkaid, who sensed they would be needed[51]— departed that evening and was back at Krueger's Cape Cretin headquarters the next day. Krueger was relieved not only because his superior was safe and sound but also because MacArthur gave him permission to exploit the landing as he saw fit. Krueger, in turn, ordered Swift to reinforce the beachhead as soon as possible with as many men as he could muster.[52]

The 4500 Japanese in the Admiralties were tired, discouraged, and hungry, but they were not about to give up. Having taken the islands in April 1942, the Imperial Army had not paid much attention to them until early 1943, when they built Momote airstrip and repaired a companion at Lorengau, over in neighboring Manus. They used the fields to ferry planes to Wewak, Rabaul, and Hollandia, but Kenney put an end to that in early February, when an AAF strike destroyed eighty of them on the ground or in the air. Ezaki's forces had been built around the 51st Transport Regiment until SWPA operations in New Britain and Saidor convinced Tokyo to order another regiment to the islands. Unfortunately, an American submarine, tipped off by Ultra, sank a transport carrying almost 3000 men from the unit in mid-January. After that the Japanese managed to slip in some 1000 more reinforcements, but that was all.[53]

Ezaki was not surprised by the SWPA landing, having intercepted messages to that effect from American submarines to the south.[54] Besides, like the Americans, he believed that the Admiralties were the key to the southwest Pacific. He had prohibited his men from firing on Kenney's planes and told them not to expose themselves so the islands would look weakly held. The ruse worked well enough to attract Chase's now isolated and outnumbered troopers. Without hope of further aid, Ezaki realized that he had to move fast to eliminate Chase's Hyane Harbor foothold before reinforcements arrived or else the battle would be lost. Unfortunately, he seriously underestimated the number of Americans in and around the beachhead at only 200 or so. Instead of concentrating all his men, he ordered a battalion to attack at once while he brought up the remainder of his command.[55]

The result, that night, was a series of uncoordinated Japanese assaults against the dug-in Americans. Infiltrating the troopers' lines by land and even sea, the Japanese cut American telephone wires and hurled grenades, especially in the southern part of the perimeter. Fortunately for the Americans, their task, though terrifying enough, was somewhat easier, consisting as it did of staying in their foxholes and shooting anyone who was not doing the same. The two destroyers Kinkaid left behind, whose guns outclassed anything the Japanese could bring to bear, also helped. The Japanese broke off the attack at dawn, leaving behind sixty-six dead, as opposed to twenty-two American casualties.

Troopers reconnoitering that day, 1 March, toward the skidway, a fifty-yard-wide low sandy spit of land used by natives to drag their canoes from Seeadler Harbor to the ocean, discovered that the Japanese were still nearby in strength. Chase got even more immediate evidence of this fact later that afternoon, when a group of Japanese infiltrators was killed almost on top of his command post. Such harassing attacks continued for the next two days as the Japanese concentrated their forces from nearby islands for an all-out assault.

The Japanese were not the only ones rushing reinforcements to Los Negros. So was Kenney, whose AAF airdropped plasma, ammunition, mines, and grenades, but not—to Chase's chagrin—barbed wire. The AAF also bombed and strafed Japanese positions, which undoubtedly raised trooper morale, at least until several of them were inadvertently killed or wounded by not-so-friendly AAF fire. To accommodate the anticipated followup wave, Chase expanded the beachhead to include the whole airfield, which his men occupied without opposition on 2 March.

Later that day the long-awaited reinforcements arrived, bringing the rest of the 5th Cav, Seabees, and engineers. The latter two spent seven grueling hours unloading the vulnerable LSTs so they could be on their way home before nightfall brought Japanese bombers. Fortunately, the hard coral, which was such a curse to the entrenching troopers, made unloading easier. Nor was that all they had to do; over the next few days the Seabees and engineers fought Japanese infiltrators, hauled supplies to Momote, and cleared fields of fire with their ubiquitous bulldozers.

These reinforcements were needed because Chase and his men were convinced that the big Japanese assault was coming soon.[56] In preparation, the troopers dug in deeper, strung tripwires of coral-filled tin cans, and sowed landmines. On 3 March, Chase ordered the landing craft in the harbor abandoned because he did not want their crews caught in the impending crossfire. It was a wise decision; that night two LCVPs were sunk—by American fire.[57]

Chase guessed right. Ezaki had wanted to attack all out the night before, but he had had too much trouble positioning his men. Now he was ready, and he hit full force on the night of 3–4 March, concentrating on the northern part of the perimeter.[58] One unit even charged singing "Deep in the Heart of Texas."[59] Japanese tapped into American phone lines and called for forward artillery observers to lift their fire. As usual, the Japanese assaults were delivered in piecemeal fashion, without much coordination, but what they lacked in organization they made up in ferocity, forcing Chase to commit his service troops to combat. In the seesaw battle, however, it was American firepower, here as elsewhere in the war, that tipped the scale, especially the destroyers in the harbor. Afterward, referring to this close-in naval assistance, Chase said, "They didn't support us; they saved our necks."[60] Dawn showed that some Japanese had penetrated the American perimeter, but they were rapidly killed or driven away. The night-long ordeal cost the Americans 61 dead and 244 wounded, but the perimeter held. The troopers counted more than 700 Japanese corpses the next day, although some of them may have fallen in earlier assaults.

Holding the perimeter, as MacArthur had foreseen, was equivalent to winning the battle. His GHQ saw it that way, too.[61] In their efforts to eradicate the American beachhead before reinforcements arrived, the Japanese spent their reserves and offensive capability.[62] From now on, they could harass and hinder SWPA but not defeat it. American strength could only increase, whereas each Japanese soldier killed was one fewer on Ezaki's already anemic roster. After 4 March, American victory in the Admiralties was a foregone conclusion.

GHQ could place a check next to the Admiralties in its list of targets on the way to the Philippines, but to the troopers, Seabees, and engineers still there, the operation was by no means over. Victory might be inevitable, but troopers killed after Ezaki's big charge were just as dead as their comrades who fell defending the Los Negros beachhead, and their survivors mourned their loss just as much.

Clearing Seeadler Harbor

The Admiralties' heart was big Seeadler Harbor, which GHQ coveted as a naval base to support its drive along the New Guinea coast. Krueger wanted it, too, but for more immediate reasons. Hyane Harbor was becoming increasingly congested as reinforcements, supplies, and equipment flowed in, and opening Seeadler would greatly relieve the pressure.[63]

Since the troopers around Hyane Harbor had their hands full coping with fanatical Japanese attacks, Krueger turned to the Navy. Barbey, however, was reluctant; Seeadler was surrounded by Japanese guns, and Kenney's AAF had strewn the place with magnetic mines the previous May.[64] Krueger persisted though, and Barbey ultimately gave way. On 2 March, the day the followup wave arrived at Hyane Harbor, four destroyers and two minesweepers tried to force their way into Seeadler Harbor.[65] The lead destroyer, the *Mullany*—coincidentally enough, under the command of one Baron J. Mullaney—led the way in an attempt to expose Japanese gun positions by attracting their fire. In this the *Mullany* succeeded all too well, and Japanese shells from points around the harbor straddled the vessel until the rest of the force came up to cover her withdrawal. A repeat performance the next day accomplished little more than damaging the destroyer *Nicholson*. On 4 March Barbey took off his gloves, so to speak, and sent in the cruisers *Phoenix* and *Nashville*, which in the following days added their weight to the destroyer assault, pounding Japanese positions in and around the harbor. In the end, the naval officers merely discovered—or, for the historically minded among them, rediscovered—that their vessels could bombard enemy positions as long as they cared to, but only infantry could physically occupy the ground where the guns stood.

Fortunately for SWPA, if not for the Navy's injured pride, those land forces were on hand, now that the Japanese had shot their bolt in front of Hyane Harbor. Krueger pressured Barbey to transport reinforcements to the beachhead as fast as possible, and this strategy soon yielded results.[66] Elements of the 7th Cavalry Regiment—George Armstrong Custer's old outfit—arrived on 4 March, and the 12th Cavalry Regiment disembarked two days later. In between another formidable force showed up: 1st Cavalry Division commander Major General Innis P. Swift.

Heavyset, vigorous, tough and hard, with a square jaw and unsmiling face, Swift was cut from the same cloth as his friend Krueger, of whom he said, "If Krueger told me to cut my left arm off up to the elbow, I cut it off. He got me out here. I am sixty-two years of age and General Krueger got the 1st Cav Division and got me out here."[67] Exactly why Swift drew the amputation line at his elbow and not, say, his shoulder, is beside the point; apparently Krueger, like MacArthur, could inspire loyalty. Swift, however, planned to give his 6th Army commander performance as well as devotion.

One reason Swift was on Los Negros on 5 March was to check up on Chase. Although on the surface Chase had functioned above and beyond the call of duty during his long and lonely five-day ordeal, Krueger was disturbed by the tone of his dispatches. Chase constantly called for reinforcements, even though he was well aware of the scheduled timetable for their arrival. He also displayed considerable jumpiness, as well as an inability to furnish vital information Krueger repeatedly requested.[68] When he met Chase, Swift discovered that Krueger's suspicions were accurate; Chase was clearly distraught. He loudly denounced GHQ for failing to warn him about all those Japanese on Los Negros, and Swift had to take him aside twice to tell him to shut up. Swift recognized that his 1st Brigade commander had been under considerable stress, but this encounter probably explains why Chase played little part in the rest of the operation, especially since Swift was full of praise for the 5th Cavalry's performance as a whole.[69]

Swift felt that the important thing was to keep the weakened Japanese on the run by attacking toward Seeadler as soon as possible, especially since the Navy was not making much progress in forcing the harbor open. To that end, soon after he arrived he reversed an earlier Chase decision and got his troopers moving from the beachhead across the skidway.[70] Although slowed somewhat by Japanese harassing fire, badly concealed mines, and their inexperience in fighting outside of their foxholes, elements of the 5th Cav crossed it that afternoon and spent much of the night firing at a host of mostly imaginary enemy soldiers.

Swift's immediate goal beyond the skidway was Salami, on Seeadler's southeastern shore. On the morning of 6 March, the 7th Cav jumped off to take it but soon got bogged down on a bad road congested with mud, vehicles, troops, mines, and Japanese-felled trees. The 12th Cav troopers, brought up in support, bypassed their stalled comrades to the west and, with the aid of nine B-25s, took Salami after an hour-long firefight against

Japanese-held bunkers and buildings. The Americans now had their foothold on Seeadler.

A foothold was not enough to open the harbor, though, so for that purpose Swift targeted Papitalai mission, Papitalai plantation, and Lombrum, all down the coast to the south and southwest, and accessible only from the sea. Unfortunately, of the five LVTs assigned for the 12th Cav's assault on Papitalai mission, only two made it through from Hyane Harbor; the others got stuck in the mud. Since the attack was part of an integrated plan that included a simultaneous landing at Papitalai plantation by the 5th Cav, the 12th Cav went ahead anyway, sending only twenty men in the initial wave. They reached Papitalai mission and dug in under Japanese fire, holding out for forty-five minutes, until twenty more men arrived to reinforce them. It went on like that all day as the two LVTs, eventually joined by a third that managed to get through the muck, slowly transported the 12th Cav and its supplies and equipment across the channel. By 2000, however, after beating off three Japanese attacks, Papitalai mission was in American hands, at the price of thirty-two casualties. To the east, elements of the 5th Cav occupied Papitalai plantation after a brisk skirmish. The 7th Cav had the easiest time of all, taking Lombrum the next day, 8 March, without opposition. With Lombrum, Papitalai mission, Papitalai plantation, and Salami in American hands, Seeadler Harbor was open to American ships once the Navy's minesweepers cleared away Kenney's mines.

While the 7th, 12th, and part of the 5th Cavs opened Seeadler Harbor, the rest of the 5th Cav spent the remainder of March mopping up Los Negros. Japanese opposition centered on Hill 260, in the southern part of the island. There the Japanese repulsed an initial assault on 11 March, mostly because the 5th Cav's mortars and flamethrowers fell behind the attacking column in the dense jungle, denying the infantry vital support. Reinforced by elements of the 12th Cav, and backed up by heavy artillery and air support, the troopers finally cleared the hill on 14 March with light losses. Scattered Japanese remained on Los Negros, but by the end of the month almost all them had been killed.

Descent on Manus

Swift's rapid occupation of Seeadler Harbor was a feat any commander could be proud of, especially considering the inexperience of his troopers. The 1st Cav general was not the type of man to rest on his laurels, though, particularly when work remained to be done both in developing the island's military facilities and in eliminating those Japanese who had thus far managed to escape the relentless American steamroller. As the last important piece of Admiralties real estate still under Japanese control, Lorengau airfield, on nearby Manus, was the focus of the bloodier of these two tasks. No one was sure, however, exactly how many Japanese were defending the place. The AAF, ranging widely over the island, saw little evidence of Japanese activity, but whatever its other admittedly positive attributes, its stock as a source of estimates for enemy strength was at best questionable after all those Japanese had stormed across the skidway at Chase's troopers earlier in the month.[71] Sifting through its own sources, the 1st Cav estimated that there were between 1700 and 2600 Japanese in and around Lorengau, but others put the figure at about 2700.[72] Either way, the troopers would soon find out.

An attack on Lorengau would not be easy, involving as it did another of those always complex amphibious landings. Swift, however, believed that two factors that would improve the odds were Hauwei and Butjoluo islands, offshore from Lorengau.[73] American artillery on both places could soften up Japanese positions before the troopers stormed ashore, and without fear of being sunk by counterfire. The Navy knew all about this danger.

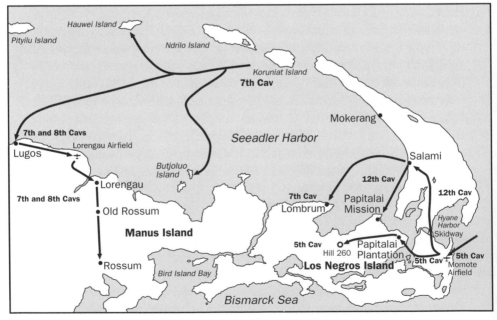

The Admiralty Islands, 29 February 1944

Enemy guns on Hauwei had given the 7th Fleet a difficult time when it had steamed into Seeadler earlier in the month, but since then Barbey and the AAF had pounded the place hard. Recent aerial photos and, perhaps more convincingly, native reports indicated that the apparently battered Japanese had evacuated the islands.[74]

Butjoluo was in fact deserted, but not Hauwei, as a twenty-six-man patrol sent to confirm the information discovered on 11 March, when it stumbled into an ambush. The accompanying PT boat abandoned the troopers after its captain, apparently deciding that in this instance discretion was the better part of valor, was shot in the ankle. Fortunately for the troopers, Sergeant James C. Breslin, commander of the LCVP that transported the patrol there, was made of sterner stuff. The LCVP quickly came under heavy fire, but Breslin brought his boat in close to shore and picked up what was left of the battered recon force just before a Japanese mortar shell sank the vessel. The survivors donned life jackets and scurried out of range of Japanese small arms fire. Although the wayward PT captain reported upon his arrival to Salami that the entire patrol was lost, a bomber sent to investigate saw the survivors treading water. Another PT boat, covered by a destroyer, picked up the patrol and the LCVP crew. Altogether, the Americans sustained twenty-three casualties, including eight killed.[75]

A Japanese-held Hauwei meant that Lorengau would also remain in enemy hands unless the Americans did something about it, which they did. The next day an entire squadron of the 7th Cavalry Regiment, supported by Australian P-40 aircraft from Momote, destroyers, a tank, and those ubiquitous amphibious engineer craft, stormed the island and its forty-three Japanese defenders, none of whom survived the resulting battle that their earlier victory provoked. Despite their numerical and material superiority, it took fifty-four casualties and twenty-four hours for the troopers to seize the place. Artillery moved in soon afterward, enabling the assault on Manus to proceed according to plan, if not to schedule.

Since reconnaissance showed lots of Japanese positions in and around Lorengau, Swift decided to avoid a costly frontal assault and instead use his naval superiority to land down the coast at Lugos. The newly won artillery sites on Hauwei and Butjoluo pounded Lorengau, fixing the Japanese there while four destroyers and eighteen B-25s worked over Lugos. The tactic worked; on 15 March the 8th Cav landed without losses. Watching the landing from a PT boat, Swift noted wryly, "Our timing was a minute and a half off; we failed to take into account the heavy sea which retarded the landing craft as they turned toward the beach. Well, that's not too bad."[76]

For the troopers, their bloodless Lugos landing was a blessing, but the engineers in the following waves saw the situation a little differently. The bank quickly turned into mud, forcing them to drag vehicles off the beach with winches. Even this proved futile when the sandbar at the river mouth washed away. Eventually the engineers gave up and moved a mile and a half east to a new beach. This one, unlike the original, lacked offshore reefs but possessed a jetty, which made unloading easier and enabled the engineers to devote more time to other equally vital chores: removing Japanese barbed wire and landmines, clearing jungle, and building roads.

The engineers were undoubtedly having a hard time, but their task was preferable to that of the 8th Cav, which spent 16 March slugging it out with the Japanese in and around Lorengau airfield. The troopers had little luck until reinforced by elements of the 7th Cav, whose men entered the battle shouting their regimental song, "Garry Owen!" Backed by considerable air and artillery fire, the two units succeeded in securing the airstrip by nightfall the next day.[77]

Lorengau airstrip was different from Lorengau village, which was in a cup-shaped valley across the twenty-yard-wide Lorengau River. The Japanese were there, too, as both a landing craft that tried to bring in supplies and a recon patrol that crossed the river discovered. Taking the village, however, turned out to be surprisingly easy, especially in comparison with the previous day's bitter struggle for the airfield. The earlier battle had sapped Japanese strength, the rolling ground provided some cover for the 8th Cav troopers storming across a sandbar in the river, and American artillery and air attacks had exposed the Japanese positions by stripping away their cover.[78] For these reasons, the village was in American hands by the end of 18 March, at the cost of only seven men wounded.

Unfortunately for the exhausted troopers, Lorengau's fall did not spell an end to the operation. Documents captured at the airstrip showed that the Japanese had fortified the road all the way down to Rossum, from which they could threaten the Americans around Lorengau.[79] The 8th Cav tried to muscle its way through but got hung up by Japanese bunkers in the caves and gullies that bordered the narrow, mine-filled road. Air strikes accomplished little, as did efforts to outflank enemy positions.

To speed up the process, the fresher 7th Cav replaced the tired 8th Cav, but the advance gained little momentum, especially when a well-placed shot at the lead vehicle on the narrow road could and did slow up the entire attack column. Old Rossum, a third of the way to Rossum, fell on 22 March, but it took three more days and reinforcements from the recommitted 8th Cav for the troopers to clear out all the bunkers and occupy

Rossum. Forcing the Rossum road cost both regiments 36 killed and 128 wounded. As always, the line officers were hardest hit; one 7th Cav troop lost 3 commanders in as many days.

Rossum's fall signaled practically the end of the Admiralties operation. By 1 April, only a few scattered Japanese remained on the islands, constantly on the run from troopers aided by friendly natives.[80] Indeed, the Admiralties became a type of training ground, called the "Reservation," for untested American units preparing for future battles on the road to Japan.[81] For its part, the 1st Cav stayed in the Admiralties until October, when it shipped out to participate in the bloody Leyte operation. Later it played a key role in Manila's liberation and finished the war fighting in northern Luzon. Throughout the conflict, it retained its reputation as the best division in SWPA.

Building the Base

In warfare, conquering enemy territory is often only the first step toward making it strategically useful. Without airfields, docks, warehouses, depots, and the innumerable other logistical apparatuses SWPA required to prosecute its war, the Admiralties were little more than so many well-placed large chunks of rock in the vast Pacific Ocean. Swift's second task, then, was to transform the islands from a geographic location into a war-waging platform. Doing so, though, proved to be more frustrating than the Japanese, who could at least be killed and thus eliminated from contention.

The problem, over and above the difficult terrain and the shortage of equipment, was an extension of the continuing interservice struggle for Pacific War dominance. SWPA had big plans for the Admiralties. GHQ wanted to build a floating Liberty ship dock, a LST pile dock, an evacuation hospital, and two petroleum tank farms to hold 37,000 barrels of oil. Most importantly, it wanted to improve run-down Momote and Lorengau airfields for bombers.[82] Most of the service troops initially deployed for these tasks, however, were Seabees from SOPAC, so Nimitz thought it was only natural that the Navy should control the completed base. MacArthur, whose paranoia toward the Navy had roots deep enough to reach the center of the earth, saw this as yet another attempt to freeze him out of the Pacific War, and he ordered all non–7th Fleet vessels out of the islands. SOPA commander William Halsey had to fly to Brisbane to calm MacArthur down and get him to rescind the directive. As it was, the JCS supported MacArthur anyway, but the episode did little to ease continuing interservice tension.

Swift may or may not have cared much about these shenanigans, which in any case were beyond his responsibilities, but such interservice strife filtered down the chain of command into the Admiralties, hindering the all-important effort to develop the islands. The Seabees were not initially placed directly under Army command, so they resented Army officers giving them orders, especially when such directives conflicted with their standard operating procedures.[83] As the Seabees understood it, they were supposed to build naval facilities, but the Army, with a different set of priorities, wanted them working on the airfields. Serviceable airfields would of course advance the war effort, but the Seabees had their pride and their orders. The hard-bitten Army engineers saw things a little differently. To them, the Seabees simply did not pull their weight; they spent too much time sightseeing and not enough at their machines. The engineers worked around the clock in shifts, unlike the Seabees, who constructed their camp before they even pitched in to other, more important duties. Most damning of all, the Seabees discriminated against the engineers in the liquor distribution. Swift, not surprisingly, had little patience for any of this and had to order the recalcitrant Seabees to fall into line.[84]

Interservice hassles, occasional enemy interference, and equipment shortages all slowed construction, but by and large the Seabees and engineers met their deadlines. Although covered with grass and a foot of topsoil, Momote airfield was repaired and ready for action on 9 March, only ten days after the troopers first stormed ashore. By 1 April, almost a week ahead of schedule, the runway was extended to 5600 feet, and a bomber group was operating there on 18 April. Lorengau, however, proved a more difficult challenge, mostly because bad terrain made it impossible to lengthen the runway. Instead, the Army abandoned the place in favor of a brand new airfield at Mokerang. Building it took time, however, and it was not finished until 21 April, although this was a day ahead of schedule. Even so, the engineers and Seabees, with the aid of some 1230 native workers, gave MacArthur the logistical facilities he needed to continue the campaign.

Evaluating the Admiralties Operation

The impact of the 1st Cavalry Division's clenched-fist assault on the Admiralties reverberated throughout the southwest Pacific to Washington. The operation was, in fact, a watershed for both SWPA and MacArthur. First of all, it fulfilled Operation Cartwheel by neutralizing Rabaul and the surrounding area, leaving its isolated garrison to spend the rest of the war scratching at the top of its American-designed and built coffin.[85] This was in and of itself much, considering the number of Americans and Australians who died to keep the communications lines between their two nations safe from Japanese forces based in their New Britain stronghold. Moreover, all those battle-hardened SOPAC troops, planes, ships, and equipment devoted to Cartwheel could now be redeployed for other operations closer to the Japanese homeland, although this slow process would not be completed until after the New Guinea campaign. Their onetime Japanese opponents, on the other hand, were permanently removed from the Pacific theater playing board.

This was important, of course, but there was more to the Admiralties operation than just surrounding a fortress on the outskirts of the Japanese empire. In this respect the islands, as MacArthur said, were a cork, but they were also a pivot that enabled SWPA to reorient its resources westward. This was especially true for the AAF. Kenney's airdromes in northeastern New Guinea were originally designed to hit Rabaul, and his planes could only with difficulty attack Japanese targets along New Guinea's north coast. The Admiralties, once the Seabees and Army engineers resolved their differences and finished the airfields, provided the perfect platform for Kenney to point his planes at new targets of opportunity along the New Guinea littoral and in the Mandates to the north.

The Admiralties were not only a cork and pivot but also a shield. In American possession, SWPA was protected from Japanese assaults from the Carolines. Barbey's sailors, transporting troops, supplies, and equipment, no doubt appreciated the fact that they did not have to strain their eyes looking for Japanese planes approaching from the north, leaving them with only two compass points to watch.

Finally, the operation laid a strategic foundation for future SWPA operations. By advancing the invasion date, MacArthur forced the JCS to take the successful operation into consideration when they debated Pacific strategy that March. Although it is hard to tell how much of an impact the operation had on JCS deliberations, such initiative could not have hurt, and it nicely counterbalanced the Navy's recent successful Marshalls operation.[86] The accelerated invasion, then, may have helped keep MacArthur in the Pacific War by convincing the JCS that it was worth underwriting a SWPA offensive.

No one disputed that the Admiralties were worth taking, yielding as they did a variety of strategic benefits, but not everyone appreciated the manner in which they were attacked. By advancing the invasion timetable,

MacArthur upset carefully laid logistical plans, so equipment arrived piece-meal, without schedule, and on commandeered ships, making base con-struction all the more difficult. Moreover, much like a mountain climber re-gretting a risky ascent after he reaches the top, some observers lamented MacArthur's dangerous gamble, despite its apparent success, by noting how close the Japanese had come to wiping out Chase's beleaguered re-connaissance-in-force. Such a disaster might have set the Pacific War back several months and could even have led to a cancellation of a SWPA offen-sive by a discouraged JCS.[87] Taking the islands on schedule, one 6th Army staffer later noted, would have been so much *easier.*[88]

That may or may not be true, but MacArthur was more interested in celerity and results than ease, and anyway it was a good staffer's job to make every operation look simple and logical in retrospect. Besides, accel-erating the invasion date meant the war would end that much sooner, thus saving American lives. To be sure, there were equipment shortages, but Momote airfield was up and running before March was half over, whereas it would have still been a weed-choked mess under the original schedule. Similarly, bombers were flying out of the Admiralties far sooner than they would have had MacArthur invaded on 1 April. Casualties were heavy, considering the number of men deployed for the operation, totaling 330 dead and 1189 wounded, but it is doubtful that the losses would have been any lighter if, as originally planned, the whole 1st Cav had stormed ashore at well-defended Seeadler Harbor.[89] Finally, and perhaps most importantly, if MacArthur had waited until April, the JCS might have limited SWPA's strategic future to New Guinea, making the Admiralties a barren prize, at least in terms of advancing the cause of Philippines liberation.

MacArthur undoubtedly had a lot going for him—Japanese disorgani-zation, enough Ultra intelligence to get some of his subordinates to take for-tunate precautions, and the solid performance of the 1st Cav—but he was smart enough to recognize that the invasion, while risky, promised a big payoff. It is, in fact, hard to picture any other American World War II com-mander undertaking such a hazardous operation. On the whole, the Admi-ralties operation stands out as a shrewd strategic move, and MacArthur himself considered the invasion one of his brightest maneuvers.[90]

HOLLANDIA: A GREAT LEAP FORWARD

MacArthur's New Guinea road to the Philippines was dotted not only by mother nature's logistical and topographical potholes but also by some half dozen similarly formidable Japanese-made roadblocks. Mother nature might be an equal opportunity tormentor, but the Japanese designed those bases up and down the New Guinea coast specifically to protect their empire by killing Americans bold or stupid enough to assail them. Together, then, these obstacles guaranteed SWPA's soldiers an exceedingly bumpy ride as MacArthur's offensive drive gathered momentum.

One of the biggest roadblocks, Hansa Bay, situated 120 miles up the coast from Allied-held Saidor, was next on SWPA's hit list. Taking it, however, would not be easy, as those in the know realized.[1] There were only 5000 mostly base personnel troops at Hansa Bay itself, but Adachi's three divisions hovered nearby, recovering from earlier ordeals, and Japanese air power was based at nearby Wewak.[2] Worse yet, beyond Hansa Bay and Wewak, farther up the coast, lurked other potentially dangerous Japanese bases for SWPA to butt its head against, if and when it overcame its immediate objective.

From this view, then, it is easy to understand planning section chief Brigadier General Bonner F. Fellers's discouragement at the end of 1943. Fellers recognized that at its current rate of advance, and against such well-defended targets as Hansa Bay and Wewak, SWPA might never reach the China-Formosa-Luzon area, let alone Japan. The thing to do, he finally decided, was to use SWPA's increasing land, air, and naval resources to go *around,* not through, Hansa Bay and Wewak, and instead attack Hollandia, some 500 miles up the coast from Saidor.[3] There was nothing new about this leapfrog strategy; SOPAC commander Admiral William Halsey and MacArthur had both used it successfully on a smaller scale in the Solomons and Papua during Operation Cartwheel, but now SWPA finally possessed the means to apply it in a big way. Kenney liked the idea, as did Willoughby, who knew that Hollandia was weakly held, at least in comparison with the Hansa Bay area.[4] Even so, most at GHQ opposed such a risky operation deep into the Japanese rear, including Fellers's boss, operations chief Stephen Chamberlin, who was dead set on storming Hansa Bay.[5] Fellers went to MacArthur anyhow, who told him to start planning. This end run around his superior, however, nearly cost Fellers his career. The normally mild-mannered Chamberlin fired him when he learned what had happened, but MacArthur, grateful for any scheme that promoted both his advance to the Philippines and his war with the Navy, stepped in and made Fellers his military secretary.[6]

Meanwhile, the war—the one against the Japanese, that is—went on. After MacArthur returned from Los Negros, Kenney, whose boldness was undiminished by recent evidence of its sometimes unfortunate consequences, urged his chief to cancel the Hansa Bay operation and go for Hollandia.[7] Encouraged by his apparently easy success in the Admiralties—easy, that is, from the strategic point of view; the 1st Cavalry troopers still had to overcome severe tactical obstacles to win—MacArthur agreed and asked the JCS for permission to do so: "Recent seizure of a foothold in the Admiralties which will shortly be followed by complete occupation presents an immediate opportunity for rapid exploitation along the north coast of New Guinea. To this end I propose to make the Hollandia area instead of Hansa Bay my next objective."[8] The JCS not only signed off on the idea in their 12 March directive announcing the continuation of the dual drive to the China-Formosa-Luzon area, but they also ordered Nimitz to supply carrier-based air support for this potentially dangerous venture. By mid-March, then, the basic outline was in place for a SWPA assault deep behind Japanese lines, and its code name reflected the risks attached to such a hazardous mission: Operation Reckless.

Target Hollandia

Hollandia, about halfway up the New Guinea coast, had once been a center for the birds-of-paradise feather trade, but its economic importance had languished after the early 1930s, until the invading Japanese found other, less peaceful uses for the place. The town itself was not as significant as the surrounding area, which included two harbors—Tanahmerah and Humboldt—twenty-five miles apart, separated by the Cyclops Mountains. Fifteen-mile-long Lake Sentani, situated on a large level plain, was to the south, and unexplored mountains loomed beyond that.

Hollandia sounded like a mundane enough place, but it offered much to SWPA. Those two harbors provided the only good anchorages between

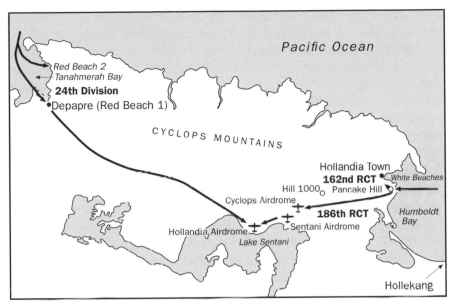

The Hollandia Operation, 22 April 1944

Wewak and Geelvink Bay; Humboldt alone could hold up to fifty Liberty ships.[9] The level plains around Lake Sentani were one of the few New Guinea sites where airfields could be quickly built. Their completion—or, more accurately, improvement; the Japanese had already constructed three there and were working on two more—would enable Kenney's AAF to range over western New Guinea and support Nimitz's mid-June Marianas operation by bombing the Palaus. That flat terrain could also hold thousands of troops, along with their supplies and equipment, for operations farther westward, and even in the Philippines, when and if the JCS came around to MacArthur's way of thinking. Finally, an American-held Hollandia would isolate Adachi's forces in the Hansa Bay-Wewak area, leaving them to wither on the vine, much like their comrades clawing at the lid of their Rabaul coffin. If successful, then, the Hollandia operation, although hazardous, promised to yield major strategic dividends by advancing MacArthur's offensive both in terms of distance and time, giving him a leg up in his race with the Navy's central Pacific offensive to the China-Formosa-Luzon area.[10]

The Japanese valued Hollandia, too, but as a place from which to repel, not advance, MacArthur's offensive. Indeed, the area's importance increased in proportion to the proximity of the relentless American war ma-

chine. To the Japanese, Hollandia served as an outer bulwark for their con-
tracting empire. Adachi, regrouping his army around Hansa Bay, saw it
that way: "Hollandia is at the final base and last strategic point of this
Army's New Guinea operations. Therefore, it is expected that if we are unable to occupy [Port] Moresby, the Army will withdraw to Hollandia and
defend this area to the last man."[11] Japanese 2nd Area Army commander
Anami recognized Hollandia's worth as well. He believed that it was only
a matter of time before MacArthur reached into his bag of tricks and attacked the place. First, however, he expected swpa to assault Hansa Bay-
Wewak. Even so, in late 1943 the Japanese began to strengthen the Hollandia area, building airfields and, at the beginning of the new year,
ordering reinforcements there from Adachi's battered army.[12]

Adachi, however, stalled. He lacked the transport to move his troops
very far, and the earliest he could get significant reinforcements to Hollandia was in late May. Like Anami, he was convinced that MacArthur would
attack Hansa Bay first—and soon.[13] As he saw it, MacArthur never assaulted Japanese positions unless they were within range of one of Kenney's
airdromes, and Hollandia was not, thanks in large part to the grim determination his tough troops had exhibited over the past year. True, Nimitz
might supply MacArthur with carrier air support, but this had never before
occurred in swpa.[14]

ghq did everything it could to reinforce Adachi's conviction that the
Hansa Bay region, not Hollandia, was next on swpa's shopping list. 7th
Fleet destroyers shelled Wewak, as if to soften up the place for an inevitable
assault, and pt boats prowled conspicuously offshore. Kenney's pilots hit
the sector hard, launching missions against the Wewak airfields almost
every day. In March alone the 5th aaf flew 2454 sorties to the area and, at
the discount price of only 16 bombers and 18 fighters lost, reduced the
place to rubble. In a series of heavy raids from 11 to 16 March, for instance, the 5th aaf dropped some 1600 tons of bombs on Wewak, crater-
ing the runways, destroying 168 Japanese planes on the ground and in the
air, and even stripping the nearby trees of their foliage.[15] In fact, the aaf
ultimately ran out of targets[16]—or said it did; bitter experience in the Pacific War showed that the Japanese could survive almost anything the aaf
threw at them—especially after the Japanese ordered their few surviving
aircraft back to the safer Hollandia airfields.

Besides ordinance, the aaf also released dummy parachutists, which,
like the empty life rafts set ashore by submarines, would, they hoped, convince the Japanese that American reconnaissance teams were sizing the
place up for an amphibious landing.[17] Such decoy tactics worked well

enough to confirm Japanese suspicions that Hansa Bay-Wewak was next on SWPA's agenda.[18] Willoughby, for his part, wanted to go even farther. He proposed that SWPA launch a large-scale feint to draw off Japanese troops before Hollandia was attacked, but Chamberlin said GHQ lacked the resources for such an operation.[19]

Willoughby had more important things to do than suggest strategy anyway. Because Hollandia was so far from SWPA bases, and because attempts to infiltrate ground reconnaissance teams into the area had failed, most intelligence about the place came from Ultra.[20] The big question, of course, was exactly how many Japanese were in the vicinity. In late March, Willoughby estimated that there were 10,000 men in the area.[21] From this estimate, he speculated that there *might* be two combat regiments, but he was not sure.[22] Next month, just before the attack, Willoughby upped the figure to 15,000 men, but he could still find no sign of those two regiments; the only combat troops he identified were 3000 men from the 6th Sea Detachment.[23] Just the same, Willoughby warned that Hollandia was receiving "considerable reinforcements."[24] Perhaps more alarmingly, those Japanese were very busy. Willoughby noted that Hollandia was "teeming with activity," which buttressed his earlier conviction that "time, no doubt, is favoring the Japanese in the development of defenses in depth."[25] SWPA, in short, better attack soon, before Hollandia became as formidable as Hansa Bay.

GHQ intended to do just that, as soon as it got its forces into place. Doing so, however, involved not only the usual intricate coordination of SWPA's various widespread land, air, and sea commands but also cooperation with Nimitz's POA. Since Hollandia was at the outer edge of Kenney's AAF radius, the JCS ordered Nimitz to supply carrier-based close air support for the landing. The problem, at least from GHQ's view, was that Nimitz was outside of MacArthur's radius of authority, so ordinary chain-of-command procedures would not work. However, MacArthur could, and did, turn on the charm when he and his subordinates met with Nimitz and his representatives at Brisbane from 25 to 27 March to hammer out the POA's role in the upcoming operation. Unfortunately for SWPA, Nimitz's first loyalty was to King and the Navy, and he insisted that his big vulnerable carriers, after softening up the Palaus, remain off Hollandia for only two days after the troops hit the beach. MacArthur thought eight was a better figure, but he could only agree. Although D-Day had originally been scheduled for 15 April, logistical problems, tides, and the POA's other duties prompted GHQ to postpone the operation until 22 April.[26]

MacArthur, thanks to Nimitz, now had forty-eight hours of close air support for his assaulting forces, but he still had to bridge the gap between the big carriers' departure and the day the aviation engineers brought Hollandia's airdromes up to snuff for Kenney's AAF. What SWPA needed, then, was an airfield nearby to support the invading forces at a moment's notice. Scouring their maps, GHQ considered Wuvulu, off New Guinea's north coast, and Tanah-Merah—which, although possessing the same name as one of Hollandia's bays, was an altogether different locale—in the south central part of the island. In the end, they rejected both places for logistical and intelligence reasons—meaning MacArthur's planners knew next to nothing about either site, and even if they did, they did not have the resources to occupy and develop them.[27]

Ultimately, GHQ zoomed in on Aitape, on New Guinea's coast halfway between Hollandia and Wewak. Aitape possessed a lightly defended Japanese airfield, and if SWPA could capture and upgrade it quickly then Kenney's forces would have a base from which to cover the troops advancing on Hollandia's airdromes after Nimitz's skittish carriers left the scene. In fact, AAF deputy Whitehead suggested that SWPA attack Aitape fifteen days before the Hollandia assault so the airfield could be ready when Reckless got under way. Krueger, however, was unwilling to surrender the element of surprise, which an American assault on Aitape would almost certainly do, so he scheduled the operation simultaneously with the one on Hollandia.[28] The problem now was finding close air support for the Aitape invasion. Fortunately, Nimitz came to the rescue and offered SWPA eight escort carriers to cover the landing, which would then move up to Hollandia to guard that beachhead after the big fleet carriers left. They would stay there until 11 May, buying the aviation engineers at Aitape more time to improve their newly possessed airfield, assuming, of course, that it was captured at all.

Such complications were not necessarily a bad thing, especially since they were in part due to the greater abundance of resources now at SWPA's disposal. The Hollandia-Aitape operation, in fact, would be the largest so far mounted in SWPA, consuming two divisions and part of two EBSRs, or a total of 84,000 men, of which 53,000 were slated to land in the first three days. Of these, 23,000 were engineers, a recognition of the logistical difficulties inherent to New Guinea warfare. The infantry divisions would bear the combat burden, of course, and they were ready to do so. Efficient, stubborn, chain-smoking, and respected Major General Horace Fuller commanded the 41st Division, based at Finschhafen. Two of its RCTs had already seen action in earlier New Guinea operations, and the division was probably the most battle-seasoned American infantry outfit in SWPA, so GHQ valued it highly.[29] One of its RCTs would land at Aitape while the other two swarmed ashore at Humboldt. Staging from Goodenough Island, the 24th Division, under quiet, austere, and unassuming Major General Frederick Irving, would assault Tanahmerah. It had not yet seen combat, but GHQ thought a lot of it anyway.[30] Together, the units attacking Hollandia, but not Aitape, were part of Lieutenant General Robert L. Eichelberger's I Corps.

Eichelberger was a very popular man, which went a long way in explaining his climb up the military ladder. As Willoughby put it, "Eichelberger was for many years the secretary of the General Staff in Washington. That was a powerful position and a position which helped him to make friends in the political field. He was also superintendent of West Point. He got that job because he had the other job. He was good-looking, smooth, polished, and socially just the thing for Washington."[31] Fortunately for SWPA, and especially for the troops under his command, there was more to Eichelberger than looks and connections. He was also intelligent, thoughtful, frank, whimsical, tough, and comfortable with his position and responsibilities. His staff thought he could do no wrong, and his courage at Buna nearly won him the Medal of Honor until a jealous MacArthur squashed the proposal.[32] On the flip side though, Eichelberger's makeup possessed a measure of belligerency and vainglory which, when mixed with MacArthur's deep-rooted paranoia, went a long way toward explaining why the Hollandia operation was his first combat command in some sixteen months.[33]

Eichelberger was sent to the southwest Pacific in late 1942 by Marshall, one of his many Washington sponsors. There he gave SWPA its first offensive Pacific victory at bloody Buna-Gona around the new year, after MacArthur told him to take the place or not come back alive. Eichelberger carried out his orders and lived to tell about it—unfortunately, the same could not be said for a good many Australian and American boys under his command—but his shabby treatment at the hands of a presumptuous GHQ embittered him. He liked the subsequent publicity better, which included prominent mention in articles in *Life* and the *Saturday Evening Post*. MacArthur, on the other hand, saw Eichelberger as a Marshall-constructed bomb designed ultimately to blow him out of his SWPA command, and the Buna victory served only to increase its potency.[34] Instead of rewarding Eichelberger, MacArthur exiled him to Australia to train troops and brought in Krueger as his ground commander.[35] Whatever Krueger's other flaws, a yearning for publicity was not one of them, or would not be once he learned of Eichelberger's fate. In the meantime, Eichelberger endured and worked hard to get back into MacArthur's good graces. Fortunately for him, MacArthur continued to value his combat abilities and several times fought off Marshall's attempts to pry him loose for an army command in Europe.[36] In late 1943, apparently convinced that Eichelberger now realized who was SWPA's top dog, MacArthur tapped him to lead the I Corps into combat.

In selling his soul to the SWPA devil, though, Eichelberger developed a jaded view of MacArthur that only increased as time went on. He respected his chief, however, more than the chief's sycophantic Bataan gang. He had small use for Sutherland, who he suspected wanted his job, and hard experience at Buna taught him to question Willoughby's intelligence estimates of Japanese strength.[37] Fortunately for Eichelberger's disposition, he did not have to deal with them much. The same could not be said for his immediate superior, the crusty Krueger, who grated on Eichelberger's nerves not only because he found the 6th Army commander pompous and overbearing but also because Krueger had the job Eichelberger believed he deserved.[38] Or maybe it was even simpler than that; Eichelberger and Krueger were as dissimilar as two men could be. Eichelberger represented a new breed of American soldier, the kind comfortable with civilians and their lingo and able to put them at ease with him. Tough Krueger, on the other hand, saw life through the lens of a soldier who had come up the hard way, without any of the advantages Eichelberger enjoyed.[39] MacArthur was aware of their differences, and he used them to his advantage by playing the two men off against each other.[40]

At any rate, Eichelberger was glad to be back in the thick of things, although he suspected that this combat assignment might prove as difficult as his last one at Buna. Like Krueger, he believed that surprise was his strongest ally; a forewarned Japanese force, using Hollandia's advantageous terrain, could easily turn any SWPA landing into a bloodbath.[41] His fears were reinforced by his I Corps intelligence officer, who, using Willoughby's ambiguous reports, estimated that there were two, maybe three regiments of tough Japanese regulars at Hollandia.[42] Even so, the I Corps commander was not the type of man to back away from a confrontation, and if the Japanese wanted a fight, Eichelberger would give them one.

Kenney's Surprise

George Kenney was not a modest man, so no one should have been surprised when, at the Brisbane conference, he breezingly stated that he would wipe out all Japanese air opposition around Hollandia by 5 April, long before Nimitz's precious carriers got anywhere near the vicinity.[43] The conference participants doubted not the nature of the boast but rather the promise itself, except for MacArthur, who had considerable confidence in his air commander.[44] The problem was that Hollandia was beyond the 350-mile radius of Kenney's P-38 fighters, and without fighter escorts the vulnerable bombers would be shot out of the sky before they could deliver their payloads. There was always night bombing, but that had proved ineffective; Hollandia was hard to spot in the dark. None of this was news to the Japanese, who were rushing planes to Hollandia, confident that they were beyond the reach of the AAF buzzsaw busy turning Japanese air power at Wewak to sawdust.[45] Indeed, Willoughby estimated that there were 116 bombers and 104 fighters at Hollandia's airdromes, and they had to be removed if Operation Reckless was to succeed.[46]

To make matters worse, Kenney was short of planes. Although in late February the 5th AAF's paper strength showed 803 fighters, 780 bombers, 173 reconnaissance aircraft, and 328 transports, at any given time only a little more than half of these planes were operational. The rest were sidelined by damage, personnel shortages, or a lack of spare parts. On 5 March, for instance, of the 265 B-24s available to SWPA, only 177 were actually with their units, and of these, Whitehead estimated that a mere 117 were available for missions.[47] Moreover, these planes had to tackle Japanese air power not only at Hollandia but at Wewak as well.

Kenney was, however, an innovative man, and now his resourcefulness, combined with American technological prowess, stood him in good stead. The confidence he displayed at the Brisbane conference was that of a man with an ace up his sleeve. In this case the ace was a rather mundane piece of equipment: 300-gallon wing tanks. These accoutrements, when attached to his P-38s, extended their range to 650 miles, placing them within striking distance of Hollandia, thus enabling them to accompany the otherwise vulnerable bombers to their target. Equipping the P-38s took time, though, and he needed a lot of them to tackle the approximately 100 Japanese fighters accumulating at Hollandia. In the meanwhile, to protect the vital element of surprise, Kenney concentrated on Wewak and forbade his P-38 pilots to fly beyond Aitape, or to remain there for more than fifteen minutes.[48] By the end of March he had collected more than 100 of the long-range P-38s, some shipped directly from the States and the balance modified in New Guinea and Townsville, Australia.

Once the pieces were in place, Kenney moved quickly, and on 30 March he sent his bombers, accompanied by those long-range P-38s, to Hollandia. By now Hollandia's airdromes held some 139 bombers and 125 fighters, but the Japanese were caught by surprise, with their aircraft lined up wingtip to wingtip. By the following day some 199 Japanese planes had been destroyed on the ground or in the air.[49] One observer noted, "Bombing gorgeous, entire target uncovered."[50] Another report said, "Bombing considered excellent. . . . [Japanese] pilots seemed to be having a great amount of difficulty with the P-38's."[51] This was true, but there was more to it than that. The Japanese pilots were timid and inexperienced, and their planes lacked spare parts.[52] Indeed, the raids were so successful that on 31 March the battered Japanese ordered their remaining planes withdrawn to the west.[53] American losses, on the other hand, were negligible. Within days Willoughby could report, "Careful planning by the enemy to restore a formidable air striking and defensive force in support of Central and Western New Guinea was nullified during the last week."[54] Willoughby was right about that; Kenney's attacks wrecked 340 Japanese planes on the ground and 60 in the air, all at a cost of only 4 aircraft lost to enemy fire.[55]

Japanese air opposition—what little there was, that is—ended after the first two days, but the AAF still had plenty to do. Kenney's pilots spent April blasting enemy airdromes, installations, dumps, and coastal defenses in and around Hollandia. There was not even much antiaircraft fire. By the time American troops landed, the place was, as Kenney later wrote, "a graveyard of aircraft, anti-aircraft defenses, wrecked and sunken vessels and barges, and smoldering piles of what had once been fuel, aviation stores and food supplies."[56] Kenney's boast that Nimitz's pilots would have nothing to do when they showed up offshore from Hollandia turned out to be right after all.[57] Japanese air power around Hollandia was no more.

The Tanahmerah Bay Bog

Everyone in SWPA benefited from Kenney's success, including Barbey, who was responsible for getting the invasion forces from their widespread staging bases to their targets. The VII Amphibious Force commander might not have to worry about large-scale Japanese air attacks on his slow-moving 164-ship convoy, but the possibility of detection by roving enemy reconnaissance planes or submarines remained. To that end, after the invasion fleet rendezvoused off northwest Manus on 20 April, Barbey headed westward, so as to deceive any lurking Japanese into thinking that the American objective was Palaus or Truk—or anyplace but Hollandia—before turning hard south after dusk for the true targets.[58] Next day the convoy split into three to assault Aitape, Humboldt, and Tanahmerah simultaneously. Barbey's actions, though prudent, were unnecessary; Japanese planes patrolled off Hansa Bay and Wewak, but they did not extend their reach much beyond that.

SWPA's range, as the Japanese would presently discover, was a good deal greater. At dawn on 22 April, off Tanahmerah, two heavy cruisers and six destroyers opened fire for forty-five minutes on the calm and sleepy coastline. Nimitz's carrier planes roamed overhead, but, as Kenney predicted, they had little to do but bomb the waterline to detonate any underwater mines before the troops headed for shore.

The soldiers of the 24th Division had a good deal more work ahead of them, but they were confident and ready for their baptism by fire.[59] So too were the battle-hardened engineers, who favorably compared the plenitude around them with last year's shoestring Nassau Bay operation, which they had undertaken with only thirty landing craft accompanied by two PT boats.[60] In this case, fortunately, their confidence was not misplaced. Except for some scattered fire from the flanks and a small island in the bay, both of which were quickly silenced by the Navy, there was no resistance when the 19th and 21st RCTs hit the landing beaches shortly after 0700. Irving, watching the landing, could breathe a sigh of relief when he saw the amber flares through the smoke that indicated a lack of opposition. He had argued hard for two landing beaches, one to the north and the other at Depapre, just in case one did not have any exit roads. The Navy, however, feared that the underwater coral obstacles around Depapre—also called Red Beach 1, to differentiate it from Red Beach 2 to the north—might rip the hulls off their landing craft, and it took all of Irving's powers of persuasion to get Eichelberger and Barbey to agree.[61]

Eichelberger would appreciate Irving's foresight later, but right now he and Barbey, like Irving, were sweating bullets on the latter's command ship, the destroyer *Swanson,* wondering whether they were steaming into a trap.[62] Both men were surprised, and elated, by the lack of Japanese opposition. So was MacArthur, who came down to Tanahmerah on the light cruiser *Nashville* after observing the equally easy landing at Humboldt Bay. MacArthur invited Eichelberger, Barbey, and Krueger aboard for ice cream sodas, and he showed his appreciation to Eichelberger for a job so far well done by giving his I Corps commander his untouched glass of ice cream after Eichelberger wolfed his own down.[63]

MacArthur's pleasure only increased when he, his staff, Eichelberger, Krueger, Barbey, and a host of journalists and photographers went ashore around 1500. On the beach, amid the clicking of cameras, MacArthur examined rocket-made craters, watched engineers unload LSTs, returned salutes of dumbfounded GIs, and—presumably out of earshot of both the press and Krueger—listened to an annoyed Eichelberger protest the 6th Army commander's heavy-handed attitude.[64] Such complaints did not change MacArthur's opinion of his recently resurrected I Corps chief. Later, back on the *Nashville,* he confided to Eichelberger that if SWPA got another field army he wanted him to command it.[65] Right now, though, MacArthur had good reason to be pleased with this risky operation, which had placed his forces in the enemy's rear with scarcely a shot being fired. "Irving's plan here was not good—it was brilliant!" he exclaimed.[66] Later, in what should have been an ominous statement, echoing as it did similar words spoken at Los Negros before all those Japanese stormed out of the jungle, MacArthur said to his subordinates, "This was one of the best executed operations I have ever seen. You have the enemy trapped now; don't let him go."[67]

Back on the *Nashville* with his chief subordinates, MacArthur's optimism grew to encompass future operations. Since things were going so well, he proposed that in three days SWPA divert its reserves from Hollandia, where they were apparently unneeded, to Wakde, up the coast, to keep the Japanese off balance and speed up his own advance. Barbey, who was accustomed to improvisation under pressure, was all for it, especially since the attack plans had already been drawn up. Krueger was noncommittal, but Eichelberger spoke out vehemently against his chief's idea. As he saw it, the followup shipping was not combat-loaded, so an assault on Wakde could only succeed if there were no Japanese opposition, and there was no guarantee of that. Moreover, SWPA had encountered no Japanese today, but those two or three regiments of tough Japanese regulars were supposed to be somewhere around Hollandia, and they might have withdrawn inland to prepare ambushes for his strung-out troops as they moved toward the airdromes near Lake Sentani.[68] Perhaps taken aback by Eichelberger's heated response, MacArthur agreed to leave the current plan in place, but he did not let this sudden discord disrupt his good mood as he headed back to Brisbane via Aitape and Port Moresby.[69]

Even as MacArthur returned to Australia, his Hollandia landing was running into trouble. The problem was not the Japanese, who were as yet nowhere to be found in strength, but mother nature, who, here, as elsewhere in New Guinea, proved to be an opponent every bit as formidable as SWPA's human enemy. The Navy was right about Depapre; the waters offshore were indeed full of undersea coral obstacles, and it was impossible for large landing craft to beach there. Indeed, Navy underwater demolition teams ultimately blasted a 500-foot–long, 60-foot–wide, and 12-foot–deep channel to Depapre, but it was not even partially ready until 26 April. In the meantime, Irving had to rely on Red Beach 2.

But this, as he quickly discovered, would not do either. The predicament was that there was no way off the beach. "Beach" was a deceptive term anyway, implying as it did the existence of a wide ribbon of sand between the jungle and the water, which there was not.[70] This made unloading hard enough, but behind the generously termed beach was a 300- to 400-yard-wide swamp, with high cliffs and a stream beyond it. There was simply no dispersal room to unload all the supplies and equipment the landing craft continuously disgorged, which quickly accumulated in piles up to 8 feet high. To make matters worse, discarded Japanese equipment was also scattered along the beach, further crowding things. One exasperated engineer officer later noted, "One bomb on the beach would probably have destroyed everything with the resultant fires and explosions."[71]

The engineer was more correct than he knew, as events would soon demonstrate elsewhere. As it was, just the congestion on Red Beach 2, even without any Japanese interference, was maddening enough. Irving assigned his assistant division commander, Brigadier General Kenneth J. Kramer, the unenviable task of straightening things out, and the engineers got to work under his supervision. The big problem was making room, and to do this the engineers had to deal with that swamp. They tried to drain it by cutting a canal across the beach to the ocean, but that did not lower its water table much, especially when it began to rain. Instead, it forced the engineers to devote resources to building a 12-foot bridge across the new canal. The engineers also tried corduroying a road across the swamp, but even after sinking three layers of palm logs covered with brush, rocks, and sand, vehicles still sank up to their axles. Tractors that should have been used to clear beach exits were diverted to pulling mired vehicles out of the muck. Nothing worked. Looking the situation over the day after the landing, Eichelberger and Barbey decided to concentrate their main effort on Humboldt, and they hoped that enough supplies would get through at Tanahmerah to keep the 19th and 21st RCTs moving toward the Japanese airdromes at Lake Sentani.[72] Irving, already under pressure from Krueger to get his men in motion, also adjusted his plans and ordered all the combat units at Red Beach 2 up to Depapre, where they would be more useful.[73]

Humboldt Bay Fireworks

Twenty-five miles to the east, across the rugged Cyclops Mountains at that other Hollandia-area bay, the veteran 41st Division's experience mirrored that of its unbloodied sister unit. The day there, as at Tanahmerah, started propitiously enough. Three light cruisers, six destroyers, Nimitz's carrier air-craft, and part of the 2nd ESB's support battery pounded what little Japanese opposition exposed itself to such a lethal barrage. One journalist, watching the preliminary bombardment, compared the scene to a fireworks display, es-pecially since the high wind blew the sound away from the convoy.[74]

After an hour of this, at 0700, men from the 162nd and 186th RCTs headed for the four smoke-covered White beaches. Emerging through the haze, they landed and found no enemy, but there was plenty of evidence that this had not been the case a short while ago. Japanese ammunition dumps, food, barbed wire bales, and trucks dotted the shoreline, much of it set ablaze by the Navy's guns.[75] One observer, surveying the destruction, said that it looked like a cyclone had ravaged the place.[76] By 0800, Pan-cake Hill, a barren grass-covered knoll that overlooked the beaches, was in American hands. Meanwhile, a reinforced battalion occupied Hamadi Is-land, in the middle of the harbor, without resistance.

To the 41st Division veterans, the absence of any enemy opposition was odd and not at all in line with Japanese behavior they had encountered pre-viously. It might, in fact, be a trick, so that night the troops dug in deep and waited, but nothing happened, at least nothing attributable to the Japanese ground forces.[77] Next day the 162nd RCT occupied Hollandia town with practically no resistance. The place was deserted except for a flock of honk-ing geese who attached themselves to the mud-spattered GIs.[78]

Behind the lines, down at the White beaches, though, things had not gone well—had, in fact, gone tragically awry. There the engineers had problems that made combat duty look positively appealing. The difficulties were similar to those that afflicted their comrades at Tanahmerah Bay. There was a swamp behind White Beach 1, and the sand was too soft for wheeled construction equipment to operate. Supplies and equipment kept arriving, and since the precious LSTs were highly vulnerable to Japanese night bombers, they were unloaded hastily and sent on their way before dark. To make the situation even worse, cargo diverted from Tanahmerah showed up, and there were not enough engineers to unload all the vessels, so untrained combat troops were pressed into duty.[79] All that captured Japanese materiel got in the way, forcing the men to push it into the water to make room for American goods.[80] By nightfall, as one observer noted, "ammunition, gasoline, and equipment of all kinds were piled in cluttered confusion the length and breadth" of White Beach 1.[81] The engineers were just asking for trouble, and they got it.

That evening a group of engineer officers met to discuss how on earth they planned to handle all the additional supplies and equipment diverted from Tanahmerah, but an air alert siren interrupted their conversation. Overhead a single Japanese bomber, undoubtedly attracted to the glow of the burning Japanese supplies on White Beach 1, dropped several bombs, one of which landed directly on an abandoned Japanese ammunition dump. The beach erupted in flames, and fire swept 100 yards up and down the shoreline in minutes, gobbling up everything in its path. Major Elmer P. Volgenau, watching the coast from an LST out in the bay, described what he saw:

> The holocaust on White Beach as viewed from the sea was so awesome and terrifying as to almost defy description. Great billowing black clouds of smoke were flung thousands of feet into the air from exploding drums of gasoline, while the oil, lubricant, rations, vehicles, and hundreds of tons of miscellaneous stores and gear burned below in a solid, hideous, frightening wall of flame five hundred feet in the air for a mile and a half along the beach. Through this dense pall of smoke and flame all kinds of ammunition set up a pyrotechnic display to end all boyhood impressions of Fourth of July fireworks. The spitting, vicious cackle of millions of rounds of small-arms ammunition, grenades, and engineer explosives permeated with increasing waves of sound the shattering, crashing, crumbling roar and rumble of barrage after barrage of heavy artillery shells. In all directions, in all colors of the rainbow, rockets, signal flares, and white phosphorus shells sprayed out. . . . The fierce eerie glare made faces look green in the half light.[82]

The engineers, and everyone else thereabouts, including a group of MPs who emerged barefooted from their bivouac to see what was happening, swung into action, much like ants responding to a small child kicking their hill.[83] Firefighting LCIs, designed for just such emergencies, moved in a futile effort to extinguish the flames. LCVPs also closed in on the shore and rescued men trapped by the fire. Other soldiers caught in the firestorm waded to safety through the crocodile-infested swamp behind the beach and emerged looking like slimy green devils.[84] Bulldozers pushed burning debris into the water, and everyone available worked to create a firebreak, using ad hoc human chains and hastily constructed roller conveyors to move supplies and equipment out of the path of the onrushing flames. For a while it looked like this might work, but the remorseless fire jumped the break and set off another ammunition dump, showering the work parties with bullets and shell fragments, which was worse than anything the infantry encountered that day.[85] Watching the scene, Volgenau noted: "Shortly after the 2nd ESB working and rescuing parties evacuated the beach due to the tremendous heat and danger of exploding projectiles of all kinds, the raging fire reached its maximum intensity in an intensity that made everyone gasp. None who saw it will ever forget the White Beach fire at Hollandia set off by one unlucky Jap bomb."[86]

The fire, which killed 24 and wounded more than 100, burned for forty-eight hours. The contents of eleven LSTs, or 60 percent of all the supplies unloaded with such difficulty the previous day, went up in smoke. One officer, disembarking on 24 April, observed in awe: "As we moved into the Bay, I saw fires the length of White Beaches One and Two. Bursts of flame and black smoke were followed by the thud of explosions. Large burning objects were thrown in the air and sparks fountained over blackened sand and charred coconut trees. Columns of smoke rose in the still air and merged into a thickening veil above. We were abreast the conflagration. Oil drums exploded. Ammunition crackled."[87] One soldier, arriving nearly two weeks later, described the scene: "A solid black line of gutted army supplies lined the beach for half a mile. The jungle near this stuff was scorched. Tires were burned right off the trucks, shovel handles right out of the shovels. The heat had been intense enough to melt metals. . . . I have never seen such a sight of utter devastation."[88]

The explosion—or, more specifically, the resulting damage—affected combat operations inland. Troops were placed on half rations and told to conserve their ammunition. Fortunately, there was not much use for the latter item. As for the engineers, they abandoned White Beach 1 and moved their operations over to White Beach 3, where supplies and equipment soon piled up as well, vulnerable to another such fiasco, despite Volgenau's subsequent admonition that "among the 'lessons learned the hard way' by all ranks was 'Do not pile more supplies on a beach than the shore working parties can handle efficiently.'"[89]

The Third Prong: Aitape

While the engineers at White Beach 1 were surveying the damage done to their logistical tail by one lucky Japanese bomber, Brigadier General Jens A. Doe, the contentious, opinionated, and stubborn commander of the 163rd RCT who had seen combat at Sanananda the previous year, basked in MacArthur's praise for a job well done.[90] Doe's task, which comprised the third spike of SWPA's multipronged Reckless operation, was to seize and repair Tadji airfield near Aitape so that Kenney's planes could better support Eichelberger's troops as they moved inland toward Lake Sentani.

Indeed, Tadji was the only thing of value around Aitape, which was just one point along a thirteen-mile stretch of exposed beach, part of a five-to

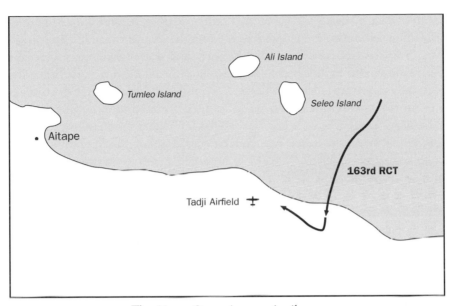

The Aitape Operation, 22 April 1944

ten-mile wide coastal plain covered in jungle and swamp. The Japanese had used Tadji to ferry planes to Wewak, but Kenney put an end to that in a series of raids that wrecked the three airstrips.[91] SWPA was unsure exactly how many Japanese were still around. In March, Krueger put the number at only 500, but just before the assault Willoughby wrote that "Aitape troop strength will fluctuate as much as 1–3000 above current G-2 estimate of 3000."[92] As it turned out, there were only 1000 Japanese from the 20th Division in the area, of whom 240 were combat troops. Krueger did not know this, however, so just to be safe, he placed the 32nd Division's 127th RCT in reserve.

Captain Albert G. Noble, commander of the naval task force transporting Doe's men, had a lot of beach to soften up before the landing, so he made sure every gun in the convoy had a target. The half-hour preliminary bombardment by naval vessels and Nimitz's carrier aircraft looked impressive enough, at least to Doe, who said, "That's that. That's the end of boredom and impatience. We know now we're going to get those strips."[93] He was right about that, but things did not go as he had planned, at least not initially. The preliminary bombardment raised so much dust and smoke that the two assault battalions lost their way and ended up coming ashore 800 yards east of their original destination.

Not that it mattered. There was little enemy opposition, and the new beach turned out to be as good as the one the troops missed, if not more so. Tadji airstrip, covered by kunai grass and dotted by fifteen smashed fighters and two bombers, fell by 1100, and the whole day cost the 163rd RCT only two men killed and thirteen wounded.[94] In fact, the escort carriers providing close air support had so little to do that half were sent to Manus to refuel, while the rest headed for Hollandia to relieve the big fleet carriers. Krueger, however, was concerned about the possibility of a Japanese counterattack from Wewak, so he ordered in the 127th RCT.[95] It was not needed, though, and despite some skirmishes in the following weeks, which contributed to the total price tag of nineteen killed and forty wounded, the operation's outcome was decided the minute the troops hit the beach, as Doe anticipated. Talking to a reporter, Doe said, "The reason for the swift, successive landing at Tadji was due to surprise and effective, powerful air and naval support. We had an excellent execution of a carefully worked out amphibious and ground plan."[96]

MacArthur agreed when he showed up the day after the landing on his way back from Hollandia. He informed Doe that he would soon be promoted to divisional command since Fuller was slated for "a position of greater responsibility," meaning I Corps chief, once Eichelberger moved up to take charge of that new field army MacArthur wanted.[97] Krueger, who arrived next day, was also pleased, although as usual less articulate in expressing his approval.[98]

Krueger's praise also stemmed in part from Doe's logistical success, which, at least at first, contrasted so sharply to Eichelberger's woes at Tanahmerah and Humboldt. Doe's engineers had seven jetties ready for unloading an hour after the troops hit the beach, and since no swamps lurked behind the beachhead, there was plenty of dispersal room. The only setback occurred just before midnight on 27 April, after Krueger left, when the half-loaded transport *Etamin* was bombed by a Japanese plane. The crew managed to save the vessel, which was hauled back to Finschhafen for repairs.

The Aitape operation, though, could not be considered successful until Doe got Tadji airdrome in working order. RAAF (Royal Australian Air Forces) engineers got to work soon after the American troops secured the place. They labored under floodlights throughout the night, so that on 24 April, forty-eight hours after the 163rd RCT landed, the strip was ready for the twenty-five RAAF P-40s that arrived that day. Unfortunately, the Australians rushed the job and neglected proper drainage techniques, so rains on the night of 25–26 April washed out the airstrip. It was not repaired until 29 April, too late to support the advance on the Hollandia airdromes but in plenty of time to help supply Eichelberger's troops while the engineers fixed the roads inland from Tanahmerah and Humboldt bays. In fact, drainage remained a big problem at Aitape, so much so that it was not until early July that Tadji could accommodate bombers, and by then its role would not be to cover Hollandia but to support troops to the east.[99]

Taking Hollandia's Airdromes

Whatever Eichelberger's woes, they paled by comparison to those of the Japanese in and around Hollandia. Since no one expected a SWPA attack anytime soon, there was no local defense plan. By mid-April, the Japanese knew from increased radio traffic volume and air reconnaissance reports that something big was up, but no one knew exactly where the Americans would strike.[100] When they did storm ashore at Humboldt, Tanahmerah, and Aitape, the local garrisons, which included almost no combat troops, scattered like chaff in the wind. The Japanese at Hollandia abandoned Lake Sentani's airdrome before Irving's and Fuller's millstones crushed them, retreating inland through New Guinea's hostile jungle. One desperate soldier, plodding south and westward, wrote in his diary:

> There is no end to this life. We are still roaming aimlessly. . . . Perhaps this is part of our fate. , , , We are beginning to hate everything in this world. We live each day sympathizing with one another. At times, we see someone in our group shedding tears. It is most pitiful. . . . The determination among our men to accept inevitable death is admirable. We live on herbs and roots of trees. . . . This is a horrible situation. . . . Sunny days are more bearable, but we would weep when it rains. Then again there are the attacks from mosquitoes. This is most annoying. I can't stand it. . . . My friends are dead. I am steadily growing lonely.[101]

By 7 May, some 10,000 Japanese survivors had gathered near Genjem, twenty miles west of Hollandia. From there they tried to move westward to the safety of the Sarmi garrison, but only a few survived the march. Most succumbed to hunger, SWPA air attacks, disease, and hopelessness. Whatever their fate, they posed no threat to SWPA.

Despite the logistical problems stemming from Hollandia's uncooperative beaches and bogs, Eichelberger could at least take pride in getting his men ashore and seizing Tanahmerah and Humboldt bays, both at minimal cost in men, if not materiel. Doing so though, as the I Corps commander knew, was merely a means to an end, the end being the conquest of those three Japanese airdromes down around Lake Sentani. Irving, too, was aware of the ultimate operational goal, and soon after the 24th Division hit the Tanahmerah beaches he sent one of its battalions inland, followed the next day by another. The two 21st RCT battalions moved cautiously, still expecting to run into those two or three Japanese regiments, but the enemy seemed more intent on avoiding than provoking hostilities, so opposition was surprisingly light. Even so, the 21st RCT offensive continued on a wide front, which, while slowing down the rate of advance, made it harder for the Japanese to infiltrate behind the front lines to attack the vulnerable supply trains trudging up from the beaches.[102]

Indeed, mother nature continued to cause more problems than the enemy. Getting vehicles to the congested beaches was hard enough, but the trail from Tanahmerah inland to Lake Sentani was all but impassable for anything on wheels. There were, for example, fourteen unbridged streams to cross in the first fourteen miles.[103] Irving had foreseen this problem, however, and he calculated that he could supply one RCT by hand as far as Dazai, halfway to the airdromes, and the AAF would have to take up the slack.[104] The AAF tried and ultimately delivered 3999 C-47 loads from Aitape, Nadzab, and Finschhafen before the Hollandia airfields were in operation, but rain interfered with the initial resupply missions.[105] Those same rains also caused landslides, making life miserable for the engineers assigned to repair the trail. Fortunately, the absence of any real Japanese resistance gave Irving a surplus of manpower, so by 26 April some 3500 soldiers from three battalions, two antitank companies, and two cannon companies were hauling supplies by hand up the muddy trail. One observer, who perhaps failed to compare mortality rates between combat and noncombat roles, noted, "It was ignominious work for highly trained combat men, but to their credit."[106] By now, Eichelberger realized that no significant opposition would develop, so he wanted those airfields quick.[107] Irving pressed on, and seeing his goal in sight, on 25 April ordered, "Indications point to enemy withdrawal. Attack vigorously tomorrow and seize Hollandia [airdrome]."[108] The 21st RCT did so and the next day easily occupied Hollandia airdrome and, late in the afternoon, contacted elements from the 186th RCT moving inland from the west.

To the east, the 41st Division faced the same problems that plagued Irving's outfit—light opposition from the Japanese, but more formidable resistance from the terrain. There, too, the inland trail crumbled under the weight of Army vehicles, except for LVTs and DUKWs, which, along with AAF airdrops, formed the backbone of the 41st Division's resupply efforts. Those amphibious craft played another, equally vital role. They served as the 186th RCT's private little navy, enabling the Americans to gain control of Lake Sentani and use that power to outflank Japanese positions along the shoreline. On 26 April, the day the 21st RCT occupied Hollandia airdrome, the 186th RCT took its two companions, Sentani and Cyclops, with little difficulty.

From that point on, the Hollandia operation consisted mostly of mopping up enemy forces scurrying for safety and turning the area into a staging base for other, hopefully equally devastating attacks against the shrinking Japanese defense perimeter. The only real fight occurred at Hill 1000, northeast of Cyclops airdrome, where on 28 April some 400 Japanese repulsed an assault by a battalion from the 186th RCT. The Americans bombed and shelled the hill until the next day, when the battalion successfully stormed it. After that, the 24th Division took over mopping-up duties after GHQ withdrew the 41st Division to Hollekang near Humboldt Bay for operations further west.

Eichelberger could be, and was, proud of his troops' accomplishments. Both the 24th and 41st divisions performed well, seizing Hollandia's airdromes four days after coming ashore, despite bad topographical and logistical conditions. To be sure, the almost complete lack of enemy resistance helped a lot, but even when the Japanese put up a fight the GIs quickly overcame all opposition. Although Fuller and his 41st Division went on to other, ultimately unhappy, New Guinea adventures, Irving's 24th Division—except for one RCT which participated briefly in the Biak operation—did not see action again until the Philippines campaign. There the unit fought through the 6th Army's bloody Leyte operation, and later in Mindanao under Eichelberger. Unfortunately, at Leyte Irving displeased Krueger and was relieved of command, but Eichelberger, who liked and respected him, gave him a job in his new 8th Army.

The Big Engineering Phase

Eichelberger could breathe a sigh of relief once Hollandia's airdromes fell to Fuller's and Irving's weary men. Their occupation marked the successful termination of the first part of the operation. Now, however, the I Corps commander had to oversee what his staff referred to as "The Big Engineering Phase," which involved turning Hollandia into a huge SWPA logistical complex that could support five airdromes and 200,000 men.[109] Moreover, he had to work fast; MacArthur needed those facilities completed quickly to continue his advance up the New Guinea road, and he had also promised Nimitz that SWPA air power would support the POA's mid-June Marianas operation.

Like Swift over in the Admiralties, Eichelberger too was hindered not
so much by the Japanese, who wanted nothing more than a chance to flee
the wide-ranging GIs, but rather by his own confederates. On 25–26 April,
for instance, he and his staff spent the night flat on their bellies as the 24th
Division platoon assigned to guard his headquarters expended 3000
rounds of ammunition in an imaginary battle with the Japanese, though the
not-so-friendly fire casualties were real enough.[110]

Usually, though, Eichelberger's problems were not quite so personal,
but irksome nonetheless. There were the high-handed Dutch colonial officials, who wanted to take over Hollandia's civil administration and treated
the Americans like hired thugs.[111] Another more serious problem was souvenir hunting by bored soldiers, which quickly got out of hand. GIs stole
anything Japanese, or that even looked Japanese—helmets, rifles, bayonets,
swords, pistols, flags, and so forth—and sold or bartered it away, usually
for fruit juices to ferment into alcohol. In fact, the troops even pilfered
Japanese coffins of their nonhuman contents, and at Tami airfield they
stripped bare a captured Japanese fighter plane.[112]

Eichelberger could shrug off these difficulties as incidents of war, but he
had more serious problems that affected his primary mission of turning
Hollandia into a logistical platform for future SWPA operations. First of all,
clearing the roads from the coast to Lake Sentani was not going well. Rain
interfered with the engineers' work, and the trail was narrow, slippery, and
vulnerable to occasional Japanese snipers.[113] Abandoned American trucks
dotted the muddy ditches along the road. One engineer reported:

> What little tonnage got over Pim Jetty [on Humboldt Bay] had to be hauled
> some 17 miles over a rough, almost impassable, track up in the jungle hills
> to Lake Sentani and thence by a circuitous trail around the east shore of the
> lake to the complex of three Jap airdromes north of it. Therefore, after an
> engineer battalion had hacked its way there and put one of the airdromes
> in roughly operable shape, avgas [aviation fuel] had to be flown first from
> Finschhafen (500 miles); then Aitape (120 miles); and finally from a
> swampy strip hastily constructed on the isolated southern shore of Hum-
> boldt Bay in order to initiate and sustain local fighter operations in the Hol-
> landia area. This put a terrific load on the theater air transport capacity but
> with all the vulnerable shipping in the harbor, it was a "must" operation in
> order to insure local fighter defense.[114]

Nor were conditions much easier on the beach, as Eichelberger learned
when a Japanese ration dump at Humboldt caught fire and, much like the
earlier disaster at White Beach 1, spread up and down the shoreline.[115]

As it turned out, even if Eichelberger had done an exemplary job, Hollandia would not have lived up to expectations. More than a month earlier, 5th AAF deputy chief Whitehead, scanning low-level reconnaissance photos, became convinced that Hollandia's soggy terrain could not support the AAF bombers GHQ planned to station there. In fact, he and Kenney had recommended that GHQ downgrade the Hollandia operation and attack Wakde-Sarmi, which would place SWPA in position to strike Biak, where bombers could be based.[116] By then, however, it was too late to change the Reckless plans. After Eichelberger's men overran the airdromes, Whitehead rushed over for a firsthand look that confirmed his worst fears. The Japanese-built airdromes were poorly constructed and drained, and it would be difficult for fully loaded bombers to clear the surrounding hills.[117] Heavy rains in May did not help the situation. Summing things up, AAF chief of staff Colonel R. E. Beebe called Hollandia a "lemon."[118] The airdromes were not completely valueless though. Cyclops was ready for fighters and transports on 29 April, and C-47s could fly out of Hollandia on 2 May, so SWPA operations further west could have fighter protection. Unfortunately, the difficult terrain would not enable the 5th AAF to fulfill MacArthur's promise to Nimitz to support the Marianas operation by bombing the Palaus.

Similarly, the Hollandia region did not live up to SWPA's hopes as a base. The area was too swampy, the road net too primitive, and the anchorages too inadequate. Looking over the place, Major General James L. Frink, in charge of SWPA's services and supplies, recommended that GHQ scale back its ambitious plans for the place. MacArthur agreed, and in the end the Americans reconstructed only three airdromes, and built 3 million square feet of covered storage and facilities for 140,000 men.[119] Even this, however, was an enormous undertaking, and engineers still had to erect dozens of docks, water supply facilities, fuel pipe lines, hospitals, warehouses, camps, and headquarters.

The Brass Moves In

To make Eichelberger's already difficult job even more trying, he had to cope with the prickly Krueger, who moved his advance headquarters from Cape Cretin to Hollandia on 24 May. To Krueger, Eichelberger was not measuring up to expectations, and he was quick to let the I Corps commander know it. As he saw it, Eichelberger was not pressing his staff or his souvenir-hungry troops hard enough, which was an unhealthy sign of an army losing its fighting edge. "In my more than 40 years as an officer I have never raised my voice to an enlisted man, but a Corps commander should know better," a fuming Krueger said to a staffer after he chewed out Eichelberger for poorly handling supply ships.[120] Eichelberger, for his part, responded to this criticism, which he considered unwarranted, with all the patience he could muster, but he found dealing with Krueger and his attitude exhausting, trying, and tedious.[121]

Eichelberger was not the only high-ranking SWPA officer under fire. So was his other arch rival, the abrasive Sutherland, who was letting his boundless ambition get the better of him. By now Sutherland was at the zenith of his power. MacArthur relied heavily on him, and he terrified many at GHQ. Not surprisingly, some believed that Sutherland was growing altogether too powerful, so that he might actually pose a threat to MacArthur himself.[122] Sutherland seemed to see things in that light. After MacArthur moved his advance GHQ to Hollandia in May, his chief of staff gazed out a headquarters window and said to a subordinate, "I am in command now. I am running this show. The General is an old man. He can't operate any more."[123]

As Sutherland would soon learn, he was considerably off the mark. Whatever his other admittedly significant flaws, MacArthur knew how to manipulate and command men. Nor did it help Sutherland that most officers at GHQ hated him and were more than willing to do whatever they could to knock him down a peg or two. Indeed, about the time Sutherland made his private inaugural speech at Hollandia, some around GHQ noticed a subtle change in MacArthur's attitude toward his chief of staff. The two had never been friends, but now MacArthur began to privately criticize Sutherland's decisions and to permit others to bypass his chief of staff and bring matters directly to him.[124]

The gunpowder, then, was already sprinkled around GHQ; all that was needed was a spark to blow the relationship wide open. This was provided by one Elaine Clarke, an Australian who was among the Women's Auxiliary Corps (WACs), Red Cross workers, and female nurses who showed up at Hollandia as part of its transformation from Japanese base to SWPA supercomplex. Clarke was Sutherland's mistress. Mistresses were not that uncommon around GHQ, but Clarke stood out. Not only was she tied to the hated Sutherland, but she was also bossy and very annoying. Worst of all, she was married to a British officer who was currently passing his time in a Japanese prisoner of war camp, and her infidelity was cause enough for any honorable soldier to despise her. MacArthur knew all about her, and he commanded Sutherland not to violate Australian law by taking her out of Australian territory. His judgment apparently clouded by Clarke's charms, Sutherland repeatedly disobeyed MacArthur's orders, until, in September, he and his commander got into a shouting match when MacArthur hauled his chief of staff on the carpet for his disobedience.[125] Sutherland remained SWPA's chief of staff, but he never had as much power again.

Evaluating Hollandia

Writing years later, when he got around to glorifying MacArthur publicly on paper, Willoughby compared the Hollandia operation to the great Carthaginian victory at Cannae, where Hannibal annihilated a Roman army twice the size of his own with a double envelopment.[126] As was usual with Willoughby, there was a good deal of exaggeration and distortion to this analogy. The most obvious were that at Hollandia the Americans outnumbered the vanquished Japanese, and that although Hannibal's great triumph yielded no long-term strategic benefits, SWPA's victory paid off big in a number of ways.

For one thing, at the minimum cost of 152 killed and 1057 wounded—the Japanese lost approximately 3300 dead and 611 captured, out of their 10,000-man garrison, which did not include the two or three combat regiments Willoughby had suspected, and Eichelberger had believed, were in the vicinity—MacArthur took another big leap up the New Guinea coast, covering in one operation more ground than he had gained the entire previous year. This placed him ahead of Nimitz's forces, which were busy preparing for the Marianas operation. Indeed, the SWPA chief estimated that his well-placed lightning strike saved him an estimated two months over his old plan.[127] This meant he could liberate his beloved Philippines that much sooner, assuming the JCS came around to his way of thinking, which dramatic victories like Hollandia made all the more likely. Moreover, now that Hollandia was in American hands, GHQ could use its staging facilities and airdromes to project SWPA's power further westward. SWPA forces from Hollandia participated not only in other New Guinea operations but also in the Philippines liberation campaign. Indeed, Hollandia remained an important base throughout the war, and even after the conflict many demobilized GIs returned home through it.

Nor were the savings only in terms of time and lives. Because of the surprising ease of the operation, SWPA did not expend as many resources as anticipated, thus easing GHQ's logistical burden. In fact, SWPA was able to reduce ship retention requirements to twenty vessels per month for June, July, and August.[128] MacArthur could spend his logistical savings on operations further west, accelerating his New Guinea offensive even more.

Finally, by occupying Hollandia, MacArthur cut off Adachi's three divisions—some 55,000 men—in the Hansa Bay-Wewak area. This was something any commander could be proud of—especially MacArthur, who had been on the receiving end of such treatment in the Philippines. Indeed, he dredged up that analogy to describe the operation to the public, saying that SWPA had thrown a "loop of envelopment" around the enemy that "reversed Bataan."[129]

This was all well and good, but the Hollandia operation also displayed some troubling tendencies that would plague SWPA throughout the New Guinea campaign and on into the Philippines as well. First, MacArthur somewhat misinterpreted the victory; his analogy to Bataan is not quite accurate. In the Philippines, MacArthur's surrounded forces tied down significant numbers of Japanese who needed to secure strategically vital Manila Harbor. Adachi's forces, now reduced to eating roots and berries, protected nothing particularly vital to SWPA, but MacArthur still had to devote lots of troops to keep an eye on them. This not only drained SWPA's always valuable resources but also ultimately provoked the New Guinea campaign's bloodiest, and most strategically useless, battle.

The operation also revealed a flaw in MacArthur's generalship that became more pronounced as time went on. Here, as in the Admiralties, the SWPA chief believed that once the assault troops were securely ashore the battle was for all practical purposes over and he could return to Brisbane to prepare for the next round. He did not recognize that Japanese troops dug in inland could tactically hinder American forces, and such interference, if sustained, could eventually cause SWPA problems at the *strategic* level, throwing a wrench into GHQ's offensive timetable. Fortunately, there was surprisingly little Japanese resistance at Hollandia, so MacArthur's assumptions proved correct, but this would not always be the case.

Finally, the Hollandia operation was only partially successful logistically. To be sure, Hollandia eventually provided staging facilities and fighter bases for future operations up the New Guinea littoral, but a major reason SWPA attacked it was to place bombers there that would support Nimitz's Marianas operation and to bomb enemy positions further west. Unfortunately, Hollandia was too far from SWPA bases for MacArthur to get a good look at its soggy terrain before GHQ drew up plans for its seizure, so he had to find additional airfields to the west to stage bombers from before Nimitz's mid-June assault date. Meeting this new deadline, however, put even more pressure on SWPA field commanders to secure their objectives quickly, which had unhappy consequences later.

Despite these problems, on the whole the Hollandia operation stands out as another of MacArthur's shining victories. Through the correct interpretation of Willoughby's sometimes ambiguous intelligence, the successful application of superior resources, the element of tactical and strategic surprise, and the recognition that the dual drive offensive would keep the Japanese Navy out of the way, MacArthur's risky assault deep into the enemy rear paid off. In part MacArthur was lucky, but mostly he succeeded because attrition had reduced the enemy to a state of strategic paralysis. Even had they managed to discern SWPA's intentions, the Japanese lacked the mobility to do much about it beyond the tactical level.

FIVE

COMBAT AND SURVIVAL IN A HOSTILE ENVIRONMENT

The Pacific War was like no other conflict ever waged by the United States. Mass American armies had fought overseas before, and would again, but in this case the distances, numbers, environment, enemy, and duration were all extreme and unfamiliar. For SWPA's soldiers, airmen, and sailors, their experience was not at all like that of their Civil War or World War I predecessors, or even akin to their compatriots fighting the Nazis in Europe. In those instances, the enemy was culturally similar and the battlefield somewhat recognizable. Everything about New Guinea, however, was alien, from the frequent tropical deluges to the unfathomable Oriental foe. The island's physical distance from the United States only served to reinforce the bewilderment, isolation, and loneliness many GIs experienced there.

Worse yet, there was no way out for the unfortunate men sucked into MacArthur's war. Once a GI reached SWPA, he was there for the duration of the conflict, unless released from his unwelcome obligations by serious injury or death, neither of which was particularly appealing, at least not at first. Except for sporadic mail, communicating with friends and family was impossible. For SWPA personnel then, the war's *outcome*, not just the war itself, was an intensely intimate matter, signifying as it did personal liberation. In the meantime, the GIs endured the strange natives, foods, climate, and diseases that helped make New Guinea a planetary purgatory.

Some of New Guinea's perils kicked in soon after soldiers, sailors, and airmen left the United States for SWPA. The first problem was not the Japanese, whose submarines were so rare along shipping lanes that most transports steamed across the Pacific unescorted, but rather tedium. Life on troopships alternated between time spent below decks and topside, depending on the weather. There was not much to do in either place during the two- to four-week trip but sweat in the heat, read, write letters, gamble, talk, watch an occasional movie, pilfer, or eat. The food left a lot to be desired, though; fresh milk and vegetables ran out quickly, so for most of the voyage the men subsisted on spam sandwiches, dehydrated potatoes, powdered eggs, hot dogs, and an occasional orange or ice cream bar.[1] The Navy tried to fill the time with unpleasant tasks like lifeboat drills, cleaning the ship, dumping garbage, and KP duty, but this hardly compensated for otherwise uneventful hours. Whatever the men did, they did together; privacy was nonexistent in such cramped quarters. One soldier wrote, "We were placed in the enclosed lower part of the ship, crammed together like cattle. One could hardly tell men from equipment."[2]

Life on board ship was hard enough, at least on minds quickly dulled by such monotony, but it was paradise compared to life in SWPA, except for those lucky enough to find themselves stationed in Australia. The towns and cities Down Under, while somewhat quaint, were clean and cool and had a certain charm. At the other end of the misery scale, some men found themselves in primitive new New Guinea camps, which were neither quaint nor cool nor clean. There GIs often had to beg, borrow, or steal—pilfering from offshore transport ships for such purposes was called "moonlight requisitioning"[3]—to set up their rudimentary installations.

Most men shipped to SWPA in 1944, however, ended up in one of New Guinea's big, well-established bases: Port Moresby, Milne Bay, Oro Bay, Finschhafen, or, later, Hollandia. These places bustled with activity as soldiers trained, loaded or unloaded ships, constructed warehouses and buildings, and repaired the implements of war. Huge piles of rations, ammunition, and crates dotted the landscape, and rows of jeeps and vehicles filled the motor pools. Despite all the activity, which radiated a degree of life altogether lacking on the transport vessels, none of SWPA's New Guinea bases was aesthetically pleasing. Bugs crawled everywhere, it rained constantly, mud was an everyday hindrance, and the heat and humidity were stifling. Of course, these installations were designed not to look good but to advance the war effort. Even though the Japanese had been driven westward, accidents made life dangerous. In late March 1944, for instance, a kunai grass fire touched off a huge AAF ammunition dump near Nadzab, filling the sky with exploding bombs, white magnesium flares, and red tracers, but fortunately killing no one.[4]

The men, like the bases, were tools of war, and employed as such. For the combat troops, training exercises that emphasized such SWPA specialties as night operations, small unit actions, and mock amphibious landings filled their days. Often, however, SWPA yanked combat units from their primary task and pressed them into unloading cargo vessels. Many of these soldiers discovered a hitherto unsuspected perquisite to such duty: pilfering shipholds. In fact, at Milne Bay Major General Franklin Sibert's 6th Division grew so proficient at such unauthorized work that it earned the nickname "Sibert and His 10,000 Thieves."[5]

Most men in SWPA, as in the American military as a whole, were not combat troops but support personnel who undertook the hard, repetitive, and unglamorous maintenance, repair, storage, transport, and planning tasks a modern army required to wage war. For them, the biggest enemy was not the Japanese, whose occasional air raids, while scary enough, at least provided a change of pace, but boredom. Miserable living conditions and grueling work often served only to underscore the perpetual monotony, which drove some men insane, or "troppo," in SWPA parlance. Most GIs, however, successfully coped as best they could with the alien environment circumstance had thrust them into.

Diversions were few in SWPA. There was rarely enough equipment for baseball, basketball, or football, and clearing the fields for such activities required resources needed elsewhere, so the men usually played volleyball.[6] Watching movies was a favorite pastime, but the reels were of poor quality and often repeatedly spliced. USO shows were better still but rare, especially near the front, where movie stars, or movie star wannabes, might be killed. To pass the time, some soldiers kept pets from New Guinea's less dangerous pool of exotic wildlife, raising and training flying squirrels, praying mantises, lizards, and tree kangaroos. Others swam, wrote letters, or read a lot. For the truly adventurous, the personnel-strapped AAF issued a standing invitation for gunners on its bomber missions.[7]

One way to a soldier's heart—at least for those not about to depart on one of Kenney's bombers—was through his stomach. In SWPA, however, Army-issued rations often were not very good.[8] Tinned fruit, canned vegetables, dehydrated potatoes with the consistency of gravel, tasteless dehydrated eggs, dried milk, and soggy pancakes filled bellies but were not very appetizing. The Army even invented a butter designed not to melt in the tropical heat, but in practice that meant it never melted at all, hence its derisive nicknames "axle grease" and "GI lubricant."[9] The Navy's rations were better, especially since their ships had refrigeration, so soldiers often traded Japanese souvenirs—or GI-created facsimiles—to wide-eyed sailors for naval goodies. Food packages from home were equally satisfying, but cookies and candy had to be consumed quickly before the rats got them. When all else failed to please, the men could eat native foods like bananas, pineapples, breadfruit, manioc, sago palm, and especially coconuts. Many soldiers, however, had trouble retrieving coconuts from the tall palm trees, so they usually paid a native a cigarette to do it for them. Stingy GIS settling for coconuts on the ground quickly discovered that these were wormy and fermented and often caused dysentery.

Food was important, but it did little to help soldiers forget their present woes. Alcohol filled that role, but it was hard to get. In order to save shipping space, SWPA at first did not even issue a beer ration, which infuriated troops ordered to unload brews for their luckier naval counterparts.[10] Even after Krueger ordered beer to New Guinea, other materials had higher shipping priority. Usually left to their own devices, soldiers fermented coconuts, canned blackberries and peaches, or vanilla extract and consumed the results. Some even poured rubbing alcohol through bread until the loaf took on a shiny waxy texture, then they wrung it out and drank the liquid straight or mixed with grapefruit juice.[11] None of these various concoctions—invariably termed "jungle juice"—tasted very good, but flavor was secondary to the wallop the potion packed.

For both drunken and sober soldiers, mail was another morale booster. It took two weeks for v-mail—photographed and miniaturized letters—to reach SWPA, or about a month for regular air mail to make the same trip. Distributing it within SWPA, however, was a big problem, and GIS received letters irregularly and in bunches. Soldiers often got dozens of letters at once and then nothing more for a long time.[12] This feast-or-famine routine was so detrimental to morale that Krueger complained to MacArthur, who explained that mail delivery was tied to the unpredictable shipping schedule, which gave priority to other things.[13]

Soldiers' letters were subject to Army censors, whose primary job was to make sure that GIS did not reveal military secrets to the folks back home. The biggest such threat to security, however, was not from the average soldier, who knew little beyond his immediate field of vision, but from senior officers, who were often indiscreet in their letters.[14] Preserving security was not the censors' only job.[15] One soldier attempted to ship a jeep home piece by piece until the censors caught on. Like a picture, an object is worth a thousand words, so each month censors confiscated a bushel basket full of Japanese skulls from GIS trying to impress—or, more accurately, deceive—friends and family as to their military prowess.[16]

Everyone liked to receive mail, except when such home front dispatches contained a Dear John letter from a faithless wife or sweetheart. When this happened, there was little the recipient could do but suffer. Although furloughs to Australia were occasionally granted, there was no stateside leave.[17] Under normal circumstances AWOL (absence without leave) would have ravaged SWPA, but in New Guinea there was nowhere to go but the jungle, which, for all its charms, was unlikely to attract many homesick Americans on the run from military authorities.

The Army, like any other institution, rewarded good work, mostly through promotions and decorations. In SWPA, unfortunately, promotions were excruciatingly slow, so officers tended to be older than their counterparts of equal rank in other, more important, theaters.[18] This was maddening enough, but an ambitious man could only with difficulty leave his present job. Officers, for instance, were not allowed to transfer out of combat units unless physically or mentally unable to perform their duties, and few people wanted into such units.[19] Krueger could, and did, assuage unappreciated feelings through decorations; he granted corps and division commanders wide authority to dispense most medals freely and quickly.[20]

Moreover, morale was further undermined, at least among ground troops, by the common conviction that the American public believed that Kenney's glamorous flyboys were winning the Pacific War single-handedly.[21] As it was, in glorifying the SWPA commander, MacArthur's voracious and self-serving publicity machine all but overlooked the contribution that hundreds of thousands of ordinary GIs and sailors made in winning the New Guinea campaign.

The biggest morale booster of them all—short of an end to the war and an immediate discharge—was also the rarest: women. SWPA was an overwhelmingly male preserve, but some 2700 WACs personnel served behind the lines as nurses, telephone and teletype operators, photo interpreters, and file clerks.[22] Many around GHQ, however, did not approve of stationing women near combat zones; they interfered with male camaraderie and required separate facilities, thus consuming scarce resources.[23] For most SWPA personnel though, the issue was moot; females were as remote and untouchable as the starlets the men watched on their movie screens.

Less distant were New Guinea's native population. Hundreds of separate tribes dotted the big island, from the headhunters and cannibals in the interior to more docile groups who had been exposed to European culture and rule. Almost everything about them was alien to the Americans. Most of the men dressed in loincloth and chewed betelnut, a mild narcotic that reddened their lips. The women, who the men kept hidden in their villages, wore grass skirts and nothing else. Many tattooed their bodies and punctured their distended ears. The GIs called them "Fuzzy Wuzzies," after their hair, and communicated with them in pidgin English. Not surprisingly, although most of the natives were friendly, they had little enthusiasm for a war that destroyed their villages and upset their way of life.[24]

Be that as it may, manpower-short SWPA saw New Guinea's natives as a valuable unskilled labor pool and tapped it. The Army hired natives as guides or to build or corduroy roads, carry supplies, clear and excavate land for airfields, cut timber, and bear stretchers. Observant engineers noticed that the natives worked best when well treated and permitted to toil with other members of their tribe.[25] Native labor, in the end, freed Americans for combat duty, thus contributing to SWPA's New Guinea campaign victory.

SWPA's environment was undoubtedly hard on the soldiers and airmen who sweated in the sticky wet heat or shivered with malaria in hospital tents, but the theater had plenty of misery left over for the Navy, Army, and merchant marine personnel who manned the ships that plied the New Guinea shoreline. To be sure, such vessels possessed none of New Guinea's mud and insects, but the blazing sun that turned steel decks into steamy griddles was almost as awful. Moreover, sailors had to be constantly alert for the sudden appearance of Japanese planes diving out of the sun to sink their vulnerable ships, or of uncharted reefs lurking beneath the water. Naval duty, in short, offered no escape from the theater's perils.

Perhaps the most monotonous burden fell on the merchant marine sailors manning the bulky Laker and Liberty vessels that carried men and materiel to SWPA before returning to the States with raw materials to feed the American war machine. Ship crews tended toward the disparate, consisting of men of every age, race, prewar profession, and temperament. Although civilians, they came under the jurisdiction of the Articles of War, and in the Atlantic the danger to life and limb from German U-boats was real enough to justify such action. In the Pacific, on the other hand, few crews ever saw combat; day-to-day existence revolved around long boring weeks on the trackless ocean or outside of crowded New Guinea ports. Considering the circumstances, it was hardly surprising that morale often deteriorated, even though the sailors received greater pay than their Army and Navy counterparts.[26]

To make matters worse, SWPA's warped logistical apparatus was enough to drive even the most patient captain and crew to distraction. Sailors liked to tell the tale of a Liberty vessel that wandered throughout the Pacific for six months looking for someone to accept its cargo of barbed wire. Everyone refused it, so the vessel finally returned in frustration to the West

Coast.[27] The story, while probably apocryphal—it is hard to imagine any equipment-strapped SWPA supply officer turning away cargo, no matter how mundane its contents or questionable its ownership—reflected the logistical confusion many seamen saw in SWPA. Indeed, one exasperated sailor composed a ditty, "The New Guinea Theme Song":

> Things are as snafu as they seem,
> Confusion and chaos reign supreme
> So chuck it back aboard and we're on our way
> To Manus, Finsch and Milne Bay
> Where we'll drop the hook and wait some more,
> Maybe then they'll know the score.
> But it's odd on end—ten to one at best,
> That they're as screwed up as the rest.
> Around for a month or so
> With our spirits drooping and our morale low.[28]

Moreover, GHQ tried to snag Liberties whenever possible and keep them in the theater, a type of impressment that prevented seamen from seeing their loved ones for the duration of the war. Such action, while perhaps unforgivable to sailors denied the opportunity to visit their families or sinful ports-of-call, reflected SWPA's appreciation of their value. Indeed, after the war MacArthur said, "They have brought us our lifeblood and they had paid for it with some of their own. I saw them bombed off the Philippines and in New Guinea. When it was humanely possible, when their ships were not blown out from under them by bombs or torpedoes, they have delivered their cargoes to us who needed them so badly."[29]

For the sailors manning the vessels of Kinkaid's 7th Fleet, merchant marine duty often seemed downright appealing. Kinkaid's Navy had a handful of destroyers and cruisers, but the bulk of the fleet was built around the LSTs, LCIs, PT boats, and other smaller craft that formed the backbone of SWPA's amphibious war. Although these vessels were designed for short trips, the logistical difficulties of New Guinea warfare often forced Barbey to keep his men and ships at sea for long durations to shuttle men and supplies to the soldiers and airmen stationed in SWPA's far-flung domain.

Under such trying and isolated circumstances, the performance of the small crews depended greatly upon the captain, who assumed the role of father figure of his close-knit naval family. Indeed, the perceptive Barbey quickly recognized that a crew was no better than its commander.[30] Unfortunately, the lack of privacy and sleep, tension-filled boredom, and hard work all conspired against crew harmony. The men quickly read all the books in their small library and watched whatever movies the captain managed to procure. The food was bland, and since each ship usually had only a small household refrigerator, the sailors ate perishables quickly. Anchoring in an isolated cove enabled the men to stretch their legs, but the dense jungle offered few other amenities. Older crewmen and the officers seemed to adjust better to this environment than their younger enlisted counterparts, perhaps because they were mature enough to accept the situation and find ways to occupy themselves.[31] Illness was rare, though sailors still came down with some of New Guinea's bountiful collection of tropical diseases, collectively known as "the crud."

Oddly enough, the prospect of combat tended to raise morale, perhaps because it provided a change of pace from the everyday boredom and served to remind everyone why they were so far away from home. Astute captains placed extra machine guns onboard, which not only ensured better protection from Japanese planes but gave more of the crew a chance to vent their frustrations on legitimate targets instead of each other.

Although most of the 7th Fleet only occasionally saw combat, this was not true of the PT boats. These small fast ships, armed with four torpedoes and automatic weapons, scoured the New Guinea coast at night in an effort to disrupt the Japanese supply line by sinking the barges that provided sustenance to the enemy's garrisons. The PT boats played a dangerous cat-and-mouse game with enemy planes and shore batteries, and they contributed greatly to the strangulation of the Japanese on the island. Off of Aitape, for instance, PT boats destroyed 115 barges attempting to supply Adachi's isolated 18th Army, at the cost of only one of their own lost to enemy fire.[32] Later, the PT boats moved on to Geelvink Bay and helped choke off Japanese barge traffic in that area, contributing to MacArthur's fast advance through the Vogelkop.

In Combat

Although prewar Army planners never envisioned fighting the Japanese in New Guinea's unforgiving jungle, they had devoted considerable time and energy to thinking about war in general. Their often bitter World War I experiences taught them the perils of waging war with a mass-based conscript army. As they saw it, simplicity was the antidote to the confusion and chaos that inevitably plagued partially trained troops in battle.[33] Army planners hoped that a few basic doctrines, combined with an emphasis on firepower, technology, flexibility, and mobility, would win the day in the next war, and they successfully pushed the Army in that direction.

To accommodate this thinking, before Pearl Harbor the Army simplified its organization by imposing triangularization at every level below corps. Each unit from division down to platoon was given one fire support and three maneuver components. This simple and uniform organization enabled the Army to emphasize to everyone, regardless of rank, the easy-to-understand holding attack, whereby one part of a unit pinned the enemy down with firepower while the balance of the force used its mobility to hit the opponent's flank or rear. The Army hoped that the holding attack, combined with firepower and mobility, would keep future battles fluid and prevent the horrendous static trench warfare that characterized World War I.

The heart of the Army's new organization and doctrine lay in its 14,200-man infantry divisions. Army Ground Forces commander General Leslie McNair wanted these divisions lean and mean, so he stripped them of specialized units and staff to cut down on the paperwork and nonessential personnel that inhibited mobility. Instead, all these specialized antitank, engineer, antiaircraft, and armored units went into a corps pool for use when and where necessary. Unfortunately, during the war divisional commanders tried hard to hold onto whatever weapons and equipment they could get, betraying McNair's intentions.[34] Moreover, in SWPA especially the RCTs also acquired this additional baggage because they were often thrust into combat without their parent divisions and the support they normally provided.

Divisions and RCTs were of course important, but the real war was fought by the infantrymen in their squads, platoons, and companies.[35] It was the infantry that gained the ground, suffered the most casualties, and lived in the worst conditions. In SWPA, the infantry's war usually took place in a dense and trackless jungle that, as one Australian put it, "drowned out the battle like an opaque green liquid."[36] The jungle obscured vision and fields of fire, crowded and overwhelmed the senses, and increased the loneliness and isolation that characterized twentieth-century battlefields. The heavy jungle foliage was ready-made for infiltration, so commanders forwent traditional battlelines and instead organized their men in tight defensive perimeters.[37] Behind these impromptu walls, American units launched daytime patrols and attacks. At night, however, the GIs dug in deep and waited for the dawn. In doing so, they surrendered the night to the Japanese, who made good use of it to infiltrate and harass the tired Americans. GIs in their two- or three-man foxholes could do little but keep a weather eye, string tripwires, and assume that anyone walking around in the inky darkness was Japanese and act accordingly.

Waging war in New Guinea's green hell was awful enough without the added difficulty of having the Japanese as the opponent. The Japanese were experts at infiltration and sniping, and their superbly camouflaged defensive positions possessed interlocking fields of fire to greet GIs moving warily up ridges or along trails. One person described a typical Japanese bunker: "Coconut trees, up to a foot in diameter, cut into logs and interlaced with boughs, vines and earth-filling, formed the roofs of whole clusters of strongposts. Infantry fire made no impression on them, and as they rose very little above the level of ground or swamps, 25 [pound artillery pieces] failed to wreck them."[38] The Japanese backed up their positions by effectively using mortar and machine-gun fire to stop American attacks in their tracks.

Prying the Japanese out of their positions was a long and arduous task that required a good deal of hard-earned skill. Once they located the Japanese—which in itself often cost any number of casualties—GIs called in artillery to destroy Japanese bunkers and pillboxes, or at least to disrupt their supply line so that the enemy abandoned the position. If that did not work—and it usually did not—or if artillery support was unavailable, the infantry moved in close under heavy covering fire and tried to lob a grenade into the Japanese position and kill its inhabitants. If possible, a flamethrower might accomplish the same thing in a more grisly manner, assuming that the weapon did not malfunction or the Japanese did not kill the unlucky soldier assigned the task.[39] This process, repeated time and time again in the Pacific War, led to considerable intermingling of American and Japanese positions, further confusing already chaotic battles.[40]

The Japanese mindset contributed greatly to the ferocity of the Pacific War. The Japanese saw surrender as dishonorable, and they frequently fought to the last man when most other soldiers would have given up. Moreover, the Japanese often tried to take as many GIs as possible with them to the next world by, for example, pretending to surrender and then opening fire. Such incomprehensible actions dehumanized them in American eyes and made suspicious GIs reluctant to take prisoners, which only served to increase and perpetuate the brutality of the conflict.[41]

This savage and bitter type of warfare led to heavy losses. Although mortars and artillery inflicted most American casualties, the shattering impact of rifle and machine-gun fire killed more men than anything else.[42] Fortunately, an American soldier wounded in World War II stood an excellent chance of survival, assuming that a medic could administer first aid and a four-man stretcher bearer team could lug him to safety, a difficult job in New Guinea's tangled terrain. Once away from the front, new medical technology such as penicillin to destroy bacteria, sulfa drugs against infections, and blood transfusions to prevent shock limited the World War II death rate to only 4.5 percent.[43] The Japanese, on the other hand, had none of these medical miracles, which contributed to their extraordinarily high losses.

Unfortunately, all that deadly fire did not always necessarily come from the other side. Friendly fire was a significant problem throughout the Pacific War. In New Georgia in the Solomons, for instance, an estimated one fourth of all Americans killed taking the island died from friendly fire. At nearby Bougainville the figure was 16 percent.[44] There were friendly fire incidents throughout the New Guinea campaign as well. During the Driniumor River operation, for example, thirty-five GIs were killed or wounded in one fell swoop by misdirected American artillery.[45] Such accidents were inevitable in the chaos and confusion of battle, but this was undoubtedly small solace to those who were inadvertently hit by their own friends.

To wage this bitter and remote jungle war, the infantry relied first and foremost on their own weapons. For the rifleman, this meant the semiautomatic M1 Garand, perhaps World War II's finest rifle. Sturdy and reliable, with a powerful punch and lots of velocity, the eight-pound Garand fired an eight round clip, for up to forty rounds per minute. Unfortunately, it also emitted gas and flame when fired, making it easy for the Japanese to spot and contributing to a high number of head wounds.[46]

Each squad usually possessed a carbine, either a Thompson submachine gun or, later, an M1 carbine. What they lacked in range they made up for in firepower. Each was automatic and capable of spraying the immediate vicinity with enough bullets to strip the foliage off the trees and guarantee that everyone was either hugging the ground or a casualty. Indeed, it was the GIs' best response to a Japanese ambush. In addition, each squad had a Browning Automatic Rifle (BAR) capable of firing 500–600 rounds per minute. Although intended to provide covering fire for advancing riflemen, the BAR was particularly effective in repelling Japanese attacks. The BAR was sturdy and reliable, but it needed constant maintenance, something often difficult to provide in New Guinea's primitive environment.

Weapons platoons and companies also possessed tools to help the infantry gain ground. The reliable .30 caliber light machine gun, for instance, fired 400–500 rounds a minute and had enough range to keep Japanese heads down from a long way off. Even more effective were the 60mm and 81mm mortars, each with a three man crew. Mortars served as the infantry's own personal artillery and indeed were sometimes the only indirect support GIs received. Unfortunately, New Guinea's overhanging trees often obscured and obstructed their fire, and carrying mortar rounds burdened the already overloaded infantry.[47]

The tank was perhaps the infantryman's best friend in the Pacific War. American armor—not only Sherman medium tanks but also armed LVT Buffaloes to clear the beaches—when accompanied by infantrymen to root out any lurking antitank guns, were a lethal combination in destroying Japanese bunkers and pillboxes. During the New Guinea campaign, American armor repeatedly broke the back of Japanese resistance, opening the way for the infantry to advance. Unfortunately, deploying tanks in New Guinea was not easy. Steep ridges, reefs, swamps, mud, fallen trees, stumps, and the chronic maintenance problems inherent in SWPA's war all conspired against the effective use of armor. Moreover, the Japanese did not give up at the sight of a tank. Antitank guns, a type of Molotov cocktail, explosives with attached magnets, and even individual infantrymen jamming rifles into a tank's suspension were all capable of knocking out American armor.[48] The Japanese, for their part, lacked the logistical capability to deploy much of their own armor, and when they did, American weaponry was generally more than a match for them, especially the 37mm guns carried by antitank and cannon companies.

Although the AAF had attained air superiority in SWPA by the time the New Guinea campaign got under way, this often did not translate into much direct air support for the infantry. Although not as gung-ho about strategic bombing as their European theater counterparts, the 5th Air Force concentrated primarily on Japan's air power and logistical network. This yielded big indirect benefits to infantrymen facing outnumbered, underfed, and ill-equipped Japanese, but the advantage was not immediately apparent to tired GIs rooting out enemy positions without any help from overhead. Moreover, frequent bad weather, unmapped and obscure jungle terrain, and communications problems made it difficult, although not impossible, to coordinate air support.

The Army's artillery was very good. Its mainstay was the 105mm howitzer, which had a 12,500-yard range, could fire four rounds a minute, and possessed enough impact to destroy most Japanese bunkers. Even more dangerous was the 155mm howitzer, or "Long Tom," with twice the range of the 105mm. Each infantry division had four artillery battalions, three of 105mm and one of 155mm howitzers, for a total of forty-eight guns. What made American artillery so effective, however, was not the quality or quantity of the guns but rather the way they were used. The Army coordinated its artillery through Fire Control Centers, which received targeting information via telephone or FM radio from spotter planes and forward observers in observation posts. Artillery commanders used this information to mass all their pieces on one target, often with devastating results. This was especially true of Time On Target firing, by which artillery commanders timed their artillery to land simultaneously and suddenly in one area, before the enemy had a chance to take cover. The Japanese possessed no such capability, and what little artillery they could deploy was vulnerable to American counterbattery fire.

The problem with using artillery in New Guinea, however, was that it was hard to deploy inland, where the decisive fighting usually took place. The jungle, mud, swamps, and lack of roads made it difficult to move the heavy pieces around. Even when they were in place, however, it was not easy to coordinate targeting in the unmapped and trackless jungle.[49] When available, however, artillery gave the Americans a vital edge and made the difference in more than one New Guinea battle.

American weaponry outclassed its Japanese counterparts in almost every respect. To compensate, the Japanese increasingly relied on their defensive skill and the undoubted tenacity of the individual soldier. This, along with their ability to use light artillery, mortars, and machine guns, helped offset American technological and materiel superiority, but it was never enough to turn the tide of battle.

The Peril of Disease

Writing home in 1943, one SWPA soldier described his condition: "I have contracted malaria fever. . . . I'm having quite a time trying to keep food in my stomach; guess it's another case of too little almost too late! My feet are pretty well parboiled and I have athletes foot pretty bad—the Doc has to lance them every morning, but don't worry as he says everything will be OK in a few weeks."[50] The letter, though postmarked from World War II New Guinea, might just as well have come from any other tropical battlefield throughout history. Indeed, until World War II, disease killed more American soldiers than enemy bullets. By the 1940s, new medical technology and techniques had reversed that trend, but disease remained an ever-present threat, especially in SWPA, which was perhaps the world's biggest pesthole.

New Guinea's innumerable microorganisms could plague or kill a man in any number of unpleasant ways. Soldiers swimming in the island's lakes, for instance, got ear infections from a fungus in the water that, if unchecked, could eat away the eardrum. The heat and humidity turned scratches into infections, then into jungle rot, a slimy oozing sore that never seemed to heal and in fact could become so severe as to require amputation. Natives warned Americans not to build in certain areas because evil spirits inhabited these places. Scoffing engineers soon realized that the "evil spirits" were rodent mites who carried scrub typhus, which, at Dobodura, killed 2 percent of those subsequently infected.[51]

The biggest, if not necessarily nastiest, biological threat, though, was malaria. Carried by mosquitoes, the disease wracked the patient with chills that never really went away. Malaria initially caused SWPA serious problems. In February 1943, for example, 23 out of every 1000 SWPA personnel were in hospital with malaria at any given time, and the average stay the following month was twenty-eight days per afflicted patient.[52] This was more than a minor annoyance; a man felled by malaria was as out of action as one with a bullet in him, and personnel-strapped SWPA, faced with daunting logistical tasks as well as the Japanese, needed every man it could get. Even worse, many of the world's known quinine sources were in Japanese hands. The only other accepted way to control the disease, by coating the stagnant water pools that attracted mosquitoes with oil, was impractical in New Guinea, where oil was valuable and water pools abundant.[53]

Clearly, something had to be done, or else soon half the American Army in SWPA would be shivering in hospital tents. MacArthur appointed Colonel Howard Smith, a former public health officer who had been the Philippines' chief of quarantine service, to bring malaria under control. Smith and other SWPA health officers introduced DDT, repellent cream, atabrine (a synthetic quinine), mosquito netting, and other suppressant and prevention measures to the theater. It was not an easy task. Troops resisted taking atabrine pills, not so much because it tasted extremely bitter and gave their skin a yellowish hue but because of false rumors that it caused impotence or sterility.[54] Officers had to order their men to swallow the pills at mealtime. The AAF freely sprayed DDT, even behind hostile beaches before amphibious assaults. Krueger insisted that his troops wear shirts at all times to prevent mosquito bites, an order which, while widely ignored, showed how serious SWPA was about the malaria problem.[55] Such stringent measures worked. In March 1944, only 2 per 1000 SWPA personnel were in the hospital for malaria at any given time, and the average stay was nine days. In fact, as of 1 April 1944, there were only 751 malaria cases throughout the entire theater.[56]

This was a remarkable accomplishment that any health official could take pride in when writing his reports. It was even more impressive, however, in comparison with the troubles the enemy faced on the other side of the island, especially as American air and sea interdiction took a toll on Japanese medical supplies. In the summer of 1944, SWPA estimated that at any given time 25 percent of all Japanese on New Guinea were incapacitated by disease, and almost all of them had malaria to one degree or another.[57] Each Japanese soldier stricken by New Guinea's diseases was one less on the firing line shooting at American soldiers.

Writing about New Guinea, one correspondent noted, "Since [the Americans] couldn't be at home, they did the next best thing and made themselves a home—at least as much as the jungle would allow."[58] Of course, they never completely tamed the island's hostile environment, but they were able to make the place bearable enough to live in and wage war on. This gave SWPA an enormous advantage over the Japanese, who increasingly succumbed to New Guinea's incredibly hostile climate, diseases, and terrain. New Guinea played no favorites, but American technology and materiel abundance enabled SWPA to use mother nature to wear out the enemy as effectively as all those planes, ships, and guns at its disposal.

SIX

WAKDE-SARMI: WHOEVER HEARD OF LONE TREE HILL?

Most of those Japanese fortunate enough to escape MacArthur's Hollandia onslaught trickled westward through the jungle, hiding from roving American planes and PT boats while fighting an almost invariably losing battle against the ravages of hunger and disease. Their goal, which few attained, was the Wakde-Sarmi area, 125 long miles to the northwest.[1] The Japanese had been there since June 1943, when they built an airstrip on tiny Wakde Island, just off the New Guinea coast, to ferry planes to Wewak. In late 1943, in response to SWPA's increasingly ominous advance, the Japanese expanded the position and began construction on two new airfields on the mainland near Sarmi at Sawar and Maffin Bay. To defend the area, Imperial Headquarters ordered two regiments from the veteran 36th Division in from northern China; they arrived in December. By the time SWPA attacked Hollandia, there were some 11,000 men entrenched in and around Wakde-Sarmi, about half of whom were battle-hardened combat troops.

MacArthur's sudden and unexpected leap to Hollandia, which in the blink of an eye emasculated Japan's forward New Guinea defenses, turned Wakde-Sarmi from a secure rearward position into an exposed and vulnerable salient. To make matters worse, reinforcing the area was difficult. There were no roads along the northern New Guinea coastline, and American submarines and planes took an increasingly heavy toll on Japanese convoys in the region. In late April and early May, for instance, American submarines, guided by Ultra, sank many of the transports carrying parts of the 32nd and 35th divisions from China to New Guinea and the Netherlands East Indies.[2] In this one swoop the Japanese 2nd Army lost all hope of creating a theater reserve in New Guinea capable of blunting MacArthur's offensive.

On 2 May, even before this tragedy, Imperial Headquarters had written off Wakde-Sarmi as strategically indefensible and concentrated their resources in the Biak-Manokwari region. A week later, after the American

Navy removed those New Guinea-bound reinforcements from the strategic chessboard, the Japanese decided to fall back even farther, to Sorong-Halmahera. Neither area was ready to receive an American assault, but they hoped those 11,000 veteran troops dug in around Wakde-Sarmi could buy their comrades the time needed to build a new defensive line along New Guinea's western edge.[3]

The Japanese viewed Wakde-Sarmi as a lost cause strategically—except, of course, to the extent its sacrifice promoted the construction of that new defensive perimeter to the west—but tactically it remained a tough nut to crack. Storming small and well-protected Wakde Island would not be easy, no matter how much firepower the Americans brought to bear, and the Japanese had already fortified the coast around Sawar and Maffin Bay. The only other way to the mainland airdromes from the east was across the Tor River and over a series of rugged hills, all of which were defended by experienced troops who had had plenty of time to prepare for an American assault. Unfortunately, these advantages were somewhat offset by the 2nd Area Army commander Anami's late April decision to send two battalions from Wakde-Sarmi eastward to attack the Americans around Hollandia. This was not only completely impractical, but it also deprived the 36th Division of nearly a third of its combat troops when the Americans swarmed ashore.[4]

MacArthur's offensive took on increased urgency—if that was possible—when GHQ discovered that Hollandia's boggy terrain could not soon provide SWPA with the bomber bases it needed to support Nimitz's mid-June Marianas operation by hitting the Palaus, as well as further advances up the New Guinea coastline toward the China-Formosa-Luzon area. By now the Admiralties were too far away to furnish short-range air cover, so GHQ had to come up with alternative airdromes fast, lest the New Guinea offensive stall at Hollandia. Poring over their maps, GHQ zeroed in on Wakde-Sarmi as a solution to their immediate problem. Taking the area would not only propel SWPA another 125 miles up the coast—and, therefore, that much closer to the Philippines, whose liberation fueled GHQ's sense of urgency—but the AAF could develop those mainland airdromes into bomber bases capable of supporting future SWPA operations. In addition, an American-held Wakde-Sarmi could prevent the Japanese from interfering with Hollandia's logistical buildup.[5]

With these considerations in mind, GHQ, even before the Hollandia assault, ordered Krueger to prepare for operations around Wakde-Sarmi. Indeed, MacArthur's suggestion at Tanahmerah Bay that Eichelberger divert his followup waves up the coast reflected his impatience to keep the offensive going, and the key to doing so was getting those bomber bases at Sawar and Maffin Bay.[6] Examining the situation, Krueger decided upon a division-sized assault, with one RCT attacking Wakde and the remaining two storming ashore around Sawar. As for manpower, GHQ told Krueger to use the 24th, 41st, or 32nd Division for the operation. Krueger wanted to employ the 32nd Division, which had not seen serious action since its Buna bloodletting almost a year and a half ago. SWPA, however, lacked the necessary amphibious shipping and staging facilities to transport it from Saidor—the 127th RCT had not yet been sent to Aitape—so instead Krueger tapped the veteran 41st Division, which was mopping up around Hollandia and Aitape.[7] The 163rd RCT, under irritable deputy division commander Jens Doe, would assault Wakde from Aitape, and Fuller's other two Hollandia-based RCTs would take Sawar and Maffin Bay. GHQ set D-Day for 15 May, three days after the AAF expected Hollandia's airdromes to be ready to supply air cover for the landing.

On 7 May, however, just a little more than a week before the intended assault, GHQ directed Krueger to change his plans and substitute the island of Biak, some 200 miles northwest of Wakde in Geelvink Bay, for Sarmi. Kenney, analyzing low altitude air reconnaissance photos of the mainland airdromes, had concluded that it would take too long for the AAF to prepare them for bombers, which would delay SWPA's fast-moving offensive.[8] Whitehead, in fact, called Sarmi a "mudhole" because its terrain, like Hollandia's, was too boggy to support bombers.[9] Moreover, he added, the area was "fuller of Nips and supplies than a mangy dog is with fleas."[10] Kenney was not much for spilt milk thinking, though, so he suggested that SWPA take Wakde as planned but simultaneously assault Biak instead of soggy Sarmi.[11] Wakde was too small to base many bombers on, but fighter planes placed quickly there could provide close air support for American troops assailing Biak, whose three airdromes would fulfill SWPA's requirements.

Attacking two widely separate places concurrently, however, was not an easy task, especially on such short notice. SWPA supply and transport officers, studying their charts, shook their heads. There was not enough shipping or time to assault Wakde and Biak simultaneously, despite Kenney's assurances that the AAF would take up the logistical slack.[12] Army engineers had doubts, too; Hollandia was already absorbing much of their men and equipment, so they did not have the resources to tackle Wakde and Biak at the same time.[13] Barbey did not like the hasty plan either, and he argued for a postponement until 21 May, which would permit more preparation and ensure better tidal conditions.[14] At a 9 May conference, SWPA representatives decided that the best course of action was to split the proposed operation into two, with an attack on Biak following the Wakde assault by ten days. MacArthur signed off on the idea the following day and also agreed to postpone the Wakde invasion until 17 May to give the 6th Army time to clear shipping out of congested Humboldt Bay.[15]

GHQ and Krueger believed that one RCT ought to be enough to handle the Wakde assault, not only because there were now no plans to assail the enemy dug in around Maffin Bay and Sawar but also because the Americans seriously underestimated Japanese strength in the entire region. Krueger prohibited ground reconnaissance because he did not want to tip SWPA's hand,[16] and while air reconnaissance revealed that the Japanese were busy fortifying the area, it did not provide hard figures.[17] Ultra, on the other hand, could generate such numbers, in theory anyway, but the Japanese changed their Army codes on 10 May, temporarily depriving SWPA of this valuable intelligence source.[18] In response, Willoughby fell back on radio traffic analysis, but he had a hard time getting an accurate lock on exactly how many Japanese were there. Refugees streaming through Wakde-Sarmi from Hollandia constantly changed the size of the garrison, making it hard for Willoughby to reconcile his various intelligence sources.[19] A week before the attack, he estimated that there were 6050–8750 Japanese, of whom he guessed as many as 6650 might be combat troops.[20] He knew there were two regiments there,[21] but he was unaware that two battalions had been dispatched to assault Hollandia. Low-powered radio transmissions from that big lost patrol escaped SWPA interception, and anyway Willoughby believed that such an attack was only a "remote possibility" because of the terrible coastal trails and wide-ranging PT boats.[22] Reading these and other reports, Krueger put the number of Japanese in and around Wakde-Sarmi at about 6000, or only a little more than half the true total.[23]

Just as serious as this underestimation of Japanese strength, in the long run, was Willoughby's misinterpretation of enemy intentions. At first he believed that the Japanese planned to make an all-out fight for Wakde-Sarmi. He noted increased activity around Sawar and Maffin Bay and wrote, "It is reasonable to assume that the Japanese are prepared to defend the area."[24] As Willoughby saw it, Wakde-Sarmi was the main outpost protecting the big and important Japanese base at Manokwari on the Vogelkop.[25] Despite some evidence that they might pull out, "It must be considered that as long as the 36th Division is in the area, it is a serious threat, capable of fighting a lengthy campaign in conjunction with other divisions that may be located west of Geelvink Bay."[26]

Willoughby changed his mind, however, after the Japanese abandoned work on the spongy Sawar and Maffin Bay airfields. To Willoughby, this indicated that the Japanese planned to pull out after they covered the escape of any of their comrades who survived the long trek from Hollandia.[27] The development of new airdromes south of Manokwari reinforced his view, convincing him that the Japanese intended to make their stand there.[28] The Wakde-Sarmi garrison, then, would probably fight a delaying action before falling back to Manokwari. Little did he, or anyone else at SWPA, realize that the veteran Japanese troops around Wakde Sarmi were there for the long haul.[29]

Arara Beach

Preparatory to the Wakde-Sarmi operation, Kenney's AAF swung into action, sweeping the area clear of all Japanese air opposition. This was not all that difficult. The Japanese, still stunned by Kenney's and Nimitz's air assaults, had withdrawn much of their air strength west of Biak, giving the AAF free rein around Wakde-Sarmi.[30] Kenney did not neglect the opportunity, and in the first two weeks of May, despite cloudy weather, his forces dropped 1500 tons of bombs on the area, destroyed twenty-seven Japanese fighters and twenty-five bombers, leveled Sarmi town, and pounded Wakde so hard that it appeared that the whole island was on fire.[31]

Such apparent success was encouraging to those in the know, but the men of Jens Doe's 163rd RCT, watching the New Guinea coast come into view on the overcast morning of 17 May, had to find solace elsewhere; maybe in God, or their officers, or their own well-honed combat abilities. Or in the Navy, whose hour-long preliminary bombardment, here as elsewhere in SWPA's far-flung operations, looked impressive enough, at least from a distance. After the shelling stopped, cruiser float planes moved in to mark the beach with colored smoke, and then rocket LCIs picked up where the destroyers left off and hammered the shoreline some more.

This morning's target was not Wakde Island—not yet, anyway—but Arara, on the mainland southwest of Wakde, beyond the island's guns. Krueger had decided that Wakde was too small to unload and store all the supplies and equipment a full RCT required to operate.[32] Arara, on the other hand, not only possessed plenty of dispersal room but would also serve as a springboard to Wakde and, should it prove necessary, Sarmi as well.

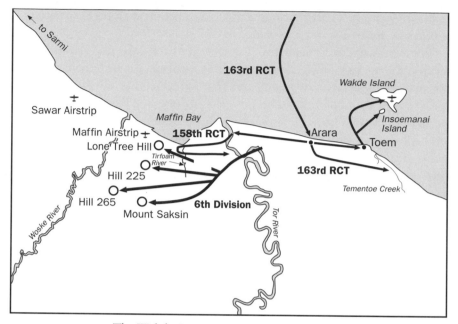

The Wakde-Sarmi Operation, 17 May 1944

That, of course, remained to be seen, but for now the men of the 163rd RCT had more important things on their minds as they descended into their landing craft and headed for shore in a light drizzle. Fortunately, as at Aitape, less than a month ago, there was no opposition, except from mother nature. The surf was high, forcing the landing craft to disgorge their human cargo fifty feet from the beach in waist-deep water. As the soldiers trudged slowly to the shore, many tripped in underwater shellholes made by the preliminary bombardment or by yesterday's AAF air strikes designed to detonate any underwater mines. To make matters worse, upon reaching the beach they had to hurdle an eight-foot-high embankment before heading inland, not an easy task in full combat regalia.[33] None of this was particularly pleasant, but it was better than being shot at.

The engineers could also take comfort in this fact as they struggled in the shallow water to unload supplies and equipment. The high surf threatened to wash away the jetties along the coast, so they had to repeatedly reinforce the bases with sandbags. The high embankment was another obstacle, but the sand track between the beach and the swampy jungle provided plenty of dispersal room, and after the engineers unloaded the LSTs they got to work turning that track into a viable road.[34]

Meanwhile, the combat battalions fanned out to secure the beachhead's flanks, one moving west to the Tor River and another heading east to Tementoe Creek. There was almost no enemy opposition, so after digging in, which they completed by noon, the soldiers ate, swam, read mail, and lounged around. One man compared the afternoon to a family reunion.[35] Two LCVPs, however, discovered otherwise when they motored into the mouth of the Tor in search of a sheltered anchorage and were ambushed. Enemy fire killed one vessel commander and wounded the other, demonstrating to the survivors, and everyone else thereabouts, that the Japanese, while out of sight, should not be placed out of mind.[36]

Doe, for one, saw it that way. He wanted the beachhead buttoned down tight before he undertook his primary task of reducing Wakde. By remaining on the defensive on the mainland, however, Doe gave the Japanese time to recall the two battalions sent toward Hollandia and to concentrate their forces in the hills beyond the Tor River.

This would have consequences all around later, but for now Doe's eyes were focused squarely on Wakde. While two of his battalions secured his flanks, the third moved into Toem, directly across from Wakde, and by 1130 it had set up artillery positions to shell the island before tomorrow's assault. One company occupied undefended Insoemanai Island, a third of a mile south of Wakde, although a coral reef forced the troops to wade the last seventy-five yards to shore. The RCT's heavy weapons companies soon followed, and before the afternoon was over their mortars and machine guns began lashing at Wakde.

The question on everyone's mind, as the afternoon wore on, was whether there was anyone over on Wakde to shoot at. Back in mid-April, Kenney's pilots reported no signs of life there, but considering the AAF's track record on such matters, there was plenty of room for skepticism.[37] Barbey, for one, did not buy it, and neither did Willoughby, who a week before the operation estimated that there were 1000 Japanese on the island.[38] The day before Doe's men hit the beach, however, Willoughby admitted that his figures could be way off.[39]

Unfortunately, proximity did little to clarify the issue. Most of the combat troops, watching three destroyers, rocket craft, artillery, machine guns, and mortars pound the place, were convinced that such heavy fire would undoubtedly kill anyone there before one American soldier set foot on the island.[40] Eichelberger's chief of staff, Brigadier General Clovis E. Byers, observing the operation from a P-39, was so convinced that the Japanese had evacuated Wakde that he and his companion tried to land on the runway. Fortunately for both men, the airstrip was too cratered for their plane to touch down or else Eichelberger would have had to look for a new chief of staff. Instead, Byers returned to Hollandia and predicted to Eichelberger that tomorrow's landing would be unopposed.[41] The commanding officer on Insoemanai agreed, and reported that he and his orderly could have waded over to Wakde and taken it single-handedly had it was not been for the orderly's sore feet.[42] Not everyone was so sanguine, though. Doe, who was responsible to Krueger for the success or failure of the operation and was undoubtedly conscious that his career depended upon its outcome, erred on the side of caution and decided to stick to the original plan, rejecting suggestions that he order an immediate assault.[43]

Such optimism, however, receded as the Japanese on Wakde, perhaps needled into action by American fire from Insoemanai, almost a stone's throw away, opened up with mortars and machine guns of their own. There were almost 800 of them there, experienced troops concealed in caves, bombproof bunkers and pillboxes with layers of coconut logs and coral rock on top, and even plane turrets buried up to their muzzles.[44] Unfortunately for them, their defenses, while impressive, were not interlocking, and they lacked clear fields of fire.[45] Even so, there were more than enough of them to give the Americans a hard time the following morning, something these veterans might have been proud of, except that within days almost all were dead.

Storming Wakde

The cold drizzle that greeted the 18 May dawn reflected the mood of the 1500 men slated to participate in the Wakde attack.[46] Four companies from the 163rd RCT's 1st Battalion boarded twenty-four LCVPs manned by an amphibious engineer company. They moved out in six waves of four landing craft apiece, followed by four tank-filled LCMs. Each soldier carried a day's rations, a canteen of water, and a unit of fire.[47] In the distance, two destroyers pounded Wakde, and twelve AAF A-20s roared out of the cloudy sky to rake targets of opportunity. As the assault waves headed for shore, rocket LCIs took station on their flanks and opened fire.

The landing craft aimed for the Wakde's south shore, which was not only closest to support fire from Insoemanai but was also free of the coral reef that surrounded most of the island. The Japanese, anticipating an assault from that direction,[48] opened fire when the first wave was 300 yards out, conclusively dispelling hopes that this landing would be as easy as yesterday's, or last month's at Aitape. One coxswain yelled, "Okay fellows, it's time to take your kneeling positions! The rules say you got to get down on your knees!"[49] Most needed no encouragement, and in fact many flattened themselves on their bellies on the bottom of their landing crafts, at least those who had the room to do so. The coxswains and bow lookouts responsible for driving the LCVPs, on the other hand, lacked that particular luxury, so they suffered especially heavy losses. Of the 120 engineers manning the landing craft, 5 were killed and 30 wounded.[50] One LCVP careened out of control into a circle when its coxswain was hit, and command of two others ultimately devolved onto men who had never operated them before, one of whom was a correspondent.[51] Enemy fire ultimately damaged eight landing craft, including one LCVP that received a total of sixty-eight shell fragments and slugs that day.[52]

In the midst of this hailstorm of bullets and shrapnel, just after 0900 the first wave descended from their landing craft into waist-deep water. They struggled for the shore and rushed for the cover of the beach shelf, where intense Japanese fire pinned down the survivors for a half hour. Three company commanders were among those killed and wounded.[53] On the credit side, however, heavy support fire from Insoemanai kept the enemy from rushing the beachhead.

Fortunately for the beach-hugging Americans, deliverance was just around the corner—or, more accurately, just behind them. The three tank-carrying LCMs—the fourth shorted out in the high surf—finally arrived and disgorged their armored cargo. One tank immediately sank in seven feet of water, but the other two lumbered out of the surf and up the beach and then swung into action. The Japanese possessed no weapons to counter the armored monsters, which, with the aid of the infantry and overhead A-20s, crushed enemy resistance along the beach in fifteen minutes. The tanks, followed by the infantry, lumbered inland, destroying pillboxes and bunkers as they went along. The supporting GIs moved from crater to crater and from blasted stump to blasted stump as they rooted out the die-hard Japanese defenders. As one man put it, "It was a matter of shifting from one log to another."[54] Down along the shore, meanwhile, reinforcements arrived: an infantry company from Insoemanai and an engineer company from the mainland.

Inland, American armor continued to work its magic, breaking down Japanese resistance that had stalled the infantry. Japanese attempts to stop the tanks, which included individual infantrymen jumping on top of them, grenades in hand, proved futile. The assault, however, was a long, drawn out process, involving a good many wounds all around. Japanese bunkers and pillboxes riddled the island, and clearing them all took a while. Even then many were overlooked, so theoretically secure areas were every bit as dangerous as the front. The Americans did not reach the airstrip until 1630, by which time the omnipotent tanks had to return to the beach for ammunition, which took an hour. In the meanwhile, one company sprinted 200 yards across the runway under fire from Japanese machine guns, which killed two men and wounded three others, but the rest got to the other side.[55] Most of the soldiers preferred the less glamorous but safer tactic of moving through ditches. Unfortunately, there were no ditches on the airstrip, so there was only one method of crossing. One soldier, forced to run the airstrip gauntlet at dusk, later recalled, "A weaving straight line is the shortest distance between two points—when you are in combat."[56]

Although the airfield was more or less in American hands, the battle was not over yet, not by a long shot. The GIs held only half of the island, and there were plenty of Japanese pillboxes and bunkers untouched or overlooked by the day's action. Worse yet, enemy infiltrators were seemingly everywhere, and that night and in the following two days they targeted American artillery positions, supply dumps, command posts, and motor pools, causing considerable damage but inflicting few casualties. Small wonder then that the 1st Battalion commander, directing his men from a shellhole, muttered over and over, "Must speed this thing up. Must finish them up before dark or it'll be a tough night."[57]

Meanwhile, back at the beach, the engineers struggled to bring order out of chaos. LSTs and barges jockeyed for position on the small and narrow beach, which was littered with debris from the preliminary bombardment. Japanese who had escaped the 1st Battalion's combined armor–infantry assault infiltrated the area, taking potshots at those who did not keep their heads down. One supposedly dead Japanese detonated a grenade that wounded a couple of sailors.[58] The engineers had to divert men from unloading and beach-clearing duty to fight off these enemy infiltrators, who, two days later, still managed to launch an unsuccessful fifty-man attack on the American beach positions.

The first night, as the battalion commander predicted, was a long one. Despite the beating they had taken, the surviving Japanese remained very much alive, shooting at everything. GIs took refuge in foxholes and ditches, but they lacked water. Supply-laden Alligators did not reach everyone, and it was too dangerous to send carrying parties back to the beachhead. Thirsty soldiers filled canteens from water-logged shellholes, or dodged Japanese sniper fire to retrieve green coconuts.[59] That night, too, a Hawaiian-born English-speaking Japanese soldier surrendered to the Americans, one of only four enemy survivors in the bitter battle. Although the Americans ground down most Japanese resistance in the first twenty-four hours, mopping up continued for days afterward. The last Japanese holed up along the rocky coast, where tanks could not reach them, so GIs had to clear them out with flamethrowers and grenades.

While the 1st Battalion mopped up, aviation engineers, when they were not fighting off Japanese infiltrators and equally annoying American souvenir hunters, worked hard to get the airstrip into working order. On 20 May, just three days after the Americans stormed ashore, a squadron of P-38s arrived, and a week later some B-24s were operating from the island. Because Wakde was SWPA's westernmost airbase and, therefore, its most important piece of real estate, Kenney stuffed it full of aircraft, even though he knew cramming too many planes in such a small area was dangerous.[60] Willoughby thought so, too, and in one of his more accurate prophesies warned that Wakde would be vulnerable to Japanese night bombers until the airfield was fully operational.[61]

The battle for Wakde was for all intents and purposes over on 20 May, when the 1st Battalion was shipped back to the mainland, although some mopping up continued until two days later. At the cost of 40 killed and 107 wounded—as opposed to Japanese losses totaling 734 dead, plus those 4 prisoners—MacArthur had the airstrip he needed to provide close air support for the Biak assault, a week away.[62] Krueger was full of praise for his men, and for Doe, who again performed well in an independent mission.[63]

GHQ was also pleased and said so in a 19 May communiqué:

> Exploiting our Hollandia operation, we have seized the Wakde-Toem area in Dutch New Guinea. The enemy was completely surprised and his defense negligible. The recent heavy air bombardment of the area has had its effect and only trifling opposition is being offered to our forces spreading eastward and westward along the coast. . . . This operation throws the enemy's rear areas in New Guinea, already dislocated and disrupted by our seizure of Hollandia, into further confusion. Possession of the Wakde airbase will give us adequate air coverage over all of Dutch New Guinea and the success of the operation presages the reconquest of the entire province.[64]

Like so many of MacArthur's communiqués, this one was not completely accurate. Seizing Wakde was undoubtedly an impressive accomplishment, but the communiqué *implied* that the operation was over and that SWPA could now move on to bigger and better things up the New Guinea coast. MacArthur could, and would, do so, but although the Wakde-Sarmi operation had achieved its primary strategic objectives by gaining SWPA an airbase to support MacArthur's attack on Biak, its bloodiest stage was yet to come.

Attack of the Green Hornet

On 21 May, the troops who would shed much of the blood spilled around Wakde-Sarmi trudged down the gangplanks onto the New Guinea beach, four days after the 163rd RCT swarmed ashore at Toem. The 158th RCT was a day early and it landed at the wrong place, which caused considerable confusion among the harried engineers, but that was a small price to pay for the added protection of another regimental combat team, even one as bizarre as the 158th.

Created from the Arizona National Guard, the 3100-man 158th RCT was probably the most heterogeneous unit in the American Army, consisting of a good number of American Indians and Mexicans, as well as whites. Scorned by some as the "Spic and Blanket-Ass Bunch," the 158th had been in SWPA for more than a year, although it had not yet seen serious combat.[65] Organizationally, it was an independent RCT, meaning that it belonged to no division.

In fact, for a week now it had belonged to fifty-year-old Brigadier General Edwin D. Patrick, who was every bit as colorful as his command. Patrick had been Krueger's chief of staff, but the two men had not gotten along well. Patrick was too abrasive for the 6th Army commander and his subordinates, so MacArthur suggested that Krueger reassign him.[66] Krueger, in turn, shipped him to the 158th RCT.

Krueger's loss, however, was not necessarily the 158th's gain. Patrick was courageous and bold in combat, but such ferocity covered up some less admirable qualities. His staff nicknamed him the "Green Hornet" because of the special green jumpsuit he wore, which, along with the big star he plastered on his helmet, made him a conspicuous target, factors that went a long way toward explaining his death at the hands of a Japanese machine gunner the following year in the Philippines. More seriously—for his troops, anyway—Patrick tended to drink coffee all day and whiskey all night, a combination that contributed mightily to his mercurial mood swings, recklessness, and questionable judgment.[67]

For all of Patrick's flaws, Krueger, and not his former chief of staff, was most responsible for the 158th's ordeal at Wakde-Sarmi. A month earlier, during the operation's planning stages, MacArthur wrote Krueger, "You are authorized to dispose of the 158th Infantry according to your judgment."[68] Now Krueger did just that. Although Wakde was now in American hands, thanks to Doe's hard-bitten GIs, Krueger did not think the American foothold was secure as long as the Japanese lurked in the rugged hills west of the Tor. From these dominating heights they could conceivably lob artillery shells at Toem, where every day busy engineers unloaded valuable and vulnerable supplies and equipment to sustain the American garrison there, as well as planned operations further west.[69] Krueger wanted the Japanese cleared out, and since the 163rd RCT might ultimately have to join its parent command at Biak, he sent the 158th in to do the job.

Unfortunately, Krueger was not sure how many Japanese were in those hills.[70] Willoughby did not think there were all that many, and just before Krueger unleashed Patrick, the SWPA intelligence chief wrote: "In the absence of determined counterattacks against our beachhead it is now believed that the enemy has withdrawn the bulk of his Sarmi forces to the west, possibly to Biak. If the Japanese had sufficient forces available to attack our positions, it is logical to assume that he would have done so promptly rather than allow us a week's time to consolidate our positions. The conclusion is, then, that he does not have enough troops available to make such an attack."[71] Willoughby's logic, here as elsewhere in his career, was flawed. He did not know about those two Japanese battalions sent east to attack Hollandia, but when he found out, two days after Patrick's offensive got under way, he wrote that the heavy opposition the 158th RCT was encountering west of the Tor was due to Japanese efforts to cover the return of the two missing battalions.[72] As for numbers, in late May Willoughby estimated that the Japanese had 4000–5000 men in the area.[73]

Whatever the number, Patrick was going after them. After relieving the 163rd RCT—Doe's men remained around Toem to guard the beachhead from any possible attack from the east—on 23 May Patrick's field commander, the stiff and austere Colonel J. Prugh Herndon, called "the old sunnatabichi" by the American Indians in his command,[74] threw two battalions across the 100-yard-wide Tor. Once on the far side, however, Japanese fire from three small lakes near the coast pinned them down for the rest of the day.[75]

Herndon made progress the next morning, but it was not easy. This was the 158th's first major combat operation, so it made rookie mistakes. The preliminary bombardment proved ineffective because one battalion commander mistook Japanese shelling for his own and ordered it stopped. Every night the Japanese hauled their artillery out of caves and blasted the American positions, then took them back inside before daylight, making them all but invulnerable to counterbattery fire. Overlooked Japanese sniped at the GIs from the rear, promoting the uncomfortable feeling that the enemy was everywhere and nowhere.

Fortunately, American technology and firepower, here as elsewhere in the war, saved the day. Two LCMs and an LCVP along the coast covered the infantry's right flank and raked enemy positions. More importantly, here as at Wakde, American armor moved in and broke the back of Japanese resistance along the Tor, then spearheaded the 158th's drive to the Tirfoam River, halfway to the hills to the west. The GIs reached the Tirfoam at 1200, and at 1330 Herndon ordered his men across. There, however, the Japanese wheeled a 37mm gun out from the jungle and in quick succession damaged three of the four tanks before the Americans knocked it out. Deprived of his armored trump card, Herndon ordered those units on the Tirfoam's west bank back across the river for the night. The day cost the 158th twenty-eight killed and seventy-five wounded.

Next morning, Herndon played another American trump card: artillery. While his big guns softened up the Japanese west of the Tirfoam, the fresh 3rd Battalion relieved the weary 1st Battalion, which had thus far led the advance. Recrossing the Tirfoam at mid-morning, the GIs discovered that their artillery had destroyed most of the Japanese positions, so they moved westward to the twisty Snaky River, where Japanese fire once again brought the GIs to a stumbling halt just short of their objective: Lone Tree Hill.

Lone Tree Hill was not as barren as its name implied.[76] It derived its inaccurate designation from a headquarters map that showed one solitary tree on it. In fact, it was covered with dense jungle undergrowth and riddled with coral outcroppings, caves, ravines, and crevices. Lone Tree was 175 feet high, 1200 yards long, and 1100 yards wide. Its north side, called Rocky Point, dropped off steeply to stony Maffin Bay; Snaky River fronted it to the east. The coastal road ran south of the hill through a defile, south of which lay Mount Saksin, Hill 225, and Hill 265, also occupied and fortified by the Japanese. The 158th had had a difficult enough time even getting to Lone Tree Hill and its companions; now it had to take them.

Herndon did his best. On the morning of 26 May, after two destroyers off the coast and all the American artillery thereabouts had pounded Lone Tree Hill, the 158th attacked. Unfortunately, the lead battalion got lost in the dense jungle, and by the time it got back on track the Japanese had recovered from any damage the artillery and Navy had inflicted and responded violently to the American assault. Inaccurate maps plagued Herndon's men, so they often did not know exactly where they were in the Lone Tree Hill labyrinth. Some units, backed by continuing heavy artillery support, managed to cross the Snaky, and others reached the defile to the south, but intense Japanese fire stopped them soon after.

Next day Herndon tried again. Heavy artillery fire drove the Japanese from Lone Tree Hill's eastern slopes, enabling one company to reach the summit, but enemy fire quickly trapped them there. Another company reported that it had seized nearby Hill 225, but it turned out that they had misread their maps and were somewhere else, although no one knew exactly where that might be. The battle reached nightmarish proportions. Fighting in small isolated groups on unfamiliar ground against an enemy securely holed up in camouflaged caves, unsure of their exact location and their supply lines but certain of the damage the Japanese were inflicting, the Americans had by now suffered some 300 casualties but were no closer to prying Lone Tree Hill from its die-hard Japanese defenders. One officer writing up the unit's official report later noted rather plaintively, "It was a very difficult situation."[77]

Herndon thought that armor might help, so next day—28 May, the day after Fuller's 41st Division splashed ashore at Biak—he ordered two LCMs to transport two tanks to the front. The LCMs reached the Tirfoam late in the morning, but there was no place to unload their cargo. An engineer platoon, defended by an infantry company, got to work blasting a landing zone out of the coral, but that took time. The Japanese quickly zoomed in on the area, however, and finally forced the company to fall back across the Tirfoam that evening, but not before the engineers completed their task. Meanwhile, to the west, Herndon got another company up to Lone Tree Hill's summit, where it was immediately trapped with its companion unit in a maze of enemy pillboxes and bunkers. Ultimately, both companies ran low on water and ammunition, but they managed to withdraw to the Snaky late in the afternoon, a couple of hours before the engineers skittered back across the Tirfoam.

Herndon now had his tanks, but armor did not counterbalance his declining will. While the engineers sweated it out along the Tirfoam, Herndon decided to call off the attack. As he saw it, his forces were already overextended, the Japanese were infiltrating around his left flank, and enemy fire made it increasingly difficult to supply his forward units. Patrick had already recalled one of his battalions to guard Toem, depriving him of a third of his infantry. If three battalions could not take Lone Tree Hill, how could two battered and bruised ones accomplish the same task? Herndon appealed to Patrick, who agreed to permit him to fall back behind the Snaky and await reinforcements before resuming the attack.[78]

Herndon was relieved by Patrick's decision, but next morning, contemplating all the Japanese fire he had thus far encountered, he began to worry anew. Calling his battalion commanders together, they agreed that Japanese resistance had been fierce, and there was no evidence of it slackening anytime soon. In fact, one battalion commander noted, they might counterattack, in which case the Snaky was a bad spot to be. The Japanese could cross it at any number of places because they knew the terrain, and they seemed to have the men to do it, whereas the bled-down 158th RCT was weaker than when it began the offensive.[79] Mulling this over, Herndon decided that the thing to do was retreat behind the highly defensible Tirfoam, which would get him away from deadly Lone Tree Hill. Herndon asked Patrick for his permission to fall back, and Patrick reluctantly agreed.[80] That afternoon the 158th withdrew to the Tirfoam without losing any men or equipment.[81]

Herndon could take pride in accomplishing the difficult tactical maneuver of a daylight retrograde movement in the face of the enemy, but such exploits did not win wars. Back at Toem, Patrick saw it that way. Although he okayed Herndon's decision, he began to fret. He did not like backing away from any confrontation, especially in his first big independent command. Moreover, Herndon sounded pretty jittery and pessimistic, hardly the type of man an RCT commander wanted to spearhead his attacks.[82] In fact, the more he thought about it, the more alarmed he became, so that afternoon Patrick drove over to Herndon's new headquarters, 1800 yards east of the Tirfoam. By then it was too late to stop the withdrawal, which was halfway complete, but Patrick could at least take action against its immediate instigator to make sure nothing like this ever happened again. "I'm relieving you of command and putting Colonel Sandlin in charge," he said to Herndon. "You will report to Finschhafen immediately."[83] Sandlin was Colonel Erle Sandlin, Patrick's aggressive, pugnacious, hard-drinking, and bullying chief of staff.[84]

With Herndon removed from the scene, Patrick was theoretically free to resume the offensive, but he did not. Not because he did not want to—after all, he had his reputation to think of, which had just been damaged by this unsuccessful attack—but because of problems above and beyond his own. On 27 May, two days earlier, Krueger ordered two of the 163rd RCT battalions guarding Toem beachhead to Biak, where Fuller's 41st Division assault was about to run into big trouble. To be sure, Krueger was robbing Peter to pay Paul, but in this case Fuller's Paul had access to three bomber airdromes, whereas Patrick's Peter could secure little more for SWPA than a series of scraggly hills. Seen in this light, Krueger's choice was clear, and the two battalions left on 29–30 May, leaving just one battalion behind to defend the Toem beachhead. Patrick did not think that was enough. The Japanese had just begun raiding the beachhead, and although he did not think this was a serious threat, he worried that these roving bands could destroy important installations.[85] To that end, Patrick, like Krueger, played the Peter/Paul game and ordered Herndon to send one of his battalions from Lone Tree Hill back to Toem.

Back at Hollandia, Krueger was concerned about Patrick's safety, now that he had only four battalions—one of which, the 163rd RCT's 1st Battalion, would on 9 June join the rest of its division at Biak—to defend his widespread positions. He had faith in Patrick, though, not only because the man, whatever his less noble attributes, was a fighter, but also because he only had to hold out a short while until help arrived in the form of the 6th Division, on its way from Milne Bay.[86] At first the 6th Division's 1st RCT was not slated to reach Wakde-Sarmi until 10 June, with the remainder of the unit appearing in mid-July, but an impatient Krueger got GHQ to provide the shipping necessary to move it there sooner.[87]

This was good news to Patrick, who saw in these reinforcements a means to redeem his earlier poor showing. As he viewed the situation, he had been on the verge of seizing Lone Tree Hill until Herndon's and Fuller's incompetence, as well as Krueger's rattled response to the latter's failures, pulled the rug out from under him.[88] He wanted another go at Lone Tree Hill, and the 6th Division would free up enough of his men for him to take that shot. Initially he planned on launching an amphibious assault around the Japanese positions to the west by landing near the Maffin Bay airstrip, but there was not enough shipping for that, so he decided to bull his way in directly, retracing Herndon's earlier route.[89] On the morning of 8 June, two days after the first elements of the 6th Division came ashore—and also two days after Eisenhower's men stormed Fortress Europe at Normandy—Patrick sent two battalions of the 158th RCT over the Tor after a short artillery barrage. The westward marching GIs met little opposition until 1100, when they encountered enemy fire from straight ahead, as well as from those three small lakes that had hindered Herndon's advance two weeks before. The Japanese, it seemed, had been busy refortifying positions previously overrun by the Americans but later abandoned during Herndon's retreat. This was disconcerting, suggesting as it did another drawn out fight just to reach Lone Tree Hill, but Sandlin dealt with the problem as Herndon had by bringing up tanks to clear the Japanese out. By the time the armor arrived, however, it was nightfall. Undaunted, Patrick ordered the offensive resumed next day, but as Sandlin was getting ready to move out a new directive came down from Toem to suspend not only this attack but the entire offensive.

These new orders were not Patrick's idea, whose whiskey-bent and hell-bound eyes were fixated on his Lone Tree Hill *bête noire*, but Krueger's. The Biak operation was not going well, so GHQ looked elsewhere for airdromes and settled on Noemfoor Island in Geelvink Bay west of Biak. Seizing it, however, would require combat troops, and the nearest ones were Patrick's 158th RCT.[90] Besides, the 6th Division could resume the battle for Lone Tree Hill when it arrived in strength. In the meantime, Krueger ordered the 158th to stay out of trouble. On 14 June, the 20th RCT relieved the 158th RCT along the Tirfoam, permitting Patrick to prepare for new and with luck more successful operations further west. The failed Lone Tree Hill assault cost the 158th 75 killed and 257 wounded, in return for which it claimed to have killed 920 Japanese. The infliction of such losses, however, was small consolation for Patrick and his men, who had suffered SWPA's first major setback in the New Guinea campaign.

"You've Got a Fighting Unit Now"

Fifteen days after the 158th RCT disembarked at Toem for its unhappy role in the Wakde-Sarmi operation, more soldiers walked off the gangplanks onto the humid New Guinea beach to replace those of Patrick's men fortunate enough to survive their ordeal at Lone Tree Hill. These newly arrived GIs belonged to the 6th Division's 1st RCT, sent in a hurry by Krueger to bolster the vulnerable Toem beachhead. Six days later, on 11 June, the 20th RCT and divisional headquarters appeared, followed by the unit's artillery and the 63rd RCT on 14 June. Krueger had slated the 6th Division for operations further westward, but he tapped it for Wakde-Sarmi because it was conveniently at hand at Milne Bay.[91] Unfortunately, overworked engineers loaded its men and equipment onto transports hastily and unsystematically, making it all the more difficult for the unit to set up shop around Toem.

Another more galling problem was the treatment the outfit received at the hands of the now battle-hardened 158th, which saw the 6th Division men and officers as a bunch of greenhorns. This was true enough; the 6th Division had been stationed in Hawaii before Nimitz shipped it to SWPA, and it had not yet seen action. Even so, its soldiers were hard-pressed to understand the 158th's arrogance, especially since the Japanese had just beaten them in battle.[92] For their part, the 158th's GIs thought that the 6th Division ignored their sage advice acquired at such heavy cost in the crucible of New Guinea combat.[93]

Such intramural tension was just another problem 6th Division commander Major General Franklin C. Sibert faced. He had seen worse. Back in 1942 he had marched out of Burma into India with Lieutenant General Joseph Stilwell in that famous exploit. He and Stilwell, however, did not get along, so he was grateful when he was transferred out of Stilwell's baili-wick. Burdened with—or, from another point of view, blessed by—a phleg-matic personality, Sibert nonetheless impressed almost everyone with his stability, tenacity, and determination.[94] He got along with Krueger well enough, which was helpful, if not easy, and in the following weeks he sus-tained his 6th Army commander's faith in his aggressive combat abilities.

Sibert did not want to repeat Patrick's mistake and commit his forces to action without adequate knowledge of both the enemy and the surround-ing terrain, so he planned to acclimate his green soldiers gradually before tackling those veteran Japanese still dug in and around Lone Tree Hill. Then, around 1 July, he hoped to launch his offensive.[95] Krueger, however, vetoed this plan. As he saw it, the Japanese were to the west in strength, and they continued to pose a threat to the logistically valuable Toem beach-head, so he wanted them removed at once, especially since the 6th Division was scheduled to spearhead the SWPA assault on the Vogelkop in late July.[96] Moreover, Krueger planned to use Maffin Bay to stage some of the men and equipment participating in those westward operations, but this was impossible as long as the Japanese held overlooking Lone Tree Hill.[97] With these considerations in mind, he ordered Sibert to move out now.

Looking over his maps and intelligence summaries, Sibert estimated that there were 2500–3000 Japanese in the area, which was pretty accu-rate.[98] Willoughby reported that there were large numbers of Japanese east of the American position but added that they were in bad condition and unlikely to pose a threat, but Sibert still had to garrison Toem anyway.[99] As for those Japanese to the west around Lone Tree Hill, Willoughby doubted that they would go on the offensive because Patrick's assault, whatever its other unfortunate results, had mauled them significantly.[100]

As Sibert saw it, his tactical options were limited. He could not bypass Lone Tree Hill, as Patrick hoped to do, because now Krueger desired nearby Maffin Bay, which those Japanese positions in the hills overlooked. If Sibert wanted Lone Tree Hill and its companions—and he did—then he would have to repeat Patrick's tactics and muscle his way straight through. This was at least a simple enough maneuver for his rookie troops to per-form, even if it promised heavy casualties. Sibert, however, was thinking more about the damage he intended to inflict, not sustain, by using his 6th Division meat ax on the Japanese spider.

On 18 June Sibert ordered the 20th RCT, commanded by Colonel George Washington Ives, across the Tirfoam, followed by elements of the 1st RCT, to retrace Patrick's steps from the previous month.[101] Like Patrick's troops, his men were inexperienced, but although the Japanese were tough veterans, the 158th had mangled them badly. After crossing the Tirfoam two days later, the 20th made good progress against minimal enemy opposition and succeeded in reaching the Snaky River around noon. Then, predictably enough, it ran into heavy fire from Lone Tree Hill, dead ahead. American tanks plodded forward, but they could not overcome the rough terrain, and flanking efforts by the infantry also failed. Even so, by the end of the day all three of the 20th RCT's battalions were up along the Snaky; from north to south, the 3rd, 1st, and 2nd battalions.

Next morning the 20th tried again. The 3rd Battalion scaled Lone Tree Hill's eastern slope without initially meeting much enemy resistance but then staggered back down the hill when the Japanese suddenly opened fire. To the south, the 1st Battalion had no better luck in its attempts to force the defile and reach nearby Hill 225.

Ives went all out the next day, 22 June. That morning, eighteen P-47s strafed Lone Tree Hill, followed by a short and intense twenty-minute artillery barrage. This seemed to do the trick. The 3rd Battalion again advanced up Lone Tree Hill's eastern slope to Rocky Point and again met minor opposition. This time, however, two companies reached its peak near Rocky Point just after 1200. By 1500 most of the rest of the battalion was on the summit, having demonstrated what American technology, materiel, firepower, and men could accomplish.

Or so it seemed. In fact, the 3rd Battalion had fallen into a trap. The Japanese laid low in Lone Tree Hill's crevices and caves and permitted the GIs to reach the top, then opened fire and cut off their escape and supply route, surrounding them near Rocky Point. The 2nd Battalion hurried up the eastern slope to rescue their colleagues, but after they had crossed a wide draw withering enemy fire pinned them down and trapped them there. The canny Japanese had just taught the 20th RCT an expensive lesson in tactics. Now they moved in to finish off the beleaguered Americans. Japanese artillery, knee mortars, and machine gun fire lashed at the GIs, and in the evening the Japanese charged the 3rd Battalion on the summit. Although hand-to-hand combat continued through the night, the American lines held. It was not easy, though; American artillery fire was restricted out of fear of hitting the surrounded men, and it was hard to dig into the coral subsoil, so the troops had to take cover in natural depressions and logs. The stench of rotting bodies permeated the area, and an overnight rainstorm drenched the surrounded GIs, although it alleviated their thirst.

On 23 June the Americans, like an insect in a spider's web, fought to escape the Japanese trap. The 20th RCT's 1st Battalion tried to relieve the surrounded 3rd but got pinned down on top of a nearby ridge. At dawn the Japanese switched targets and attacked the 2nd Battalion, but the GIs beat off the assault and inflicted heavy casualties. After that they managed to wiggle out of their trap, withdraw down the hill, regroup, and try again to relieve the still-entangled 3rd Battalion. This they did, but only with the greatest effort. By 1400, however, the 2nd and 3rd battalions had linked up on Lone Tree Hill's summit.

Meanwhile, Sibert, informed that two thirds of his lead RCT was isolated behind enemy lines, resorted to desperate measures and ordered a small-scale amphibious landing behind Lone Tree Hill that he hoped would rescue the surrounded battalions. Next day, 24 June, two companies from the 1st RCT's 3rd Battalion, backed by the 6th Reconnaissance Troop, left the mouth of the Tirfoam on board twenty-three LVTs, ten of which carried infantry, and the remainder sporting 37mm guns. Both companies landed by 1200 below Rocky Point, where their comrades on the hill were freeing themselves from their traps. Withering Japanese fire, however, quickly stopped them on the narrow beach and sunk an LVT full of wounded men, although all were saved. The rising tide reached the boots of the troops prone behind the clay ledge on the shore. Four tanks moved in, but they could not get off the beach. Instead of rescuing the stranded battalions above, the two companies now found themselves in need of salvation.

While this amphibious ordeal was going on, the 2nd and 3rd battalions spent the day clearing Japanese from Lone Tree Hill's caves, crevices, and bunkers, as well as opening a supply line. This protracted out process required the generous use of flamethrowers, demolition charges, gasoline, and grenades, especially since the enemy had to be quite literally rooted out of the ground. To the north, American artillery fire gradually broke down Japanese resistance along the beach, permitting the two companies there to contact their comrades on the summit. In escaping the Japanese trap, the 20th RCT also broke the back of enemy resistance on Lone Tree Hill, much like an insect wrecking a web in its violent attempt to escape.

Although Lone Tree Hill was in American hands, the Japanese still held several other positions, notably Hill 225, Mount Saksin, and Hill 265.[102] On 26 June, units from the 1st and 63rd RCTs relieved the bloodied and bruised 20th and pressed the assault on those other, subsidiary, Japanese positions. Although the American conquest of Lone Tree Hill removed the keystone from the Japanese defensive arch, the GIs still had to knock down the upright stones, which was not easy. Hill 225 held out until 4 July, and the GIS seized Mount Saksin the following day. The inexperienced 63rd RCT's initial attack on Hill 265 failed, but finally a company worked its way between the peak and the Woske River and assaulted it from the west with the help of tanks and artillery. Japanese resistance collapsed on 12 July, uncovering Maffin Bay for American use. After that the GIS pushed west to the Woske, discovering lots of abandoned Japanese equipment, dumps, and positions. One platoon crossed the river, but the balance of American forces remained on the east bank, bringing an end to the 6th Division's role in the Wakde-Sarmi operation.

Sibert, of course, could be and was proud of his division's performance in its first combat role,[103] even if it achieved its objectives with something akin to sledgehammerlike precision, which, while hardly a thing of tactical beauty, was not out of step with the consequences of the American way of war. It had not, however, been easy. In the last ten days of June, the 6th Division lost 114 men killed, 284 wounded, and more than 400 evacuated for noncombatant injuries, illness, and fatigue. Moreover, not all the casualties were physical. The divisional quartermaster, for example, watching American dead stack up before him, suffered a mental breakdown because he believed his inability to adequately supply the GIS was the cause of so much death.[104] By way of compensation, the GIS got Lone Tree Hill, its companions, and Maffin Bay, which is what Krueger had asked of them, and they also killed some 940 Japanese, which was that many fewer facing MacArthur's offensive. The operation also turned the 6th Division into an experienced outfit, at least for those who survived, and this would be helpful when it faced tougher challenges to the west. Krueger seemed to see it that way. Visiting the area later, the 6th Army commander asked about officer casualties in the battered 20th RCT. When told that they had been heavy, Krueger expressed his approval, and added, "Well, I know you've got a fighting unit now."[105]

Evaluating the Wakde-Sarmi Operation

Hill 265's fall marked an end to large scale fighting around Wakde-Sarmi, although patrolling and skirmishing continued for the rest of the year. Having fulfilled his assignment, Krueger pulled the 6th Division out of the area later that month, and he used the now experienced unit in the Sansapor-Mar operation in the Vogelkop. In the meantime, someone had to guard the Toem beachhead against what remained of those two Japanese regiments, so Krueger sent in two RCTs from the inexperienced 31st Division—

the 155th and 167th; the remaining RCT, the 124th, was undergoing its own adventure on the Driniumor River around Aitape—under Major General John C. Persons. The two RCTs relieved Sibert's men on 18 July and spent the next six weeks patrolling, building bridges and roads and fortifications, unloading ships, and fighting off occasional Japanese harassing attacks. Like the 158th RCT and the 6th Division, Krueger used Wakde-Sarmi to teach the green unit about war, although in this case the lessons were not nearly as expensive as their predecessors'. As one Navy captain put it: "Any time the Army wanted to give new troops just in from the States some actual contact with the enemy, they would just march them westward until they met the Japs, and in that way they got some very good jungle training. . . . The Japanese did not bother the Americans unless the Army came close for some tactical exercises, in which case they would cooperate."[106] On 1 September the rookie 33rd Division replaced Persons's men—the 31st went on to take part in the Morotai operation—and they too got a taste of combat before tackling bigger tasks further west. The 33rd left for the Philippines in early 1945, where they participated in operations in Luzon for the rest of the war. Wakde-Sarmi reverted to an inactive backwater, and eventually SWPA abandoned the mainland and relegated once valuable Wakde airstrip to an emergency field. As for those two Japanese regiments, or what was left of them, they remained around Sarmi for the remainder of the conflict.

Like those battered Japanese, the Wakde-Sarmi operation became something of a forgotten chapter in SWPA's war. In his memoirs, for instance, MacArthur completely glosses over the event, noting, quite inaccurately, that Japanese opposition ended with Wakde's fall, as if Lone Tree Hill had never existed.[107] Such selective, if not as complete, amnesia infected other postwar accounts, most of which concentrate on the advantages accrued from seizing Wakde.

In fact, the operation seemed to yield significant strategic benefits. Wakde airstrip, once in American hands, gave SWPA the close air support it needed to storm Biak, enabled some bombers to soften up the Palaus for Nimitz's assault on the nearby Marianas, permitted Kenney's pilots to range more easily over western New Guinea, and provided protection and security for all-important Hollandia. Maffin Bay supplied staging facilities for operations against Noemfoor and Sansapor, easing SWPA's logistical burden and in so doing advancing MacArthur's offensive timetable. Without Maffin Bay, SWPA would have had to stage its western New Guinea operations from far-off Hollandia, which would have required more shipping and time, neither of which was a luxury MacArthur could afford if he wanted to beat the Navy to the China-Formosa-Luzon area. Finally, the operation not only destroyed two veteran Japanese regiments but also gave green American units and commanders good training and experience for future challenges in New Guinea and the Philippines.[108]

But was it worth the high price? The Wakde-Sarmi operation cost SWPA 630 men killed, 1742 wounded, and 41 missing.[109] The Wakde half is easily justifiable; SWPA had to have an airbase quickly to continue its offensive, and Doe's smartly conducted assault enabled SWPA to seize one relatively intact with moderate losses. Once Wakde was in SWPA's hands, GHQ used it as a platform to rapidly extend American power throughout the west New Guinea littoral.

It is more difficult to justify the Sarmi part of the operation. Much of the responsibility for the 158th RCT and 6th Division attacks rests with Krueger. As he saw it, the enemy was nearby, and although there were not all that many of them, they could pose a threat to the Toem beachhead and jeopardize MacArthur's stringent offensive timetable. It was better to attack them as soon as possible than sit idly by and await events. To be sure, Krueger, thanks to Willoughby's ambiguous intelligence assessments, underestimated enemy strength in the area, but even had he known exactly how many Japanese were in and around Lone Tree Hill, he probably would still have ordered the offensive because the same threats and pressures remained. He might, however, have committed more men, assuming, of course, that SWPA had the logistical capabilities to move them there without sacrificing more important operations further west. Had Krueger used a bigger force in the initial attack on Lone Tree Hill, the position might have fallen in May, sparing the 6th Division its ordeal the following month.

On the other hand, Krueger might have tried alternative methods to prevent the Japanese on Lone Tree Hill from shelling vital Toem, such as air strikes, but there was no guarantee that such tactics would have been successful. Moreover, had these measures failed, the resultant disruption of operations around Toem would have slowed down MacArthur's offensive, a cardinal sin in SWPA. Also, air strikes would not have gained SWPA Maffin Bay, which contributed to the acceleration of SWPA operations to the west.

Krueger's actions, in short, merely reflected MacArthur's desire to move along the New Guinea road as quickly as possible for both military and interservice political reasons. A slower offensive pace that did not require Maffin Bay, for instance, might have spared many of those lost American lives, but MacArthur would argue that the sooner he got to the Philippines, the sooner the war would end, thus saving more lives in the long run than all those who fell in and around Wakde-Sarmi. The problem, of course, is that this excuse can be used to justify any costly military operation. MacArthur sacrificed those men not so much to win the war as to win his race with the Navy so he could liberate the Philippines.

SEVEN

BIAK: A BELATED AND UNHAPPY VICTORY

Dawn broke bright and clear off Biak on 27 May, the same day Patrick's rattled men tried for a second time to storm bristly Lone Tree Hill. Naval and air strikes, however, quickly blotted out the New Guinea sun as bombers from the Admiralties dumped 317 tons of ordinance on Biak's southern coastline. Destroyers and cruisers then moved in and threw 6100 shells of various caliber at the same target.[1] Shortly before 0715, after the forty-five-minute preliminary bombardment, troops from Horace Fuller's 162nd and 186th RCTs, 41st Division veterans of the recent Hollandia operation, headed for the shore, the 186th to the east, and the 162nd to the west.

Their immediate objective was a 1400-yard strip of beach at Bosnek, about ten miles to the east of Biak's three airdromes, SWPA's ultimate operational goal. Things went wrong from the start. Three LCI rocket ships, accompanying the assault waves, shot off their 684 rockets too soon, forcing the landing craft to travel the last 1000 yards to the beach without any fire support, except from some armored Buffaloes.[2] Worse yet, the westerly current, combined with the smoke and dust raised by the preliminary bombardment that blinded the coxswains, forced some units from the 186th RCT onto a swamp-ridden beach two miles west of its original destination, to the left of its sister RCT. Some naval control boat officers, peering through the haze, saw the error soon after it developed. They decided, however, that it was too late to recall the wayward assault craft without completely wrecking the landing plan.[3]

As it was, the mistake cost the Americans a lot of lost time. Colonel Oliver P. Newman, the 186th RCT commander, saw it that way. Once Newman got his bearings straight on the beach, he called Fuller and suggested that his RCT, which was now the furthest westward American unit, take over the 162nd's assignment and spearhead the attack toward the three airdromes up the coast.[4] Fuller rejected Newman's recommendation, however, and ordered the 186th to move overland back to its originally assigned beach.

All this took a while, but it did not seem to matter much. Here, as at Hollandia, there was no Japanese opposition at the waterline, although an offshore coral reef forced the first GIs to wade the last 100 yards to the beach. Followup waves, for their part, landed dry shod. LSTs, although unable to reach the shore because of that reef, unloaded bulldozers, which moved to the beach with water up to the drivers' shoulders and only their elevated exhaust pipes showing. Once ashore, these bulldozers constructed and repaired coral jetties, so LVTs, LCIs, and DUKWs, which could cross the coral reef, were able to ferry men and equipment directly onto the beach.[5] Two pontoon causeways also contributed to rapid unloading. Better yet, there was plenty of dispersal room behind the beaches, once engineers removed a few scattered mines. Some congestion resulted nevertheless because many MPs were reluctant to exert their authority. Later that afternoon, a few Japanese bombers attacked the new American beachhead, but they inflicted little damage.

Meanwhile, the scattered troops sorted themselves out and spread up and down the beachhead. Back on the troopships, officers had warned their men that Biak would not be a pushover like Hollandia, but the lack of enemy opposition convinced many otherwise, leading to a carelessness the Japanese would soon correct.[6] Nor was this overconfidence restricted to the lower ranks. Back at Hollandia, Barbey, for one, concluded that the Japanese had evacuated the island.[7] MacArthur was even more optimistic. A GHQ communiqué issued the next day noted the absence of Japanese resistance and proclaimed SWPA victory not only on Biak, but in all of western New Guinea: "For strategic purposes this [Biak operation] marks the practical end of the New Guinea campaign. . . . Compared with the enemy our offensive employed only modest forces and through the maximum use of maneuver and surprise has incurred only light losses."[8]

As events would soon demonstrate, this was a good deal from the total truth. The New Guinea campaign had yet to run its course, and a lot of Americans would die before it did, many of them right here on Biak. Not everyone was so blinded by the first day's success. One correspondent, flying in an A-20 over the beachhead on D-Day—or Z-Day, as GHQ called it, to differentiate it from that other landing in that other war—noted prophetically: "A quick view of the area left an impression of emptiness somewhat ominous in its implications. This is too rich a plum to be thrown away. It might be bait set out to ambush the American invaders."[9]

He was right about that.

To the Japanese Army, Biak, like Wakde-Sarmi on the mainland, was now little more than an isolated outpost whose primary purpose was to buy time to develop a new defensive line around Sorong and Halmahera. It had not always been that way. Originally the Japanese had seen Biak as an integral part of their New Guinea strategy. With that in mind they not only built three good airdromes there beginning in late 1943, but they also garrisoned it with a regiment from the veteran 36th Division, whose comrades gave the 158th RCT and 6th Division such a hard fight at Wakde-Sarmi. MacArthur's Hollandia operation, however, rolled the Japanese defensive line back to New Guinea's western edge, placing Biak and its defenders beyond the strategic pale.

It was not at all unusual for the Japanese Army and Navy to work at cross-purposes, and Biak exemplified this unfortunate tendency. The Japanese Navy saw Biak as strategically important in its own right, not just as another platform from which to temporarily delay an American amphibious juggernaut that seemed to defy the laws of entropy by gathering up momentum as it went along, chewing up or bypassing Japanese garrisons thrown in its path. Naval officers, adhering to their prewar doctrine, were in mid-1944 preparing for a climactic battle with their American counterparts, probably in the Palaus, or maybe in the Marianas. No matter which locale hosted the encounter, Biak would be important to the Imperial Navy. In Japanese possession, land-based planes from Biak's three airdromes could cover the Navy's right, or southern, flank by lashing at the advancing Americans from that quarter. On the other hand, if SWPA captured Biak before the big battle began, then the Americans could use its airdromes in conjunction with Nimitz's forces to attack the oncoming Japanese fleet from two directions. From the Navy's point of view, then, the Japanese had to hold onto Biak until Nimitz showed his hand.

Fortunately for both the Japanese Army and Navy, Colonel Naoyuki Kuzume, commander of the Biak garrison, planned to accommodate each service's goals by stymieing any SWPA assault. His 10,700-man defense was centered on the 36th Division's 222nd regiment, but he also had some antiaircraft units, light tanks, aviation engineers, and naval guards.[10] Moreover, he could count on reinforcements from nearby Noemfoor and Manokwari, assuming they could slip past American naval and air patrols. In the meantime, Kuzume deployed his men on Biak's southern coast around those three airdromes, dug in, and prepared for SWPA's assault, which he expected in June.[11]

MacArthur was more than willing to oblige Kuzume, and in fact did so in May, not June. The SWPA commander wanted those three airdromes, which, unlike Hollandia's and Sarmi's, could immediately accommodate bombers. He had promised Nimitz that SWPA bombers would help soften up the Palaus for the POA's mid-June assault on the Marianas. It was now late May, and, except for small Wakde, which could not contain that many planes, no matter how many Kenney stuffed into it, he did not have the bases from which to fulfill that pledge unless his forces took Biak. Mostly though, MacArthur was thinking of his own future. As he saw it, Biak's three airdromes were the last significant *military* obstacle between him and the Philippines.[12] He believed that taking the island would for all intents and purposes end the New Guinea campaign, enabling him to concentrate even more on the *political* obstacles that prevented him from liberating the archipelago. Indeed, he could use his military successes at Biak and elsewhere along the rugged New Guinea road as more evidence that his strategic conception was superior to anything the Navy presented. MacArthur could not convincingly play this military card, however, until Biak was in American hands, so as usual he wanted to move fast.[13]

Considering the circumstances, it did not seem like MacArthur was asking all that much from his soldiers. Willoughby estimated that there were only 4400 Japanese on Biak, of whom maybe 2500 were combat troops.[14] Unfortunately, his codebreakers had trouble deciphering Japanese radio messages on the island, so he could not rely so much on Ultra.[15] Krueger, as usual, forbade ground reconnaissance for fear of tipping off the Japanese. Air reconnaissance, while revealing a lot about beaches, airdromes, and defensive positions, was of only limited utility in counting enemy personnel.[16] Despite these problems, Willoughby not only coughed up numbers, he also warned, "Biak would be of the most importance to the Allies and it is probable that it will be defended very strongly."[17] A week later, just after the Americans landed on the island, Willoughby wrote, "The local quality of resistance may be stubborn probably on Biak, because relatively fresh units are involved with the usual combat quality of organized infantry."[18] Even so, both GHQ and Krueger believed that two veteran American RCTs ought to be enough to wipe out any such opposition.

Willoughby and others also worried—accurately enough, as the situation worked out—about Biak's peculiar topography.[19] Millions of years ago, volcanic disturbances created the island by pushing long narrow coral ridges up above the waterline. These jungle-covered ridges formed almost unbroken barriers along the coastline up to 330 feet high. The ridges were highly defensible, and so were the innumerable caves of all sizes that honeycombed the island. There were no harbors and almost no streams; the island drained through seepage. This, combined with the island's heat and humidity, made the Biak operation a thirsty one for participating American soldiers. As events would soon demonstrate, though, thirst was the least of their problems.

In fact, for some members of Colonel Harold Haney's 162nd RCT, disillusionment began to set in before Z-Day was even over. After establishing themselves on the beach, at around 0900, part of the 162nd plunged westward along the coastal road toward Biak's three airdromes. Along the way, they occupied Ibdi, where Haney dropped off his 1st Battalion to secure his rear. Although one company tried to protect the advancing column's right flank by moving along the ridges overlooking the coastal road, almost impassable terrain hindered their march. Rather than have the wayward company slow down the main advancing column, Haney recalled them, although this exposed his men to any Japanese who might be up in those ridges. Haney, however, was thinking more about those airdromes up ahead than any damage the enemy might inflict on him.[20]

At 1300 the 162nd's 3rd Battalion encountered Japanese fire 7000 yards west of Bosnek, at a big coral ridge that ran to within 40 yards of the coast: the Parai Defile. This piece of geography came as a surprise, not only because of its formidable dimensions—it was not one ridge at all, but rather seven sharp ones all paralleling the coast, separated by 50–75 yards, with deep gullies full of jungle-covered potholes, caves, and crevices in between each crest—but because it was not on any map.[21] Even so, the Japanese were there, and although they did not seem all that numerous, it still required six tanks, naval gunfire, much of the 3rd Battalion, and two hours to knock them loose.

Next morning, bright and early, the 162nd's two battalions started out again, determined to occupy those airdromes.[22] The 3rd Battalion, leading the advance, reached Mokmer village without much opposition. Mokmer airdrome, the operation's main objective, lay just ahead. At a road junction 1500 yards to the west, however, the Japanese ambushed the GIs as they crossed a gully to occupy the lower of two ridges. While the troops took cover, American artillery opened fire and by 0845 seemed to have beaten down the enemy opposition. The advance continued, and indeed one company got within 200 yards of the airdrome, but that was all. Increasing Japanese resistance rocked the Americans back on their heels, prompting one lieutenant to state simply, "Our men are pretty badly chewed up."[23]

Haney was up by now, having arrived just after the GIs reached Mokmer village. He was a short, slender, energetic man, not the type to flinch

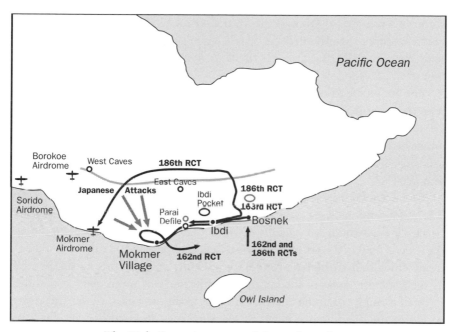

The Biak Operation, 27–29 May and 1–7 June

in the face of adversity, but the situation did not look very promising. In fact, it rapidly got worse as the Japanese increased the tempo and intensity of their attacks throughout the afternoon, driving a wedge between the 3rd Battalion and the 2nd Battalion to the east. Around 1400 a runner dashed toward Haney's Mokmer command post and yelled, "Jap tanks are coming!"[24] This was all but unheard of in SWPA, but American antitank bazooka men and two destroyers offshore swung into action and knocked them out.

Repulsing substandard and antiquated Japanese armor was one thing, but stopping the infantry was something else. Throughout the afternoon the 3rd Battalion's situation deteriorated. The enemy cut the wire lines and only one radio worked, making it difficult to direct artillery fire. Worse yet, the naval support fire officer was killed early on, so calling on the two destroyers offshore became increasingly problematic. Casualties mounted sharply, and those GIs too injured to man machine guns were laid out in caves. The troops ran low on ammunition and supplies. The battalion commander shouted over the radio, "They're plastering hell out of us. One of my three tanks was knocked out by a lucky hit. The other two are out of gas. Send me ammunition, blood plasma, morphine and water. It's urgent!"[25] Back at the 162nd RCT's Mokmer village command post, one major grimly pledged, "Hell, I can supply those people, if they'll send me some [B]uffaloes. Tell them to stay where they are, I'll supply them."[26]

Fortunately for the beleaguered battalion, help was on the way, just the type the stern major wanted. Ten supply-and ammunition-laden Buffaloes arrived at mid-day, but they had trouble reaching the 3rd Battalion beach under heavy Japanese fire. They finally moved in one at a time, while the others provided covering fire, delivering their cargo and evacuating the wounded.

By nightfall both Haney and Fuller had read the writing on the wall. The 3rd Battalion clearly could not advance—that is what got them in their current mess—and it was equally obvious that they could not remain where they were, isolated and only spasmodically supported. This left only re-treat, which Fuller ordered around 1600. Under cover of four tanks, as well as the ESB craft, most of the battalion infiltrated out in an orderly manner in small groups down the coastal road, or along the beach under the cover of one of the overhanging cliffs. By the time they reached the comparative safety of the 2nd Battalion's lines, they had suffered sixteen killed and eighty-seven wounded.

Back at Bosnek, Fuller was disconcerted by this sudden evidence of Japanese resistance, which had mauled his spearheading battalion. Even before the landing he had had doubts about this operation, and now they seemed to be coming true.[27] Clearly it was not going to be easy to take those airdromes, especially with the limited forces at hand. That evening he radioed Krueger and asked for his third RCT, the 163rd, now guarding the Toem beachhead after wrestling Wakde from the Japanese. Krueger had al-ready alerted the unit for movement, but he promised Fuller that he would order two of its battalions to leave for Biak the next day, 29 May. More-over, just in case things got out of hand, he also promised to ready the 503rd Parachute Infantry Regiment for deployment.[28]

The men of the 162nd's 3rd Battalion, now resting behind the 2nd Battalion's perimeter, would have appreciated news of imminent rein-forcement, had they known. As it was, their ordeal was by no means over, as they and the 2nd Battalion discovered next morning, when the Japa-nese attacked all-out. The day's events, in fact, replayed yesterday's, only on a larger scale, but with similar results. The 162nd threw back three major Japanese assaults, including one spearheaded by tanks. American armor was up to the task, however, and knocked the Japanese tanks out one by one—destroying seven in all—as they clanked up the coastal road.

More ominously, around 1200 the Japanese cut the coastal road east of
the Parai jetty, isolating most of the 162nd from the 186th at Bosnek. An
American counterattack drove them out and reopened the road, but the
situation continued to deteriorate. One correspondent, watching the action, reported:

> By late afternoon Mokmer village was crowded with maimed and dying
> American soldiers. Boys with shattered legs, bloody head wounds and faces
> half shot away were stretched out under every available shelter. With shock-
> ing frequency, I saw medical aides shake their heads and draw a blanket
> over a shattered form. Most of the seriously wounded were victims of the
> wicked Japanese knee mortars. Some men without a scratch—dazed and
> speechless—huddled in the shade.[29]

Just like the day before, all available naval craft hurried to the 162nd's
rescue, but only LVTs, LCVPs, and DUKWs could cross the coral reef. Watching his defensive perimeter shrink, Haney decided to travel personally to
Fuller's Bosnek headquarters to explain the situation. There the two men,
facing the same limited options they had confronted the day before,
reached the same conclusion: retreat. One battalion and most of the other
escaped overland down the coastal road, but hundreds of men waded
through the water to the edge of the coral reef to the relative safety of LCVPs
and LCMs. Other LCVPs and DUKWs removed the wounded directly from the
beach. Amphibious engineers covered the retreat with their ubiquitous
landing craft. Although Parai jetty, up the coast, was outside the shrinking
162nd RCT pocket, Fuller evacuated it, too. The day cost the Americans fifteen killed and ninety-six wounded. After two days the 162nd, or what was
left of it, was back where it started.

After the forty-eight-hour ordeal, 186th RCT commander Newman visited a rattled Haney, who had no plans for another attack, having had his
fill of Japanese for now. Newman, whose role had thus far been mostly that
of spectator and was presumably that much less disillusioned, proposed
that the 186th attack the airdromes across the ridges, avoiding the coastal
road gauntlet. Fuller, however, said no. He needed Newman's men to protect the all-important Bosnek beachhead, although he reconsidered once
the 163rd RCT arrived from Toem.[30]

To be sure, Fuller and Haney deserved much of the blame for the 162nd
RCT's fiasco. In their urgency to attack the airdromes, neither man took the
time to conduct an adequate reconnaissance that might have discovered all
those Japanese in the ridges overlooking the coastal road.[31] In the largest
sense, however, the blame belonged to MacArthur, who initiated the pressure for celerity over caution. MacArthur wanted Biak fast and, as events

would presently show, was not very tolerant of delay. His men paid, and would continue to pay, for his hastiness.

To make matters worse for the beleaguered Fuller, the Japanese Navy was about to add to his present woes, at least indirectly. To the Imperial Navy, Biak was the key to the immediate Pacific situation, and its fall would jeopardize not only their impending Mahanian battle with the American fleet but also Japanese control of all of New Guinea. As one Japanese naval officer put it: "Many airstrips can be built on Biak Island, and then it will be very hard for us to maintain airstrips on the western end of New Guinea. Palau will also be within his striking range, so movements of the task fleet east of Mindanao will be impossible. Finally, Operation A [the planned climactic battle with Nimitz's fleet] will be made impracticable. Therefore, Biak is the most critical crossroad of the war."[32]

To that end, soon after the American landing, the Imperial Navy sent reinforcements to the Manokwari-based 23rd Air Flotilla from the Philippines, Marianas, and Carolines. Unfortunately, most of the pilots were inexperienced, and many came down with malaria as soon as they reached the pestilent-ridden island. Equally as important, the Navy decided to apply its naval power to prevent SWPA from quickly seizing Biak's three airdromes. The Japanese fleet, in short, was about to enter MacArthur's theater in a big way for the first and only time in the New Guinea campaign in an operation they termed "Kon."

Throughout the New Guinea offensive, MacArthur, with only the small 7th Fleet at his disposal, depended on Nimitz's substantial naval resources to tie down the Japanese Navy in the central Pacific and keep it away from his theater. This was one of the advantages the SWPA commander garnered from the much-maligned dual drive strategy, although he of course did not talk about it, if he even saw it in those terms. As MacArthur's and Nimitz's offenses converged on the China-Formosa-Luzon area, however, the Japanese Navy found it increasingly difficult to view either thrust in isolation. Some in SWPA recognized this and concluded that GHQ could no longer automatically discount Japanese sea power. One of Kinkaid's naval officers, for instance, warned Willoughby that Biak was uncomfortably close to the nexus of substantial Japanese air and sea forces. Moreover, the island was far enough away from Nimitz's fleet, which had hitherto held that latter threat in check, to permit the Imperial Navy to concentrate suddenly on SWPA.[33]

Willoughby, in turn, observed that to counter any Japanese naval sortie SWPA would have to rely primarily on its overstretched AAF, which was currently limited to a handful of airfields in Hollandia and Wakde. From Ultra he knew that the Japanese were planning for a Mahanian battle somewhere in the western Pacific, so he recommended that MacArthur delay the Biak invasion until Nimitz's Marianas operation began, which would presumably divert Japanese naval resources in that direction.[34] MacArthur of course rejected Willoughby's suggestion, which would slow down the fast-moving stride his forces had recently attained on the New Guinea road, a loss of momentum that could cause him to lose his race with the Navy. Instead, he relied on the forces at hand—the 7th Fleet, Kenney's AAF, and Willoughby's intelligence service— to counter any Japanese naval threat.

Willoughby, however, proved more adept at counting and tracking Japanese naval resources than discerning the motivation and intentions behind their movements. On the day Fuller's soldiers swarmed ashore on Biak, Willoughby stated that, "The enemy has thus far shown no inclination to risk his surface units in an area dominated by Allied aircraft."[35] This was true enough, but the AAF was too far from Biak to completely dominate the island. Besides, it was Japanese naval doctrine, not Kenney's admittedly formidable AAF, that had hitherto kept the Imperial fleet locked in the central Pacific. Soon, however, SWPA intelligence picked up evidence that this might not be the case for long. Willoughby knew that the Japanese were concentrating air and naval reinforcements in western New Guinea and the Philippines, but he was not sure what role they would play in the forthcoming encounter with Nimitz's fleet.[36] Indeed, once Kon began, Willoughby confessed that "information concerning the enemy convoys to the north east of Halmahera is at the present time quite confusing."[37]

To implement Kon, the Japanese planned to use elements from their main fleet to convoy some 2500 men from Mindanao to Biak, as well as to cover barges that would transport other soldiers from Manokwari to the besieged island. The hope was that these men would help Kuzume keep Biak's airdromes out of American hands long enough for the Imperial Navy to fight its Mahanian battle with its American counterpart. To carry out this plan, the Japanese amassed an old battleship, three heavy cruisers, one light cruiser, and eight destroyers at Davao on 1 June. As for air support, by the beginning of the month there were 166 planes in the Vogelkop ready to contest the AAF. Kenney's superior forces, on the other hand, were hampered by the inadequate number of airdromes at their disposal in the region.

On 2 June, as part of Kon, Japanese planes struck at the Bosnek beachhead, concentrating especially on the vital and vulnerable LSTs. Bad weather around Wakde and Hollandia prevented the AAF from responding to all these attacks, which, although largely unsuccessful, hindered resupply efforts. Even so, the bombing runs cost the inexperienced and malaria-ridden Japanese pilots heavily, especially when AAF fighter planes managed to put in an appearance.

Despite its lack of success, Japanese air power at least kept the AAF busy, which, considering Kenney's killer instinct, was something of an accomplishment. The AAF, however, was only one American weapon the Japanese had to neutralize to successfully implement Kon. Another was Task Force (TF) 74, under Australian Rear Admiral Victor Alexander Charles Crutchley, whose destroyers and cruisers contained the bulk of the 7th Fleet's fighting power. Fortunately for SWPA, intelligence told Kinkaid that the Japanese might launch some type of naval sortie toward New Guinea, so he had warned Crutchley to be ready to engage any enemy force of equal or inferior strength, ordered increased aerial reconnaissance over New Guinea's waters, and told landing craft around Biak to seek cover under Fuller's batteries.[38]

Although Crutchley was on the lookout for the enemy, the AAF struck first on 3 June after both submarine and naval air reconnaissance spotted the Japanese convoy, but their attack caused no real harm. Japanese air power took its best shot at TF 74 the following day, but it too inflicted little damage. By that time, however, the Imperial Navy had suspended Kon and withdrawn their forces without landing any troops on Biak. The Japanese, upon sighting American reconnaissance aircraft and submarines, concluded that SWPA knew their location. In addition, inaccurate reports of carriers—inexperienced Japanese pilots probably mistook LSTs for flattops—in the area persuaded them that SWPA possessed the tools to use this recently acquired intelligence to sink their convoy.[39]

By the end of 3 June, however, further reconnaissance convinced the Japanese that there were no American carriers nearby. In response to this good news, the Japanese Navy decided to reactivate and refurbish Kon. This time they hoped to reinforce Biak with 600 men protected by four task forces totaling 6 destroyers, 1 light cruiser, 1 heavy cruiser, and smaller vessels for a quick run on 7 June, covered by planes from the 23rd Air Flotilla. American intelligence quickly picked up on the movement, if not its destination, but such foreknowledge was somewhat counterbalanced by Japanese air success. On the night of 5–6 June, 2 Japanese bombers slipped into Wakde and dropped their ordinance on the more than 100 aircraft Kenney had crammed into the small island. Estimates of the resulting damage varied, but everyone confirmed that most of the planes were knocked out.[40]

Everyone also agreed that the Japanese had struck a serious blow, especially with the enemy fleet on the prowl. Willoughby, for one, wrote: "Suddenly shifting his night air attacks against the Biak area to the Wakde airdrome, the enemy over 5/6 June scored probably his most successful strike against an Allied field in this theater. . . . [B]ombs caused nine casualties, destroyed six planes and damaged a large number [of] others by touching off an Allied bomb dump."[41] Wakde was out of action for days to come, stripping SWPA of one of its best weapons against Japanese naval power.

Fortunately, SWPA still had other arrows in its quiver, one of them being TF 74. Although the task force had only one heavy cruiser, three light cruisers, and ten destroyers, it still packed a punch, especially since Crutchley was ready and the Japanese did not try to cover this latest Biak reinforcement run with battleships. Nor was the AAF completely out of action, despite the beating it took at Wakde. On 8 June ten B-25s and their P-38 escorts, flying from battered Wakde, struck the Japanese destroyer screen off the Vogelkop, sinking a destroyer and injuring another. That evening, moreover, five Japanese destroyers attempting to make the run to Biak ran into Crutchley's task force. The Japanese had sent their slow cruisers back in an effort to increase the convoy's speed, so Crutchley outgunned them. The Japanese retreated, pursued throughout much of the night by American destroyers. Although some 1300 rounds were exchanged, only one shell hit—a Japanese destroyer, lightly damaged—and the Japanese got away, ending Kon's second round. During the fracas, however, barges managed to slip through to Biak to land a few reinforcements.

Now the Japanese Navy decided to go all out to get reinforcements to Biak. As Vice Admiral Jisaburo Ozawa, commander of the First Mobile Fleet, put it, "The battle of Biak has taken an unfavorable turn. If we should lose the island, it would greatly hinder our subsequent operations. I am therefore in favor of sending reinforcements, especially since this might draw the American fleet into the anticipated zone of decisive battle."[42] On 10 June the Japanese assembled two battleships, three heavy cruisers, two light cruisers, and seven destroyers to transport 800 men in two destroyer transports and smaller craft to Biak on 15 June. They wanted not only to reinforce the island garrison but also to bombard the 41st Division beachhead and tempt the American Navy into a decisive battle.[43] Willoughby knew something big was in the air, but not exactly what.[44] The 7th Fleet could not begin to match the Japanese behemoth arrayed against it, especially since Japanese air strikes had recently put the light cruiser *Phoenix* out of action and there would be little air support from Wakde.

Fortunately, SWPA was rescued by, of all things, the dual drive offensive MacArthur frequently derided. Nimitz's forces began their preliminary bombardment of the Marianas on 13 June, convincing the Japanese that it was time to fight their showdown battle now, with Biak's airdromes still out of American hands. They recalled their fleet and sailed off to a disastrous encounter with Nimitz's fleet at the Battle of the Philippine Sea.

Operation Kon showed both the fruits and perils of the dual drive Pacific offensive. Here, for the first and only time in the New Guinea campaign, the Japanese, in an admittedly haphazard and ill-organized manner, attempted to take advantage of their interior lines to concentrate their inferior forces on one of the American offensive thrusts to achieve local superiority. Fortunately for SWPA, Japanese aims were limited to keeping Biak's airdromes out of American hands before their climactic battle with Nimitz; they were not trying to roll back MacArthur's offensive. Militarily then, even had the Japanese somehow managed to defeat the 7th Fleet and cut off Fuller's men from the rest of SWPA, the gains would have been transient. Reinforcements rushed in from SWPA and elsewhere would have quickly restored the American position.

Even so, the consequences might have been far more serious for MacArthur politically. By tripping the SWPA chief up on the New Guinea racetrack, a Japanese victory, however short term, might have enabled Nimitz to reach the China-Formosa-Luzon area first. This might have convinced the JCS to underwrite a POA offensive against Formosa and relegate SWPA to a sideshow attack on Mindanao.[45]

Ironically enough, however, in the end the dual drive strategy also helped save MacArthur's offensive. Although the POA offensive, as well as King's hostility, deprived MacArthur of significant naval resources, Nimitz's fleet pinned down its Japanese counterpart in the central Pacific, keeping it for the most part out of New Guinea waters. Moreover, when the Japanese did venture into SWPA for Kon, Nimitz's Marianas offensive lured them back north.

In the largest sense, however, Kon's failure lay with the Imperial Navy. Japanese naval officers remained focused on a decisive battle with the POA and refused to grasp the opportunity the dual drive offensive presented them to defeat the Americans in detail. They saw Kon not so much as an independent operation in its own right but as part of a larger plan for a confrontation with Nimitz. Moreover, during Kon the Imperial Navy committed significant air resources to New Guinea that might have helped it in the Battle of the Philippine Sea. By way of compensation, such as it was, the Japanese managed to slip into Biak some 2000 troops over the next month to help Kuzume fight an ultimately losing battle. Kon, in short, exemplified the strategic confusion that plagued the Japanese war effort.

Mokmer Airdrome Ambush

For Fuller's men, the last two days of May were a time of rest and inactivity, at least in comparison with the previous three, during which the Japanese had taught the Americans an expensive lesson in the value of adequate reconnaissance. Fuller was not going to repeat that mistake, so he had his men out patrolling while he waited for those two 163rd RCT battalions from Toem that Krueger had promised. Their arrival at the Bosnek beachhead would free up the 186th RCT for deployment elsewhere, enabling Fuller to feed its three fresh battalions into the Biak hopper.

Fuller's new plan, a modified version of Newman's 29 May suggestion, was made possible not only by those reinforcements on their way from Toem but also by the discovery of two trails that led over the ridges from Bosnek to Biak's three all-important airdromes. Fuller proposed to send the 186th overland across the ridges while the 162nd again tried to bulldoze

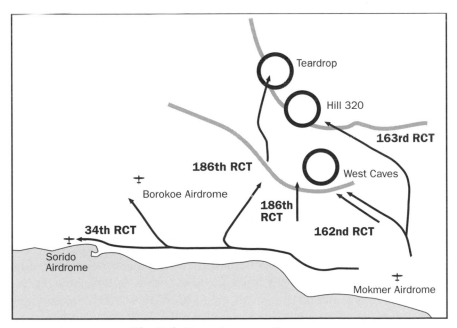

The Biak Operation, 9–27 June 1944

its way down the coastal road. This time, however, the 162nd's flank would be covered by the advancing 186th, ensuring Haney's men a degree of protection altogether lacking last time. Krueger's G-3, Colonel Clyde Eddleman, visiting the beachhead to impress on Fuller the need to move fast so MacArthur could get those airdromes into action soon, listened to the scheme and upon returning to Hollandia told his boss that it would work if carried out aggressively.[46] Krueger hoped so. He was conscious of GHQ's desire to wrap up this operation quickly, and if he was not, MacArthur would soon make him so.

Whatever faith Krueger had in Fuller and his plan, he was not about to rely on it completely, not with the MacArthur dragon breathing down his neck. If Fuller could not take an airfield immediately, then SWPA would build one. To that end, Krueger ordered Fuller to investigate the possibility of constructing an airfield north of Bosnek, where the Japanese had surveyed for one earlier. Looking over the area, engineer officers said it would take too long to complete, and Fuller added that anyway he would need those engineers once his men took the three airdromes, which he believed would be very soon.[47]

Krueger accepted that explanation but not the underlying presupposition, so on 2 June he told Fuller to occupy Owi Island, off Biak's south coast, with elements from the newly arrived 163rd RCT. Owi was ideal for an airfield: flat, well-drained, clear, and, as events showed, unoccupied by the Japanese. Krueger had not ordered the place taken earlier because it would have been too difficult to mount simultaneous landings on it and Biak.[48] Although a company of the 163rd seized the island on 1 June, aviation engineers were not sent there until 7 June, when it became increasingly clear that the three Japanese airdromes would not be ready for SWPA use by the 15 June deadline. As it turned out, Owi was not ready by then either, although fighter planes were using the airfield there only three days later.

Meanwhile, Fuller started his new offensive on 1 June, the day after the 163rd disembarked at Bosnek. For the men of Newman's 186th RCT, the march up the foot trail over the ridges was a grueling experience. The twelve-foot high scrub grass cut off any breeze, making it unbearably hot. Worse yet, there were no streams, and blasting for wells yielded nothing but dirt. All water had to be hand-carried, limiting the thirsty soldiers to a canteen a day, hardly enough to compensate for the stifling heat. Fortunately, there was almost no enemy opposition, most likely because the Japanese expected an amphibious assault on the airdromes and had redeployed their men with that in mind.[49]

By 2 June Newman's troops were abreast with the 162nd's line of advance. When the 162nd ran into heavy Japanese opposition at the Parai Defile, Fuller sent one of its battalions over to help the faster-moving 186th. This compensated for the battalion Newman sent back the next day to aid the engineers hand-carrying supplies over the rough trail.

Despite the continuing lack of Japanese opposition, rough terrain and overbearing heat, as well as a twenty-four-hour halt Fuller called while waiting the outcome of Kon's first sortie, slowed the 186th advance over the next few days. Newman was puzzled that Fuller did not devote more engineers to building a road over the ridges, which would have considerably alleviated his logistical problems.[50] In fact, the attachment of the 162nd RCT battalion to the 186th's advance only exacerbated Newman's supply difficulties, without much commensurate gain, since there were no Japanese around to deploy it against.

The farther Newman's soldiers got from Bosnek, the harder it was to supply them, and on the night on 4–5 June, his men received no water whatsoever. Next morning, against the advice of his staff and battalion commanders, Newman ordered the advance continued. He figured that since his men would be thirsty no matter what they did, they may as well march. Within hours, however, the troops were exhausted, and Newman ordered a halt at 1000 while he pondered what to do.[51] Fortunately, mother nature smiled on the Americans. At 1200 it began to rain, enabling the GIs to catch water in their ponchos and quench their parched throats. Thus refreshed, the advance continued, and by evening some of Newman's men could glimpse Mokmer airdrome down below, ripe for the plucking.

Fuller saw it that way and ordered an immediate assault, which, if successful, would secure for SWPA the bomber platform MacArthur had been seeking for the past three months. Newman was not so sure, and neither was the recently arrived Doe. Both men wanted to clear the overlooking ridges of any Japanese before they marched on the airdrome. Fuller, however, under pressure from Krueger to get the airdromes up and running, refused. This provoked a long and heated argument with Newman at Fuller's headquarters. Krueger's chief of staff, Colonel George C. Decker, on another fact-finding mission for his boss, walked in soon afterward. Queried about the plan, Newman had a hard time choking back his rage. When Decker asked what would happen if there were indeed Japanese in the ridges overlooking Mokmer airdrome, Newman responded, "We are going to catch hell."[52]

This got through to Fuller, who perhaps remembered what happened to Haney when he failed to conduct an adequate reconnaissance. He agreed to let Newman spend a day—D-Day, over in that other war against that other opponent—bringing up supplies, looking for a trail down to the airdrome, and reconnoitering the overlooking ridges. Newman, in turn, ordered one of his battalion commanders to scout the area, but the GIs found no Japanese. Newman would later have cause to regret that he did not personally oversee the reconnaissance, but for now he accepted the report at face value and prepared to move on Mokmer airdrome on the next day, 7 June.[53]

The following morning, after a half hour of shelling and air strikes, two of Newman's battalions jumped off down the ridges to the airdrome. By 0850 they had taken their objective without opposition. Mokmer airdrome was in American hands, a little late perhaps, but still in enough time for aviation engineers to turn it into another platform for Kenney's AAF to terrorize the Japanese from the Marianas to the Philippines.

Or so the Americans thought. Around 0945 Newman and some of his staff were standing in the center of the runway, savoring their victory and watching GIs move into defensive positions. Suddenly the Japanese in those not-so-abandoned surrounding ridges opened up with everything they had, lashing the Americans with rifle, machine gun, mortar, and artillery fire. Newman leaped into a nearby crater and called for his own artillery fire, but the liaison officer was wounded, his radio missing, and Newman's walkie-talkie lacked the range to reach Bosnek.[54] Eventually Newman made contact with 41st Division artillery, and soon shells rolled in and slammed the overlooking hills. The Japanese guns fell silent, probably to conserve ammunition.

As Newman had feared, the Japanese had lured the Americans into a trap, with the airdrome as bait. For the Japanese up in the surrounding ridges, the Americans were like fish in a barrel. Fortunately, in this case the fish had considerable firepower of their own, which, although less accurate than that of the Japanese, was a good deal heavier. For the Americans, their choices were limited to retreat, stay put, or attack. Considering the stakes, it was not surprising that Fuller chose the last option. In the meantime, Newman brought all his men down from the ridges, abandoned his tenuous overland supply line, and dug in. Fuller would have to supply him over the beach. This was easier said than done. The Japanese were entrenched up and down the shoreline, and initial attempts to clear them out failed until tanks arrived to do the job.

Whatever the circumstances, the Americans still possessed Mokmer airdrome, so Fuller ordered in aviation engineers to put it into shape for the hopefully not-so-far-off day when his men drove the Japanese out of their overlooking positions. The engineers landed on the night of 9–10 June, but the tide came in so quickly that much of their equipment was waterlogged, so they had to pull it ashore and dry it out before they could use it. This was a tedious enough task, but it was better than being shot at, which occurred frequently over the next four days as the engineers worked grueling, twelve-hour shifts. By 13 June they had completed 4000 feet of runway. Even so, continuing Japanese fire made further work impossible, so they were withdrawn until the combat soldiers cleared out the enemy from the Mokmer ridges, which took until 20 June. Fighter planes began flying out of Mokmer on 22 June, but by then it was too late to support Nimitz's Marianas operation.

While the 186th RCT unknowingly walked into the Japanese trap, the 162nd RCT was having problems of its own in carrying out its part of Fuller's two-pronged attack.[55] Advancing down the unhappily familiar coastal road on 3 June against sporadic enemy resistance, the 3rd Battalion ran into heavy fire from Japanese entrenched in Parai Defile, that huge mass of coral outcroppings that dominated the route to Mokmer airdrome. Although backed by air strikes, armor, and a bulldozer, the GIs retreated after a two hour fight. In the course of the next several days, Haney's men cleared the Japanese from much of the surrounding area, but they could not advance overland until they rooted the enemy out of the defile.

Fuller, however, wanted the overland route opened soon so he could more easily supply Newman's men, who were about to advance on Mokmer airdrome. On 7 June, the day the 186th walked into the Japanese trap, Fuller ordered two companies from the 162nd onto LVTs for an amphibious assault near Parai jetty that he hoped would cut the enemy off from that direction. The two companies landed without opposition but ran into heavy resistance as they moved eastward back to the defile. At the jetty area, meanwhile, tanks and a cannon company also landed, but increasing Japanese fire prevented LSTs and LCMs from approaching the beach until nightfall.

Despite such problems near the jetty, Fuller believed that he had found the key to reducing the Parai Defile, or at least to getting around it. He sent most of the 162nd by sea to the jetty area, and while one battalion remained behind to continue the effort to clear the defile, the rest of the RCT marched westward to Mokmer airdrome to join Newman's partially besieged men in their efforts to clear the Japanese from the overlooking ridges. Ultimately the 163rd RCT came down from Bosnek to take up the difficult task of reducing the defile, which one soldier described as a ghastly white mass of rocks and boulders covered with big trees.[56] Or it was until

American artillery and air strikes stripped the vegetation away, although that did not bring the GIs any closer to victory. In fact, the Japanese in the defile held out until late July.

Mokmer Ridge Bloodletting

Mokmer airdrome was in American hands, but its value was considerably diminished by all those Japanese in the surrounding heights. The thing to do, Fuller knew, was to sweep the enemy away, but this was much easier said than done and would obviously require a considerable number of men and guns. To that end, Fuller brought two battalions from the 162nd RCT to Mokmer and on 9 June sent them and Newman's soldiers up against those ridges.[57] After some initial progress, the offensive sputtered to a halt. Fuller ordered the assault renewed. The attacks continued for the next three days but with little success. The Japanese frequently counterattacked and constantly infiltrated the GIs lines at night through the bushes and shellholes.[58] The Americans stopped their assaults every day around mid-afternoon so the GIs would have enough time to entrench in the rough coral before night brought on the inevitable Japanese raids.

In fact, the offensive rapidly degenerated into a grinding battle of attrition, which under normal circumstances would inevitably lead to American victory. In this case, however, the stakes were not territory but time. SWPA's occupation of Biak was all but inevitable once Fuller's men established themselves on the island—Kon was never intended to roll back MacArthur's offensive, only to delay it—but the longer the Japanese kept those airdromes out of SWPA's hands the better chance they had of winning the climactic battle on which their Navy was banking. MacArthur, for his part, wanted the island seized quickly in order to continue his race with the Navy to the China-Formosa-Luzon area. Viewed from that perspective, attrition, which was almost by definition a long and tedious process, worked in Japan's favor.

Fuller did not like the look of things, and neither did Doe, who after a quick inspection of the troops confirmed that this type of warfare cut both ways. Doe, however, had a new plan, which was to send two battalions around the Japanese left, or north, flank and knock them out of those ridges. Fuller okayed it, and the attack jumped off on 14 June. Although some men reached the vital West Caves area, the major enemy strongpoint on the Mokmer ridges, an enemy counterattack that included tanks drove them off. American small arms fire and artillery destroyed or scattered the enemy armor, but the Japanese continued to cling to those ridges. Doe wanted to renew the offensive and attack the West Caves head on, but he was overruled, not by Fuller but by the new American commander on Biak: Lieutenant General Robert L. Eichelberger.

Eichelberger to the Rescue

Throughout the New Guinea campaign, MacArthur worked hard to convince the public and his superiors that a successful amphibious landing signified the practical conclusion of an operation. GHQ usually termed subsequent fighting inland "mopping up," even though the Japanese concentrated most of their forces in the interior and the Americans suffered the bulk of their casualties there as well. MacArthur tried to fit Biak into this familiar pattern and was for the most part successful, even though the initial landing was only the first step in a lengthy and bloody struggle that killed a good many soldiers long after GHQ had declared the operation over. In fact, even Marshall fell for the deception, to an extent anyway. After Fuller occupied Mokmer airdrome, the chief of staff wrote MacArthur: "With the capture of Mokmer airfield I send you my personal congratulations on the Aitape-Hollandia-Maffin Bay-Biak campaign which has completely disorganized the enemy plans for the security of eastern Malaysia and has advanced the schedule of operations by many weeks."[59]

Possessing Mokmer airdrome, as Fuller quickly discovered and Marshall eventually learned, did not mean that the AAF could use the place, though. One correspondent, remaining on Biak after his colleagues took MacArthur's communiqué at face value and departed from the theoretically secured island, wrote sardonically after the Japanese ambushed Newman's soldiers, "Obviously it will require additional reinforcements to achieve the resounding victory proclaimed ten days ago by General MacArthur."[60]

MacArthur was hardly a stranger to self-delusion, especially when it came to his own causes, abilities, and accomplishments. In this case, however, despite his rosy communiqués, he recognized that he could not continue his westward race to the China-Formosa-Luzon area without the air support that only Biak's airdromes could immediately provide. As June wore on and the Japanese continued to stymie Fuller's efforts, MacArthur grew increasingly impatient and took his frustration out on Krueger. He repeatedly pressured his ground commander to wrap the operation up in a hurry so SWPA could move on to bigger and better things. On 5 June, as

Newman's thirsty men approached Mokmer airdrome overland, MacArthur radioed Krueger, "[I] am becoming concerned at the failure to secure the Biak airfields. The longer this is delayed the longer our position there will be exposed to enemy air attack with the possibility of heavy loss therefrom. Is the advance being pushed with sufficient determination? Our negligible ground losses would seem to indicate a failure to do so. Request your views immediately."[61] Krueger might dispute the exact definition of "negligible," but instead he replied the same day:

> Fuller had been directed repeatedly to push his attack with the utmost vigor. Since it appeared to me some time ago that his operation was not progressing as satisfactorily as I desired, I seriously considered relieving him. Before taking that action I awaited reports from my G-3 Colonel Eddleman and other senior staff officers whom I sent at various times to Biak to observe the action. Their reports did not warrant such action. The terrain over which the advance had to be made consists of a narrow Defile along the beach and a series of alternating cliffs, shelves and ridges paralleling the coast. The shelves and ridges are covered with dense vegetation, are deeply pitted coral and contain innumerable caves. The terrain difficulties rather than strong Jap resistance have retarded the advance except in the Defile where the enemy was able to bring enfilade fire to bear. A radio [message] that is not entirely clear indicated that the patrols . . . reached the ridge north of Mokmer drome. . . . Clarification has been requested. I am awaiting a full report on the situation from my Chief of Staff before taking any further action.[62]

This was hardly a ringing endorsement of Fuller's abilities, and in fact it sounded a lot like a subordinate trying to shift blame for failure onto someone else's shoulders by building up a record against him. Krueger continued this strategy three days later, after Decker returned from Biak, in another message to MacArthur. Krueger again emphasized the island's difficult terrain and Fuller's recognition that speed was invaluable, but he praised both the 41st Division commander's overland assault and his plan to clear the enemy from the Mokmer ridges. On the other hand, Krueger criticized the 162nd RCT advance up the coastal road on 27–29 May—although he admitted that Fuller lacked the resources to mount a larger attack at the time—and acknowledged that some units and personnel had displayed a lack of aggressiveness and leadership. Even so, he assured his boss that these deficiencies had been corrected. Fuller, he noted, had undoubtedly made mistakes, and although other officers might have done better, he was glad he had not relieved him because all evidence indicated that he was on the verge of a victory that would sweep the Japanese from the ridges overlooking the all-important airdromes.[63]

Despite such tepid praise—or perhaps because of it—Krueger was considerably more disappointed with his 41st Division commander than he let on in his messages to MacArthur. He wanted to go to Biak for a firsthand look at the situation, but he did not feel that it was safe for him to leave his Hollandia command post. Not only was most of his staff still back at his old Cape Cretin headquarters, but things were touch-and-go at Wakde-Sarmi, and the Japanese were making noises around Aitape.[64] Biak, in short, was merely one responsibility among many the 6th Army commander faced.

Krueger could and did send some of his senior staffers over to Biak for a look, and he was not at all happy with their reports. Decker, for instance, said that the biggest problem was not the Japanese but the heat. He did not recommend anyone's relief, but he believed that Fuller needed some help. Decker added that Fuller's plan to take Mokmer airdrome would succeed if pushed aggressively enough.[65] But to Krueger that was one of the problems, along with a lack of coordination, determination, and even competence.[66] Krueger simply did not like the way Fuller was running things. Why had not Fuller reconnoitered before sending the 162nd RCT on its abortive advance down the coastal road? Why was Fuller not making better use of the battle-tested Doe? Krueger doubted that Fuller was up to the job of clearing the Mokmer ridges, but he was certain of all the pressure MacArthur was exerting on him for results.[67]

On 13 June, after four days of unsuccessfully battering the ridges overlooking Mokmer airdrome, Fuller asked Krueger for another RCT. He explained that his troops were tired and intelligence reports indicated that Japanese reinforcements were infiltrating from Noemfoor and Manokwari. Krueger did not credit the report of enemy reinforcements, although it was true,[68] but he ordered in the 24th Division's 34th RCT from Hollandia.[69] In the meantime, Krueger continued to pressure Fuller for more speed, but he was rapidly losing both confidence and patience in his 41st Division commander.[70]

In fact, the more Krueger thought about it, the more convinced he became that Fuller was overburdened with responsibilities that prevented him from concentrating fully on the battlefield. The thing to do, he decided, was to send Fuller some help, although he later claimed that he had no intention of relieving his 41st Division commander, despite statements to the contrary in his messages to MacArthur.[71] It was MacArthur, however, who brought the issue to a head and provoked Krueger into action. On 14 June a frustrated SWPA chief radioed to Krueger, "The situation on Biak is unsatisfactory. The strategic purpose of the operation is being jeopardized by the failure to establish without delay an operation field for aircraft."[72] That broke the camel's back, and Krueger replied later that day, "General Eichelberger and his staff have arrived. Upon their arrival General Eichelberger will assume command [on Biak,] relieving General Fuller."[73] As Krueger saw it, Eichelberger would take over Fuller's administrative burden, permitting the 41st Division commander to focus on driving the Japanese from the Mokmer ridges.[74]

On the afternoon of 14 June, while Krueger was wrestling with his thorny Biak problem, Eichelberger and staffer Colonel Harold Riegelman were on a launch on southern Lake Sentani speculating on the number of Japanese starving in the surrounding hills. Riegelman asked his I Corps commander how long they would remain in Hollandia, and Eichelberger guessed about three months.[75] Eichelberger, however, was not being completely honest with Riegelman. Just four days before, Krueger had told him that he had considered sending him to Biak, but he had decided it was no longer necessary now that Fuller had seized Mokmer airdrome and would soon clear the Japanese from the overlooking heights.[76]

Krueger had said nothing since then, but Eichelberger knew from illegitimate but authoritative sources that the situation on Biak had deteriorated. For several weeks I Corps had been intercepting secret radio messages between GHQ and 6th Army headquarters, so Eichelberger knew all about MacArthur's and Krueger's frustrations with Fuller.[77] Eichelberger's staffers defended the practice by saying that Krueger's headquarters never told them anything, but such eavesdropping probably had more to do with their boss's suspicions that Krueger was out to get him, and to be forewarned was to be forearmed. Eichelberger, then, was hardly surprised when after dinner his chief of staff, Brigadier General Clovis Byers—recovered by now from his close call over Wakde, where his carelessness nearly cost him his life—took a call from a 6th Army staffer ordering Eichelberger to Krueger's headquarters. Byers informed Eichelberger, who asked knowingly, "What do you think it is?"[78]

Krueger's Hollandia headquarters was far from Eichelberger's, which probably suited both men just fine. Eichelberger and Byers drove six miles by jeep to Pim jetty, took a crash boat across Jaufeta Bay, then motored another five miles to Krueger's command post at Hollekang beach. There the gruff Krueger explained the situation on Biak—Eichelberger, of course, already knew most of the details, having in effect tapped his superior's phone—and told Eichelberger to take his I Corps headquarters to Biak tomorrow. He was to supersede, but not replace, Fuller, although Krueger gave him the authority to relieve the beleaguered 41st Division commander if he believed it was necessary. Eichelberger, however, hoped it would not come to that.[79] When Eichelberger asked whether the I Corps would return to Hollandia after the operation, Krueger simply replied, "We never draw backwards," leaving his subordinate to mull over the hidden implications, if any, in that cryptic phrase.[80] Later, just before Eichelberger left, Krueger was a little more forthright and told his I Corps commander, "Now, don't go and get yourself killed."[81]

Eichelberger could appreciate these parting words more than most men, having been through a similar trial a year and a half ago, when MacArthur shipped him off to Buna with instructions to take the place or return a corpse.[82] Krueger's sendoff, although not as dramatic, at least expressed a degree of personal concern altogether lacking in MacArthur's earlier admonitions. Back at their headquarters, the I Corps staff hurriedly prepared for the move. Next morning Eichelberger and a few key subordinates left for Biak on two Catalinas. They were met by an LCM off the island just after noon, but they had lots of trouble transferring their gear, and in fact the pilot fell into the ocean and nearly drowned. The rest of the I Corps personnel showed up three days later, on 18 June.

For Fuller, the past week had been trying, to say the least. It was bad enough watching his attacks break in blood on the crests of those ridges frowning over Mokmer airdrome, whose empty runways seemed to mock the Americans. Krueger's constant badgering, however, was even worse and was enough to alienate a man much less stubborn and opinionated than Fuller. As early as 5 June, for instance, Krueger radioed: "The slow progress of your advance, in view of your light losses and minor hostile opposition during the past two days is very disturbing. It is imperatively necessary that you push forward with the utmost energy and determination and gain your objective quickly."[83] Krueger was still at it a week later: "I again must urge you to liquidate hostile resistance with utmost vigor and speed to permit construction on Mokmer and other [air]dromes to be undertaken. Since you have not reported your losses, it is assumed that they were not so heavy as to prohibit advance."[84]

Just as MacArthur's 14 June message provoked Krueger into sending Eichelberger to Biak, word of Eichelberger's imminent arrival prompted action on Fuller's part, although of a different sort. As he saw it, Krueger's constant pestering, as well as Eichelberger's appointment, indicated a lack of confidence in him, so he quit. In fact, he stated that he would submit his resignation every half hour until it was accepted.[85]

Arriving at 41st Division headquarters ahead of Eichelberger, Byers tried to talk Fuller out of leaving. When Fuller saw Byers, the divisional commander said, "This is a hell of a thing to have to happen on the anniversary of the day you graduated from West Point."[86] Byers explained that Krueger was not relieving him but rather expanding the operation. Fuller had already sent his resignation to 6th Army headquarters, but Byers offered to have his friend Decker intercept it. Fuller initially accepted this plan, but as Byers headed for the signal station one of Fuller's aides caught up with him and said that his boss had changed his mind again.[87] Eichelberger showed up while Byers was on his way to the signal shack, and he repeated Byers' plea, but to no avail. Fuller, who by now was crying, simply said, "The dignity of man stands for something. I'll take no more insulting messages."[88] Eichelberger, who also found dealing with Krueger a trial, sympathized with Fuller. He believed that the 41st Division commander had not been given enough troops for his assignment and those he was sent were committed piecemeal, but there was nothing more he could do.[89]

Four days later, Riegelman paid Fuller a visit that he later compared to a condolence call. Fuller looked distressed, with tight lips and deepened lines. Riegelman said he was sorry and tried to persuade him, even at this late date, to stay on, but Fuller said the division had lost confidence in him, that Krueger simply did not know what was going on, and that one more RCT would have won the battle.[90]

Fuller's distress echoed up the chain of command. When Eichelberger returned to Hollandia later in the month, Krueger angrily demanded to know why he had permitted Fuller to quit. Eichelberger said he had tried to prevent it, but it was Krueger's hectoring messages that provoked Fuller's resignation.[91] Later Fuller met with MacArthur and had good things to say about everyone but Krueger. Although he stood ramrod straight, his jaw trembled, and he broke down when MacArthur promised him a Distinguished Service Medal. In Australia he suffered appendicitis, and although MacArthur appointed him head of the Pacific Strategy Board, his career as a combat soldier was over.[92]

The Pacific War was as hard on the spirit as on the body, as both Fuller and Herndon, over at Wakde-Sarmi, discovered. Fuller failed because he could not win the Biak battle the way MacArthur wanted it won—fast. Krueger merely responded to MacArthur's pressure. Analyzing the issue later, Krueger's subordinates defended their boss, saying he never meant to relieve Fuller, and in any case Fuller was a little too old for his command.[93] This all might have been true, but perhaps the best explanation for Fuller's downfall came years later from fellow division commander Joseph Swing: "Horace Fuller was a great friend of mine. . . . He just didn't have it, if you know what I mean. It is hard to teach people how to be leaders. You got it or you haven't got it."[94] In the final analysis, the Biak maelstrom showed that, for all his ability, Fuller did not have what it took to prosper in MacArthur's theater.

With Fuller removed from the scene, Eichelberger had to find a new commander for the 41st Division. Doe was the obvious choice, but Eichelberger had reservations. Doe was undoubtedly a fighter, and he possessed plenty of battle experience, having commanded independently and successfully at Aitape and Wakde. He was, however, also cantankerous, hypercritical, stubborn, and had in the past spoken negatively about former National Guard divisions like the 41st. In the end, Eichelberger decided to designate Doe temporary commander and planned to make the appointment permanent if Doe proved himself by quickly clearing the Japanese from Mokmer ridges.[95]

Finding a replacement for the departed Fuller was only one of Eichelberger's difficulties as he settled in on Biak. The biggest problem, of course, was winning the battle soon, and Krueger made sure Eichelberger knew this. Two days after Eichelberger got to the island, Krueger turned up the heat, warning him that SWPA's New Guinea offensive depended on opening Mokmer airdrome quickly.[96] Subjected to the same pressures that broke Fuller, Eichelberger responded with typical resentment. He was hard put to understand how Krueger, who had not even been to Biak to look things over, could make such demands on him.[97] In a carefully worded message, Eichelberger explained that he had just got to Biak and was ignorant of the tactical situation. The 41st Division was intermingled and exhausted from heavy fighting and unsuccessful frontal assaults, so he wanted to take a day to sort things out and give the troops a breather.[98] Krueger grudgingly accepted the delay, mostly because he had no real choice. With that flank secured, at least for now, Eichelberger turned his attention to those Japanese holed up in the Mokmer ridges.

Eichelberger's Offensive

Before doing anything else, Eichelberger wanted to acquaint himself with his new command, as well as with the unfamiliar terrain, which he did while Doe's offensive ran its course. In each case, he did not like what he saw. Biak possessed the worst ground he had ever seen, except for Buna, which was saying a lot.[99] Even the scarce water was hostile, tasting as it did of melted coral, and chlorine tablets did little to improve it.[100]

Bad terrain and bad water, however regrettable, were incidences of war, and Eichelberger could accept them as such. He was, on the other hand, not at all impressed with the 41st Division officers, who were supposed to be well-trained components of the mighty American war machine. In fact, *he* had taught them, back in Australia during his time in exile, so he knew they could do better. As he saw it, Doe was not keeping in contact with his men, a mortal military sin in Eichelberger's book.[101] Moreover, most American artillery fire went to waste because no one knew exactly where the Japanese were.[102] An inspection tour showed that the Japanese still held ridges that were supposed to be in American hands. This helped convince Eichelberger that the RCT commanders knew as little about the tactical situation as he did, although his short time on the island provided him with an excuse the others lacked.[103]

Officers could be replaced, although Eichelberger refrained from such drastic action, but enlisted men could not, so he had to work with what he had. Despite his report to Krueger, the men were not as tired and discouraged as he expected, considering their recent ordeals.[104] He was, however, noticing signs of an old tendency among the GIs to feel sorry for themselves and forget their jobs and the enemy's woes.[105] Taken together, then, it was small wonder that Eichelberger canceled Doe's offensive when the new 41st Division commander wanted to assault the West Caves area directly with the 162nd RCT.

Despite these problems, Eichelberger, ever the optimist, thought that he could quickly drive the Japanese off the Mokmer ridges.[106] As he saw it, the 41st Division had relied too much on nibbling attacks, which, while safe enough in the short run, would not win the battle anytime soon.[107] Like any good American soldier, Eichelberger believed in firepower, but he wanted to maneuver his forces into a position from which they could employ their guns most effectively. To that end, he planned on flanking the Japanese not from the north, as Doe tried, but from the south, around the enemy's right.[108] Newman's 186th RCT would spearhead the attack, moving north to seal off the Mokmer ridges, while the 162nd RCT continued its direct assault on the West Caves area. On the left flank, the newly arrived 34th RCT would occupy deserted Borokoe and Sorido airdromes. At the other end of the line, the 163rd RCT would take strategically vital Hill 320, which dominated the right flank and in Japanese hands could provide a wonderful platform from which to shoot at the advancing 186th. In fact, the Americans had taken Hill 320 on 7 June, but for some reason they had recently abandoned it.

Looking over the plan, Doe did not like it at all and tried to talk Eichelberger out of implementing it. He feared that the Japanese would mortar the spearheading 186th RCT to death long before it reached its objective.[109]

Eichelberger's mind was quite made up, however; he needed results fast, or he too might find himself without a combat command.

Since he might well only have one chance at success before Krueger's ax swung, Eichelberger wanted things done right, so he gave his men all of 18 June—a Sunday, ironically enough—to redeploy, reconnoiter, and rest. Next morning, after a preliminary bombardment, the 186th RCT jumped off for its immediate objective, a low ridge 1000 yards northeast of Borokoe airdrome.[110] As Doe feared, the Japanese mortared some units on the way, but at 1130 the 2nd Battalion successfully stormed the ridge. Newman quickly ordered up the rest of his men, although one battalion got held up by the rough terrain.

Next day, 20 June, the 34th RCT took Sorido and Borokoe airdromes with almost no opposition, and a company from the 163rd RCT seized vital Hill 320. Despite these accomplishments, Eichelberger did not think the 41st Division was pushing hard enough, so he yelled at everyone and hoped for a better tomorrow.[111] He was not disappointed; that day the 186th and 162nd RCTs converged on the West Caves area, sealing off Mokmer ridges.

The heart of the West Caves area was the Sump, an eighty-foot-deep and 100-foot-wide pothole that had once been a cave. Caverns at the bottom led to an underground maze full of Japanese. In better times, the enemy there possessed plenty of supplies and ammunition, underground brooks, electric lights from gas generators, wooden floors, and ladders. These positions were all but immune to American artillery and air strikes. In fact, it took a while for the Americans even to locate the place. Aerial photos were of little help, so Eichelberger finally sent his operations officer and his assistants up in cub scout planes, and from there they pinpointed the strongpoint by flying over Japanese lines at low altitude.

Finding the exact location of the West Caves was one thing, but rooting out its defenders was something else again. Skip bombing did not work, and flamethrowers were of limited value because they did not penetrate far enough into the cave interior and were likely to flashback on their operators. The GIs eventually learned to drive the Japanese inside the caves with tanks, mortars, and grenades, and then seal them off by dumping hundreds of barrels of gasoline into the caverns and igniting it, or by throwing in lots of TNT. It was a tricky and dangerous task, though. Handling so much explosive was risky under the best of circumstances, and Japanese infiltrators, who knew the terrain well, were always on the prowl.[112]

Still, the Americans got the job done, although not without a good many wounds all around. The GIs launched their first attacks on the West Caves on 20 June, and resistance collapsed three days later, but the last

Japanese in the area was not killed until 27 June. Colonel Kuzume was among the West Cave casualties, but accounts differ on whether he committed suicide or died fighting. By now, however, for most Japanese the two options amounted to the same thing. The Americans finally entered the caverns on 27 June and discovered a chamber of horrors full of decomposed and fried bodies, or their various components, and even a butcher shop for cannibalistic purposes. One officer who explored the Sump wrote later:

> I organized a small party and prepared to enter. The north sump was almost forty paces across and forty feet deep. A small cave opened off to one side. . . . Within the mouth I followed an incline ending somewhat below the floor of the sump, at a cavern which appeared to have been used as a kitchen. One side of the cavern showed a drop of ten feet to a shelf. . . . From the shelf we peered into a large pit, the floor of which, twenty feet below, was covered with wood planks. A ladder led to that level. . . . The chamber in which we found ourselves was large, dark, unbearably hot, fetid, and swarming with flies. All of us were dripping perspiration. . . . I found a passage at the point indicated by the map. It was barely wide enough for one man to squeeze through. I worked my way along this damp, foul corridor, feeling for a precarious footing on the slimy, jagged rock floor, until a breath of cooler air warned me that I was about to enter the main net.[113]

Eichelberger's offensive broke the back of Japanese resistance by jarring them loose from the Mokmer ridges, finally enabling the AAF to use the airdromes Fuller had seized more than two weeks before. Even so, there was still a lot of mopping up to do, although not by Eichelberger. Krueger, apparently forgetting his earlier admonition that his men "never draw backwards," told Eichelberger he and his I Corps headquarters could return to Hollandia whenever he thought his job was complete. Eichelberger remained on Biak until 29 June and then left, proud of his accomplishment. Krueger did not seem to see things in that light, and in fact the 6th Army commander remained silent as he and Eichelberger took a boat trip to I Corps headquarters, but before Krueger got into a jeep and drove away he said, "I congratulate you on the job you have done."[114]

Sour grapes probably explain Krueger's lukewarm praise. MacArthur had decided to create a new field army in SWPA, the 8th, and would appoint Eichelberger the commander. Krueger, however, did not feel another army was necessary.[115] Even so, he had to learn to live with it, and at least it got the quarrelsome Eichelberger out of his command; conversely, it also removed him from 6th Army control and turned him into even more of a rival. Eichelberger, for his part, next year led his new 8th Army with distinction in the southern Philippines in a series of tactically brilliant but strategically valueless amphibious operations. As for his old I Corps, which went on to fight in Luzon, its new commander was Major General Innis P. Swift, conqueror of the Admiralties.

Mopping Up Operations

For Eichelberger, the Biak operation more or less ended after his men drove the Japanese from Mokmer ridges, permitting the AAF unrestricted access to the airdromes down below. For the rest of the GIs on the island, mopping up continued throughout June and well into July. The Americans had clearly broken the back of Japanese resistance, but the flailing victim was still capable of inflicting a lot of damage. In fact, in July alone the Japanese killed 70 Americans and wounded another 257.[116]

Among the first targets for the Americans mopping up was the Teardrop, a 300-yard-long and 100-yard-wide cul-de-sac just off the northwest corner of Hill 320. Elements of the 163rd RCT floundered around there from 20 to 23 June, until Newman's men came in hard to seal it off the next day. Or so they thought; next morning the Japanese were gone, having slipped through American lines that night.

The 41st Division had initially ignored the Japanese stronghold in the East Caves, north of Parai Defile, because the enemy could not use it to pound Mokmer airdrome. Even so, it was a threat to the coastal road, so Fuller had committed parts of the 163rd RCT to its reduction before Eichelberger arrived. Like its counterpart to the west, the Americans employed lots of air strikes and artillery to drive the Japanese underground, then finished them off with TNT and gasoline. Although the 163rd opened the road as early as 13 June, mopping up in the area continued until 5 July, and the last Japanese were not killed for another two weeks.

The Ibdi pocket, also north of the Parai Defile, was the last site of organized Japanese resistance. Getting there was not easy, though, and the GIs had to use trees to climb the steep cliffs before even coming to grips with the enemy. Initial assaults in late June were unsuccessful, and fierce Japanese opposition stymied the 163rd until a two day bombardment cracked the position on 22 July.

Mopping up and patrolling continued through July and involved a series of minor amphibious landings along Biak's coast that helped keep the Japanese on the run. In mid-July the 34th RCT returned to Hollandia, so the 41st Division did most of the remaining work. Even so, scattered Japanese continued to hold out in the interior until the end of the war. As for the 41st, it remained on Biak until 1945, when it participated in Eichelberger's 8th Army operations in the southern Philippines at Palawan Island, the Sulu Archipelago, and on the Zamboanga peninsula.

For SWPA, Biak's value lay in its airdromes, from which the AAF could project its power all the way to the southern Philippines. Once Eichelberger's offensive knocked the Japanese loose from Mokmer ridges, aviation engineers, who, except for their four-day attempt to work under enemy fire on the runway, had spent much of their time building jetties, widening the coastal road, carrying water for the infantry, and maintaining trails to the front, moved in and got to work putting the airdromes into working order.[117] Mokmer airdrome was ready for fighter planes on 21 June, and Owi opened completely nine days later. Neither, however, was in action in time to support the Marianas operation. Fortunately, the POA did not need such assistance.

Even without Japanese interference, constructing the airdromes was not easy. Biak was on SWPA's military frontier and had a long supply line, so there was a constant shortage of spare parts. Engineers even set up sawmills to provide some of their own lumber.[118] Moreover, an impatient Kenney gave shipping priority to planes and their pilots, so there was soon a dearth of maintenance crews and equipment, which grounded lots of planes.[119] Despite such problems, Mokmer was ready for bombers on 2 August, and soon the AAF was flying missions to the Netherlands East Indies and Mindanao, as well as supporting operations in western New Guinea and the Palaus. Borokoe, Sorido, and Owi were also completed in August.

Biak, however, possessed more than just airdromes. Engineers also turned the island into an advanced SWPA base, with Liberty ship docks, sixty miles of road, warehouses, bivouacs, and a hospital. This took a while, not only because the airdromes had higher priority but also because the engineers had to devote a lot of time to supporting the combat troops, especially early on. To make matters worse, scrub typhus, carried by mites on rodents, broke out on Owi and quickly spread to Biak. The epidemic peaked in August, striking 1025 men, of whom a dozen died. Here, as on the New Guinea mainland, natives warned that the area designated for development was "tabu," but the engineers ignored them. Faced with the unhappy consequences of their unwise actions, the Americans responded with alacrity. The troops burned or cleared all the brush around their bivouacs, kept out of the undergrowth, and impregnated clothing with dimethylphthalate, which eventually brought the disease under control.[120]

Evaluating Biak

The Biak operation cost SWPA more than 400 killed and 2000 wounded, as well as a good number of noncombat injuries from scrub typhus, heat-stroke, and what not.[121] Although the losses were not nearly as great as those concurrently registered in Normandy, in that other war, they were high in proportion to the number of men engaged, which never exceeded four RCTs. Enemy casualties were even more severe, and a good deal harder to calculate. No matter how many Japanese managed to escape into the interior, however, they contributed little to the further defense of their homeland.

Even so, the Japanese defenders, those who escaped and succeeded in eking out a squalid existence at any rate, could take pride in their accomplishments, having stalled MacArthur's New Guinea offensive for nearly a month. Because the Japanese garrison had been written off by Imperial Headquarters after Hollandia fell, there was never any chance that its defenders could actually defeat the Americans once the GIs established themselves ashore—even Kon did not envision this goal—but that was not the issue for either side.

What was at stake was not territory but time. The Japanese wanted to hold onto Biak as long as possible so they could build a new defensive line in western New Guinea and fight a climactic battle with Nimitz's POA without the AAF lashing at their right flank from Biak's airdromes. They succeeded—to an extent. The Imperial Navy went into battle at the Philippine Sea with Biak still in friendly hands, although it did not help them much in the end, and they lost most of the aircraft they indirectly committed to Biak's defense. Kuzume's rugged defense slowed MacArthur's advance, but not enough, as events turned out, to enable the Japanese to build a defensive line in western New Guinea capable of resisting the SWPA onslaught.

For SWPA, too, time was the determining factor. MacArthur wanted Biak's airdromes fast to support Nimitz's Marianas operation and to promote further operations toward the China-Formosa-Luzon area as part of his effort to convince the JCS to permit him to liberate the Philippines. MacArthur failed to help Nimitz, but in the end Nimitz did not need his assistance. Moreover, despite the month-long battle, SWPA was still able to reach the China-Formosa-Luzon area on time, enabling MacArthur to reopen the Philippines issue with the JCS.

Biak, in short, was on the whole a SWPA victory, albeit a belated and unhappy one. Despite the delay, it yielded MacArthur significant strategic benefits. Not only did it advance SWPA farther up the New Guinea road, but it also helped protect Hollandia and contributed to the isolation of the big Japanese base of Manokwari on the Vogelkop.[122] Moreover, many in SWPA, like MacArthur, saw the Biak operation as the conclusion of the New Guinea campaign.[123] Patrick, for example, wrote to Krueger that the operation "just about puts everything in the bag."[124] After falling for MacArthur's deceptive communiqué, correspondent William Dunn broadcast on 28 May: "The Japanese are through in New Guinea. . . . The landings on Biak . . . are rightly described as the cork in the bottle, and as soon as the three enemy airfields on the island are in our possession the 5th Air Force will be in operation from bases less than a thousand miles from the southern tip of Mindanao."[125]

These observers were partially right but still a good deal from the whole truth. To be sure, after Biak there was no effective Japanese opposition to SWPA's subsequent westward advances, but this was as much due to MacArthur's shrewd leapfrog strategy that surrounded Manokwari as to the Biak operation. While contributing to the implementation of this policy, the Biak invasion was merely one factor among many that made its execution possible.

Looking back at the Biak operation after the war, most SWPA officers attributed their problems to skilled Japanese use of the island's peculiar terrain, which was ready-made for defense.[126] This was true, but there was more to it than that. Throughout the operation's early stages, inadequate intelligence and reconnaissance, faulty tactics, overconfidence, and a lack of communications between Fuller and his subordinates, who did not understand MacArthur's desire for speed, hindered the American effort. All these problems, when combined, played a role in preventing SWPA from winning the battle on time. Even so, since the New Guinea offensive was ultimately successful and MacArthur used this victory to talk the JCS into underwriting a Philippines liberation campaign, Biak, like Wakde-Sarmi, faded from memory.

EIGHT

NOEMFOOR: MOVING CLOSER TO THE TARGET

Even before Fuller's troops splashed ashore onto Biak, ignorant of the ordeal they would soon confront, GHQ was mulling over whether to occupy Noemfoor Island, seventy-five miles further west. Kenney and Whitehead liked the idea. Even with Hollandia, Wakde, and Biak in American possession, Kenney's forces still needed additional airfields to station their 5th AAF and RAAF units, as well as all those 13th AAF planes in the process of redeployment from the Solomons and Admiralties.[1] Noemfoor was near SWPA's front lines, so planes positioned there would be more valuable to future operations than those still located in far-off eastern New Guinea. In addition, the island possessed three partially completed Japanese airfields—Kamiri and Kornasoren in the north, and Namber on the west coast—that, if captured, the AAF could quickly convert to American use. Operating from Noemfoor, the AAF could easily strike at the Vogelkop, slated for SWPA invasion in late July, and Halmahera Island, the last major roadblock before Mindanao.[2]

Fuller's Biak troubles helped to tip the balance in favor of invading Noemfoor. The Japanese were using the island as a way station to infiltrate men and materiel to Biak, prolonging the struggle there.[3] A SWPA attack would put an end to that. Moreover, in American hands, Noemfoor could act as a shield for SWPA's forces in the Geelvink, enabling the AAF to dominate the sea lanes to the west, making it all the more difficult for the Japanese to launch another Kon-like naval sortie. It all made sense to MacArthur, who on 15 June authorized an assault by the end of the month. In a letter to Marshall, MacArthur summed up his thinking: "Possession of [Noemfoor's] airfields will give added breadth and depth to our air deployment and will further penetrate and dislocate enemy's main supply and defense axis."[4]

As usual, it was Krueger's job to translate MacArthur's directives into reality. GHQ told the 6th Army commander to use an RCT from the 6th Division, now fighting at Wakde-Sarmi, for the operation. Krueger, however, wanted Sibert's men for the Vogelkop assault, so he got MacArthur to substitute instead Patrick's 158th RCT, now recovering from its horrific Lone Tree Hill experience. As for reserves, Krueger put the 34th RCT and 503rd Parachute Infantry Regiment on standby, just in case anything went wrong. Altogether, the 6th Army commander planned to throw some 13,000 combat and service troops at Noemfoor, surely enough to overwhelm its meager 2000-man Japanese garrison.

In this operation, SWPA had another thing in its favor besides numbers: topography. For military planners, Noemfoor was easy on the eyes, especially in comparison with its Geelvink Bay companion to the east. Spherical in shape, twelve to fifteen miles in diameter, and almost totally flat, Noemfoor was covered with rain forest and little else. It possessed no dominating coral ridges or highly defensible caves to make things difficult for attacking GIs. Mother nature's only real obstacle, in fact, was a thick coral reef that surrounded most of the island.

These topographical and numerical advantages, however, were somewhat offset, at least in theory, by local garrison commander Colonel Suesada Shimizu's knowledge that the Americans were going to attack soon.[5] Krueger reasoned that with American forces now on Biak, it would be obvious to everyone, including the Japanese, that Noemfoor was SWPA's next target, so he sent in the Alamo Scouts to supplement the AAF's often faulty air reconnaissance photographic intelligence.[6] On 23 June the Japanese spotted one of the two scouting parties near Kamiri, searching for information on the island and its reef, and Shimizu quickly deduced SWPA's intentions. He initially expected an attack in the Kamiri area, but he eventually shifted his attention to Kornasoren as the likelier target.[7] The Scouts had been there for two days, and although they measured the reef and decided that Japanese strength was centered on Kamiri, they did not get much intelligence on tidal movements, the depth of the water over the reef, or possible boat channels.[8] This prompted Barbey to later observe that aerial and submarine reconnaissance could have done a better job—and without alerting the Japanese.[9]

In addition to the Alamo Scouts, SWPA used its other intelligence sources, most notably air reconnaissance and Ultra. In fact, it was an AAF photo recon mission that had first discovered the three airfields, back in late March, and revealed that two of them were in good enough shape to be worth taking.[10] Ultra, for its part, worked well enough to enable Willoughby to estimate with reasonable accuracy that there were about 1700 Japanese troops on Noemfoor, of whom around 700 were combat personnel.[11] Krueger accepted this figure but believed that the Japanese might reinforce the island to as many as 3250 men by the time SWPA invaded.[12]

Ultra also told Krueger that Shimizu expected an attack, which was why he anticipated that the Japanese might strengthen the garrison. GHQ, however, thought this unlikely since Noemfoor, like Wakde-Sarmi and Biak, was beyond the enemy's strategic pale.[13] At any rate, Krueger wanted to take the island fast, before any reinforcements showed up, so he was eager to meet MacArthur's 30 June deadline.[14] Unfortunately, logistics thwarted the 6th Army commander. In mid-June SWPA was stretched thin, with continuing operations on Biak, Wakde-Sarmi, and along the Driniumor River near Aitape. There was not enough amphibious shipping to go around, which was one reason why Krueger placed the 503rd Parachute Infantry Regiment in reserve. In addition, the Navy's destroyers and cruisers were busy refueling and rearming in the Admiralties. Besides, Barbey believed that the troops required more rehearsal time.[15] Kenney also wanted a delay so he could bring more of Biak's airstrips into action to better support the operation. Thus browbeaten, Krueger agreed to postpone the attack until 2 July, and got MacArthur to okay his decision.

If Krueger could not rely on celerity to take Noemfoor quickly, then he would resort to that old American Army standby: overwhelming firepower. Eschewing all tactical subtlety, Krueger decided to blast his way through the heart of the Japanese defenses at Kamiri airdrome. This, he thought, would help cut American losses by splitting the hopefully dazed enemy between there and Namber airfield to the south, enabling Patrick's men to deal with the isolated segments one at a time.[16] Besides, the reef was narrowest there, and getting ashore intact, as Krueger knew, was half the battle. To accomplish this task, simple to envision but hard to implement, Krueger arranged for the heaviest preliminary bombardment SWPA had ever undertaken. It would last an hour longer than usual, giving the Navy, ESBs, and AAF plenty of time and daylight to work over the beach. That was the plan and the reasoning behind it, but when a young officer asked Colonel Erle Sandlin, the 158th infantry commander, why they did not simply land directly east of the airfield and avoid the Japanese defenses, the battle-hardened Sandlin replied, "Because it's too damn far to walk."[17]

Kenney no doubt would have appreciated Sandlin's humor and determination, but he did not like Krueger's idea at all. Like Krueger, he and Whitehead believed that the Japanese were reinforcing Noemfoor. They did not think that the 158th RCT would be able to take the island by itself. In fact, Kenney wrote to Whitehead, "If it were not for the confidence that I have in your flattening the defenses before the infantry gets in, I would be willing to bet that the show would be a flop."[18] As MacArthur's air chief saw things, the infantry would need all the AAF support it could get. Fortunately, Kenney, who felt that air power could cure the common cold if someone was willing to take the time to discover the connection, was ready to provide it. Throughout late June AAF planes from Wakde, Owi, Hollandia, and Biak pounded Noemfoor and other Japanese targets in western New Guinea, as well as all the barges they could find. By the end of the month there were only fifty-seven enemy planes in northwest New Guinea, of which twelve were serviceable.[19] Krueger's men might face opposition, but not from the air. Nor did AAF support cease on D-Day at the water's edge. That July Kenney's men flew 402 sorties and dropped 375 tons of ordinance on Noemfoor.[20]

Overwhelming Application of American Firepower

In his heart of hearts, Kenney undoubtedly believed that his AAF played the key role in the New Guinea campaign, but of course SWPA operations were interservice affairs involving land, sea, and air forces to varying degrees. All three elements, however, shared a common affinity for massive firepower. Such firepower, in theory at least, permitted the military to expend metal in lieu of soldiers, whose voting and taxpaying families took a dim view of high casualties when some other solution, no matter how expensive, presented itself.

To be sure, as Nimitz and his subordinates over in the POA could attest, this firepower-for-manpower formula did not always work. Indeed, it was often counterproductive in that it made the soldiers overly dependent on artillery and air support, stifling individual initiative. Krueger may or may not have been aware of these drawbacks, but he was in a hurry to get Noemfoor's airfields. He did not have the inclination or logistical luxury to overwhelm the island's Japanese defenders with manpower, or the time to maneuver, so instead he relied on firepower.

To that end, on the morning of 2 July, Kenney's B-24s, B-25s, and A-20s pounded the Kamiri area hard, including the almost simultaneous detonation of 300 1000-pound bombs just before the landing. Offshore, the 7th Fleet moved in to work over what remained. One heavy cruiser, two light cruisers, eighteen destroyers, and three LCI rocket ships threw 12,000 shells and 800 rockets at Kamiri and other targets. In all, the preliminary

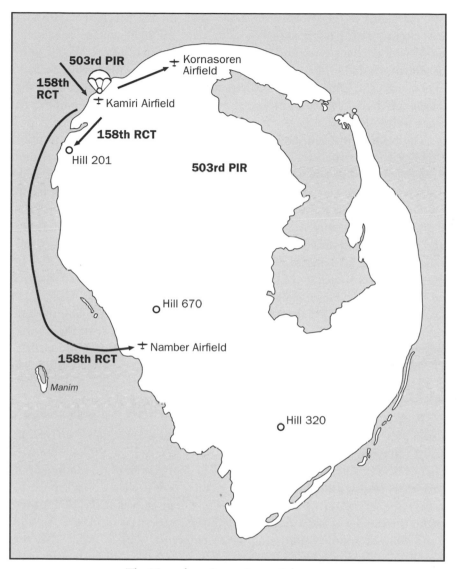

The Noemfoor Operation, 2 July 1944

bombardment was nearly three times heavier than military planners considered necessary to attack a lightly defended area.[21]

In this case, such a massive application of firepower had its intended effect, although Japanese demoralization and disorganization helped a lot. Except for a few scattered mortar rounds, not a shot greeted the two 158th

RCT battalions as they headed the 2000 yards for the beach. The morning was cloudy, with passing showers, calm seas, and light winds. This, combined with all the smoke and dust kicked up by the big preliminary bombardment, obscured the beach. SWPA, however, had learned from its Biak experience. This time control boats pointed white flood lights toward the beach, and buoys placed in the water beforehand marked the landing craft route to the shore.

The biggest problem, however, was not the Japanese or beach identification but rather the 150-yard-thick coral reef between the task force and Kamiri airfield. The reef was full of hidden potholes and fissures, some very deep, which helped mire landing craft. Even so, the troops got through, and on land all went well. The 2nd Battalion, disembarking on the left, or east, flank, encountered some forty shellshocked Japanese, who ran out of a cave and milled around until killed by the GIs' fire. The 158th RCT quickly overran Kamiri and set up a defensive perimeter. Buffaloes proved invaluable in mopping up resistance to the east of the airstrip, serving as armored support and outflanking Japanese defensive positions there from the rear.[22] Red grenade smoke marked the advance of American forces, enabling the ESB support battery to keep a step ahead of the attacking GIs with their hardhitting rockets. By the end of the day, not only was valuable Kamiri airfield in American hands, but its acquisition had cost SWPA only three killed, nineteen wounded, and two injured, demonstrating that overwhelming firepower, when applied against a disillusioned foe, can yield fast results.

Back at the beach things went well, too, despite that reef, which naval demolition teams went to work blasting channels through. Even so, six trucks, five small trailers, and two jeeps sank in unseen potholes, although engineers later retrieved most of them. The reef was hard on landing craft propellers, hulls, and shafts as well. In fact, in less than a week only 16 LCMs were serviceable. By 1750, when shore activity was suspended for the night, the engineers had safely unloaded some 7100 men, 500 vehicles, and 2200 tons of supplies and equipment, emptying 5 of 8 LSTs.[23] Nearby Kamiri airstrip proved useful by serving as a lateral road, freeing up engineers for other tasks. Scattered enemy mortar fire in the morning set ablaze a DUKW and exploded a truckload of ammunition, but this reminder of Japanese capabilities probably speeded up, rather than retarded, the unloading process.[24] Finally, the complete lack of any enemy air opposition also made the engineers' job easier. Kenney's AAF had destroyed most of those Japanese aircraft not diverted to the Marianas, and a weather front sealed Noemfoor off from the west and south, shielding the island from the few remaining enemy planes.

Tragic Airdrop

By mid-morning then, the Noemfoor operation seemed to be going well. Patrick, however, was nervous. A prisoner claimed that there were as many as 3500–7000 Japanese on the island, considerably above SWPA estimates of enemy strength.[25] The 158th RCT commander, perhaps still haunted by his Lone Tree Hill ordeal a little more than a month before, when he ran into far more Japanese than he expected, decided better safe than sorry. That morning he radioed Krueger for help. He wanted the 503rd Parachute Infantry, which could get there fast, and added that Kamiri airstrip would make a good dropzone.[26] Krueger, for his part, had always intended to deploy the 503rd on Noemfoor unless Patrick refused it, so that afternoon he okayed the request and ordered the unit readied.[27]

By the end of the day, Patrick had second thoughts about his prisoner's information. Other captured Japanese, as well as a Javanese slave laborer, who was presumably more trustworthy, did not confirm the earlier report of all those enemy forces. Back at GHQ, Willoughby also doubted the one prisoner's report. He wrote, "This [figure] is considered very high in view of the absence of any strong opposition to our landing and during our early advance inland."[28] Even so, Patrick still wanted the 503rd, which under his command could permit him to seize Noemfoor's two remaining Japanese-held airfields quickly, to blot out his recent failure at Lone Tree Hill once and for all.[29] So now, although he suspected that there were no large numbers of Japanese to deploy the 503rd against, he believed he could still use the unit productively.

The 503rd Parachute Infantry Regiment was a longtime SWPA outfit and had a good fighting reputation, having done well in combat the previous year at Nadzab.[30] Besides, airborne outfits, with their selectively chosen personnel and rigorous training, tended to have great morale. For Krueger, the immediate problem was that the logistics-strapped AAF lacked the aircraft to send the whole unit in at once. Instead, Krueger ordered them to Noemfoor a battalion at a time, one a day, with the 1st Battalion leading off the next day, 3 July.

Jumping that morning, one paratrooper described his experience: "After leaving the plane my chute carried me toward the jagged wreckage of a Jap airplane. I barely had time to climb my risers (spill air from one side of the parachute) so as to slip (drift) away from the wreckage. I let the chute snap full open again, and hit the coral airstrip just as the chute popped full open. This was the softest landing ever, like jumping off a 2 or 3 feet chair."[31] Unhappily, many others were not so lucky. Although Kamiri airfield was in American hands, Patrick's men had not had time to remove from the runway all the wreckage and debris the Japanese left behind. Realizing this, Patrick wanted the C-47s to fly in single file so the paratroopers could land on a narrow strip already cleared. Unfortunately, the 503rd did not get the message in time, so the planes came in two abreast and dropped the men over a wider area, scattering them amid debris, wreckage, and blasted trees. An AAF smokescreen, designed to protect the descending paratroopers from Japanese snipers, blew back over the airfield, further obscuring their view. To complicate matters even more, the planes came in at only 400 feet, which, while improving landing accuracy, gave the paratroopers little time to slow their descent. In the end, of the 739 men who jumped, 72 were injured by debris or the rapid descent onto the coral airstrip, including 31 severe fractures.[32]

Not surprisingly, Krueger, who, for all his gruffness empathized with the average GI more than most officers, having been one himself way back before the turn of the century, was upset by the incident when he learned the details that afternoon. He wanted things done right next day for the 3rd Battalion, so he ordered Patrick to remove all the debris from Kamiri and made sure that this time the C-47s flew in single file. On 4 July only fifty-six men were injured in the drop, most from hitting the hard coral strip at such a low altitude. It was an improvement over yesterday's performance, but not by much, and it was certainly nothing to be proud of.[33] In fact, the 503rd had lost more men on Noemfoor than the 158th, and without hearing a shot fired in anger. Among the 503rd's casualties were one battalion and three company commanders. Looking the situation over, 503rd chief Colonel George M. Jones recommended that Krueger ship his remaining battalion over. Krueger agreed, and the 2nd Battalion was flown to Biak and taken to Noemfoor on LCIs. It arrived on 11 July, long after it was needed; if, indeed, it had ever been needed at all.

In fact, the 158th probably could have successfully mopped up Noemfoor on its own. Although the 503rd made the job easier and quicker, once the airfields were in SWPA's hands the operation was, from GHQ's strategic point of view, over. To be sure, SWPA had no other pressing business for the paratroopers, but supplying them at Noemfoor took up logistical resources needed elsewhere.

Pursuing Shimizu

The GIs of the 158th RCT may or may not have looked sympathetically upon the paratroopers' plight, but if they did, such forbearance did not last long. As far as Patrick's men were concerned, they were doing most of the fighting and suffering the bulk of the casualties. Aside from breaking a good many bones, the 503rd seemed most proficient at garnering publicity that rightfully belonged to the long-suffering 158th.[34] So, while the paratroopers picked themselves up from Kamiri—or, in all too many cases, were picked up on a litter by someone else—the 158th got back to the business of taking those airfields. Kamiri was already in American hands, of course, having been overrun, quite literally, on D-Day. The Japanese, however, still held Kornasoren and Namber, so Patrick turned his attention to those targets. The 158th's 3rd Battalion seized Kornasoren on 4 July with little opposition. Namber, farther down the coast, took a little longer, and in fact required a shore-to-shore amphibious assault by the 158th's 2nd Battalion on 6 July. Backed by three destroyers, six B-25s, and an LCI rocket ship, the GIs landed unopposed on the airfield's northern strip and occupied it with practically no enemy resistance.

While the 158th's 2nd and 3rd battalions assaulted Patrick's primary objectives, the 1st Battalion fought the operation's only real battle, just south of Kamiri at Hill 201, named not for its height but for the number of Japanese killed there.[35] The hill overlooked the Japanese Garden, an area 500 yards in diameter cultivated by the enemy for food. Except for the hill itself, there were few trees around but lots of tall papaya, taro, and cassava plants. The 1st Battalion moved in on 4 July and established a defensive perimeter for the night. Commander Lieutenant Colonel Paul Shoemaker, seeing some Japanese in the vicinity, suspected that the enemy might attack his unit, so he made sure his men were ready. He was right; the Japanese assaulted the southwest perimeter just after moonset, around 0500. The enemy charge was poorly organized and coordinated, and the GIs, who withheld their fire until the last minute, cut them down in droves. After two hours, the surviving Japanese withdrew. American losses were negligible. In fact, the engagement was so one-sided that troops manning other parts of the line did not even know there was a battle going on and at dawn were shocked by the number of enemy corpses scattered at the point of attack.

Hill 201 broke the back of Japanese opposition on Noemfoor. Or, more accurately, it decimated a garrison already tottering from demoralization, the impact of repeated AAF attacks, and a brutal preliminary bombardment. From that point on, the combat phase of the operation consisted of mopping up scattered Japanese, with the 158th clearing the island's southern half and the 503rd patrolling the north. Normally troops undertook such activity with a minimum of enthusiasm, but in this case their interest was sparked by rumors that Japanese commander Colonel Shimizu possessed a 300-year-old jeweled sword, ripe for the taking by any GI who could pry it from his dead hand and keep it away from overly curious officers.[36] Throughout July and into August, the GIs chased Shimizu's dwindling force, fighting skirmishes at Hill 670, Hill 380, and elsewhere. They were aided by natives, who eagerly helped guide American patrols and capture enemy soldiers in revenge for poor treatment at the hands of the Japanese.[37] In the end, the 158th and 503rd secured the island, but they never found Shimizu or his jeweled sword, both of which are presumably still in the Noemfoor interior, assuming that the latter ever existed anywhere beyond some morale officer's imagination.

While combat patrols beat the bushes in search of a glint of ruby or sapphire, Patrick got busy repairing those three airdromes. This was not an easy task. Kamiri was in adequate shape, but Namber was so rough and ungraded that the aviation engineers abandoned work on it in favor of Kornasoren. Even Kornasoren, however, was described as "only a location," not an airfield.[38] Still, by working around the clock with the aid of natives and combat troops, the engineers got the airfields in condition in time to support SWPA's attack on the Vogelkop. Kamiri was ready for fighters on 16 July, and the first bombers landed at Kornasoren ten days later.

Noemfoor itself, or its coast anyway, made the aviation engineers' job all the more difficult, at least indirectly. Noemfoor was the worst unloading point in all of SWPA. Even after Navy demolition teams blasted channels for LSTs, the thick reef continued to torment landing craft. By 22 July, 80 percent of the DUKWs, vital for unloading, were out of action, and there were no spare parts to fix them.[39] The eccentric tides did not help matters much either. Since top priority went toward building the airfields, there was not enough manpower to unload vessels, although combat troops and natives were both pressed into duty. Many of the former, as usual, used the opportunity to pilfer shipholds.[40] By 13 July the GIs were unloading only 1500 tons a day, and as late as 12 August AAF movement into the island was 69 percent behind schedule for personnel, 76 percent for vehicles, and 66 percent for most everything else.[41] Not surprisingly, Noemfoor never became a major SWPA base.

Strategic Evaluation

Krueger declared the Noemfoor operation over on 31 August, after the Americans suffered 65 killed and 343 wounded.[42] Japanese losses included the entire 2000-man garrison, as well as the three airfields, whose acquisition was SWPA's primary goal. In American hands, Noemfoor's airstrips not only extended AAF range throughout western New Guinea, Halmahera, and Netherlands East Indies but also reduced aircraft congestion on Biak and Wakde. Moreover, Noemfoor's occupation put an end to Japanese infiltration into Biak.

As for the assaulting troops, both the 158th and 503rd went on to fight in the Philippines. The 158th landed at Lingayen Bay and later liberated Luzon's Caramoan peninsula, and the 503rd spearheaded the bloody assault on Corregidor in Manila Bay. Patrick also went to the Philippines, but not with the 158th. Promoted to command the 6th Division, he served in Luzon until a Japanese machine gunner put an abrupt end to his career and his life.

The decision to invade Noemfoor must be viewed in the context of the concurrent Biak operation. In the end, it is doubtful that attacking Noemfoor to eliminate haphazard and sporadic enemy infiltration to Biak was worthwhile, especially since Eichelberger had broken the back of Japanese resistance on the island by the time Patrick's men went ashore. When MacArthur made the decision to assault Noemfoor, however, affairs on Biak were still touch and go. Also, while better intelligence might have shown the shabby condition of Noemfoor's airfields, SWPA believed, correctly, that it was easier to storm and improve the island's substandard airfields than to build new ones from scratch. And, as Kenney had hoped, once repaired, these airfields extended AAF range and alleviated congestion elsewhere. Noemfoor, in short, was another step along SWPA's road to the China-Formosa-Luzon area. Although not as successful as, say, the Hollandia operation, it still moved MacArthur closer to his target.

NINE

DRINIUMOR RIVER: A STRATEGICALLY WORTHLESS OPERATION?

While MacArthur's amphibious juggernaut rolled westward, gobbling up or bypassing scattered enemy garrisons along the way, Lieutenant General Hatazo Adachi pondered his 18th Army's plight in its Hansa Bay–Wewak bastion. Right after SWPA struck Hollandia, 2nd Area Army commander Anami, back at Manokwari, instructed Adachi to withdraw his forces to western New Guinea. The orders were canceled in mid-May, leaving Adachi and his 55,000 troops to their fate, or at least their own devices.

Adachi, however, was not about to surrender his destiny without a fight. Although he admitted, "I cannot find any means nor method which will solve this situation strategically or technically," he went on to add, "Therefore, I intend to overcome this [strategic dilemma] by relying on our Japanese Bushido."[1] If this sounded ominously like Adachi was contemplating an army-wide banzai charge, it was because he had something like that in mind. Isolated in eastern New Guinea, the 18th Army possessed a finite and dwindling supply of manpower, ammunition, equipment, and rations. Adachi realized that to remain where he was, passively on the defensive, was a form of deferred suicide, especially with the Australians clawing at his forces from the east. On the other hand, taking the offensive might serve Japan by siphoning resources from SWPA's westward advance, slowing down MacArthur's campaign and buying time for his compatriots to build up their defenses in western New Guinea.[2]

Scanning his maps, Adachi zeroed in on Aitape as his most practicable target. Ideally, he would have liked to attack Hollandia, the nexus of SWPA operations, but he lacked the resources to do so. Aitape, was comparatively close at hand, however, and assaulting it might convince the Americans that its seizure was the first step in a Japanese offensive toward all-important Hollandia. This, in turn, might cause SWPA to hurry reinforcements to the area that were otherwise slated to attack the Japanese defense line in western New Guinea.[3] As Adachi put it, just before he launched his offensive, "The presence of the enemy in Aitape affords us a last favorable chance to display effectively the fighting power which this Army still possesses, and to contribute toward the destruction of the enemy's strength. It is obvious that, if we resort from the first to mere delaying tactics, the result will be that we shall never be able to make effective use of our full strength."[4]

In May, then, elements of the 18th Army's three divisions lurched into motion, heading westward. It was not easy, though. Adachi's forces had enough supplies and equipment for one operation, but his men were short of trucks, so they had to carry almost everything by hand through the almost trackless New Guinea jungle, a slow and laborious process. To make matters worse, SWPA planes and PT boats, prowling in the air and offshore, shot up Japanese concentrations whenever the opportunity presented itself. Nevertheless, the 20th, 41st, and part of the 51st divisions, some 20,000 men, gradually closed in on Aitape throughout May and June.

Early Skirmishes

Krueger worried about Aitape's vulnerability to just such a Japanese attack.[5] Shortly after Doe's 163rd RCT seized the place as part of the multi-pronged Reckless operation, Krueger reinforced it with the 32nd Division's 127th RCT. Doe's men left soon after to pursue bigger adventures further west at Wakde and Biak, so to fill the resulting gap at Aitape Krueger ordered in the rest of the 32nd Division, commanded by Major General William H. Gill.

The 32nd Division, built from the Wisconsin and Michigan national guards, did not have a very good reputation, although in all fairness it was more sinned against than sinning. It had been in SWPA a long time and had participated in the Buna operation back in late 1942. The inexperienced unit won the battle through brutal attrition, but it suffered enormous casualties and had to be withdrawn to Australia for retraining, reorganization, and refurbishing. Gill worked hard to get it back into shape, both physically and mentally, and now both he and GHQ felt it was ready to fight again. One GHQ report stated, "It is believed that this division is anxious to give an excellent account of itself in its next combat action."[6] This remained to be seen, but the outfit was full of fresh battle-experienced officers and men, including some who had seen action at Saidor earlier in the year. As Gill saw it, his primary mission was to defend Aitape's Tadji airfield.[7] Upon learning that the Japanese were slowly closing in, he requested reinforcements. He knew that the 43rd Division was on its way, but it was not scheduled to arrive until July, and by then the Japanese might have already overrun both Aitape and his rebuilt division.[8]

Gill's urgency was spurred on by a series of skirmishes between his men and the approaching Japanese in May and early June.[9] Elements of the 127th RCT, stationed at Nyaparake, east of both Aitape and the Driniumor River, ran into Japanese troops in mid-May. Japanese pressure told, and some American units were surrounded in the subsequent fighting, but they managed to cut their way out and fall back to Yakamul, down the coast. After that Japanese activity inexplicably declined until the end of the month, when they hit American positions at Yakamul and in the interior around Afua, at Driniumor River's headwaters. On 4 June the Japanese assaulted units of the 126th RCT at Yakamul, inflicting some 100 casualties. The American garrison there evacuated the place by sea the following day under heavy fire, carrying away or destroying everything of value just before the final enemy rush. The Japanese advanced to the Driniumor, skirmishing with the retreating Americans, but on 6 June they broke off contact again and melted back into the jungle.

Willoughby's Ambiguous Intelligence Warnings

Later that fall, long after the guns along the Driniumor had cooled, one of Willoughby's subordinates wrote: "Perhaps the most outstanding intelligence furnished by Central Bureau, Brisbane, concerned the Aitape and Wewak operations. . . . G-2 has said that never has a commander gone into battle knowing so much about the enemy as did the Allied commander at Aitape on 10–11 July 1944."[10] As usual with Willoughby's operation, this was a good deal from the whole truth. To be sure, MacArthur's G-2 predicted correctly that the Japanese would attack Aitape, but he had a hard time determining the assault date. His inaccurate divinations confused American field commanders along the Driniumor, contributing to early Japanese successes.

Throughout May, Willoughby kept a close eye on Adachi's forces. Initially he doubted that the 18th Army would assault Aitape, especially after SWPA seized Wakde, which completely sealed off Adachi's men. As Willoughby saw it, the Japanese had little to gain strategically or logistically from assuming the offensive, although as usual he covered his tracks by adding that the desperate foe might try anything.[11] To Willoughby, the lack of Japanese patrol activity, their immense supply problems, and the difficulties in concentrating forces under the nose of American naval and air power all ruled out an assault on Aitape.[12] He said, "If the enemy had intended to attack Aitape, it is believed that he would have done so much earlier."[13] MacArthur's G-2 failed to realize that Adachi was trying not to win territory but to buy time—time for the Japanese to build a new defensive line on the western part of the island to protect the homeland from the relentless American onslaught.

Willoughby began to change his mind in late May as Ultra and other intelligence sources picked up signs of Adachi's impending offensive. Aitape was the obvious target, and Willoughby noted that the Japanese goal was probably to eliminate its garrison:[14] "Japanese pressure on our eastern flank at Aitape is increasing. Intelligence reports indicate that the enemy has strong forces (remnants of the 20th and 41st Divisions) moving in this direction."[15] Japanese skirmishing around Yakamul and Afua seemed to back this up. Besides, the enemy had the resources to undertake such an assault; he estimated that there were some 51,000 Japanese in Wewak, although the 6th Army put the figure at 60,000–65,000 men.[16]

Willoughby's certainty increased throughout June. The Japanese were clearly concentrating men and supplies, undoubtedly for an assault on Aitape.[17] As Willoughby viewed things, such Japanese activity "seem[s] tactically sound from which the intended attack on Aitape could develop. The present absence of active patrolling by the enemy may indicate that he is not yet prepared to launch an attack, but renewal of his former aggressiveness should be watched for, as it will probably mean that he is ready to commence the attack."[18] Putting all his information together, Willoughby concluded, "It appears that the attack on Aitape is scheduled for some time early in July or late June."[19]

Late June came and went, but the Japanese offensive failed to develop. Reevaluating his intelligence, Willoughby reset the attack day for between 1 and 10 July, and then, as the month wore on, he narrowed the date to 10 July.[20] By way of justifying his earlier error, he wrote, "The lack of any significant ground activity in our perimeter indicates that enemy preparations for an attack, if such is the plan, are not yet complete."[21] In the meantime, Willoughby watched and waited.

SWPA Prepares

To GHQ, the impending Japanese assault on Aitape was not so much a military as a political threat. Adachi lacked the power to stop the New Guinea amphibious juggernaut, but he could slow it down by compelling SWPA to divert resources from operations further west. From MacArthur's point of view, the deceleration of his advance was almost as bad as its termination. Unless he got to the China-Formosa-Luzon area ahead of or at the same time as Nimitz's POA offensive, he could not effectively argue in favor of a SWPA-led Philippines liberation campaign. Moreover, an active Japanese presence behind his lines could provide his innumerable enemies with ammunition against his future plans; MacArthur could hardly undertake the enormous task of liberating the Philippines when overlooked Japanese units like Adachi's possessed the power to threaten SWPA's lines of communication in New Guinea.

On this issue, however, MacArthur had Marshall's support, although for a different reason. Marshall wanted the 18th Army left alone if possible, and explained to MacArthur, "So long as 18th Jap army remains physically isolated and in radio communication with other Jap units it will continue to afford us valuable source for cryptoanalytic assistance. To the extent that it will not interfere with your present operations it is highly desirable that this situation be preserved and fully exploited."[22] Such forbearance from the chief of staff, whatever its cause, was comforting, but Marshall was only one voice among four on the JCS, and the others could still use Adachi's offensive as an excuse to pinch off MacArthur's offensive at Mindanao. Besides, the 18th Army *was* interfering with SWPA operations by slowing them down, so MacArthur wanted Adachi's forces eliminated as soon as possible.[23]

As usual, MacArthur's operational problem was Krueger's to solve. Like his chief, Krueger hoped to exterminate the Japanese threat to Aitape as quickly as possible. Doing so, however, required forthright and decisive action. As he saw it, SWPA should not wait around for Adachi to show up outside of Aitape before engaging him in battle. This not only would take too much valuable time but would also mean surrendering the initiative to the enemy, a cardinal military sin.[24] Instead, Krueger wanted to slug it out with the Japanese as far to the east as possible, enabling SWPA to maintain the initiative and prevent Adachi from possibly bypassing Aitape and striking directly at vital Hollandia.[25]

As evidence of an imminent Japanese assault accumulated, Krueger responded by sending reinforcements to Aitape, even though this stretched SWPA's logistical resources and diverted men from operations further west. The 43rd Division was already on its way from New Zealand, and Krueger got GHQ to speed up its movement. To fill the intervening gap, Krueger sent in the 112th Cavalry and 124th RCT. In all, Krueger planned to deploy eight RCTs against Adachi's two depleted divisions, assuming they all got there before the Japanese showed their hand. By forcing Krueger to concentrate SWPA forces on Aitape, Adachi succeeded in his mission, at least to an extent, even before his men got near their objective. Had it not been for Adachi's offensive, Krueger would have been able to deploy fresh American troops further west, sparing tired units like the 41st Division and the 158th RCT from repeated commitment to battle.

Brigadier General Julian W. Cunningham's 112th RCT, which arrived at Aitape on 28 June, was not really an RCT at all but a glorified independent cavalry regiment of some 1500 men formed from the Texas National Guard. The unit was dismounted before it was shipped overseas in July 1942, and in fact many of its men remained disgruntled about this.[26] Since their arrival in SWPA they had seen some action around the turn of the year at Arawe in New Britain. Although small in size, they were a welcome addition to the apprehensive Aitape garrison.

So too was the 31st Division's 124th RCT, under Colonel Edward M. Starr, which began disembarking on 3 July. Krueger had wanted to keep the 31st intact for future operations, but since the 112th was so small and the 43rd Division would not arrive at Aitape until mid-July, after the Japanese were supposed to attack, he ordered Starr's men in.[27] The 124th had reached New Guinea from the States on 20 February, ahead of the rest of the division. It had not seen any action, and in fact had not received any jungle training until it was shipped overseas.[28] Nevertheless, it had made a good impression on most observers. Whether or not it would live up to expectations remained to be seen.[29]

To command all these troops, Krueger ordered recently arrived Major General Charles P. Hall and his XI Corps headquarters to Aitape. The fifty-seven-year old Hall, nicknamed "Chink" by his fellow officers, was a solid professional with a reputation for good judgment, and he was highly regarded by almost everyone. Marshall thought a lot of him, as did MacArthur, who called him "entirely satisfactory."[30] He managed to get along with the prickly Krueger, mostly by obeying his orders, which is all the 6th Army commander asked of anyone.

One person who did not think much of Hall, however, was 32nd Division chief Gill, whom Hall superseded as commander at Aitape. Hall initially relegated Gill to mostly administration and supply duties, which only exacerbated the resentment he felt at being supplanted. Gill was hard put to understand how Hall and his people, fresh off the boat, could handle an assignment that called for an in-depth knowledge of jungle fighting. "Hall and his staff were untrained in this thing from the top down." Gill later said. "They had never had any combat like this. They didn't know anything about jungle fighting."[31] Gill's disillusionment only increased when the Japanese attack commenced, and he later claimed that Hall never really understood what was going on.[32]

Hall would have disagreed with Gill's assessment, of course, had he known about it. As it was, he had more important things on his mind than mollifying a disgruntled subordinate. On 27 June, the day he reached Aitape, he met with Krueger and Gill. Gill suggested that his men confront the Japanese at Aitape, not to the east. As he saw it, the Americans lacked the manpower for an attack, and supplying troops in the trackless jungle would be a logistical nightmare. The best thing to do, he said, was to let the Japanese beat their heads against well-prepared and -marked positions around the Aitape perimeter, which would maximize Japanese casualties while minimizing SWPA's. Krueger, however, said no. Hiding behind the Aitape defenses meant surrendering both time and initiative to the Japanese. Krueger had stretched SWPA thin to provide Hall with reinforcements, so he wanted results fast, and those results could only be gained by taking the offensive.[33] Hall's job, he said, was to protect Aitape and Tadji airdrome, conduct an active defense, and follow it up with a vigorous counterattack when his strength and tactical position permitted.[34] Krueger estimated that 20,000 Japanese would attack in three days, so Hall had better brace himself.[35]

Hall wanted to accommodate his superior's wishes, especially when the expected Japanese attack failed to materialize. Looking over the situation, he did not believe that the Japanese were as strong as Willoughby's intelligence indicated.[36] He hoped to use the newly arrived 124th RCT for an amphibious assault at Nyaparake on 13 July, which would link up with the attacking 32nd Division and the 112th RCT.[37] Caught between this amphibious anvil and the overland sledge, Adachi's forces would be pounded to pieces.

In the meantime, Hall reorganized the defenses around Aitape for all those newly arrived reinforcements. He established two defensive lines, one around Aitape to protect Tadji airdrome, and the other to the east on the Driniumor River, which was supposed to absorb the shock of any Japanese attack and then serve as a launching point for an American counterattack. In addition to the 126th RCT, the 533rd EBSR, and other engineer and logistical support units, Hall placed the 124th RCT around Aitape, from which it could act as a reserve for the Driniumor line and still be handy when he launched that amphibious assault he was planning. To the east, Hall deployed—or more accurately in the former case, kept—

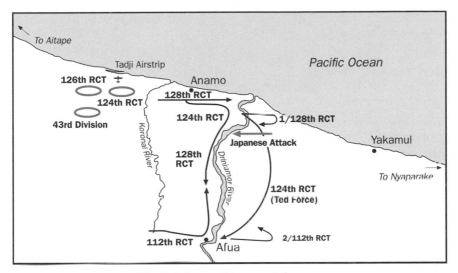

The Driniumor River, 10 July 1944

32nd Division elements and the 112th RCT along the Driniumor, with Cunningham's troopers to the south around Afua. He appointed 32nd Division assistant commander Brigadier General Clarence A. Martin to oversee the Driniumor line, and told him, "You will take vigorous action to provide maximum resistance to any westward movement between Driniumor and Nigia Rivers without sacrificing your command."[38] Hall thought he was ready to receive an attack, and if the Japanese would leave him alone for a little while longer, he would beat them to the punch.

Hall's decision to divide his forces between Aitape and the Driniumor was a serious tactical mistake. He deployed his troops along the river as if he expected them to act as a tripwire defense that would sound the alarm for the balance of his forces around Aitape. Krueger, however, believed that the units along the Driniumor should be able to repel a Japanese assault on their own and then swing over to the offensive to crush Adachi.[39] Martin, with the small 112th and only parts of the 32nd Division at his disposal, lacked the power to do this, and his orders implied otherwise anyway. By placing so many men back at Aitape, a prudent Hall undoubtedly strengthened the place and made it all but impossible for Adachi to seize it. In doing so, however, he not only weakened the Driniumor line, rendering it vulnerable to Japanese penetration, but also crippled his ability to carry out Krueger's orders. As events would demonstrate, Martin's undermanned force lacked the strength to seize the initiative when the Japanese showed up. Instead of a quick and decisive victory, Hall found himself locked in a brutal six-week battle of attrition.

The Big Japanese Assault

While Hall perfected his plans, the 32nd Division and 112th RCT continued to dig in behind the Driniumor. There was nothing spectacular about the river; it was like most others in New Guinea, with an inconsistent depth, width, and flow rate, depending on the season. Right now it was about 100 yards wide and shallow enough to wade across. In fact, the Driniumor was probably the friendliest landmark around. Dense jungle extended as far as the eye could see, which was not much. There were no vantage or observation points and no fields of fire. The area was not the friendliest environment for the mobility- and firepower-loving Americans to fight in, at least not until their weapons worked over the jungle enough to provide the clear view they required to inflict something more than collateral damage. In the meantime, the Americans relied on photo maps to locate their positions and targets. As it turned out, such maps were valueless unless they showed the strip of ocean at the top.[40] Supplying troops in the dense jungle was difficult unless they were stationed near the ocean. Native supply trains frequently got lost or were ambushed by Japanese infiltrators, and airdrops were inaccurate. The hot, humid, and suffocating climate contributed to the miserable environment. One officer said, "The terrain is undescribable."[41] It was not a good place to fight a battle, but neither were most places in New Guinea.

Even worse for the GIs, in early July the tempo of fighting between American and Japanese patrols beyond the Driniumor increased, as did enemy infiltration, which put soldiers as far away as Aitape at risk.[42] The Japanese gradually drove American patrols back across the river, sealing themselves off from prying enemy eyes. Superb Japanese camouflage tactics also made it hard for the AAF to see what was going on, and Willoughby's intelligence, now predicting a 10 July attack, had been wrong twice already.

All remained quiet on the Driniumor in early July except for incessant skirmishes. Neither Krueger nor Hall was surprised. By now Krueger did not expect a Japanese attack.[43] Hall, for his part, did not anticipate one anytime soon.[44] As Krueger saw it, if the Japanese were not going to come out of the jungle, then the Americans should go in after them. First, however, XI Corps had to find out exactly where behind the Driniumor the enemy was hiding, so on 8 July Krueger ordered Hall to send a reconnaissance-in-force out to locate them.[45] Hall thought this was a bad idea,[46] but orders were orders, so he told Martin to dispatch the 128th RCT's 1st Battalion and the 112th's 2nd Squadron across the Driniumor for a look. Hall doubted that they would run into much trouble because he did not think the Japanese were deployed for battle.[47]

Gill, Martin, and Cunningham were not nearly so sure. Since, unlike Krueger and Hall, they were not privy to Willoughby's information—Gill later called G-2 intelligence "very slim"[48]—they relied mostly on those American patrols the Japanese had pushed back across the Driniumor. As Gill and Martin saw it, the Japanese were going to attack—and soon. Indeed, on 10 July a Japanese soldier captured near Yakamul said that an assault was imminent, which merely confirmed Gill's and Martin's views.[49] Neither of them liked the reconnaissance-in-force idea at all, especially since the dispatched patrols would severely deplete the Driniumor position.[50] Hall was reluctant to move reinforcements up to the river from Aitape to replace the departing men because he was not sure the Japanese were even out there, and he wanted to keep the 124th RCT nearby for his amphibious assault.[51] Gill and Martin hoped to wait until the 43rd Division arrived before they sent any troops across the Driniumor, but Hall, under pressure from Krueger, refused, although he permitted a two-day delay.[52]

On the morning of 10 July the 2nd Squadron and 1st Battalion crossed the Driniumor in search of Japanese. Leaving Afua, the 112th troopers encountered no enemy. Rough terrain hindered their march, however, so they moved only two miles before digging in for the night. To the north, the 1st Battalion had a more eventful time. They pushed eastward down the coast until they ran into Japanese roadblocks. Heavy artillery fire shook the enemy loose, but resistance increased as the day wore on. By nightfall the 1st Battalion was a mile short of Yakamul, where it dug in. Back at Aitape, Hall was unhappy with both reconnoitering units. He suspected that they had not pushed hard enough, so he ordered them to continue the advance next day.[53]

Gill and Martin were right. Adachi was about ready to attack, having accomplished the logistically impressive feat of moving his two-plus divisions and their equipment nearly 100 miles across the dense jungle terrain almost entirely by hand—and under the noses of American air and sea power. Looking over the American position, now that his troops had driven the American patrols back across the Driniumor, Adachi decided on a two-pronged assault. The 41st Division would lead off by driving straight across the Driniumor while the 20th and part of the 51st enveloped the

American line around Afua. He scheduled the attack for the night of 10–11 July, only hours after Hall stripped his Driniumor line to supply the men for the reconnaissance-in-force Krueger ordered.

All day long on 10 July Americans along the Driniumor of all ranks and stations picked up indications that the Japanese were about to launch a big attack, and all took actions in accordance with their positions. Martin ordered his men to keep alert, although this hardly compensated for the troops Hall had removed for Krueger's reconnaissance-in-force. Just before midnight, right after Hall radioed 6th Army headquarters that the reconnaissance-in-force had discovered nothing, the Japanese attacked after a short but intense artillery barrage.[54] Adachi aimed at the center of the Driniumor line, throwing a whole regiment at the 128th RCT's 2nd Battalion. Previously registered American artillery, machine-gun, and mortar fire responded vigorously. Exploding shells blasted away the underbrush and, in conjunction with the tracers and starshells, exposed the massed enemy soldiers. The Japanese struggled across the waist-deep river and got hung up by American barbed wire. Even so, they managed to cut American communication lines, making it hard to coordinate the defense or even find out exactly what was happening.

Despite American firepower, which bloodied the Driniumor in a most gruesome fashion, enemy numbers told, and by 0300 the Japanese had broken a 1300-yard-wide hole in the center of the Driniumor River line and established themselves on some wooded high ground. The effort, exhausted the Japanese, however, so the night quieted for a couple hours while Adachi's men caught their breath. A new attack at 0500 expanded the gap in American lines to 2000 yards and placed a regiment on the west bank. The cost was high; some 3000 Japanese were killed or wounded that night, and in some places their dead dammed the river.[55] Dawn showed American and Japanese units intermingled up and down the length of the Driniumor, except to the south, where the Japanese had not made a serious effort. Even so, the Japanese had their bridgehead, and they laboriously began to swing their units north to Anamo, on the coast west of the Driniumor, and south toward Afua, to cut off American units still clinging to the river line.

Martin was not surprised by the Japanese assault, but he had a hard time figuring out what was going on. He knew the enemy had punched a hole in the line but not how big it was. He was, however, well aware that he had no reserve to plug it. As Martin saw the situation, he and his men had done their job, serving as a tripwire to warn of and slow down the Japanese offensive. Now he wanted to fall back two or three miles to the X-Ray-Koronal Creek area, as soon as he withdrew the two reconnaissance-in-force units, which were now behind enemy lines. From this new position, and with reinforcements, Martin believed that the Americans could repel the Japanese assault.[56]

Hall took a somewhat different view. He was conscious that a Japanese breakthrough might discredit MacArthur's entire offensive in the JCS's eyes, so he wanted to do things right, especially since his own career was on the line.[57] He did not think that the situation was as serious as Martin indicated.[58] In fact, he wanted the two reconnaissance-in-force units to remain where they were so they could continue the advance the next morning. Later, however, he changed his mind and told them to withdraw. Shortly after midnight he ordered Martin to fall back, but only if attacked by overwhelming numbers. Afterward Gill noted that in jungle combat it was impossible to discern enemy strength until it was too late, so Hall should simply have told Martin to retreat without any strings attached.[59] Gill and Martin were relieved by Hall's withdrawal order, but not the tough Cunningham, who wanted to stay at the Driniumor and fight it out, even if the AAF had to supply him by air.[60]

Cunningham would get his chance to test that proposition later, but for now he prepared to obey orders and fall back. As for Hall, right now he was worried about another subordinate. Martin's jittery reaction to the Japanese attack raised doubts in the XI Corps chief's mind as to his fitness to command. Martin had served bravely throughout the Buna operation, and most saw him as brilliant.[61] To Hall, however, Martin appeared played out, and he did not seem willing to put up the hard fight required to wrest the initiative from the Japanese and win the battle quickly. Hall suggested to Gill that they bring Martin in from the Driniumor for a rest. Gill, who perhaps saw an opportunity to get back into the thick of things, offered to take over at the front, and Hall agreed.[62]

Meanwhile, next morning along the Driniumor the Americans struggled to disengage. The 128th's 1st Battalion, near Yakamul, got its orders at 0135 and pulled out within the hour, reaching the Driniumor at dawn. Once there, Martin, still in command for now, ordered it to attack to the south to try to restore the river line. The Americans quickly ran into an ambush, so Martin told them to join the retreat westward, which they did. The tired Japanese did not interfere much as the Americans fell back. ESB landing craft scoured the coast, picking up isolated GIs cut off by the battle.

To the south, the other reconnaissance-in-force patrol, the 2nd Squadron, did not get its withdrawal orders until 0800 because of a communication breakdown. It still managed to get back to the Driniumor without much trouble, though. At the river, where they listened nervously to the ferocious battle to the north, Cunningham's men, including the 127th RCT's 3rd Battalion, fell back in two echelons to the X-Ray River, about 4000 yards to the west. The Japanese left them alone, but there was still a lot of confusion, and a driving rain did not help. Even so, by 12 July the Americans had successfully regrouped west of the Driniumor.

Back at Brisbane, Willoughby announced triumphantly, "The enemy counterattack on Aitape has commenced."[63] Next day MacArthur's G-2 congratulated himself: "From the above cumulative intelligence, it can be seen how logically the attack was built up and reported, giving us a very clear picture of the enemy's plan of attack prior to it actually being launched."[64] Hall's weary men, slogging westward in retreat, would probably have disagreed.

Closing the Gap

Krueger traveled to Aitape by Catalina plane the day after the big Japanese attack, breathing fire. As he saw it, the withdrawal was completely unnecessary; Martin's men should have held on at the Driniumor. Now the Japanese possessed the initiative, enabling them to threaten Tadji airfield, Hollandia, and even MacArthur's efforts to compel the JCS to underwrite a Philippines liberation campaign.[65]

Hall had expected such a reaction and so was ready with a counterattack formula designed to reclaim the initiative and mollify his boss. He planned to drive the Japanese back to the Driniumor in a two-pronged assault. A Northern Force, under Brigadier General Alexander N. Stark, Jr., would advance to the Driniumor along the coast with elements from the 128th and 124th RCTs. At the other end of the Driniumor, a Southern Force, under Cunningham—also known as "Baldy Force," after its commander's bare scalp—would retake Afua with his 112th RCT and part of the 127th. The 126th RCT would remain in reserve around Aitape. Once back along the Driniumor, Hall could concentrate on eliminating the Japanese in the area once and for all, removing this thorn in the side of MacArthur's New Guinea offensive. This satisfied Krueger, who returned to Hollandia to await the results.

Hall was prompt. Two days later, on 13 July, he kicked off his counteroffensive. Along the coast, a battalion from the 128th RCT attacked down the coastal trail at 0730. The spearheading unit ran into an enemy ambush at the outset. Tank destroyers and LCMs moved in to rake the

Japanese position, but it was really artillery that shattered the opposition, permitting the advance to continue. Fortunately for the GIS, ESB assault craft covered their left flank, lashing at Japanese units from the sea. By 1800 the 128th was back on the Driniumor, where it dug in.

To the immediate south, two 124th RCT battalions, without the luxury of either naval support or previous combat experience, had a rougher time. On 11 July its troops were preparing for Hall's amphibious assault on Nyaparake when the XI Corps commander ordered them to counterattack to restore the Driniumor line. Loaded into trucks next morning for a ten-mile ride to their concentration point, they jumped off with the 128th on 13 July, and immediately ran into a Japanese roadblock. The GIS overcame it with the help of artillery and thereafter made surprisingly steady progress, picking up along the way scattered and very relieved 32nd Division men cut off behind enemy lines by the big attack. They reached the Driniumor on 15 July, two days after the 128th, and ran into heavy opposition as they dug in and tried to clear the west bank.

The Southern Force, at the other end of the line, had the easiest time of all. The Japanese had not pushed as hard there, mostly due to communication breakdowns, so the 112th RCT reoccupied Afua against ineffective resistance within hours after starting out. Once there, parts of the 127th RCT moved up to reinforce it.

The American counterattack was helped not only by Japanese exhaustion and logistical difficulties but also by AAF and naval support. On 13 July, Task Force 74, consisting of two Australian heavy cruisers and four destroyers under Australian Commodore John Collins, showed up off Aitape, sent by Kinkaid to help Hall out. Huddling with Hall and AAF representatives, Collins and the Americans decided that his big ships could best help the XI Corps by interdicting Japanese truck traffic behind the lines. Collins and his sailors spent the next ten days doing so before leaving to support the Sansapor-Mar operation on the Vogelkop. They did a good job, but they often lacked targets or had trouble locating them.[66] ESB assault craft also contributed to American success, moving ahead of ground troops and shooting up thickets and huts that might contain Japanese troops—or natives, but that did not seem to enter into anyone's thoughts. In addition to such mobile fire support, the ESBs ran resupply missions, although beached and unloading landing craft were prime targets for Japanese fire.

Meanwhile, overhead the 5th AAF also did its best to make the Japanese miserable, flying 3228 sorties and dropping 1917 tons of ordinance during the operation. Kenney's pilots played other less glamorous but equally im-

portant roles as well. Spotter planes directed artillery fire and relayed radio
messages from the ground; the dense jungle limited radio range, and the
Japanese often cut overland lines. AAF airdrops frequently supplied troops
on the ground because distance, Japanese infiltrators, and rough terrain
made conventional resupply efforts all but impossible. There were rarely
enough suitable dropzones in the jungle, and those that were used had to
be frequently changed because broken rations attracted flies and contami-
nated the area. Unfortunately, it took a while for inexperienced XI Corps
staffers to catch on to this.[67]

Hall was proud of what his men had accomplished in only a few short
days. He was highly impressed with Gill, Starr and his 124th RCT, and
American artillery, whose weight so frequently shattered Japanese resistance.[68] Even so, the XI Corps commander was aware that the battle was
only half over. He wanted to clear the Japanese completely from the Driniumor's west bank, wait for the 43rd Division, and locate the elusive enemy
20th Division before crossing the river for other adventures that he hoped
would lead to the complete destruction of Adachi's forces.[69]

The Japanese did not make it easy for him. Adachi fought hard to hold
onto his west bank bridgehead, maintaining a gap between the Northern
and Southern forces. In the days following the XI Corps counterattack to
the Driniumor, there were many small uncoordinated actions along the
river as the Americans tried to close the gap and squeeze out the Japanese
bridgehead. Cunningham and Starr were convinced that neither was doing
his fair share to contact the other. Each commander believed that his flank
rested on Afua, not realizing that there were two Afua villages, an old and
a new.[70] On 17 July the 112th reached the 124th after a day-long fight, but
a Japanese counterattack shattered the troopers' lines, so the next day the
124th repeated the process, only from the opposite direction. Not until the
end of 18 July did the Americans at last have a reasonably solid line on the
Driniumor's west bank.

The Japanese were not giving up, though, and they continued to launch
attacks across the river. On the night of 21–22 July, for instance, a minia-
ture version of the original big Japanese assault—this time with an accompanying smokescreen—succeeded in splitting the 124th and cutting off
many of its units. The Japanese infiltrated behind the 124th's lines and attacked them from behind. A newly arrived battalion from the 43rd Division came in hard and together with the 124th pried the Japanese loose,
sending the survivors scurrying back across the river and restoring the
American line. The GIs repulsed scattered attacks the following days with
machine gun, mortar, and especially artillery fire.

Although the Americans were back along the Driniumor, there was plenty of danger behind the lines. As late as 30 July, an estimated 500–700 Japanese infiltrators remained between the river and Aitape, targeting supply trains, Tadji airfield, and artillery positions.[71] Since the infantry was needed elsewhere, support personnel were pretty much on their own. In fact, after the operation was all but over a sniper almost killed Gill while he was shaving, hitting a small mirror nailed to a palm tree. Gill's orderly grabbed a rifle and shot the sniper out of his tree, leaving his body to dangle suspended, a reminder to everyone of the long reach of the Japanese army.[72]

Afua Slugfest

As Cunningham's and Starr's soldiers struggled to eradicate the Japanese foothold on the Driniumor's west bank, Adachi took stock. The big Japanese assault had succeeded in crossing the Driniumor, but at the cost of heavy casualties that prevented Adachi from exploiting his early gains. In fact, the Japanese barely had time to catch their breath when Hall's roaring counterattack pushed them back across the Driniumor, erasing their hard-fought achievements. Clearly Aitape and Tadji airfield were now beyond Adachi's reach. On the other hand, not all was lost. The Japanese could still cripple SWPA forces along the Driniumor, and each casualty inflicted on the Americans was one less GI available for MacArthur's westward drive. To wreak the kind of havoc he had in mind, Adachi planned to throw his comparatively fresh 20th and 51st divisions against the right American flank around Afua.[73] If successful, the Japanese could crumble the entire American defensive line.

Willoughby quickly picked up on the new scheme:[74]

> Failure to achieve success by his Driniumor river crossing on 11 July and subsequent losses in killed and wounded, presumably forced the enemy to some change in plans and reorganization, thus accounting for considerable observed activity up to 19 July. However, the general overall static condition presently prevailing, particularly in the Afua area, may infer that realignment has been or is now completed, and points to impending offensive action.[75]

Unfortunately, MacArthur's G-2 did not realize that the movement he predicted—sort of predicted; as usual, Willoughby couched his estimates in ambiguous language designed to provide adequate cover should things go wrong—was already under way.

After a reasonably quiet night on 13–14 July on Cunningham's Southern Force front, Japanese activity increased dramatically around Afua.[76] Looking the situation over, Cunningham came to a conclusion he rejected days earlier, when the 32nd Division caught the brunt of the Japanese assault: retreat. Hall and Gill refused, however, and told Cunningham to hold on. In response, the 112th RCT commander bent his right flank back at an angle and prepared to fight it out. Heavy Japanese pressure forced the 112th to surrender Afua rather than fall back from the river. Hall, suddenly taking note,[77] on 20 July sent the rest of the 127th RCT south, and Cunningham fed it into the hopper as soon as it arrived. Even so, the Americans continued to give ground, and as the end of the month approached the Japanese had surrounded Cunningham's Southern Force along the Driniumor. Hand-to-hand fighting ensued as Americans and Japanese struggled for possession of the AAF dropzones that supplied the Southern Force with rations and ammunition. GIs went hungry, wore tattered uniforms, and got jungle rot, but they held on grimly to prevent the Japanese from unhinging the entire Driniumor line.[78]

To make matters worse, Cunningham had almost as much trouble with his superiors back at Aitape as with the Japanese all around him. For one thing, he did not think much of the 32nd Division, which he believed was timid and clique-ridden, hardly the type of unit he wanted on his flank or under his command.[79] Although his forces consisted of two RCTs—his own 112th as well as the 127th—Cunningham felt he needed more men to stave off the enemy.[80] Hall and Gill failed to see the situation that way. They did not think there were all that many Japanese around Afua, so Cunningham obviously was not trying hard enough.[81] Not until the end of the month did Hall come around and recognize the extent of the Japanese threat on his right flank.[82]

By then Hall had plans that would relieve the pressure on Cunningham as an incidental aspect of his larger aim of annihilating the Japanese along the Driniumor. Until Hall could implement them, however, Cunningham and his men were pretty much on their own, and on their own they gradually turned the tide of the battle their superiors denigrated. In late July Cunningham concentrated on opening dropzones and a supply line, as well as rescuing various surrounded components of his command. It was not easy though, and his men had to slug it out with the Japanese for possession of the high ground to the south and west. No sooner did they succeed in this exhausting task than the Japanese went over to the offensive again in early August, launching a number of attacks on his pocket along the Driniumor. There was lots of hand-to-hand combat, but American artillery, here as elsewhere in the operation, tipped the scale. The Japanese broke off their assaults on 4 August in order to confront Hall's latest maneuver, but by then the Southern Force had suffered some 1000 casualties, including those evacuated due to illness.

Ted Force Counterattack

Hall fretted throughout late July as Cunningham's weary men grappled with the Japanese. He hoped to obey Krueger's instructions and launch a counterattack that would sweep the enemy away from the Driniumor and eliminate Adachi as a threat to MacArthur's offensive once and for all, but both man and nature seemed intent on frustrating his efforts to do so.[83] The immediate problem was the 43rd Division, which Hall wanted to use to deliver his Sunday punch. The 43rd, created out of New England's National Guards, had first seen action the previous year in New Georgia in the Solomons. Like the 32nd Division, its baptism by fire was nothing short of horrific, but unlike Gill's men, other units had to rescue them and complete the job.

Hall was not as much concerned about this—he liked the 43rd's commander, the two-fisted, hard-fighting Major General Leonard F. Wing, and he believed that the unit would perform better next time around[84]—as he was with GHQ's inability to get the unit to Aitape in one piece.[85] No one told the 43rd that they were going off to New Guinea to fight, so their ships were not combat loaded.[86] The outfit arrived at Aitape in driblets, with unserviceable or worn-out weapons, and equipment crated or cosmolined. In addition, unloading Wing's men in Aitape's high surf in the continuous rain slowed things down even more, especially since landing craft propellers were twisted and shafts bent from months of constant wear and tear.[87]

All this was frustrating enough without the added burden of dealing with the increasingly impatient Krueger, who was notoriously intolerant of excuses.[88] In fact, on 23 July the 6th Army commander attempted to visit Aitape to pressure Hall into action, but his pilot mistakenly believed that American artillery was testing in the area, so he called off the landing. Hall probably appreciated the respite from his superior, although of course he assured Krueger otherwise.[89] In the meantime, Hall decided to act without the 43rd Division, which, although now on the scene, was not yet in any condition for full-scale action. Instead, he turned to the 124th RCT, which had performed amazingly well in its first combat action.[90] Hall planned to use it and a battalion from the 43rd's 169th RCT to cross the Driniumor and sweep south to cut Adachi's supply and communication lines with his Wewak base.[91] Since the 124th was commanded by Colonel Edward Starr, the attack column was code-named "Ted Force."

Not surprisingly, Gill did not like the idea, believing it was beyond XI Corps' means. To Hall, this was just another reason to give the assignment to Starr and not the 32nd Division. He thought Gill was a good man but far too cautious for the type of operation Krueger wanted him to conduct.[92] Instead, the 32nd would stand along the Driniumor while the 43rd sorted itself out in Aitape.

After a three-day delay, Ted Force jumped off on the last day of July, with the three 124th battalions crossing the Driniumor abreast and the 169th's wayward contribution covering the right flank by bringing up the rear. There was no opposition; the Japanese had pulled out. As Gill's men moved up to occupy the 124th vacated positions, Starr plunged eastward against scattered resistance, mostly in the form of snipers. "We haven't seen over five Japs, but the bullets are coming from every direction," one battalion commander wryly reported.[93] The terrain was more of a hindrance. American artillery fire over the past few weeks had shattered the area, scorching the wildlife and tearing the ground apart. Advancing 100 yards in an hour across such hostile and exhausting terrain was an accomplishment. To spare the troops, officers rotated lead companies every three hours, platoons every hour, and squads every fifteen minutes.

On 3 August, Starr wheeled to the right, or south, to cut off any Japanese still along the Driniumor. Isolated from the rest of the XI Corps, Ted Force was on its own. Battalions repeatedly got separated from one another. The GIs moved out every morning at 0700 and stopped at 1600 to establish a perimeter for the night. Mortars moved into position and registered while the troops cleared out the brush for bivouacs and fields of fire. Usually battalion headquarters was established at the center of the encampment, and two thirds of the troops manned the perimeter. At first five men huddled in each foxhole, but this number was reduced to two or three when the GIs realized that an unlucky enemy shell could kill or wound a handful of men in one fell swoop. No one was allowed outside of the perimeter at night, and anyone moving around inside was liable to be shot by jittery troops. The Japanese seemed to be everywhere and nowhere in the alien jungle environment. Enemy infiltrators wreaked the most havoc, and stopping them was very difficult. One soldier wrote, "No matter how small the perimeter or how close the men were on the positions, Japanese inevitably got through."[94]

Moreover, once Ted Force turned south, away from the ocean, there was no way to evacuate the wounded, so they had to be carried along on litters, which reduced the number of men available for combat and slowed down the march, as did the extra clothing and ammunition the soldiers carried. Starr brought along additional radios to maintain contact with the outside world, but in the dense jungle their range was less than two miles. This, combined with those highly inaccurate maps, made it hard to coordinate with artillery based behind the Driniumor. Inadequate radios, as well as bad weather, also made it difficult for the AAF to airdrop supplies, especially when hungry Japanese copied American tactics and used white smoke grenades to attract the supply-laden planes. C-47 aircrews kicked their supplies out at 300 feet without parachutes, and during the march falling rations and equipment killed seven incautious or unlucky GIs.[95]

On 6 August Starr changed course again, veering southwest toward the Afua area. Japanese resistance increased as the Americans approached Adachi's main supply line. Unfortunately, Starr's men were attacking the Japanese rear guard. As far back as 31 July, the Japanese commander, recognizing that he had lost the battle, had ordered his men to fall back to Wewak. The early August assaults on Cunningham's battered soldiers were designed more to cover the retreat than to destroy the Southern Force, although this would have been a nice upbeat coda to conclude an otherwise unhappy operation. Starr's offensive did more to accelerate than stop the Japanese withdrawal. To cover the retreat, Japanese rear guard units skirmished with Ted Force amid the jungle-ridden gullies, swamps, and ridges as Starr closed in on Afua. By now exhaustion and all those litter cases, as well as terrain and the Japanese, had slowed the American advance. On 8 August, a pilot approaching the Driniumor mistook Ted Force for Japanese and called in 32nd Division artillery, which subsequently killed or wounded thirty-five men. Despite this friendly fire setback, Starr's soldiers reached the Driniumor and linked up firmly with Cunningham's men on 10 August, ending their eleven-day adventure.

Starr's men could be, and were, proud of their exploit.[96] At the cost of 61 killed and 180 wounded they had inflicted some 1800 casualties on the Japanese and swept them away from the Driniumor.[97] MacArthur, for one, called their march "a feat unparalleled in the history of jungle warfare."[98] This, however, was spreading it a bit thick. For all of its accomplishments, Ted Force failed in its primary mission of destroying Adachi's army, which, although battered and bloodied, escaped back to Wewak. In the meantime, the 43rd Division moved up to the Driniumor to mop up those Japanese still lingering in the area, replacing Gill's, Starr's, and Cunningham's tired men. For all practical purposes, the Driniumor River operation was over.

The operation might be over, but the war was not, and the Driniumor operation veterans went on to other campaigns and battles. Gill remained 32nd Division commander and led the unit in Leyte and Luzon. The 112th RCT ultimately joined the 1st Cavalry Division and fought in Leyte before landing at Lingayen Gulf. Starr and his 124th RCT returned to their parent 31st Division, commanded eventually by recently relieved Clarence Martin, ironically enough, and saw action in Mindanao under Eichelberger.

Strategic Evaluation

The Driniumor River operation cost the Americans 597 killed, 1691 wounded, and 85 missing.[99] By way of compensation, SWPA inflicted more than 8800 casualties on the enemy, stripped the 18th Army of its offensive power, safeguarded Aitape and Hollandia, and gave American combat units and commanders battle experience that they would put to good use later.

Nevertheless, the operation raised some troubling questions about MacArthur's New Guinea campaign strategy. For MacArthur, heavy American casualties along the Driniumor was the price SWPA had to pay to eliminate the Japanese attempt to divert forces from his westward drive. A less aggressive strategy that permitted Adachi's men to batter themselves against the Aitape defenses, as Gill advocated, would probably have been less costly to SWPA, but it would have taken longer, and time was one luxury MacArthur could not afford in his race with the Navy to the China-Formosa-Luzon area. From MacArthur's view then, American losses were justifiable in that they contributed to the implementation of a strategy—his—that would best enable the United States to defeat the Japanese most effectively.

Those who supported a Navy-led offensive to Formosa might see things differently. From this point of view, MacArthur's job was simply to tie down Japanese resources that might otherwise interfere with the POA central Pacific drive. To them, American losses along the Driniumor resulted from MacArthur's vainglorious desire to liberate the Philippines, a strategy that would not advance Japan's defeat but would undoubtedly kill a good many American boys. The pressure MacArthur's surrogate Krueger exerted on Hall for a quick victory wasted American lives that might have been saved by a more prudent strategy that permitted the Japanese to pound fruitlessly against Aitape's strong defenses. Instead, Hall stepped out into the jungle to grapple in a hostile environment that sacrificed the American advantages of firepower and mobility. This, combined with Hall's and Krueger's tactical errors, made the Driniumor River operation one of SWPA's most useless.

In the end, although Adachi forced SWPA to deploy units from its westward drive, he failed to appreciably slow the American offensive. Instead, GHQ simply had other outfits take up the slack, which, although rough on the men and equipment subsequently denied rest and repair, permitted MacArthur's advance to roll on along the New Guinea racetrack, Adachi or no Adachi.

SANSAPOR-MAR AND MOROTAI: MOPPING UP THE CAMPAIGN

Much like a well-aimed stone hurled through a window, April's Hollandia operation shattered the Japanese New Guinea defense system. In response, the Japanese scrambled to build a new defense line on the western part of the big island. From their point of view, Wakde-Sarmi, Biak, and Driniumor River were rearguard actions designed to delay SWPA while the Japanese Army constructed defenses further west. For MacArthur, these positions were merely obstacles on his route to the China-Formosa-Luzon area. For both sides, the issue was *time,* not territory.

Unfortunately for the Japanese, SWPA came on in a rush, crushing or bypassing enemy positions in Geelvink Bay, so by July MacArthur was ready to tackle the still unprepared Japanese positions on the Vogelkop. Taking the peninsula would end the New Guinea campaign for the Japanese, at least as far as their hopes for halting the Americans were concerned. To MacArthur, the Vogelkop was just about the last piece of New Guinea real estate he needed to place him in a position to demonstrate to the JCS that he was willing and *able* to liberate his beloved Philippines.

Except as another stepping stone to the China-Formosa-Luzon area, the Vogelkop, like all of New Guinea, possessed little strategic importance for SWPA, but this was not always so. Earlier in the war, American planners had focused on undeveloped oil fields around Klamono, southeast of Sorong, as possible targets in and of their own right. The JCS and GHQ believed that there were 5.4 million barrels of oil under the ground there. With the right men and equipment, SWPA could extract up to 3000 barrels of the stuff a day.[1] After removing excess naphtha, the Navy could use the unrefined oil for its ships, easing the immense logistical burden of hauling fuel from the States. In mid-1943 the JCS ordered military personnel to begin training to develop Klamono. By April of the following year, some 2000 men in California were ready to go.[2]

Soon after, however, the JCS changed its mind. Since MacArthur's and Nimitz's offenses were picking up speed, it appeared increasingly likely that the war might end before mid-1946, the earliest possible date that the Klamono oilfields could start yielding crude. It now seemed uneconomical to put so much time and effort into developing oilfields that might not prove necessary, so in the summer of 1944 the JCS canceled the plan.

Even so, MacArthur still wanted the Vogelkop, if not for its oil then for platforms on which to construct airdromes to propel him to the China-Formosa-Luzon area. The peninsula, however, did not seem like an easy nut to crack. Willoughby estimated that the big Japanese base at Manokwari, to the east, contained 4500 combat troops and 10,500 service personnel. Sorong, at the other side of the peninsula, held 12,500 Japanese, of whom 5150 were infantry or artillerymen.[3] No one at GHQ wanted to tackle either of those strongpoints, especially with the Biak experience fresh in everyone's mind. Instead, MacArthur decided to land at Sansapor-Mar, halfway between the two Japanese bases. As MacArthur saw it, the surrounding dense jungle would make it all but impossible for the Japanese to interfere with an American landing, especially since SWPA controlled the air and seas. Once established, AAF personnel could get to work building airfields which would cut off Manokwari and extend SWPA's reach to the Netherlands East Indies and the Philippines. There were almost no Japanese there, so MacArthur anticipated a trouble-free operation, at least as far as combat was concerned.[4] On 30 June GHQ gave Krueger his final orders to prepare to attack Sansapor-Mar exactly a month later.

In military operations, as in most everything else in life, the devil is in the details, and as usual it was Krueger's job to wrestle MacArthur's Beelzebub to the ground. The very thing that attracted GHQ to Sansapor-Mar—namely, its lack of Japanese defenders—made its occupation problematic for the 6th Army commander. There were reasons why the Japanese had decided not to garrison the area. Sansapor-Mar was surrounded not only by dense forest but also by mountains that extended almost to the beach, limiting the amount of flat land available to maneuver or build on. Moreover, it was vulnerable to northern monsoons and still pretty far from the Philippines. The coast was mostly reef free, but swamps and intersecting small rivers lurked inland, and there were no roads.[5]

This hostile topography, not the Japanese, concerned Krueger most.[6] Could the place support airfields? Could the assault troops easily reach the beach? To Krueger, the available topographical intelligence was as usual far too general.[7] Because Kenney gave priority to combat planes, there were not many photo reconnaissance aircraft in the westernmost SWPA airdromes to take a look at the proposed target. Bad weather frequently obscured the area anyway. Because there were no Japanese in the vicinity, Alamo Scouts, naval personnel, and aviation engineers extensively reconnoitered Sansapor-Mar throughout late June and into July, but their vague findings failed to appease Krueger. Everyone agreed that an amphibious landing was practicable, but consensus broke down over where to construct the all-important airfields. Ultimately, the aviation engineers decided to wait until Sansapor-Mar was in SWPA's hands before making a final decision on airdrome sites.[8]

Despite these problems, most other planning went smoothly, especially now that every major SWPA commander but MacArthur, still at Brisbane, was headquartered at Hollandia. Although the Japanese had recently increased their air power in the region, Kenney did not think his pilots would have any problem maintaining air superiority because the Vogelkop was within easy range of his newly captured Noemfoor airdromes.[9] For the assault, Krueger decided to use Sibert's 6th Division, recovering from its brutal baptism by fire at Lone Tree Hill. The 6th Army commander planned to throw 14,000 combat soldiers, 7050 service personnel, and 7000 AAF troops at the undefended target. Krueger felt that all the support and AAF personnel were necessary to quickly build the airfields that were the point of the whole operation. Besides, better safe than sorry. After all, Sansapor-Mar was closer to Sorong and Manokwari than to any SWPA base, and Adachi's troops were in the process of showing that the Japanese could perform logistical miracles in moving men and equipment through theoretically impassable jungle, so Sibert's GIs might be needed. Furthermore, Krueger wanted to push as many men as far westward as possible, so they could be readily available for future operations.[10]

A Quiet Landing

On 29 July, the day before the scheduled amphibious assault, Kenney's pilots swept over the Sansapor-Mar area. Their target was not the Japanese—not today anyway; there were none around—but another, equally implacable foe: mosquitoes. The AAF dropped tons of DDT up to a mile inland, paving the way for what they hoped would be a malaria-free operation. Next morning, without the psychological support of the customary preliminary bombardment, elements of the 63rd RCT waded ashore unopposed

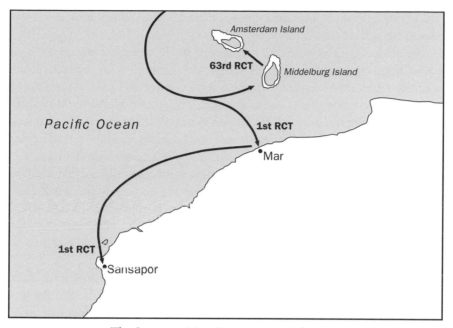

The Sansapor-Mar Operation, 30 July 1944

on Middelburg Island, north of Mar. Then they reboarded their assault craft for another Japanese-free landing at Amsterdam Island, just to the northwest. Here, however, one GI was fatally wounded by the accidental discharge of an LVT's 37mm gun, but this was the only dark incident in an otherwise trouble-free attack.

An hour after the 63rd RCT swung into action, the 1st RCT prepared to carry out its part of the operation. Here, too, there was no preliminary bombardment, for the simple reason that there were no Japanese present to pummel. At 0830 the GIs headed for shore across the calm, clear sea. Because of those two islands to the north, now possessed by the 63rd, the landing approach was angled. Colored lights pointed the way, and submarine chaser vessels marked the precise turning point for the assault craft. With such perfect weather and thorough preparations, the latter the result of hard-won experience over the past year and a half, the 1st RCT had little trouble getting ashore and fanning out. GIs spotted a few Japanese inland, but they were easily scattered. The heat was stifling and there was nothing of value or interest along the beach, but it was better than being shot at. Many of the GIs did little but relax, gamble, and speculate on their next landing. In one area the only shots fired were at a scared rabbit. Looking around, one grinning soldier quipped, "Well, why don't we choose up sides?"[11]

Sibert no doubt appreciated the ease of the landing and the absence of enemy opposition, although he had expected as much. With the beachhead secured, engineers moved in to unload the Liberties and LSTs, a task made simpler by the lack of reefs and heavy surf. The soft and loose sand bogged down some vehicles, but tractors moved in to pull them out. Bulldozers cut beach exits and used the leftover material to construct ramps for the LSTs. There was not a lot of dispersal room, and the engineers had to use the beach as their coastal road, but these were minor problems compared to the 6th Division's last operation. To speed up the unloading process, Sibert pressed some of his lounging infantry into duty. With such reinforcements, all the ships were unloaded within twenty-four hours, although the fact that some pilfered vessels contained only half the supplies and equipment their manifests indicated certainly accelerated the process.[12]

Next day a battalion from the 1st RCT moved over water from Mar down to Sansapor to set up a radar site and PT boat base, although the latter installation was later shifted to Amsterdam Island. There was no opposition, here as elsewhere. In the following weeks, 6th Division patrols skirmished with scattered Japanese, but these stragglers seemed more intent on reaching the safety of Manokwari or Sorong than on combating SWPA's latest advance. Danger was not, however, completely absent. The Japanese mounted nightly air raids, but they usually consisted of one plane and caused little damage, although they hindered sleep and kept everyone on edge. GIs called the nocturnal bomber "Washing Machine Charlie" and cheered him on, though always remaining close to their foxholes. Such laughter subsided, for a while anyway, when Charlie hit the divisional command post, killing five and wounding another eight. Fortunately, the attack spared Edwin Patrick—the Green Hornet—now serving as Sibert's chief of staff, but everything except him and his cot was hit with shrapnel.[13] Antiaircraft guns threw everything they had at the nightly visitor, but without success.[14]

The 6th Division's experienced GIs could take Charlie in stride, having seen so much worse during their pointblank confrontation at Lone Tree Hill back in June. They were a veteran unit now and went on to prove it next year in hard fighting on Luzon. As for Sibert, MacArthur rewarded his fine performances here and at Lone Tree Hill by promoting him to command the new X Corps. Sibert led the corps through the brutal Leyte campaign with Krueger and then served capably under Eichelberger in the southern Philippines by spearheading the Mindanao operation. He had a harder time getting along with Eichelberger than Krueger, who was more his style.[15]

All this, however, was in the future. For now, the GIs had little to do, as far as combat was concerned. In fact, the Sansapor-Mar operation was so trouble-free that a week after the landing Willoughby could accurately report: "It is interesting to note that since our landing at Sansapor . . . there has been no observed enemy reaction. However, this may be explained by the fact that, once again, we have caught him off balance. . . . The rugged terrain which stands between our units and our beachhead and our control of the air and sea approaches in this area create a situation which is not conducive to the successful attainment of any enemy offensive.[16]

The Americans now possessed a foothold on the Vogelkop, and there was apparently nothing the Japanese could do about it short of sending Washing Machine Charlies to entertain the troops. Whether or not SWPA could make the operation pay off was now up to the aviation engineers.

Building the Airdromes

Looking over SWPA's newly acquired real estate, 13th AAF Brigadier General Earl W. Barnes decided to concentrate his resources on Middelburg Island. Neighboring Amsterdam was too hilly for any airstrip, and building an airdrome at Mar would take a while. Working around the clock, aviation engineers had Middleburg ready for fighters on 17 August, a day ahead of schedule. Mar took longer. The area was full of underbrush and small trees, and it was poorly drained. Engineers had to dredge the ocean for coral to firm up the water table. There were not enough lightbulbs, so the men worked at night under searchlights. Despite these topographical and logistical handicaps, the engineers had 6000 feet of runway ready on 3 September, and the airstrip could support bombers six days later, in time for the Morotai operation.

The aviation engineers' logistical problems stemmed, at least in part, from the rapid deterioration of Sansapor beach, which made it increasingly difficult to unload cargo. As one general described it, "[Sansapor-Mar] was the meanest and most exposed beach in the Pacific. . . . From October onward an onshore wind set in and swells from the full sweep of the Pacific were continuous. Surf was never less than four feet high and reached heights of 20 feet in storms. It was the most forbidding and unfriendly shore we have ever been on."[17] The rough surf made it impossible to build piers, so DUKWs had to transfer everything to the shore, a slow and cumbersome process under the best of circumstances and all the more frustrating when there were deadlines to meet.

To make matters worse for SWPA's westernmost garrison, on 9 August scrub typhus and a fever of unknown origin struck the troops. GIS contracted the former disease by sleeping on the ground in clearings surrounded by high, rodent-infested grass. As its *nom de guerre* implied, no one knew where the latter affliction came from, although there was no doubt as to its impact. The fever downed 530 men, while scrub typhus cases raised the total to 805. The 1st RCT was especially hard hit, and its commander, Colonel Forbie H. Privett, was among the sick. The epidemic was no laughing matter; scrub typhus not only killed but permanently weakened those afflicted, putting them out of action as effectively as Japanese bullets. The diseases overwhelmed medical facilities, so drivers and mess personnel were put to work in the wards. By now, however, SWPA was thoroughly familiar with scrub typhus. Officers responded quickly, ordering grass and brush burned, bivouacs cleared, clothing impregnated with dimethylphthalate, and full uniforms worn at all times. The epidemic abated in late August, but by then 9 men were dead and 504 had been evacuated, many never to return.

Strategic Consequences

Despite the noncombat casualties, the Sansapor operation yielded SWPA major strategic benefits. At the minimal cost, exclusive of sickness, of fourteen killed, twenty-nine wounded, and two missing,[18] American forces surrounded Manokwari, neutralized Sorong, and eliminated the Vogelkop as a barrier to SWPA's advance to the China-Formosa-Luzon area. For the Japanese, New Guinea was now no longer a defensive shield but just another example of the consequences of opposing the mobile American war machine.

For MacArthur, the Vogelkop meant a good deal more. The week before Sibert's troops waded ashore, MacArthur journeyed to Hawaii to meet with Nimitz and President Roosevelt on the future of the Pacific War. SWPA's anticipated lodgment on the Vogelkop—no one expected otherwise—as well as those other victories throughout New Guinea, enabled MacArthur to push for a Philippines liberation campaign by stating that SWPA was willing and *able* to do so. At Pearl Harbor, MacArthur advocated the occupation of Leyte, after Mindanao's conquest, as a prelude for an invasion of Luzon, the Philippines' heartland. Although MacArthur came away convinced that he had swayed FDR,[19] the JCS was by no means won over. Nevertheless, New Guinea's conquest enabled MacArthur to get his foot in the Philippines liberation door by demonstrating that SWPA was in a position to liberate the archipelago. Now he had to persuade the JCS to let him kick it in.

Right Face

Although the Sansapor operation neutralized the Vogelkop as an obstacle on MacArthur's road to the Philippines, one last major military hurdle remained between SWPA and Mindanao: Halmahera Island, just off the Vogelkop's northwest tip. Halmahera served as a linchpin between New Guinea, the Netherlands East Indies, and the Philippines. SWPA could not make the jump from the former to the latter without dealing with the big island. The Japanese knew this, and in early 1944 they began to fortify and reinforce Halmahera, packing it with some 30,000 troops by late summer. This was three times the number that had blocked SWPA's Biak assault for almost a month. MacArthur could not afford to waste that much time again; the JCS had slated the Mindanao operation for 15 November, so he had to make that target date if he wanted to convince his superiors that he could go on to liberate Leyte and Luzon.

GHQ was well aware of Halmahera's potential to trip up SWPA's fast-moving offensive. In June MacArthur's intelligence estimated that the island would possess anywhere between 12,000 and 24,000 Japanese by the time it got within SWPA's range.[20] Willoughby wrote, "The enemy's realization of the strategic importance of Halmahera, astride our line of advance, continues to be evidenced through his extensive construction of ground defenses in all key sectors."[21] Obviously, the thing to do was to use American naval and air power to bypass and isolate the island, much as SWPA had recently neutralized Manokwari, reducing its garrison to a squalid, pestilent-ridden existence while the American military machine rolled on by. The problem, of course, was not *what* to do, but rather *how* to do it. Scanning their maps, GHQ zoomed in on mountainous Morotai, a tiny island just off Halmahera's northeastern tip, as the solution to their problem.

Morotai possessed a minuscule Japanese garrison and an abandoned airstrip, which was all to the good, of course. More important, at least to GHQ, if not to the GIS assigned to occupy it, was the forty-square mile Doroeba plain on the island's southwestern corner, ripe for AAF airdrome construction. In American hands, Morotai and its airfields could neutralize

Halmahera and cover SWPA's left flank from Japanese attacks from the Netherlands East Indies, provide bomber bases to support the Mindanao operation, and dominate the approaches to the Philippines. Moreover, it lay within range of Sansapor's newly constructed airdromes, enabling Kenney's pilots to control the surrounding airspace. This clearly was the way to go, and on 21 July GHQ ordered Krueger to prepare plans for Morotai's occupation, which MacArthur okayed eight days later. GHQ set the invasion date for 15 September, the same day Nimitz's forces were slated to attack the nearby Palaus, enabling the Pacific fleet to extend its protective blanket over both invasion forces.

As with Sansapor-Mar, Krueger believed that the biggest complication would be the topography, not the Japanese. Morotai was surrounded by coral reefs, possessed narrow and sandy beaches, and lacked entry channels. Barbey did not like this one bit, but he knew that his skilled crews and staff, with the aid of amphibious tractors and demolition teams, could overcome such obstacles.[22] Krueger did not like the situation much either, especially since he lacked information on the exact details of those topographical problems. Such ignorance was self-inflicted; Krueger as usual prohibited beach reconnaissance so as not to tip off the Japanese, who might rush reinforcements to the island. GHQ thought differently, and back in late May, without Krueger's knowledge, it had sent in a reconnaissance team by submarine, but no one ever heard from it.[23] The Japanese might or might not have done them in, but if so, they took no further action. In fact, in early September Willoughby wrote: "It may be concluded that the enemy's appreciation of the tactical importance of Morotai has either been wanting, or that he has been forced to ignore its development because of the necessity of consolidating his troops at key points on Halmahera to avoid dissipating them to outlying bases."[24] Morotai, in short, was ripe for the picking, at least as far as its minuscule Japanese garrison was concerned, although whether mother nature would be equally generous remained to be seen.

In addition to worrying about Morotai's mysterious topography, Krueger also had to tackle SWPA's logistical devil, a perpetual problem. SWPA was so logistically strapped that initially there were not enough LSTs for the invasion, although GHQ eventually scraped together the balance.[25] Krueger wanted to stage the entire operation from Maffin Bay, but the place was too small, so he had to mount the invasion from a half dozen New Guinea ports, which further complicated the always complex logistical plan. At first he devised a simultaneous landing on both sides of Morotai's Gila peninsula, but Barbey scotched that idea by protesting that it would hamper the preliminary bombardment and that the eastern coast was too rough and deep for amphibious craft anyway.[26] Instead, Krueger decided upon two landing beaches on the base of the Gila peninsula's western side.

Krueger assigned the task of taking Morotai to the XI Corps, commanded by Chink Hall, who had just received his SWPA baptism by fire at Driniumor River. Hall had at his disposal the 31st Division, part of which—the 124th RCT—had performed magnificently outside of Aitape. The other two RCTs had seen some limited action at Wakde-Sarmi, and there was no reason why they should not do as well as their sister unit. In all, and counting reserves from the 32nd Division, Hall had 37,900 combat soldiers, 12,200 service personnel, and 16,900 AAF troops on hand, more than enough, Krueger thought, to overcome all obstacles, Japanese, topographical, logistical, or any combination of the three.

Hung up on the Coral Reef

Here as elsewhere in the New Guinea campaign, SWPA's superior air and naval power gave MacArthur the luxury not only to choose his targets but also to seal those targets off from outside aid before he pounded the now isolated Japanese defenders to a pulp. In September MacArthur applied this familiar formula to Morotai. Kenney's AAF concentrated on grinding down Japanese air power in the eastern Netherlands East Indies but ignored Morotai until invasion day, when his pilots dumped DDT behind the landing beaches to eliminate one of SWPA's prime biological enemies. Fifty miles to the north of the island, one of Nimitz's big carrier task forces worked over Japanese airfields in the region on 15–16 September. Moreover, for the first time since the Hollandia operation, nearly five months before, Barbey also had flattops under his command. Nimitz lent him six escort carriers for antisubmarine duty, fighter cover, and close air support, although there was not much call for any of these tasks. The preliminary bombardment set afire some native villages but did not hurt the Japanese much, mostly because there were none in the area.

The 31st Division touched ashore at two beaches—dubbed "Red" and "White"—at the western base of the Gila peninsula. There were several small islands offshore, so the assault craft had to make an angled approach, as at Mar, but this did not cause any problems. At 0830 the 155th and 167th RCTs began landing at Red Beach, to the north, while the 124th RCT did the same at the other site to the south. Watching the tiny, sticklike

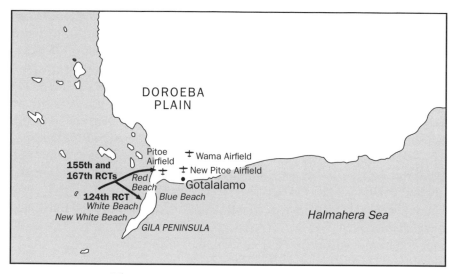

The Morotai Operation, 15 September 1944

figures struggle out of the landing craft, a relieved Barbey said, "Whenever we can get three waves ashore safely, I know the day is won."[27]

That may have been true, but as events turned out there was a good deal more to this landing than Barbey initially believed. The problem was not the Japanese, who fortunately neglected to put in an appearance, but mother nature—or, more specifically, the offshore coral reef, which air reconnaissance photos failed to do justice. Many—but not Hall and his XI Corps staff, who had worried about it from the start[28]—were deceived into thinking that it would not be much of an obstacle. But it was. Located 100 yards from the beach, the reef was not only much wider than anyone expected but also a foot or two higher at its seaward than landward side, making it impossible for landing craft to cross. Instead, coxswains disgorged their men at the reef's edge, and after traversing it the GIs waded the last 100 yards to shore in shoulder-deep water. The reef was riddled with coral spikes and formations and covered with a muddy paste of decomposed coral beneath a thin layer of white sediment. There was no uniform depth; one minute the water might barely lap over a GI's boot, but the next step might land him in a ten-foot deep hole. At White Beach the commander of the first LCVP wave was so appalled by the reef that he moved his craft 300 yards north, but conditions were no better there. For now there was nothing to do but deal with the reef as it was.

Getting the first waves of infantry and engineers ashore was difficult but not impossible. Humans are self-propelled, as it were, and capable of reaching the beach on their own accord. Equipment and supplies, however, were another matter. LVTs could navigate the reef, but LSTs certainly could not. Human chains unloaded bulk cargo in neck-deep water. Landing craft disgorged vehicles in the surf, but only a fourth made it to the beach under their own power, the rest sinking.[29] Coming ashore more than two days later, one officer said, "When I landed at H plus 60, the water approach to the beach was littered with vehicles stuck as far as two hundred feet offshore. Even though the water was up to the hood of these vehicles many were still running."[30] In the meantime, infantrymen sorted themselves out before heading inland, beachmasters barked orders, radios squawked, and engineers sweated at their machines.

In the midst of all this chaos, several hours after the first landings, an immaculate Douglas MacArthur waded through fifty yards of surf up to his thighs with Barbey to have a look.[31] The SWPA commander accompanied the operation mostly to get away from his desk and have a look at his far-flung theater.[32] MacArthur was in a good mood, despite all the problems around him, which, from his lofty point of view, were merely incidental to an operation that was for all practical purposes won.[33]

MacArthur's current state of elation stemmed not from SWPA's unopposed Morotai landing—although surely this was somewhat gratifying, since it was another Philippines-bound hurdle overcome at small cost—but rather from Admiral William Halsey, former SOPAC chief but now commanding Nimitz's 3rd Fleet. Halsey had just carried out a series of carrier raids against the Palaus and Philippines, which not only destroyed a lot of enemy ships and planes but did so against almost no resistance. The impulsive Halsey interpreted this to mean that Japanese strength in the Philippines was minimal, so the archipelago was wide open to American attack. He recommended to Nimitz that the JCS cancel the Mindanao operation and strike directly at Leyte. Nimitz thought it was a good idea and passed the message on to the JCS. The JCS also liked the proposal and radioed MacArthur for his opinion. MacArthur was traveling with the Morotai invasion force under radio silence, but Sutherland responded positively in his name. The JCS reset the Leyte invasion date for 20 October, a little more than a month away, abandoning all intermediate operations, including the Mindanao operation.

There was more here than met the eye. By accelerating the Leyte operation, the JCS tacitly all but abandoned the possibility of attacking Formosa. Planning and mounting a Formosa invasion would take several months, and the JCS was unlikely to permit the Pacific War to stall for that long. Moreover, the JCS was increasingly convinced that conquering Formosa would require an inordinate amount of time, resources, and casualties. Finally, a major reason for invading Formosa was to help protect B-29 airfields in southern China, but the deteriorating situation there forced the AAF to look to the Marianas for bases for its big bombers. With Formosa eliminated from consideration, the obvious next stepping stone to Japan was Luzon, in the heart of the Philippines. Halsey, in short, provided MacArthur with the boot he needed to kick open the Philippines liberation campaign door. After returning from Morotai, MacArthur clinched the debate by promising that he could invade Luzon around the beginning of the new year, long before the Navy could get to Formosa. On 3 October the JCS signed off on MacArthur's proposal, officially sanctioning the invasion of Luzon after Leyte, giving MacArthur what he had long wanted.[34]

All this was in the future as MacArthur explained Halsey's recommendation to Barbey on Morotai beach. For now, he was confident that the JCS would accede to Halsey's suggestion, and he clearly perceived his opportunity to press for a Luzon invasion.[35] Small wonder, then, that the SWPA chief was in a good mood.[36] Perhaps with this in mind, before he left the island he reportedly gazed northward and said to an aide, "They are waiting for me there. It has been a long time."[37]

Whether this was a threat to the Japanese or a promise to the Filipinos, or a combination of both, MacArthur did not say, but he was clearly thinking along those lines. None of this, however, meant much to Hall's men—not yet, anyway—as they struggled to overcome that reef. Something had to be done to make room for the LSTs, or else the engineers would not have the equipment and supplies necessary to build the all-important airdromes. To overcome the mud, engineers spread matting along the sea floor and held it down with sandbags, which worked reasonably well.[38] They also diverted bulldozers from jetty and road construction to winch and tow sunken vehicles to shore with cables. Navy demolition teams, for their part, tried to blast away coral heads that threatened to rip the hulls out of landing craft, but without much luck.[39] In mid-morning a reconnaissance party located a better landing beach several hundred yards south of White Beach, so four LSTs were sent there. This helped, but in the afternoon the engineers decided to abandon both Red and White beaches as soon as possible in favor a better landing place discovered on the other side of the peninsula, dubbed "Blue Beach."

Fortunately for SWPA, the reef was the only real obstacle to the American landing. Beyond the beach there was plenty of good, well-drained dispersal room, and bulldozers had an easy time pushing aside the secondary jungle growth. Equally fortuitous was the almost total lack of Japanese opposition, although inexperienced troops fired at a good many coconuts in trees.[40] A battalion of the 124th RCT occupied all of Gila peninsula by midafternoon, and to the north the 167th RCT took abandoned Pitoe airstrip around 1300. Scattered Japanese resistance wounded seven men, but this was a very small price to pay for a piece of real estate that sealed off 30,000 enemy troops on Halmahera and placed SWPA within striking distance of the Philippines. Indeed, Willoughby noted the day after the assault: "In view of the limitations which have been imposed on any enemy movements toward the fulfillment of his intervention capability from bases outside the Moluccas, it is believed that the enemy is not in a position at present to mount any offensive operations from these bases."[41] Willoughby was right; the Japanese occasionally harassed the beachhead, but the military phase of the operation was over the minute the first GIs came ashore.

Krueger had decided against trying to occupy all of Morotai and instead ordered Hall to establish a perimeter on the southwestern part of the island.[42] The first perimeter proved too small to accommodate all the planned supply dumps, bivouacs, and runway space, so on 20 September Hall expanded the perimeter further without enemy opposition.

Hall's Base

Despite that difficult reef, Hall could be proud of his Morotai victory, which differed strikingly from his recent Driniumor River ordeal in terms of the amount of blood spilled and the strategic advantages gained. Once securely ashore, the XI Corps commander got to work turning the island into another SWPA platform from which to torment the Japanese far and wide. Although the pattern was familiar to almost everyone involved, this did not make the job any easier. The original plan called for a fighter strip to be ready on 17 September, forty-eight hours after the troops came ashore, but this proved unrealistic. Airdrome construction was delayed for two days not only because the engineers had to get their equipment across that reef to shore but also because they concluded that run-down Pitoe airstrip was unsuitable for the kind of work they had in mind. Instead, they decided to build the bomber strip near Gotalalamo village. Heavy rains that turned roads and fields to mud, Japanese night air attacks, and a lack of good surfacing material—Morotai seemed to consist either of fine sand or big hard boulders, but nothing in between—delayed construction, so

Wama airfield, as the bomber strip was dubbed, was not ready for fighter planes until 4 October, and not until six days later could it handle bombers. Another bomber strip to the north—called Pitoe airfield, but different from the abandoned Japanese one—was partially finished a week later. Even so, a lack of adequate gasoline storage facilities prevented Morotai-based bombers from directly supporting the Leyte landings,[43] although they later hit targets in Mindanao, the Visayans, and Balikpapan.

For the Morotai garrison, life consisted of occasional skirmishes with the enemy, construction and unloading duty, and sweating out nightly Japanese air attacks. Mountains to the north and the Halmahera Island land mass to the south made it easy for Japanese bombers to avoid American radar, so nocturnal attacks were common. In fact, they raided the beachhead eighty-nine times in the first three months, usually attacking around 2000.[44] Although the enemy bombers inflicted little damage, they were annoying.

For Hall, the Morotai operation, for all its logistical problems, was certainly more trouble-free than his recent Driniumor operation battle. After Morotai, he went on to command the XI Corps in the Philippines. Working under the more genial Eichelberger, Hall participated in the liberation of Manila and then went on to fight in the southern Philippines.

The Morotai operation was one of MacArthur's finer strategic moves. At the cost of only thirty killed and eighty-five wounded,[45] SWPA slipped around the big Japanese Halmahera garrison assigned to guard the door to the Philippines. In American hands, Morotai not only protected SWPA's flank for the Leyte operation but also conclusively terminated the New Guinea campaign in an almost bloodless fashion.

CONCLUSIONS

On the morning of 20 October 1944, a little more than a month after Hall's XI Corps stumbled onto the Morotai beach, Douglas MacArthur left the cruiser *Nashville* and boarded a landing craft that took him, his staff, Philippines President Sergio Osmeña, and a gaggle of newsmen and hangers-on ashore at Leyte. The party waded through the surf to the beach, which the veteran 1st Cavalry and 24th Divisions had seized a few hours earlier. Once on solid ground, the SWPA chief strode to a signal corps microphone and intoned in an emotional voice, "People of the Philippines, I have returned."[1]

MacArthur's walk through Leyte's surf was the direct result of his seven-month long advance across the New Guinea littoral. Each operation, from the Admiralties to Morotai, had been designed to move his forces along the coast closer to his coveted archipelago. New Guinea itself, as well as its Japanese defenders, was of little or no concern to him, except to the extent that it impeded his advance. For MacArthur, the New Guinea campaign was more about making time than seizing territory or inflicting casualties. It was just a means to an end, a racetrack that he had to traverse as rapidly as possible in order to place his forces in a position to liberate the Philippines and dominate the war against Japan.

Unlike MacArthur, most American military planners believed that a Navy-led offensive across the central Pacific was the fastest and most cost-effective way to defeat the Japanese, and the JCS's 12 March directive reflected this viewpoint. Even so, through both public and private pressure, as well as the JCS's own inclinations, MacArthur successfully lobbied for a New Guinea offensive. Because the compromise JCS directive advocated a dual drive to the vaguely defined China-Formosa-Luzon area, he planned to use a successful New Guinea campaign to pressure the JCS to narrow its focus to Luzon, in the heart of the Philippines.

Before MacArthur could fight his big battle with the JCS over Pacific War strategy, let alone win it, he had to be in a military position to assail the Philippines ahead of or at the same time that Nimitz reached the China-Formosa-Luzon region. To do so, he drove his forces hard across New Guinea, often accepting otherwise unnecessary casualties and risks in his desire for speed. He was successful, however, and by July, with his men about to splash ashore at Sansapor-Mar, he continued the strategic debate in Hawaii. Later, after Halsey's successful carrier strikes convinced the JCS that the Philippines were vulnerable to attack, only SWPA's forces were in a position to take advantage of the JCS desire to accelerate the Pacific War. Had MacArthur's New Guinea offensive stalled at, say, Biak, he would have been unable to promise the JCS that he could take Leyte and invade Luzon before 1945, and the Joint Chiefs might have waited until Nimitz's forces were in position to attack Formosa. Instead, MacArthur won his race and reaped his reward.

Pacific War strategy was not a zero-sum game, although MacArthur and the Navy often seemed to think in those terms. The New Guinea campaign not only reflected MacArthur's strategic designs but the JCS's as well. By 1944 some sort of New Guinea offensive was all but inevitable, MacArthur or no MacArthur. Because of the Cartwheel campaign toward Rabaul—begun, ironically enough, at King's behest in 1942, when the CNO insisted on invading Guadalcanal[2]—lots of men and materiel were scattered throughout the southwest Pacific. Moving these forces to the central Pacific—assuming that enough room could have been found for them all— would have taken a great deal of time, delaying the full prosecution of the war and giving the Japanese breathing space to build up their defenses. Indeed, just redeploying SOPAC forces after Cartwheel ended took months, and the 43rd Division was the only major SOPAC ground unit that participated in the New Guinea campaign. From the JCS's point of view, it was better to use these men and equipment where they were and keep them advancing toward Japan rather than to waste all the time and effort required to move them elsewhere.

Logistical and temporal constraints, however, were not the only reasons the JCS underwrote a New Guinea campaign. They saw other, more positive, advantages as well. For one thing, they hoped that a SWPA offensive through New Guinea would cover Nimitz's southern flank and disperse Japanese resources. And in the end they were correct. The Japanese Army saw MacArthur's offensive as the greater threat, and they concentrated their forces in that direction, limiting the number of men and materiel available to stuff in those hard-to-take central Pacific islands. Also, Nimitz never had to worry about an exposed left flank as he advanced across the central Pacific. In fact, bombers from SWPA bases in the Admiralties and along the New Guinea coast supported POA operations.

In addition to military advantages, the New Guinea campaign served the JCS politically as well. In endorsing a New Guinea offensive to the

China-Formosa-Luzon area that left open the possibility of the eventual liberation of the Philippines, the JCS essentially bought MacArthur's cooperation for the time being, bringing a degree of peace to Pacific War strategy that would not have otherwise been possible if the JCS had explicitly targeted Formosa over Luzon. Had the JCS denied MacArthur his New Guinea offensive, the temperamental general might have fulfilled his threat to appeal to Roosevelt, whose amateurish forays into grand strategy had already caused the JCS considerable grief.

Finally, the New Guinea offensive provided the JCS with a degree of strategic flexibility, giving them more options in their axis of attack toward the Japanese homeland. When Halsey's successful carrier strikes convinced the JCS that the Philippines were open to American assault, MacArthur, thanks to his New Guinea campaign, was in a position to take advantage of the opportunity. The Navy, for its part, was not only far away from its Formosa target but also in no position to attack the Philippines on its own. A single thrust offensive through the central Pacific would not necessarily have advanced sufficient numbers of troops far enough forward to mount an immediate invasion of the archipelago, but a dual drive that included a New Guinea campaign could and did accomplish this.

To be sure, an argument can be made in favor of some sort of single thrust offensive across the Pacific that overlooked or downgraded a New Guinea campaign. Such scenarios, however, ignore the inescapable interservice rivalries that plagued the Pacific War effort. Neither MacArthur nor the Navy was willing to take a subordinate role in the conflict with Japan. MacArthur demanded a Philippines liberation campaign, and the Navy insisted on a major offensive that would utilize all its resources—aircraft carriers, battleships, the Marines and their amphibious abilities, and so on—to bring about a climactic and redemptive battle with its Japanese counterpart. The New Guinea campaign was the result of this interservice struggle, but both MacArthur and the JCS were in the end able to make it serve their purposes by integrating it into their strategic plans.

Winning the New Guinea Campaign

Considering the logistical realities and interservice rivalries confronting the JCS, the New Guinea offensive was all but inevitable. Although in the long run it advanced the American Pacific War effort from both MacArthur's and the JCS's point of view, this does not explain *why* SWPA won the campaign. One reason was that the JCS's dual drive offensive paid big dividends

for MacArthur's, as well as Nimitz's, offensive. Not only did Navy submarines sink many New Guinea-bound Japanese convoys—most notably
transports carrying the parts of the 32nd and 35th divisions right after the
Hollandia operation—but Nimitz's attack through the Mandates siphoned
away lots of enemy air and naval power from SWPA, reducing Japanese mobility in the area. Without such mobility, Japanese garrisons from the Admiralties to Halmahera were reduced to static positions. Such garrisons
could, and did, inflict heavy damage on SWPA, but only when MacArthur's
forces attacked them head on, as at Biak and Wakde-Sarmi. Otherwise,
these positions remained inert, much like landmines that could be avoided.
Manokwari and Hansa Bay-Wewak, for instance, were strongly held, but
their defenders lacked the mobility to contest a SWPA offensive that swept
around them. Except for Adachi's abortive Driniumor River assault, the
Japanese in New Guinea lacked the will and the means to mount large-
scale offensives. Since MacArthur always possessed the strategic initiative,
he had the luxury of choosing battles he was pretty sure he could win. A
setback, as at Biak, might slow down his advance and jeopardize his
timetable, but it could not reverse the strategic tide.

Although the dual drive strategy certainly contributed to SWPA's New
Guinea victory, there was more to it than that. MacArthur and King hated
one another, but MacArthur and Nimitz cooperated well enough to contribute to SWPA's rapid advance. Nimitz's carriers covered both the Hollandia and Morotai operations, providing invading SWPA forces with close air
support. In each case, however, such assistance proved unnecessary; Kenney's pilots had already achieved almost total air superiority. Nimitz aided
MacArthur most simply by prosecuting his central Pacific offensive, which,
as the JCS had foreseen, diffused Japanese resources and prevented them
from concentrating on SWPA.

Overt interservice cooperation was more vital within SWPA, where naval
forces had to transport and support Army troops from operation to operation. MacArthur recognized early on that the New Guinea offensive
would be a triphibious campaign, requiring the integration and cooperation of land, air, and sea forces.[3] Despite bad blood between MacArthur
and King, the 7th Fleet served the SWPA chief well, mostly due to Kinkaid's
and Barbey's efforts. The former did his best to get along with the prickly
MacArthur, and the latter's amphibious talents fitted nicely with SWPA
plans. In addition, King sent so few naval resources to SWPA—most promi-
nently, he refused to give MacArthur any aircraft carriers—that Kinkaid
had little choice but to play a subordinate role in an overwhelmingly Army-
dominated theater. In his effort to limit MacArthur's control over his naval

forces, King also in effect defanged the 7th Fleet, making it next to impossible for naval officers to challenge SWPA strategy.

The AAF also fell into line behind GHQ. Of course, despite its considerable autonomy, the AAF was still part of the Army, so it was easier for MacArthur to exert his authority over it. More importantly, Kenney's views of the AAF's role pretty much dovetailed with MacArthur's own. Kenney saw war through an aerial lens, but he still viewed the 5th AAF's primary task as spearheading and supporting the ground force's advance up the New Guinea coast.[4] During the New Guinea campaign, Kenney's bombing missions were geared toward making the Army's lot easier, not toward bringing the Japanese to their knees on his own.

Since the AAF and Navy were unwilling or unable to challenge MacArthur's strategic vision, Krueger, who was responsible for coordinating the complex amphibious operations, usually had little trouble gaining a consensus for his plans.[5] Disagreements generally revolved around the logistical means, not the strategic or operational end. Barbey, for instance, did not dispute the need to seize the Admiralties, but he questioned the way that MacArthur undertook the operation. Similarly, while Krueger frequently grumbled about the number of AAF personnel he had to find room for in invasion convoys, he accepted the fact that an AAF presence was necessary to develop and man the airdromes that SWPA's advance depended upon. MacArthur's hands-off attitude at the operational level probably contributed to this interservice cooperation. Since Kenney, Krueger, and Kinkaid were free to run their operations as they saw fit—within broad limits, of course—they were generally more willing to compromise than they would have been had MacArthur tried to place the AAF and Navy directly under Krueger's command.

Interservice cooperation was vital in winning the New Guinea campaign, but so were technology and tactics, which in SWPA usually went hand in hand. Because amphibious warfare was such a complex and, to the Army, new undertaking, it lent itself well to change and innovation. Moreover, MacArthur and his subordinates proved eager to experiment so as to increase the pace of their offensive. The New Guinea campaign saw the development or improvement of landing craft, disposable fuel tanks for Kenney's fighters, colored smoke and lights to mark landing beaches, artillery observers in spotter planes, ESBs and their rocket ships, a variety of preventative health measures such as DDT and mosquito netting, Alamo Scouts, and naval demolition teams. These innovations played roles in every landing from the Admiralties to Morotai, providing MacArthur with a degree of tactical and operational flexibility he would not have otherwise possessed. In fact, without them SWPA's amphibious offensive would probably have ground to a halt. MacArthur and his subordinates, however, were savvy enough to recognize that American technology not only went a long way in overcoming both the Japanese and New Guinea's terrain but could do so quickly.

None of this technology was worth anything unless SWPA could obtain and deploy it. Although MacArthur conducted his New Guinea offensive on a logistical shoestring, his logistics still beat anything that the Japanese had, and it played a big role in winning the campaign. Australia's resources, brilliant operations like Hollandia that required little fighting and therefore little shipping, and lucky breaks that freed up vessels from the European War all made the New Guinea campaign logistically possible. Such logistics, combined with technology, enabled SWPA to keep its men and equipment in order and helped turn New Guinea into a war-waging platform. Labor-saving devices like bulldozers permitted SWPA not only to upgrade old Japanese airdromes at Wakde and Biak, for instance, but also to build new ones from scratch, as at Sansapor-Mar and Morotai. Moreover, aviation engineers usually completed such construction quickly, providing MacArthur with enough air cover to move rapidly to the next operation, despite SWPA's lack of aircraft carriers. Logistics gave SWPA the tools with which to change New Guinea in a way most conducive to the American way of war.

MacArthur's prosecution of the New Guinea campaign was helped considerably by intelligence, especially Ultra, which permitted the SWPA commander to read, to varying degrees, his opponent's cards. Willoughby undoubtedly made several serious intelligence blunders. For instance, he failed to make clear the almost complete absence of Japanese combat troops at Hollandia; he misread enemy's intentions around Sarmi; and he was unable to discover the exact date of Adachi's attack along the Driniumor in enough time to help Martin's troops much. These were certainly egregious errors, and a good number of GIs died as a result of them. Even so, on the whole Willoughby's intelligence served MacArthur well, perhaps because it was simply impossible *not* to glean some valuable information from Ultra. Willoughby's intelligence told MacArthur the identity and location of most enemy units in New Guinea, that the enemy expected an attack at Hansa Bay-Wewak and not Hollandia, that the Imperial Navy was concentrating nearby for the Kon operation, that Adachi's forces were deploying for an attack on Aitape, and, perhaps most importantly, that the Japanese had in effect surrendered the strategic initiative by concentrating on the development of a new defensive line in the western part of the island. This was much, and it enabled MacArthur to deploy his forces accordingly. Ultra was not foolproof, but in conjunction with other intelligence methods, it was a valuable tool that contributed mightily to MacArthur's New Guinea victory.

Finally, MacArthur was aided immensely by Japanese strategic mistakes. After 1942 the Japanese surrendered the strategic initiative in the hope that they could construct a defensive line that would wear down the Americans while they rebuilt their forces for a decisive battle later. Doing so, however, permitted the Americans to develop a military juggernaut capable of overwhelming any Japanese obstacles. Moreover, MacArthur took advantage of his strategically quiescent and increasingly immobile enemy to attack targets of his own choosing, secure in the knowledge that his opponent would not strike back on a strategic or operational level.

Of equal importance, the Japanese never took advantage of their interior lines to concentrate their naval and land forces against MacArthur and his limited naval forces. The one possible exception, the Kon operation, was designed more to support the Imperial Navy's planned climactic naval battle in the Marianas than to wreck SWPA's offensive. For all the difficulty that MacArthur and the Navy had in getting along, the JCS provided a mechanism for cooperation that the Japanese lacked. Moreover, the Japanese Navy, which by 1944 alone possessed the mobility to regain the initiative in New Guinea, remained so wedded to a Mahanian battle with its American counterpart that it neglected an opportunity to shatter MacArthur's vulnerable and far-flung offensive prong. Instead, SWPA was able to undertake its advance up the New Guinea littoral with minimal naval support.

MacArthur the Commander

It is impossible to separate MacArthur from the New Guinea campaign. He advocated it, planned it, undertook it, and won it. MacArthur believed that the most important thing was not New Guinea itself but the time it took him to advance across the island.[6] To reach the China-Formosa-Luzon region as rapidly as possible, MacArthur frequently pressured Krueger to push his men harder than the immediate situation warranted, leading to tactically unnecessary casualties at, for instance, Lone Tree Hill, Biak, and the Driniumor River.[7] Even so, to MacArthur such losses were strategically essential. Only by reaching the China-Formosa-Luzon area quickly could he implement what he believed was the most cost-effective plan to win the

Pacific War. From MacArthur's view, the strategic end—liberating the Philippines—justified the sometimes unfortunate tactical means. Therefore, the tactically unnecessary casualties suffered by, say, the 41st Division at Biak, were strategically justifiable because in the long run his overall strategic plan promised the best and cheapest route to victory.

The problem with this line of thinking, however, is that there were other, equally feasible alternative strategies toward defeating the Japanese. Those who believed that Nimitz's central Pacific route provided the best means to beat Japan could plausibly argue that MacArthur's reckless strategy wasted American lives and resources. From this point of view, fewer Americans would have died in New Guinea had MacArthur played the role the JCS originally envisioned for him by using his troops simply to tie down Japanese forces, and the United States still would have prevailed. There is no doubt that MacArthur won the New Guinea campaign, but it is possible to question *how* he won it.

Despite such tactically unnecessary losses, MacArthur and his supporters frequently argued that the New Guinea campaign was cost-effective in terms of time and lives, especially in comparison with Nimitz's bloody drive across the central Pacific, and certainly in contrast with Eisenhower's campaign in northwest Europe.[8] There is considerable truth to this. SWPA losses from the Admiralties to Morotai totaled some 11,300, whereas Nimitz's casualties in his mid-1944 Marianas campaign cost the soldiers, sailors, and Marines under his command close to 20,000 killed and wounded. Fewer combat units participated in the POA offensive than in SWPA's, so Nimitz's troops also suffered greater casualties proportionally than MacArthur's. In addition, without MacArthur's aggressive offensive, the American war effort might have stagnated in late 1944 because the Navy was in no position to take advantage of perceived Japanese weaknesses in the China-Formosa-Luzon area.

On the other hand, there were big differences between the two campaigns that contributed to Nimitz's heavier losses. The Marianas were strategically more valuable than New Guinea and contributed more to the Pacific War effort than serving merely as stepping stones to other targets. The Japanese certainly saw it that way; Nimitz's attack on Saipan, not MacArthur's in New Guinea, provoked the collapse of the Tojo government. The Marianas campaign not only lured the Japanese fleet into a big battle with its American counterpart, a longtime JCS goal, but also provided the AAF with bases from which to strike the Japanese homeland. New Guinea, however, was little more than a road to the Philippines that could grind down already immobile Japanese resources. In short, New Guinea cost less than the Marianas, but it was worth less as well, and any comparison between the two should take this into account.

MacArthur and his supporters often pointed to the SWPA chief's leapfrog strategy as a key to the New Guinea campaign's success, one that helped keep casualties low.[9] Here, too, there is substantial truth to their assertions. SWPA successfully used American air and naval superiority to rapidly bypass and neutralize big Japanese bases at Halmahera, Sorong, Manokwari, and, especially, Hansa Bay-Wewak. Part of the reason MacArthur could undertake such leapfrog operations, however, was that Nimitz's concurrent central Pacific offensive stripped away Japanese air and naval forces, reducing Japanese mobility in New Guinea. Without Nimitz's offensive, it would have been far more difficult to isolate these Japanese bases. Moreover, and ironically enough, MacArthur himself admitted that the very lack of adequate support in SWPA compelled him to use the leapfrog strategy. Writing after the war, he said, "The paucity of the resources at my command made me adopt this [leapfrog] method of campaign as the only hope of accomplishing my task."[10] In other words, had MacArthur possessed more resources, he would have been more willing to assault Japanese strongholds directly, with a commensurate increase in American casualties.

In addition, MacArthur did not always adhere to this leapfrog strategy. At Wakde-Sarmi and Biak, for example, he attacked entrenched Japanese forces head on and suffered comparatively heavy losses. To be sure, MacArthur did not intend to assault such strongpoints directly, but he underestimated and misread Japanese strength and intentions. MacArthur's supporters would undoubtedly argue that in these instances the SWPA chief had little choice if he was to secure the airfields he needed to advance his campaign. Even so, MacArthur could have built his own airdromes in places unoccupied by the enemy, but doing so would have taken time, and during the New Guinea campaign MacArthur valued time more than the troops under his command. The SWPA chief believed that gaining time now, whatever the cost to his men, would undoubtedly save more lives down the road.

MacArthur's command style both contributed to and detracted from the prosecution of the New Guinea campaign. MacArthur gave his field commanders considerable autonomy to plan and conduct their operations, but he intervened when their actions interfered with his strategic timetable, as at Biak and Driniumor River. In his desire to maintain his fast pace, he frequently pressured his subordinates either in ignorance or defiance of the immediate tactical situation. At Biak, for instance, he demanded that Fuller take Mokmer airdrome quickly and refused to accept explanations for delays. There is something to be said for a general who keeps his eye on the big picture, as MacArthur certainly did, but not at the expense of losing touch with battlefield conditions.

Although MacArthur sometimes lost sight of the tactical situation, he kept a firm grasp of SWPA strategy. He often proved recalcitrant at the tactical level when heavy Japanese opposition threatened his timetable, but he demonstrated a shrewd understanding of New Guinea's strategic role. MacArthur recognized that the island was merely a means to an end, and he treated the campaign accordingly. He did not care how he got across New Guinea as long as he did so quickly. Consequently, he displayed remarkably flexibility in his planning. He readily accepted Kenney's suggestion for an immediate invasion of the Admiralties; he gladly abandoned the long-planned assault on Hansa Bay when Fellers presented a better idea; and he proposed that Krueger and Eichelberger divert their followup forces from Hollandia to Wakde when SWPA encountered minimal resistance during the Reckless operation. Such flexibility undoubtedly contributed to SWPA's swift advance and low casualty rate and demonstrated MacArthur's strategic abilities and priorities.

On the whole, and despite some blunders, MacArthur's New Guinea generalship proved beneficial to the American war effort. MacArthur recognized and utilized SWPA's technological, intelligence, and strategic advantages to overcome Japanese resistance and move his forces closer toward the Japanese mainland. Unfortunately, instead of learning from his New Guinea campaign mistakes, MacArthur went on to repeat them, on a larger and more tragic scale, later in his career. Indeed, MacArthur's conduct during the New Guinea offensive mirrored his behavior before and after the campaign.

Throughout the New Guinea offensive, MacArthur maintained a political and strategic agenda independent of the JCS's. Most American military planners believed that the best way to defeat Japan was by attacking through the central Pacific. MacArthur, however, felt that liberating the Philippines was the way to go. Despite repeated JCS directives to the contrary, MacArthur continued to hold firm to and act upon his own views, even to the point of threatening to disrupt the Pacific War. He saw JCS instructions as open to interpretation and debate, not as orders to be obeyed. Fortunately for MacArthur, the New Guinea campaign fulfilled both his and the JCS's strategic hopes. By September the strategic situation had changed in a manner favorable to MacArthur, causing the JCS to change its mind and permit a Philippines campaign.

There was nothing new in MacArthur's independent posture. As chief of staff he had openly clashed with Roosevelt on budgetary issues and force strength, and throughout World War II he adhered to his own agenda. Later in Korea, however, MacArthur's independent political agenda contributed to his downfall. He advocated expanding the war to China, even though the Truman administration and the JCS wanted to limit the conflict to the Korean peninsula. As things turned out, these two programs proved to be incompatible. MacArthur's continued public adherence to his viewpoint ultimately alienated Truman, who believed that MacArthur's policies, if implemented, might lead to World War III. Since the stakes were so high, Truman was not as tolerant of MacArthur's stances as the JCS and FDR were during the Pacific War, so he relieved the general of his command.

MacArthur made other mistakes in the New Guinea campaign that would come back to haunt him and the men under his command. He frequently disregarded or downplayed tactical or operational setbacks when they interfered with his strategic visions. At Wakde-Sarmi, for instance, he pronounced the operation over after Wakde fell and completely ignored the bitter struggle for Lone Tree Hill. He got away with this because the Japanese had surrendered the strategic initiative. A setback such as Lone Tree Hill might slow down his offensive, but it could not stop it, at least not for long.

Here, too, MacArthur had a long history of ignoring battlefield realities that did not fit in with his strategic or political mindset. After the Japanese invaded the Philippines, for instance, he insisted that the untrained Filipino troops were fighting effectively, even though this was far from the truth. Later, in Korea, MacArthur ignored increasing battlefield evidence of large-scale Chinese intervention because it conflicted with his strategic goal of ending the war before Christmas 1950. In this case, unfortunately, the Chinese seized the strategic initiative and attacked a stunned MacArthur, driving American and Allied forces back down the peninsula south of Seoul. The Americans and Allies suffered thousands of casualties in the process, losses that might have been avoided had MacArthur paid closer attention to what was happening on the battlefield and not on what he wanted to happen there.

During the New Guinea campaign, MacArthur frequently deceived both his superiors and the public to promote his own agenda. At Biak, for instance, he assured both Marshall and the American people that the operation was over once the GIs firmly established themselves ashore, even though the hardest fighting was yet to come. In encouraging outsiders to believe that his campaign was progressing better than it in fact was, he could build upon this perception of success to promote a Philippines liberation campaign. In a way he was right; once SWPA forces got ashore most operations were over in a strategic sense because the Japanese could not possibly defeat the Americans, but tactical setbacks could and did delay his all-important timetable.

MacArthur's pattern of deception existed before the New Guinea campaign and continued long afterward. As far back as his West Point cadet days he had lied to a congressional committee about the extent of hazing at the military academy. Years afterward, as chief of staff, he exceeded his instructions in his dealings with the Bonus Army. Such disobedience continued through the Korean War. For example, he permitted the Far East Air Force to bomb north of the 38th parallel before Truman signed off on the idea.[11] Later he intentionally kept the JCS in the dark as to the specifics of the Inchon landing and disregarded their wishes by sending American troops north to the Yalu River. Such deception, no matter how successful in advancing the military situation, took its toll and undermined the JCS's confidence in MacArthur's willingness and ability to carry out their orders. When Truman finally relieved the general, no one in the JCS stood up for him.

During the New Guinea campaign, MacArthur repeatedly scattered and dispersed his troops up and down the big island's coast. At one point SWPA troops were fighting simultaneously at Lone Tree Hill, Biak, and along the Driniumor. Such a strategy was arguably militarily sound because the Japanese had surrendered the initiative, and Ultra could theoretically clue MacArthur in to any Japanese attempts to infuse resources from outside the theater to resume the offensive. Even so, as Kon demonstrated, Ultra did not always completely reveal enemy motivations. If the Japanese had more forcefully pushed the operation, they might have snapped SWPA's offensive prong at Biak before Nimitz's naval units came to the rescue. To MacArthur, however, such risks were worth taking if they accelerated his advance across the island.

There was nothing new to MacArthur's tendency to scatter his forces. He repeatedly advocated an offensive into the remote Arafura Sea until the JCS scotched the idea, and in the Philippines he sent Eichelberger's entire 8th Army to liberate the archipelago's southern islands, even though the Japanese there posed no particular threat to American operations. MacArthur tried the same thing in Korea, but with much unhappier consequences. After the Inchon landing, for example, he pulled out the 1st Marine Division and sent it around the peninsula by boat to North Korea's east coast. In dividing his forces between the 8th Army in the west and the X Corps in the east, MacArthur permitted the Chinese to defeat him in detail. Unlike the Japanese in New Guinea, the Chinese possessed both the will and means to seize the strategic initiative, and they did so. By driving the Americans and their allies down the peninsula, the Chinese shattered the image of MacArthur's invincibility, contributing to the JCS's and Truman's decision to relieve him.

As a military commander, MacArthur had both significant strengths and weaknesses. In New Guinea, many circumstances beyond the realm of personal leadership—Ultra intelligence, materiel and technical superiority, and Japanese strategic errors—helped counterbalance MacArthur's military failings and contributed greatly to his victory. MacArthur's ultimate success in the campaign and as a commander, however, was due to his self confident ability to recognize and take advantage of the American military's assets. Unfortunately, years later in Korea, MacArthur continued to behave as if he possessed similar advantages over the communist Chinese, which he did not. MacArthur, in short, played the game the same way no matter how strong or weak his hand was. From this perspective, then, Allied victory in New Guinea was the result of the fortunate convergence of a skilled commander possessing substantial military advantages and an already demoralized and beaten foe.

Assessing MacArthur's Subordinates

Although MacArthur intentionally kept his subordinates out of the limelight, they played a major, and largely positive, role in winning the New Guinea campaign. MacArthur gave his field commanders considerable autonomy to plan and conduct operations, and Kenney, Kinkaid, and Krueger used this independence to reshape and improve, as well as implement, GHQ directives.

To be sure, Kenney frequently misread Japanese intentions and strengths, most notably in the Admiralties, but his aggressive and innovative tactics contributed enormously to SWPA's victory by wrecking enemy air power throughout New Guinea. His surprise air strike on Hollandia's airdromes displayed considerable ingenuity, deftness, and enterprise. During the New Guinea campaign, Kenney used his AAF to pave the way for the ground offensive by destroying Japanese air power, isolating Japanese garrisons, and softening up Japanese positions. Although he valued air power above all else, he recognized the need to integrate his AAF's mission with naval and ground forces, thereby helping to synthesize SWPA's triphibious military machine.

Kinkaid also contributed to MacArthur's successful New Guinea campaign. Not only did Kinkaid give Barbey free rein to develop and apply his creative amphibious skills, but he recognized that the 7th Fleet was supposed to supplement and support the Army's advance. Kinkaid, however, did not back down when challenged by the Japanese Navy during the Kon operation. He recognized the Japanese naval foray and moved decisively to meet it, despite his limited naval resources and AAF setbacks. Equally important to the campaign's success was Kinkaid's ability to serve both MacArthur and his arch enemy King without irrevocably alienating either man.

Despite the large role naval and air power played, ground forces bore the heaviest burden in the New Guinea campaign. Of MacArthur's three subordinates, Krueger undoubtedly had the most important job. As SWPA ground commander, Krueger had the uncomfortable task of reconciling MacArthur's rigorous timetable with operational realities. Krueger juggled these often incompatible assignments successfully enough to fulfill MacArthur's strategic goals without suffering exceedingly heavy losses. To do so, however, Krueger sometimes had to twist and bend MacArthur's orders. During the Admiralties invasion, for instance, Krueger's actions probably reduced American casualties and helped ensure the operation's success. In addition, Krueger acted as a buffer between an impatient MacArthur and his often beleaguered field commanders. During the Biak operation he tried to explain Fuller's problems to his boss while at the same time projecting an aggressive posture. Even so, in the end Krueger's job depended upon MacArthur, and he frequently pressured his subordinates on his chief's behalf to complete operations quickly, even though this sometimes led to otherwise unnecessary losses. He refused, for instance, to permit Sibert and Hall to delay their offenses at Sarmi and Driniumor River, although he was motivated as much by a belief in maintaining the operational initiative as by his desire to appease MacArthur. Krueger often seemed inflexible with his subordinates, but he successfully coordinated SWPA's complex triphibious operations with Kenney and Barbey, and only rarely did he have to appeal to MacArthur's ultimate authority. Krueger's selective application of tact and brusqueness, appeasement and firmness, and aggressiveness and caution contributed significantly to the New Guinea campaign's success.[12]

Finally, the New Guinea offensive would not have succeeded without the solid performance of SWPA's corps and divisional commanders, as well as their troops. During the campaign, SWPA's high-ranking officers repeatedly demonstrated a desire to get the job done, and if they did not exhibit much tactical finesse in doing so, this is hardly surprising in a mass-based American Army that often resorted to firepower and materiel. Despite MacArthur's rigid timetable, only one SWPA divisional or corps commander—Fuller at Biak—was relieved of command. By contrast, in Europe Eisenhower and Bradley repeatedly replaced subordinates who failed to achieve their objectives, even in their first combat actions. The European battlefields were undoubtedly far more fluid and unstable than New Guinea's, where American mobility, firepower, and materiel superiority enabled SWPA to beat into oblivion immobile and isolated Japanese positions. Such relatively controlled battlefield actions gave MacArthur's combat commanders an advantage in their on-the-job training that their European theater comrades lacked and contributed to SWPA's relatively low turnover rate throughout the campaign.

Indeed, the most successful field commanders—Eichelberger, Sibert, and Swift, for example—were those who fulfilled MacArthur's demand for speed and showed a willingness to grapple with the enemy under less than ideal circumstances, and all three went on to bigger and better things. Equally important, these men applied their enterprise and energy toward developing New Guinea logistically. Swift and Eichelberger, for example, oversaw the rapid construction of big SWPA bases at the Admiralties and Hollandia, overcoming topographical and human obstacles every bit as irksome, if not as deadly, as the Japanese. To succeed in SWPA, a field commander had not only to win military and logistical battles but win them MacArthur's way—fast.

Similarly, the American GI performed well in New Guinea. In the European War many American units stalled when confronted by the Wehrmacht, but SWPA's combat outfits stood up to their Japanese opponents quite well. To be sure, the Japanese Army in New Guinea was not nearly as formidable as its German counterpart, but this should not disparage the solid performance of the 1st Cav, 6th, 24th, and 31st divisions in their first fights, especially since the hostile terrain often compensated for any advantage the Wehrmacht had over its Japanese allies. Even outfits with dubious reputations, like the 32nd and 43rd divisions, managed to win their battles. Support units such as engineers, the 7th Fleet, and the AAF also worked very well, despite logistical and topographical constraints. In New Guinea, SWPA was able to fight *its* type of war, providing American soldiers, airmen, and sailors with a valuable advantage.

The New Guinea Campaign and the American Way of War

The New Guinea campaign was one of many the American Army undertook in World War II. Although the Army entered the conflict with a common doctrine, commanders, terrain, and the enemy all interacted to modify or distort prewar tenets. The New Guinea offensive was no exception, but despite its unique commander and battleground, SWPA's American Army by and large stayed true to its principles. Instead, SWPA commanders used Army doctrine in ways that best promoted the type of war MacArthur wanted to wage.

Since the Civil War, the American Army had utilized firepower to destroy its opponents. MacArthur was no different, and firepower played a large role in winning the New Guinea campaign, especially in getting SWPA's troops onto the beach. Except at undefended Sansapor-Mar, heavy air and naval bombardments preceded every SWPA landing. Even when there were not a lot of Japanese around to pummel, as at Hollandia, Aitape, and Toem, the massive preliminary bombardment at least boosted morale among the landing troops. Often, however, it did more than that; at Noemfoor, for instance, naval and air strikes shattered the disheartened Japanese garrison before Patrick's GIs even got ashore. Moreover, naval and air support helped defend the always vulnerable beachheads, and at Los Negros the 7th Fleet probably saved Chase's weary troopers from being overrun. Once inland, air, naval, and artillery support, when the Americans managed to deploy it, again and again shattered enemy resistance, providing SWPA with a card the Japanese could not trump.

MacArthur undoubtedly relied a lot on firepower, but the peculiar nature of New Guinea warfare, with its emphasis on amphibious operations into a remote and hard-to-reach jungle-covered environment, forced SWPA to develop new ways to employ it. To bridge the gap between the preliminary bombardment and the landing of troops, ESBs used LCI rocket craft, a tactic unique to the Pacific War. Since it was difficult to maneuver tanks in New Guinea's jungle terrain or across coral reefs, the Army frequently substituted Buffaloes, which, although not as heavily armored as tanks, could still overcome almost everything the Japanese threw at them.

Like firepower, mobility had been a constant part of American military doctrine. MacArthur used it also, but here too SWPA had to find new ways to deploy it in New Guinea's peculiar environment. SWPA clearly could not maneuver much on the island itself because it possessed lots of impassable jungle and almost no roads, so the Americans took to the sea. All those amphibious craft were designed specifically to move men and equipment over water from one point to another. By early 1944 the worn out and battered Japanese had nothing comparable, so SWPA could with reasonable safety employ this amphibious mobility to neutralize Japanese garrisons such as Hansa Bay-Wewak. MacArthur's field commanders also used their landing craft on a tactical level to outmaneuver the Japanese. Fuller's 41st Division, for example, deployed landing craft on Lake Sentani to bypass Japanese positions defending Hollandia's airdromes. Swift and Sibert both used their amphibious craft in the Admiralties and around Lone Tree Hill to outflank stubborn Japanese defenses. Prewar Army doctrine did not devote a lot of time to the role of landing craft, but SWPA's amphibious mobility proved enormously valuable in winning the New Guinea campaign.

On the other hand, several times during the campaign the Army eschewed tactical maneuvering and instead attacked the enemy head on, as at Lone Tree Hill and Biak. To be sure, such simplistic plans were easiest for SWPA's new and relatively untrained conscript forces to implement in the confusing New Guinea jungle, but this lack of imagination often led to tactical stalemate, which hindered MacArthur's hopes for a swift advance. Instead, SWPA had to resort to massive firepower to destroy the Japanese. The Army did this very well, but in theory firepower was supposed to be only one aspect of a multifaceted doctrine that also included mobility. Unfortunately, in the confusion and pressure of battle, mobility occasionally went by the wayside.

Finally, the American Army had traditionally emphasized materiel superiority over the enemy. By taking advantage of massive American industrial capacity, the Army could simply overwhelm the enemy with bullets, shells, grenades, tanks, artillery, planes, ships, and every other weapon of war. Theoretically, expending materiel would obviate the necessity of throwing valuable American soldiers at enemy positions, although this was not always the case. New Guinea's remoteness made it hard to supply the theater with everything from LSTs to grenades, but thanks to the American logistical network, SWPA still had more of almost everything than the beleaguered Japanese, except for casualties.

During the New Guinea campaign the Army remained largely true to prewar doctrine, although SWPA often modified those principles to fit within the New Guinea framework. The biggest difference between SWPA and the Army's other World War II theaters, however, was the reason for utilizing all that firepower, mobility, and materiel. Throughout the conflict, most American military commanders applied their advantages to wear down the enemy. While it was true that most Army officers sought a decisive breakthrough that would lead to victory, the result in the end was usually a slugging match that enabled the American war machine to grind down its Japanese or German opponents. Such methods took time, however, and MacArthur did not believe he had that luxury. He was not interested in attrition, so he took operational risks most American commanders shunned. For example, rather than hazard a long drawn out Admiralties operation, MacArthur attacked the place ahead of schedule, even though doing so placed Chase's troopers in considerable jeopardy. Most American military commanders tacitly accepted attrition because it was safer, but MacArthur realized that it was also slower, and celerity was his prime concern in the New Guinea campaign. To be sure, SWPA operations sometimes led to attrition, as at Lone Tree Hill, but MacArthur did his best to avoid it and leave the Japanese to the not-so-tender mercies of the Australians and mother nature.

MacArthur's successful Philippines liberation campaign, as well as the high-profile Marine invasions in the central Pacific, overshadowed SWPA's comparatively small-scale New Guinea operations. Not only did the Philippines campaign permit MacArthur to fulfill his pledge to liberate the oppressed archipelago, but it also gave the Navy its opportunity to destroy the Japanese fleet at the Battle of Leyte Gulf. Once in American possession, the Philippines enabled MacArthur's and Nimitz's forces to cut Japan off from its Netherlands East Indies oil supplies and to stage American resources for the planned big invasion of the enemy homeland.

The New Guinea campaign is one of World War II's forgotten episodes, even though it played a major role in the implementation of American Pacific War strategy. The campaign saw the conquest of no great cities, the destruction of no enemy fleets, and—thanks to MacArthur's publicity machine—the emergence of no notable field commanders. The New Guinea offensive, in the final analysis, was a means to an end, a road to something far greater than itself.

NOTES

Abbreviations

ASOOH   "U.S. Army Senior Officer Oral Histories." Frederick, Maryland. University Publications of America, 1989.

DMMA   Douglas MacArthur Memorial Archives. Norfolk, Virginia.

KP   Walter Krueger Papers. United States Military Academy, West Point, New York.

RERC   Robert L. Eichelberger Research Collection. Duke University, North Carolina.

RJCS   Record of the Joint Chiefs of Staff, Part 1. Frederick, Maryland: University Publications of America, 1982.

USAMHI   United States Army Military History Institute. Carlisle, Pennsylvania.

WNRC   Washington National Records Center. National Archives and Records Administration, Suitland, Maryland.

WTSJD   Wartime Translations of Seized Japanese Documents: Allied Translator and Interceptor Service Reports, 1942–1946. Bethesda, Maryland: Congressional Information Services, 1988.

Introduction

1. Columbia Broadcasting System, *From Pearl Harbor into Tokyo: The Story as Told by War Correspondents on the Air* (New York: Columbia Broadcasting System, 1945), pp. 169–70.

2. Murlin Spencer, *St. Louis Post-Dispatch*, 28 May 1944.

3. "Southwest Pacific Area Operations," *Army and Navy Journal*, 1944, 82(15):76.

4. Ibid., p. 130.

5. Curtin said, "With relatively little loss of life and the minimum of frontal assaults by Ground Forces, enemy strongholds have been bypassed, rendering possible a new conception of offensive power in the realm of strategy, tactics, and logistics." Ibid.

6. Marshall to MacArthur, 9 June 1944, Correspondence with the War Department, DMMA, RG 4, Box 17, Folder 1.

7. See, especially, Charles A. Willoughby and John Chamberlain, *MacArthur: 1941–1951* (New York: McGraw-Hill, 1954), pp. 189, 204–8; Courtney Whitney, *MacArthur: His Rendezvous with History* (New York: Knopf, 1964), pp. 114–15; Douglas MacArthur, *Reminiscences* (New York: McGraw-Hill, 1964), pp. 169–70, 195.

8. For a sampling, see Stephen E. Ambrose, "MacArthur: The Man and the Legend," *American History Illustrated*, January 1968, 11(9):52; Gerhard L. Weinberg, *A World at Arms: A Global History of World War II* (Cambridge: Cambridge University Press, 1994), p. 653; John F. Shortal, *Forged by Fire: General Robert L. Eichelberger and the Pacific War* (Columbia: University of South Carolina Press, 1987), p. 75; Samuel Eliot Morison, *History of United States Naval Operations in World War II*, vol. 8: *New Guinea and the Marianas, March 1944–August 1944,* (Boston: Little, Brown, 1953), pp. 144–45; and John Costello, *The Pacific War* (New York: Atlantic Communications, 1981), p. 491.

9. For instance, see B. H. Liddell Hart, *History of the Second World War* (New York: Putnam's, 1971), pp. 613–14; D. Clayton James, *The Years of MacArthur,* vol. 2 (Boston: Houghton Mifflin, 1975), pp. 489–91.

10. See, for example, Dan van der Vat, *The Pacific Campaign: World War II, The U.S.–Japanese Naval War, 1941–1945* (New York: Simon and Schuster, 1991), pp. 312–13; Peter Calvocoressi and Guy Wint, *Total War: Causes and Courses of the Second World War* (London: Penguin Press, 1972), pp. 772–73.

11. There are, however, official Army, Navy, and Army Air Forces histories that cover the campaign in some depth, although they are difficult to read and generally eschew personalities and controversy. See, especially, Wesley Frank Craven and James Lea Cate, eds., *The Army Air Forces in World War II: The Pacific,* vol. 4: *Guadalcanal to Saipan: August 1942 to July 1944* (Chicago: University of Chicago Press, 1950); Morison, *New Guinea and the Marianas;* Robert Ross Smith, *Approach to the Philippines* (Washington, D.C.: Government Printing Office, 1953); and Major General Hugh J. Casey's eight volumes on engineering operations in the southwest Pacific.

12. Based on statistics from "Summary of Operations for the Month of September 1944," DMMA, RG 3, Box 167; Smith, *Approach,* pp. 16, 577; John Miller, Jr., *Cartwheel: The Reduction of Rabaul* (Washington D.C.: Government Printing Office, 1959), p. 348; Samuel Eliot Morison, *History of United States Naval Operations in World War II*, vol. 6: *Breaking the Bismarcks Barrier, 22 July 1942–1 May 1944* (Boston: Little, Brown, 1950), p. 447; Robert Wallace, *The Italian Campaign* (Alexandria, Virginia: Time-Life Books, 1981), p. 33. Figures include the Admiralties operation.

13. Indeed, it is interesting to note how often the metaphor pops up in postwar memoirs; for example, both Walter Krueger and Robert L. Eichelberger use this analogy in their book titles. See Walter Krueger, *From Down Under to Nippon* (Washington, D.C.: Combat Forces Press, 1953); and Robert L. Eichelberger, *Our Jungle Road to Tokyo* (New York: Viking Press, 1950).

14. Although the Vogelkop oil deposits played a role in early JCS and SWPA planning, their importance receded as the campaign progressed.

15. Named after influential turn-of-the-century American Rear Admiral Alfred Thayer Mahan, who believed "the enemy's ships and fleets are the true objects [of war] to be assailed on all occasions." Quoted from Russell F. Weigley, *The American Way of War: A History of United States Military Strategy and Policy* (Bloomington: Indiana University Press, 1977), p. 175.

16. Interview with Clyde Eddleman, Clyde Eddleman Papers, USAMHI, Interview 2, p. 29.

17. The JCS consisted of Army chief of staff General George C. Marshall, chief of naval operations Admiral Ernest J. King, Army Air Forces commander General Henry H. Arnold, and President Roosevelt's chief of staff Admiral William Leahy. It was responsible for determining, coordinating, and directing the American war effort. Decisions were made by consensus.

18. MacArthur, *Reminiscences*, p. 166; Interview with Clyde D. Eddleman, 29 June 1971, 1971 Interviews, James Collection, DMMA, RG 49, Box 1, pp. 21–22.

19. See, for example, Harold Riegelman, *The Caves of Biak* (New York: Dial Press, 1955), p. 160; Edward Coffman and Paul H. Hass, eds., "With MacArthur in the Pacific: A Memoir by Philip F. La Follette," *Wisconsin Magazine of History,* 1980–81, 64(2):94–95; Robert L. Eichelberger, "Remarks on MacArthur as a Great Soldier," RERC, Box 73; General Albert C. Wedemeyer, *Wedemeyer Reports!* (New York: Holt, 1958), p. 241; Interview with Brigadier General William L. Ritchie, 24 June 1971, 1971 Interviews, James Collection, DMMA, RG 49, Box 4, pp. 21–22.

20. Daniel E. Barbey, *MacArthur's Amphibious Navy: Seventh Amphibious Force Operations, 1943–1945* (Annapolis: United States Naval Institute, 1969), pp. 24–25.

21. In his book on the Pacific War, Costello, for instance, mentions Eisenhower more often than either of MacArthur's two chief subordinate ground commanders, Walter Krueger and Robert Eichelberger. See Costello, *Pacific War,* pp. 725, 731.

22. Eichelberger, "Public Relations Policies of GHQ, Particularly with Reference to Other Leaders besides Gen. MacArthur," Dictations, RERC, Box 73, No. 5; Coffman and Hass, "With MacArthur," pp. 93–94.

23. According to Eichelberger, MacArthur once confessed to him that he did not know much about the minutiae of soldiering, which may explain why he gave his subordinates so much operational freedom. See Eichelberger, "Debunks MacArthur as a 'Great Soldier' as Pictured in Books by Willoughby and Frazier Hunt; MacArthur as Strategist," Dictations, RERC, Box 73, pp. 126–34.

24. Thomas Kinkaid, *The Reminiscences of Thomas Cassin Kinkaid* (New York: Columbia University, Oral History Research Office, 1961), p. 334.

25. For an excellent account of MacArthur's relationship with his subordinates throughout the Pacific War, see William Leary, ed., *We Shall Return!: MacArthur's Commanders and the Defeat of Japan, 1942–1945* (Lexington: University Press of Kentucky, 1988). In addition, many of MacArthur's subordinates also wrote their memoirs. See especially Krueger's *From Down Under to Nippon,* Eichelberger's *Our Jungle Road to Tokyo,* Barbey's *MacArthur's Amphibious Navy,* and George C. Kenney, *General Kenney Reports: A Personal History of the Pacific War* (New York: Duell, Sloan, and Pearce, 1949).

1. Strategic Background

1. In September 1943, Brigadier General William Ritchie, after visiting MacArthur, warned Marshall about the SWPA commander's rampant suspicion that he was being undermined. See Ritchie to Marshall, 22 September 1943, Correspondence with the War Department, DMMA, RG 4, Box 16, Folder 4.

2. Forrest C. Pogue, *George C. Marshall: Organizer of Victory, 1943–1945* (New York: Viking Press, 1973), p. 323.

3. Robert L. Eichelberger, "Some Thoughts about Sutherland and Krueger," Dictations, RERC, Box 73, pp. 570–77.

4. Frazier Hunt, *The Untold Story of Douglas MacArthur* (New York: Devin-Adair, 1954), pp. 313–14.

5. Paul P. Rogers, *The Bitter Years: MacArthur and Sutherland* (New York: Praeger, 1991), p. 61.

6. Indeed, Marshall delivered; he got Army Air Force commander Hap Arnold to send fifty P-38s and promise to bring SWPA's bomber force up to full strength. See Marshall to MacArthur, 31 December 1943, Correspondence with the War Department, DMMA, RG 4, Box 16, Folder 5.

7. There is no written record of this meeting, although MacArthur left an account of it in his autobiography. According to MacArthur, Marshall claimed that the Navy demanded the dominant role in the Pacific War, and there was little he could do about it, especially since Admiral King was supported by Secretary of the Navy Knox, President Roosevelt, Admiral Leahy, and even Arnold. It is hard to believe, however, that Marshall would confide such information to MacArthur. See Douglas MacArthur, *Reminiscences* (New York: McGraw-Hill, 1964), pp. 183–84.

8. Interview with Thomas H. Handy, 8 September 1971, 1971 Interviews, James Collection, DMMA, RG 49, Box 3, pp. 10–14.

9. For a good discussion of this problem, see Edward S. Miller, *War Plan Orange: The U.S. Strategy to Defeat Japan, 1897–1945* (Annapolis: Naval Institute Press, 1991); and Charles O. Cook, Jr., "The Strange Case of Rainbow-5," *US Naval Institute Proceedings*, August 1978, 104(8):67–73.

10. See, for instance, H. H. Arnold, *Global Mission* (New York: Harper, 1949), p. 348; and Ritchie Interview, 24 June 1971, 1971 Interviews, James Collection, DMMA, RG 49, Box 4.

11. Maurice Matloff, *Strategic Planning for Coalition Warfare: 1943–1944* (Washington, D.C.: Government Printing Office, 1959), pp. 32–33; Samuel Eliot Morison, *History of United States Naval Operations in World War II*, vol. 6: *Breaking the Bismarcks Barrier, 22 July 1942–1 May 1944* (Boston: Little, Brown, 1950), p. 6. As its name implies, the CCS consisted of both the American and British service commanders.

12. Before the war, New Guinea was divided into three administrative units: the western part, which was part of the Netherlands East Indies; Northeastern New Guinea, which Germany ruled until Australia conquered it in World War I; and the Papua, which refers to the southeastern part of the island controlled by the Australians since the nineteenth century. According to an agreement ironed out at Pearl Harbor in March 1943, MacArthur would directly command American and Australian forces fighting in Papua New Guinea, while Admiral William Halsey con-

ducted an autonomous drive up the Solomons ladder. See Matloff, *Strategic Planning*, pp. 91–97.

13. Handy Interview, pp. 25–26.

14. JCS 353, "Future Campaign Operations in the Pacific Ocean Areas, Memorandum by King," 10 June 1943, RJCS, pp. 3–5.

15. JCS 353/1, "Future Campaign Operations in the Pacific Ocean Areas," 14 June 1943, RJCS, pp. 9–15.

16. Although a retired naval officer, Leahy believed that MacArthur should be placed in overall Pacific command. See William D. Leahy, *I Was There: A Personal Story of the Chief of Staff to Presidents Roosevelt and Truman Based on His Notes and Diaries at the Time* (New York: McGraw-Hill, 1950), pp. 152–53.

17. "Corrigendum to JCS 353/1," 15 June 1943, RJCS, p. 1.

18. There were three main JCS planning bodies: the Joint Strategic Survey Committee (JSSC) consisted of retired generals—elder military statesmen—who could honestly evaluate strategic proposals without jeopardizing their careers; the Joint Staff Planners (JPS) served as the JCS's gatekeeper and reviewed the Joint Chiefs' strategic decisions to make sure that they were consistent and practicable; and the Joint War Plans Committee (JWPC), which worked for the JPS by developing detailed military plans for projected interservice operations.

19. JCS 304, "Operations in the Pacific and Far East in 1943–44," 12 May 1943, RJCS, pp. 1–2.

20. JPS 67/5, "Strategic Plan for the Defeat of Japan," 26 May 1943, RJCS, pp. 83–90.

21. Ibid.

22. Ibid.; JCS 304, "Operations in the Pacific and Far East," pp. 24–25.

23. JWPC 46/5, "Appreciation and Plan for the Defeat of Japan," 9 July 1943, RJCS, pp. 106–9.

24. JCS 386/1, "Strategy in the Pacific: Report by the Joint Staff Planners," 19 July 1943, RJCS, p. 5.

25. JPS 67/5, "Strategic Plan for the Defeat of Japan," pp. 97–98; JWPC 46/5, "Appreciation and Plan for the Defeat of Japan," pp. 69–70, 106–12.

26. CCS 417/2, "Over-all Plan for the Defeat of Japan," 23 December 1943, RJCS, pp. 1–2.

27. For a psychological explanation of MacArthur's obsession with the Philippines, see Carol Moris Petillo, *Douglas MacArthur: The Philippine Years* (Bloomington: Indiana University Press, 1981).

28. Wesley Frank Craven and James Lea Cate, eds., *The Army Air Forces in World War II: The Pacific*, vol. 4: *Guadalcanal to Saipan: August 1942 to July 1944* (Chicago: University of Chicago Press, 1950), p. 615.

29. In a letter to King in March 1944, Nimitz described MacArthur's fanatic commitment to liberating the Philippines and his paranoia about the issue during a meeting between the two men: "[MacArthur] blew up and made an oration of some length on the impossibility of bypassing the Philippines, his sacred obligations there—redemption of the 17 million people—blood on his soul—deserted by American people—etc., etc.,—and then a criticism of 'those gentlemen in Washington, who, far from the scene, and having never heard the whistle of the pellets, etc., endeavor to set the strategy of the Pacific War.'" Quoted in Ernest J. King and Walter

Muir Whitehill, *Fleet Admiral King: A Naval Record* (New York: Norton, 1952), p. 538. Eichelberger confirmed this as well in Eichelberger, "Letter to Dr. Samuel Milner," 8 March 1954, Dictations, RERC, Box 73. See also Thomas Kinkaid, *The Reminiscences of Thomas Cassin Kinkaid* (New York: Columbia University, Oral History Research Office, 1961), pp. 256, 368; William T. Ritchie to Marshall, 22 September 1943, Correspondence with the War Department, DMMA, RG 4, Box 16, Folder 4.

30. Hunt, *Untold Story*, pp. 307–8.

31. Daniel E. Barbey, *MacArthur's Amphibious Navy: Seventh Amphibious Force Operations, 1943–1945* (Annapolis: United States Naval Institute, 1969), p. 183.

32. Ritchie Interview, 24 June 1971, 1971 Interviews, James Collection, DMMA, RG 49, Box 4, p. 5.

33. Interview with Robert G. Wood, ASOOH, Tape 30, p. 20.

34. Ritchie to Marshall, 22 September 1943, Correspondence with the War Department, DMMA, RG 4, Box 16, Folder 4.

35. MacArthur to Marshall, 31 October 1943, Correspondence with the War Department, DMMA, RG 4, Box 16, Folder 4.

36. Ibid.; Barbey, *MacArthur's Amphibious Navy*, p. 22; MacArthur, *Reminiscences*, p. 185.

37. *The War Reports of General of the Army George C. Marshall, General of the Army H. H. Arnold, and Fleet Admiral Ernest J. King* (New York: Lippincott, 1947), pp. 219–20.

38. MacArthur to Marshall, 31 October 1943; Matloff, *Strategic Planning*, p. 315.

39. Hunt, *Untold Story*, pp. 314–15; MacArthur, *Reminiscences*, p. 172.

40. MacArthur to Marshall, 31 October 1943. In his memoirs, MacArthur claimed that he would have been willing to take a subordinate role, but his actions and statements during the conflict indicated otherwise. See MacArthur, *Reminiscences*, p. 172.

41. MacArthur, *Reminiscences*, pp. 166–67.

42. Hunt, *Untold Story*, p. 307.

43. MacArthur, *Reminiscences*, p. 166; Kinkaid, *Reminiscences*, p. 253.

44. Clay Blair, Jr., *Silent Victory: The U.S. Submarine War against Japan* (New York: Lippincott, 1975), p. 552.

45. Ibid., pp. 816–17.

46. JCS to MacArthur, 24 January 1944, Correspondence with the War Department, DMMA, RG 4, Box 16, Folder 5.

47. Indeed, almost all newspapers openly stated that the Philippines were the goal of MacArthur's New Guinea offensive.

48. Edward Coffman and Paul H. Hass, eds., "With MacArthur in the Pacific: A Memoir by Philip F. La Follette," *Wisconsin Magazine of History*, 1980–81, 64(2):93–94.

49. Douglas MacArthur, *A Soldier Speaks: Public Papers and Speeches of General of the Army Douglas MacArthur* (New York: Praeger, 1965), pp. 129–30. In fact, MacArthur used this weapon against FDR when the two met in Hawaii in July 1944 to discuss Pacific War strategy.

50. The MacArthur propaganda machine was mighty. When schoolchildren in Nassau County, New York, heard that MacArthur was short of fighter planes, they organized a campaign to purchase twenty-five planes for him as a Christmas present. Leone D. Howell, Chairman of the Nassau County War Finance Committee, to MacArthur, 10 November 1943, SWPA Correspondence Messages, 1942–1945, DMMA, RG 3, Box 3. See also Hunt, *Untold Story*, p. 308.

51. For an overview of the Pearl Harbor conference, see Hunt, *Untold Story*, p. 315; Matloff, *Strategic Planning*, p. 456; Grace Person Hayes, *The History of the Joint Chiefs of Staff in World War II: The War against Japan* (Annapolis: Naval Institute Press, 1982), pp. 546–47; E. B. Potter, *Nimitz* (Annapolis: Naval Institute Press, 1976), pp. 280–82; and Robert Ross Smith, *Approach to the Philippines* (Washington, D.C.: Government Printing Office, 1953), pp. 7–8.

52. George C. Kenney, *General Kenney Reports: A Personal History of the Pacific War* (New York: Duell, Sloan, and Pearce, 1949), p. 371.

53. MacArthur to Marshall, 2 February 1944, Correspondence with the War Department, DMMA, RG 4, Box 16, Folder 5.

54. Hayes, *History*, pp. 549–50; Matloff, *Strategic Planning*, p. 456.

55. Quoted from Potter, *Nimitz*, pp. 282–83.

56. Matloff, *Strategic Planning*, p. 456; King and Whitehill, *Fleet Admiral King*, p. 444.

57. JCS 713, "Strategy in the Pacific: Report by the Joint Strategic Survey Committee," 16 February 1944, RJCS, pp. 1–8.

58. JWPC, "Requirements for Pacific–Far East Operations, 1944," 29 February 1944, RJCS, pp. 1–7.

59. JPS 713/1, "Future Operations in the Pacific: Report by the Joint Staff Planners," 10 March 1944, RJCS, pp. 10–24.

60. Ibid.

61. Barbey, *MacArthur's Amphibious Navy*, p. 183.

62. JCS 713/2, "Future Operations in the Pacific: Memorandum by the Commander in Chief, United States Fleet and Chief of Naval Operations," 11 March 1944, RJCS, pp. 30–32.

63. Memorandum from the Commanding General, Army Air Forces, "Basic Decisions Which Will Give Strategic Guidance for the Conduct of the War in the Pacific," 8 March 1944, RJCS, pp. 1–3.

64. Craven and Cate, *Guadalcanal to Saipan*, p. 554; Hayes, *History*, p. 552.

65. "Reno IV," 20 January 1944, Bonner Fellers Papers, DMMA, RG 44, Folder 5.

66. MacArthur to Sutherland, 16 February 1944, Sutherland Papers, DMMA, RG 30, Box 5, Folder 10; MacArthur to Sutherland, 26 February 1944, Correspondence with the War Department, DMMA, RG 4, Box 16, Folder 5.

67. MacArthur to Sutherland, 26 February 1944, Radios (Personal), Sutherland Papers, DMMA, RG 30, Box 7, Folder 6.

68. Ibid.

69. Craven and Cate, *Guadalcanal to Saipan*, p. 554.

70. JCS 151st Meeting, 11 March 1944, RJCS, p. 4.

71. Ibid., pp. 9–10.

72. Sutherland's views are detailed in ibid., pp. 1–7; MacArthur to Sutherland, 8, 26 February 1944, Correspondence with the War Department, Sutherland Papers, DMMA, RG 4, Box 16, Folder 5.

73. JCS 151st Meeting, 11 March 1944, RJCS, p. 10.

74. The Navy view, like Sutherland's, is in ibid., pp. 1–2, 9.

75. There is no record of what went on behind those closed doors.

76. MacArthur, in turn, gave the job to Halsey's SOPAC, which took the island easily on 20 March 1944.

77. JCS 713/4, "Future Operations in the Pacific," 12 March 1944, RJCS, pp. 36–38.

78. See Charles A. Willoughby and John Chamberlain, *MacArthur: 1941–1951* (New York: McGraw-Hill, 1954), p. 177.

79. See, for example, Dan van der Vat, *The Pacific Campaign: World War II, The U.S.–Japanese Naval War, 1941–1945* (New York: Simon and Schuster, 1991), pp. 312–13; Peter Calvocoressi and Guy Wint, *Total War: Causes and Courses of the Second World War* (London: Penguin Press, 1993), pp. 772–73; John Ellis, *Brute Force: Allied Strategy and Tactics in the Second World War* (New York: Viking Press, 1990), pp. 500–510; Ronald Spector, *Eagle against the Sun: The American War with Japan* (New York: Free Press, 1985), p. 230.

80. For a good argument that Roosevelt disregarded JCS advice, see Kent Roberts Greenfield, *American Strategy in World War II: A Reconsideration* (Baltimore: Johns Hopkins Press, 1963), pp. 49–79. The best example of this Roosevelt tendency was his insistence on the North African invasion in 1942. Forrest Pogue quotes Marshall's frustration with Roosevelt on that issue in *George C. Marshall: Ordeal and Hope, 1939–1942* (New York: Viking Press, 1966), pp. 329–30: "We were largely trying to get the President to stand pat on what he had previously agreed to. The President shifted, particularly when Churchill got hold of him. . . . My job was to hold the President down to what we were doing. It was difficult because the Navy was pulling everything toward the Pacific. . . . The President's tendency to shift and handle things loosely and be influenced, particularly by the British, was one of our great problems." There is little doubt that Marshall's jaded view of FDR's strategic conceptions continued throughout the war. See also Arnold, *Global Mission*, pp. 323, 355–56.

81. CCS 417, "Over-All Plan for the Defeat of Japan," 2 December 1943, RJCS, pp. 1–2.

2. MacArthur Gears Up

1. Sy M. Kahn, *Between Tedium and Terror: A Soldier's World War II Diary, 1943–1945* (Chicago: University of Illinois Press, 1993), p. 9.

2. Ibid., p. 25.

3. Ibid., p. 138.

4. Walter A. Luszki, *A Rape of Justice: MacArthur and the New Guinea Hangings* (New York: Madison Books, 1991), p. 14.

5. E. M. Flanagan, Jr., *The Angels: A History of the 11th Airborne Division* (Navato, California: Presidio Press, 1989), p. 79.

6. Jules Archer, *Jungle Fighters: A GI Correspondent's Experiences in the New Guinea Campaign* (New York: Julian Messner, 1985), pp. 38–39.

7. "Southwest Pacific Area Operations," *Army and Navy Journal,* 1944, 82(15):76.

8. Daniel E. Barbey, *MacArthur's Amphibious Navy: Seventh Amphibious Force Operations, 1943–1945* (Annapolis: United States Naval Institute, 1969), p. 10.

9. Interview with George C. Decker, George C. Decker Papers, USAMHI, Interview 2, p. 13.

10. William H. Gill, as told to Edward Jaquelin Smith, *Always a Commander: The Reminiscences of Major General William H. Gill* (Colorado Springs: Colorado College, 1974), p. 57.

11. Division Public Relations Section, *The 6th Infantry Division in World War II, 1939–1945* (Nashville: Battery Press, 1983), p. 37.

12. Interview with Bruce Palmer, Jr., ASOOH, p. 325.

13. Barbey, *MacArthur's Amphibious Navy,* pp. 24–25.

14. Edward Coffman and Paul H. Hass, eds., "With MacArthur in the Pacific: A Memoir by Philip F. La Follette," *Wisconsin Magazine of History,* 1980–81, 64(2):94–95. Another subordinate added, "There's nobody in our age who had more stuff stored away up here that he could use from the English language to football statistics; information would just come out of that head like an encyclopedia. He just had the cerebrum to go with the personality and physical appearance." In Interview with Joseph Swing, 26 August 1971, 1971 Interviews, James Collection, DMMA, RG 49, Box 4, pp. 27–28.

15. Roger Olaf Egeberg, *The General: MacArthur and the Man He Called Doc* (New York: Hippocrene Books, 1983), p. 33.

16. Joseph C. Goulden, *Korea: The Untold Story of the War* (New York: McGraw-Hill, 1982), pp. xx–xxi.

17. Once MacArthur brought along a group of photographers while he and Eichelberger inspected soldiers training in Australia. When published, the photo captions claimed to show MacArthur leading troops in combat in New Guinea. Later in the war, referring to the distorted captions, he laughingly said to Eichelberger, "Bob, those were great days when you and I were fighting in Buna, weren't they?" In Robert L. Eichelberger, "MacArthur's Love of and Handling of Publicity," Dictations, RERC, Box 73, pp. 30–41.

18. Quoted in Michael Schaller, *Douglas MacArthur: The Far Eastern General* (New York: Oxford University Press, 1989), p. 74.

19. Barbey, *MacArthur's Amphibious Navy,* p. 24.

20. Interview with Richard J. Marshall, 27 July 1971, 1971 Interviews, James Collection, DMMA, RG 49, Box 4, p. 5.

21. Interview with Charles A. Willoughby, 30 July 1971, 1971 Interviews, James Collection, DMMA, RG 49, Box 4, p. 5. See also Weldon E. (Dusty) Rhoades, *Flying MacArthur to Victory* (College Station: Texas A&M University Press, 1987), pp. 203–4; Paul P. Rogers, *The Bitter Years: MacArthur and Sutherland* (New York: Praeger, 1991), p. 92.

22. Interview with George C. Kenney, 16 July 1971, 1971 Interviews, James Collection, DMMA, RG 49, Box 3, pp. 5–6; William Leary, Interview with Clyde Eddleman, 24 August 1984, KP, Box 40, p. 1.

23. Egeberg, *The General,* p. 41; Ritchie Interview, 24 June 1971, 1971 Interviews, James Collection, DMMA, RG 49, Box 4, p. 8. According to Krueger's daughter, when a deathbed-ridden Krueger learned that Sutherland had died, he said, "It was a good thing for humanity." See Eddleman Interview, Eddleman Papers, USAMHI, Interview 4, pp. 3–6.

24. Kenney Interview, 16 July 1971, 1971 Interviews, James Collection, DMMA, RG 49, Box 3, pp. 5–6; Robert L. Eichelberger, *Dear Miss Em: General Eichelberger's War in the Pacific, 1942–1945,* edited by Jay Luvaas (Westport, Connecticut: Greenwood Press, 1972), p. 98.

25. Eddleman Interview, p. 6.

26. Indeed, Krueger once said to a subordinate, "You know the trouble with the Army is the officers. They're a necessary evil." In Palmer Interview, ASOOH, p. 26.

27. Interview with Clovis E. Byers, 24 June 1971, 1971 Interviews, James Collection, DMMA, RG 49, Box 2, p. 9; Decker Interview, Decker Papers, USAMHI, Interview 2, p. 18.

28. Barbey, *MacArthur's Amphibious Navy,* p. 27; Interview with James F. Collins, James F. Collins Papers, USAMHI, Interview 2, p. 40.

29. Willoughby Interview, 30 July 1971, 1971 Interviews, James Collection, DMMA, RG 49, Box 4, p. 11.

30. Rogers, *Bitter Years,* p. 93.

31. *6th Division,* p. 18.

32. R. M. MacGregor, 31 August 1964, KP, Box 40, p. 1.

33. Robert L. Eichelberger, "Some Thoughts about Sutherland and Krueger," Dictations, RERC, Box 73, pp. 570–77.

34. Rogers, *Bitter Years,* pp. 55–56.

35. Decker Interview, pp. 31–32; Rogers, *Bitter Years,* pp. 55–56.

36. Rhoades, *Flying MacArthur,* pp. 204–5.

37. Douglas MacArthur, *Reminiscences* (New York: McGraw-Hill, 1964), p. 166.

38. Barbey, *MacArthur's Amphibious Navy,* p. 27.

39. Ritchie Interview, p. 10.

40. Eddleman Interview, 29 June 1971, "Miscellaneous Brief Oral Reminiscences, Part 2," James Collection, DMMA, RG 49, Box 1, pp. 27–28.

41. Marshall to MacArthur, 27 October 1943, Correspondence with the War Department, DMMA, RG 4, Box 16, Folder 4.

42. Thomas Kinkaid, *The Reminiscences of Thomas Cassin Kinkaid* (New York: Columbia University, Oral History Research Office, 1961), pp. 250–52.

43. Kinkaid appreciated Barbey's amphibious talents, but he believed that his subordinate was after his job. See ibid., p. 357.

44. Major General Hugh J. Casey, *Engineers of the Southwest Pacific, 1941–1945,* vol. 3: *Engineer Intelligence* (Washington, D.C.: Government Printing Office, 1950), pp. 89–92.

45. Ibid., pp. 92–93.

46. Ibid., p. 93.

47. Ibid., pp. 94–95. See also "Hurricane Task Force (Biak), G-2 Estimate of the Situation," WNRC, RG 407, Box 1573, pp. 1, 3; "Operations Report, Aitape Operation, 32nd Infantry Division," WNRC, RG 407, Box 9020, p. 1.

48. Elliott R. Thorpe, *East Wind, Rain: The Intimate Account of an Intelligence Officer in the Pacific, 1939–49* (Boston: Gambit, 1969), p. 139.

49. Major General Hugh J. Casey, *Engineers of the Southwest Pacific, 1941–1945,* vol. 8: *Critique* (Washington, D.C.: Government Printing Office, 1959), p. 225.

50. See John W. Dower, *War without Mercy: Race and Power in the Pacific War* (New York: Pantheon, 1986); Oliver P. Newman, "Notes on US Army Actions in SW Pacific in World War II up to and including the Papua and Biak Campaigns," Oliver P. Newman Papers, USAMHI, p. 10; Capt. Robert J. Bulkley, Jr., *At Close Quarters: PT Boats in the United States Navy* (Washington, D.C.: Naval History Division, 1962), p. 240.

51. Edward J. Drea, *MacArthur's Ultra: Codebreaking and the War against Japan, 1942–1945* (Lawrence: University Press of Kansas, 1992), p. 92.

52. Various American intelligence organizations called these military intercepts by different names; "Ultra" is used to avoid confusion. The interception of Japanese *diplomatic* traffic was called "Magic."

53. For an excellent account of Ultra's impact in SWPA, as well as its strengths and weaknesses, see Drea's *MacArthur's Ultra.*

54. Rhoades, *Flying MacArthur,* p. 205.

55. Robert L. Eichelberger, "Thoughts on Military Intelligence," Dictations, RERC, Box 73, pp. 515–24.

56. Handy Interview, 8 September 1971, 1971 Interviews, James Collection, DMMA, RG 49, Box 3, p. 7.

57. Major General Hugh J. Casey, *Engineers of the Southwest Pacific, 1941–1945,* vol. 2: *Organization, Troops and Training* (Washington, D.C.: Government Printing Office, 1953), p. 90; Major General Hugh J. Casey, *Engineers of the Southwest Pacific, 1941–1945,* vol. 1: *Reports of Operations* (Washington, D.C.: Government Printing Office, 1947), p. 201.

58. Casey, *Organization, Troops, and Training,* p. 120.

59. Ibid., pp. 95, 146–47, 150.

60. 6th Army Headquarters, "Wakde-Biak Operation," 25 February 1945, KP, Box 24, p. 42.

61. Walter Krueger, "Remarks of Various Officials," Arthur G. Trudeau Papers, USAMHI, p. 1.

62. Spare parts were so important that Krueger's chief of staff, Colonel George C. Decker, wrote to MacArthur, "No single factor affects the rapidity of airdrome construction as much as efficient and timely distribution of spare parts." In Major General Hugh J. Casey, *Engineers of the Southwest Pacific, 1941–1945,* vol. 7: *Engineer Supply* (Washington, D.C.: Government Printing Office, 1947), p. 71.

63. Casey, *Reports of Operations,* p. 199.

64. Casey, *Organization, Troops, and Training,* p. 151; Major General Horace Fuller, "Remarks of Various Officials," Trudeau Papers, USAMHI, pp. 1–3.

65. Robert W. Coakley and Richard M. Leighton, *Global Logistics and Strategy, 1943–1945* (Washington, D.C.: Government Printing Office, 1986), p. 483.

66. For an overview on landing craft, see Barbey, *MacArthur's Amphibious Navy,* pp. 14–15, 19, 359–63.

67. Major General Hugh P. Casey, *Engineers of the Southwest Pacific, 1941–1945*, vol. 4: *Amphibian Engineer Operations* (Washington, D.C.: Government Printing Office, 1959), p. 248.

68. Casey, *Critique*, p. 152.

69. MacArthur, for instance, refused to give up the 3rd ESB when Marshall suggested he send it to Nimitz. See MacArthur to Marshall, 18 September 1943, Correspondence with the War Department, DMMA, RG 4, Box 16, Folder 4. As for their value, see Casey, *Amphibian Engineer Operations*, p. 255; "Report on Combat Operations," 30 June 1944, Decker Papers, USAMHI, p. 1.

70. Casey, *Organization, Troops, and Training*, p. 82.

71. Major Elmer P. Volgenau, "Training Notes on Amphibious Operations in the Southwest Pacific Area," Sutherland Papers, DMMA, RG 30, Box 26, Folder 4. For an example of the positive impact that rockets had on morale, see Egeberg, *The General*, p. 50.

72. Coakley and Leighton, *Global Logistics*, pp. 460–61; Joseph Bykofsky and Harold Larson, *The Transportation Corps: Operations Overseas* (Washington, D.C.: Government Printing Office, 1957), p. 443; John Edwin Grose journal, 6 March 1944, John Edwin Grose Papers, USAMHI.

73. Casey, *Engineer Supply*, p. 66.

74. Ibid., p. 71.

75. Kahn, *Tedium and Terror*, pp. 33–34; US Army, 33rd Infantry Division Historical Committee, *The Golden Cross: A History of the 33d Infantry Division in World War II* (Washington, D.C.: Infantry Journal Press, 1948), p. 44.

76. Coakley and Leighton, *Global Logistics*, p. 475.

77. William C. Chase, *Front Line General* (Houston: Pacesetter Press, 1975), p. 43.

78. For a detailed examination of Pacific War logistics, see Coakley and Leighton, *Global Logistics*.

79. Bykofsky and Larson, *Transportation Corps*, p. 429.

80. Coakley and Leighton, *Global Logistics*, p. 471.

81. Quite often black labor units did such unloading chores, which explains the stigma some white troops associated with the task. See *Golden Cross*, pp. 41–45.

82. Coakley and Leighton, *Global Logistics*, pp. 455–57.

83. JCS 762/1, "Amended Shipping Requirements for Pacific Operations," 29 March 1944, RJCS, p. 2; JCS 762/2, "Amended Shipping Requirements for Pacific Operations," 4 April 1944, RJCS, pp. 1, 10–12.

84. Commanding General, Rear Echelon, GHQ SWPA to War Department, 31 March 1944, RJCS, pp. 19–20.

85. "Review of JCS 762/3: Shipping Requirements and Availabilities for Pacific Operations," 2 May 1944, Richard J. Marshall Papers, USAMHI, Box 2.

86. Coakley and Leighton, *Global Logistics*, p. 464.

87. Ibid., p. 465.

88. JCS 762/3, "Shipping Requirements and Availabilities for Pacific Operations: Report by the Joint Military Transportation Committee," 25 April 1944, RJCS, pp. 21–22; JCS 762/4, "Shipping Requirements and Availabilities for Pacific Operations: Report by the Joint Military Transportation Committee," 5 May 1944, RJCS, pp. 34–36; JCS 762/7, "Shipping Requirements and Availabilities for Pacific Operations: Report by the Joint Military Transportation Committee," 7 June 1944, RJCS, p. 52.

89. For instance, in July 1944, American troops along the Driniumor River received some 671 tons of airdropped equipment from the AAF, and at one point that month the AAF was supplying 4500 surrounded soldiers. See Major General Hugh J. Casey, *Engineers of the Southwest Pacific, 1941–1945*, vol. 6: *Airfield and Base Development* (Washington, D.C.: Government Printing Office, 1951), p. 240; Wesley Frank Craven and James Lea Cate, eds., *The Army Air Forces in World War II: The Pacific*, vol. 4: *Guadalcanal to Saipan: August 1942 to July 1944* (Chicago: University of Chicago Press, 1950), pp. 613–14.

90. Lieutenant Colonel Millard G. Gray, "The Aitape Operation," *Military Review*, July 1951, 31: 60; Major Edward O. Logan, *The Enveloping Maneuver of the 124th Infantry Regiment East of the Driniumor River, Aitape, New Guinea, 31 July–10 August 1944* (St. Augustine, Florida: State Arsenal, 1988), p. 21.

91. Logan, *Enveloping Maneuver*, pp. 35–37; Salvatore Lamagna, "Silent Victory, WWII: Fox-Company, 169th Regimental Combat Team, 43rd Infantry Division," Lamagna Papers, USAMHI, p. 5.

92. Barbey, *MacArthur's Amphibious Navy*, p. 6.

93. Casey, *Engineer Supply*, p. 105; Karl C. Dod, *The Corps of Engineers: The War against Japan* (Washington, D.C.: Government Printing Office, 1966), p. 554.

94. Walter S. Robertson to MacArthur, 11 April 1944, Correspondence with the War Department, DMMA, RG 4, Box 17, Folder 1.

95. "Southwest Pacific Area Operations," *Army and Navy Journal*, 1944, 82(15):130.

96. Handy Interview, p. 15.

97. Marshall to MacArthur, 6 September 1943, Correspondence with the War Department, DMMA, RG 4, Box 16, Folder 4.

98. Lieutenant General Brehon Somervell, "Memorandum for General Marshall," 3 October 1943, Bonner Fellers Papers, DMMA, RG 44, Folder 5, pp. 1, 4.

99. Coakley and Leighton, *Global Logistics*, p. 461.

100. Krueger to Major General J. L. Frink, 20 August 1944, Decker Papers, USAMHI, #52, pp. 1–2.

101. This fact is especially emphasized in John Ellis, *Brute Force: Allied Strategy and Tactics in the Second World War* (New York: Viking Press, 1990). As the commander in-chief of the Japanese Navy, Isoruku Yamamoto, put it in September 1940, "If I am told to fight regardless of the consequences I shall run wild considerably for the first six months or the first year, but I have absolutely no confidence for the second and third years." The following summer another admiral, Osami Nagano, repeated this view: "As for war with the United States, although there is now a chance of achieving victory, the chances will diminish as time goes on. By the latter half of next year it will already be difficult for us to cope with the United States; after that the situation will become increasingly worse." Quoted in Ellis, *Brute Force*, p. 443.

102. H. P. Willmott, *Empires in the Balance: Japanese and Allied Pacific Strategies to April 1942* (Annapolis: Naval Institute Press, 1982), p. 88.

103. Ellis, *Brute Force*, p. 472.

104. See "Japanese Army-Navy Central Agreement Concerning the Central and South Pacific Operations, with Supplement, 30 September 1943," in Louis Morton, *United States Army in World War II: The War in the Pacific: Strategy and Command: The First Two Years* (Washington, D.C.: Government Printing Office, 1962), pp. 657–60.

105. In late 1943, for instance, one Japanese report said, "All shipping [to New Guinea] must be suspended if the present situation does not improve. The percentage of shipping losses in harbours and on voyage reached 65% in March." Quoted in Information Request Report 104, n.d., Congressional Information Services, WTSJD, pp. 3–4.

106. Quoted in MacArthur, *Reminiscences*, p. 167.

107. Morton, *First Two Years*, pp. 590–91; Samuel Eliot Morison, *History of United States Naval Operations in World War II*, vol. 8: *New Guinea and the Marianas, March 1944–August 1944* (Boston: Little, Brown, 1953), p. 66.

108. Bulletin 1108, 29 November 1943, WTSJD, pp. 8–15; United States Army, Military Intelligence Division, *Disposition and Movement of Japanese Ground Forces, 1941–1945* (Washington, D.C.: War Department, 1945), part 17, p. 8.

109. Charles Willoughby, *Reports of General MacArthur: Japanese Operations in the Southwest Pacific Area*, vol. 2, part 1 (Washington, D.C.: Government Printing Office, 1966), pp. 257–58.

110. Robert Ross Smith, *Approach to the Philippines* (Washington, D.C.: Government Printing Office, 1953), pp. 88–89.

111. In the Japanese Army, an area army and an army were the equivalent of an American army and corps.

112. Morison, *New Guinea and the Marianas*, p. 66.

113. Morison notes that Japanese Commander Masataka Chihaya said after the war that the idea of a Mahanian battle with the American fleet dominated Japanese naval thinking throughout the conflict. See ibid., pp. 11–13, 67.

114. Information Request Report 104, 27 March 1944, WTSJD, pp. 6–9.

115. *Disposition and Movement of Japanese Ground Forces*, part 17, p. 13.

116. For a good discussion of Australia's contribution to MacArthur's war, see David Day, *Reluctant Nation: Australia and the Allied Defeat of Japan 1942–45* (Oxford: Oxford University Press, 1992); and D. M. Horner, *High Command: Australia and Allied Strategy, 1939–1945* (Canberra: Allen & Unwin, 1982).

117. MacArthur, *Reminiscences*, p. 151.

118. Decker Interview, p. 18; Byers Interview, p. 9.

119. Willoughby Interview, p. 16.

120. "Summary of Operations for the Month of September 1944," DMMA, RG 3, Box 166.

121. MacArthur to Marshall, 9 August 1944, Correspondence with the War Department, DMMA, RG 4, Box 17, Folder 2.

122. Day, *Reluctant Nation*, pp. 243–44; Horner, *High Command*, pp. 274–79.

123. Eddleman Interview, 29 June 1971, "Miscellaneous Brief Oral Reminiscences, Part 2," James Collection, DMMA, RG 49, Box 1, pp. 21–22.

3. The Admiralties: An Unnecessary Risk?

1. "Aircraft Reconnaissance Reports," 23/24 February 1944, Sutherland Papers, DMMA, RG 30, Box 14, p. 3.

2. George C. Kenney, *General Kenney Reports: A Personal History of the Pacific War* (New York: Duell, Sloan, and Pearce, 1949), pp. 353, 360.

3. John Miller, Jr., *Cartwheel: The Reduction of Rabaul* (Washington D.C.: Government Printing Office, 1959), p. 320.

4. Kenney, *General Kenney Reports,* pp. 359–60.

5. "Aircraft Reconnaissance Reports," 24/25 February 1944, Sutherland Papers, DMMA, RG 30, Box 14, p. 3.

6. Kenney, *General Kenney Reports,* pp. 358–60.

7. Douglas MacArthur, *Reminiscences* (New York: McGraw-Hill, 1964), p. 188.

8. Ibid.; Charles A. Willoughby, *Reports of General MacArthur,* vol. 1: *The Campaigns of MacArthur in the Pacific* (Washington, D.C.: Government Printing Office, 1966), p. 137; Daniel E. Barbey, *MacArthur's Amphibious Navy: Seventh Amphibious Force Operations, 1943–1945* (Annapolis: United States Naval Institute, 1969), pp. 148–51; Roger Olaf Egeberg, *The General: MacArthur and the Man He Called Doc* (New York: Hippocrene Books, 1983), p. 24.

9. Barbey, *MacArthur's Amphibious Navy,* pp. 148–51; "G-3 [Daily] Operations Reports," 25 February 1944, DMMA, RG 3, Box 159, p. 2. A report summing up the destroyer sweep said, "Enemy impotence in the Bismarck Seas and the waters north of it has perhaps never so far been so strikingly demonstrated." In "MIS Daily Summary #702," 22/23 February 1944, DMMA, RG 3, Box 32, pp. 4–5.

10. "MIS Daily Summary #693," 13/14 February 1944, DMMA, RG 3, Box 32, p. 3.

11. "MIS Daily Summary #695," 15/16 February 1944, DMMA, RG 3, Box 32, Appendix ii.

12. "MIS Daily Summary #704," 24/25 February 1944, DMMA, RG 3, Box 32, p. 4.

13. "MIS Daily Summary #706," 26/27 February 1944, DMMA, RG 3, Box 32, p. 4.

14. "MIS Daily Summary #707," 27/28 February 1944, DMMA, RG 3, Box 32, pp. 4–5.

15. Edward J. Drea, *MacArthur's Ultra: Codebreaking and the War against Japan, 1942–1945* (Lawrence: University Press of Kansas, 1992), pp. 101–3.

16. Marshall Interview, 27 July 1971, 1971 Interviews, James Collection, DMMA, RG 49, Box 3, p. 14.

17. Courtney Whitney, *MacArthur: His Rendezvous with History* (New York: Knopf, 1964), p. 107.

18. Eddleman Interview, Eddleman Papers, USAMHI, Interview 2, pp. 25–26; Barbey, *MacArthur's Amphibious Navy,* p. 151.

19. See Walter Krueger, *From Down Under to Nippon* (Washington, D.C.: Combat Forces Press, 1953), p. 48; "Historical Record of the Admiralties," WNRC, RG 407, Box 1446, pp. 1–2.

20. "Report of Operations for Brewer," WNRC, RG 407, Box 1446, p. 5; U.S. Army, Historical Division, *The Admiralties: Operations of the 1st Cavalry Division* (Washington, D.C.: Government Printing Office, 1945), p. 18; Barbey, *MacArthur's Amphibious Navy,* p. 147; "Alamo Force, Operation 'B,' Brewer (Admiralty) Operation, Diary of the Admiralty Islands Campaign," WNRC, RG 407, Box 1446, p. 2.

21. William C. Chase, *Front Line General* (Houston: Pacesetter Press, 1975), p. 47; Barbey, *MacArthur's Amphibious Navy,* p. 151.

22. Kenney, *General Kenney Reports,* pp. 360–61; Harry A. Stella to Eddleman, 23 July 1985, KP, Box 40, p. 2.

23. Eddleman Interview, pp. 25–26. Not that MacArthur's normally persuasive rhetoric helped; days later Krueger was still complaining about the operation, even though it appeared successful. See Robert L. Eichelberger, Eichelberger Diaries, 2, 4 March 1944, RERC, Box 1. Krueger claimed in his memoirs that he was upset because MacArthur planned to accompany the risky operation, but his protests to Eichelberger and others after MacArthur returned from the beachhead do not support this explanation. See Krueger, *From Down Under*, p. 49.

24. Krueger's Official Orders, 28 November 1943, KP, Box 7, No. 42, p. 7.

25. See Lieutenant Sugai, Alamo Force 2044, 28 February 1944 diary entry, WTSJD, p. 12; Sergeant Hashi to Sergeant Major Muranaka, Bulletin 911, 28 January 1944 letter, WTSJD, p. 5; Gibson Niles, *The Operations of the Alamo Scouts . . .* (Fort Benning, Georgia: General Subject Section, Academic Department, The Infantry School, 1948), pp. 9–11; Lewis B. Hochstrasser, *They Were First: The True Story of the Alamo Scouts,* in KP, Box 25, pp. 21–24; "Report of Operations for Brewer," WNRC, RG 407, Box 1446, p. 9.

26. Kenney, *General Kenney Reports,* p. 361.

27. Chase, *Front Line General,* p. 48.

28. Reports differ as to whether the Scout leader was flown by plane or shipped via PT boat to the task force. Chase's memoirs and some official reports state the former, but other reports hold to the latter position. See ibid., pp. 49–50; "Alamo Force, Operation 'B,' Brewer (Admiralty) Operation, Admiralty Island Operation," p. 4; "Brewer Operation," WNRC, RG 407, Box 1446.

29. Barbey, *MacArthur's Amphibious Navy,* p. 151.

30. Ibid., pp. 146–51.

31. The total number was 4539 Japanese on the islands. See Swift to Krueger, 12 April 1944, KP, Box 8, No. 47, p. 12.

32. See "1st Cavalry Division," Fellers Papers, DMMA, RG 44, Folder 5; Swift to Krueger, 19 November 1943, KP, Box 8, No. 47; Barbey, *MacArthur's Amphibious Navy,* pp. 145–46.

33. Interview with Joseph P. Cribbins, Joseph P. Cribbins Papers, USAMHI, pp. 17, 28, 34; Barbey, *MacArthur's Amphibious Navy,* pp. 145–46; "1st Cavalry Division."

34. Frazier Hunt, *The Untold Story of Douglas MacArthur* (New York: Devin-Adair, 1954), p. 318.

35. MacArthur, *Reminiscences,* p. 188.

36. Krueger, *From Down Under,* p. 49.

37. Samuel Eliot Morison, *History of United States Naval Operations in World War II,* vol. 8: *New Guinea and the Marianas, March 1944–August 1944* (Boston: Little, Brown, 1953), p. 436.

38. Ezaki, Alamo Force 2045, 29 February 1944, WTSJD, pp. 4–7.

39. "Aircraft Operation Reports," 26/27 February 1944, Sutherland Papers, DMMA, RG 30, Box 11.

40. Miller, *Cartwheel,* p. 326; Samuel Eliot Morison, *History of United States Naval Operations in World War II,* vol. 6: *Breaking the Bismarcks Barrier* (Boston: Little, Brown, 1950), p. 458.

41. *London Daily Mirror,* 2 March 1944, Charles V. Trent Papers, USAMHI; Robert Shaplen, *Newsweek,* 13 March 1944, pp. 30–36.

42. Captain Walter Karig, Lieutenant Commander Russell L. Harris, and Lieutenant Commander Frank A. Manson, *Battle Report: The End of an Empire*, vol. 4 (New York: Rinehart, 1948), p. 171.

43. Corporal Bill Alcine, *Yank,* 14 April 1944, 2(43):3.

44. Chase, *Front Line General*, pp. 50–51.

45. Bertram C. Wright, *The 1st Cavalry Division in World War II* (Tokyo: Tappan, 1947), p. 18; *Admiralties*, p. 31.

46. Alcine, *Yank*, p. 2.

47. Chase, *Front Line General*, p. 51; Egeberg, *The General*, pp. 28–30; William B. Dickinson, *New York Times*, 1 March 1944.

48. Shaplen, *Newsweek*, pp. 30–36.

49. Chase, *Front Line General*, p. 51; Dickinson, *New York Times*.

50. Chase, *Front Line General*, p. 51.

51. Karig, Harris, and Manson, *Battle Report*, p. 172.

52. Krueger, *From Down Under*, p. 50; Weldon E. (Dusty) Rhoades, *Flying MacArthur to Victory* (College Station: Texas A&M University Press, 1987), p. 190; "Alamo Force, Operation 'B,' Brewer (Admiralty) Operation, Admiralty Island Operation," p. 5.

53. Charles A. Willoughby and John Chamberlain, *MacArthur: 1941–1951* (New York: McGraw-Hill, 1954), p. 174; Alamo Force 2034, n.d., WTSJD, p. 5; Drea, *MacArthur's Ultra*, pp. 100–101.

54. Morison, *Breaking the Bismarcks Barrier*, p. 437.

55. Ezaki, Alamo Force 2045, 29 February 1944 message, WTSJD, p. 4; Ezaki, Bulletin 790, 2 February 1944 message, WTSJD, pp. 1–2; Major General Hugh P. Casey, *Engineers of the Southwest Pacific, 1941–1945*, vol. 4: *Amphibian Engineer Operations* (Washington, D.C.: Government Printing Office, 1959), p. 225.

56. *Admiralties*, pp. 43–44; Charles Willoughby, *Reports of General MacArthur: The Campaigns of MacArthur in the Pacific,* vol. 1 (Washington, D.C.: Government Printing Office, 1966), p. 140; Miller, *Cartwheel*, p. 333.

57. Casey, *Amphibian Engineer Operations*, pp. 234–35.

58. Ezaki, Alamo Force 2045, 2 March 1944 message, WTSJD, p. 7.

59. Many scholars later doubted this, but the troopers found a Japanese phonograph next day, so it is not impossible. See "Diary of the Admiralty Islands Campaign," 3–4 March 1944, Trent Papers, USAMHI, p. 10; Lee Van Atta, "Yelling Japs Mowed down in Battles on Los Negros," *Atlanta Journal,* 7 March 1944, Trent Papers, USAMHI.

60. Barbey, *MacArthur's Amphibious Navy*, pp. 156–57.

61. "MIS Daily Summary #715," 6/7 March 1944, DMMA, RG 3, Box 33, p. 3.

62. Ezaki, Alamo Force 2045, 4 March 1944 message, WTSJD, p. 7.

63. Krueger, *From Down Under*, p. 51.

64. Ibid.; Krueger, Lecture at the Armed Forces Staff College, 18 April 1947, KP, Box 12, No. 73, p. 4.

65. The Navy's efforts are detailed in "Historical Record of the Admiralties," WNRC, RG 407, Box 1446, p. 4.

66. Barbey, *MacArthur's Amphibious Navy*, p. 156.

67. Collins Interview, Collins Papers, USAMHI, Interview 2, p. 40.

68. Krueger to Swift, 4 March 1944, Decker Papers, USAMHI, No. 31.

69. Swift to Krueger, 8 March 1944, Personal, KP, Box 8, No. 47. Despite Krueger's concerns, Chase went on to command the 38th Division in the Philippines.

70. Ibid.

71. "MIS Daily Summary #719," 10/11 March 1944, DMMA, RG 3, Box 33, p. 3.

72. "MIS Daily Summary #720," 11/12 March 1944, DMMA, RG 3, Box 33, p. 4; Casey, *Amphibian Engineer Operations,* pp. 242–43; *Admiralties,* p. 76.

73. "Alamo Force, Operation 'B,' Brewer (Admiralty) Operation, Diary of the Admiralty Islands Campaign," p. 15.

74. William F. Heavey, *Down Ramp!: The Story of the Army Amphibian Engineers* (Washington, D.C.: Infantry Journal Press, 1947), p. 113; Casey, *Amphibian Engineer Operations,* p. 240; William F. Heavey, "Amphibian Engineers in Action," *Military Engineer,* July 1945, 38(237):254.

75. Heavey, *Down Ramp!,* pp. 112–14; *History of the Second Engineer Special Brigade* (Harrisburg, Pennsylvania: Telegraph Press, 1946), pp. 71–72; Wright, *1st Cavalry,* pp. 26–27; Heavey, "Amphibian Engineers in Action," p. 254; Robert J. Bulkley, Jr., *At Close Quarters: PT Boats in the United States Navy* (Washington, D.C.: Naval History Division, 1962), p. 228; "Alamo Force, Operation 'B', Brewer (Admiralty) Operation, Diary of the Admiralty Islands Campaign," p. 15.

76. Wright, *1st Cavalry,* p. 28.

77. "Report of Operations for Brewer," WNRC, RG 407, Box 1446, pp. 15–17; *Admiralties,* pp. 92–94.

78. Miller, *Cartwheel,* pp. 347–48.

79. *Admiralties,* p. 97.

80. Here as elsewhere in the southwest Pacific, the Japanese had not treated the natives very well. See Ezaki, Bulletin 790, 2 February 1944 message, WTSJD, pp. 1–2; Asamori to Lieutenant Sugawara Moto, Bulletin 899, 25 June 1943 letter, WTSJD, p. 7.

81. Morison, *Breaking the Bismarcks Barrier,* p. 447; "Summary of Operations for the Month of April 1944," Monthly Summary of Operations, April–September 1944, DMMA, RG 3, Box 165, p. 1.

82. Krueger, *From Down Under,* p. 55.

83. Karl C. Dod, *The Corps of Engineers: The War against Japan* (Washington, D.C.: Office of the Chief of Military History, Government Printing Office, 1966), pp. 525–26; John H. Dudley, ASOOH, p. 22.

84. Dod, *Corps,* pp. 525–26; Dudley, ASOOH, pp. 7–8. However, in an article written before the end of the war, Dudley and Major William G. Staggs wrote, "Engineers lived and worked under Seabees and Seabees lived and worked under Engineers. The interchange was carried out with complete harmony. The Engineer and Seabee operators and mechanics seemed to enjoy working with each other." See Dudley and William G. Staggs, "Engineer Troops on Airdrome Construction," *Military Engineer,* October 1945, 37(120): 386.

85. This included some 70,000 men in Rabaul itself, 31,000 in Bougainville, 8000 on New Ireland, and some 53,000 naval shore personnel scattered among the three, for a total of about 161,000 men. See Charles Willoughby, *Reports of General MacArthur: Japanese Operations in the Southwest Pacific Area,* vol. 2, part 1 (Washington, D.C.: Government Printing Office, 1966), p. 248.

86. Marshall sent MacArthur the following message: "Congratulations on the skill and success with which the Admiralty Islands operations has been carried through. Please accept my admiration for the manner in which the entire affair has been handled." In MacArthur, *Reminiscences*, p. 189.

87. See especially Barbey, *MacArthur's Amphibious Navy*, p. 157.

88. Eddleman Interview, p. 26.

89. "Historical Record of the Admiralties," WNRC, RG 407, Box 1446, p. 5. MacArthur's G-3, Richard J. Marshall, later said, "[MacArthur] was always concerned about casualties. He didn't want to go into the Admiralty Islands until he was assured that the Japs weren't going to slaughter a lot of our men there. There were many recommendations to go on. The only thing that finally moved him into going in there was that Kenney gave him the assurance that the Japanese were so scattered that we wouldn't have serious resistance. Of course, we got a lot of casualties." See Marshall Interview, 27 July 1971, 1971 Interviews, James Collection, DMMA, RG 49, Box 3, p. 14.

90. Egeberg, *The General*, p. 37.

4. Hollandia: A Great Leap Forward

1. See Harold Riegelman, *The Caves of Biak* (New York: Dial Press, 1955), pp. 87–88; Robert L. Eichelberger, "Debunks MacArthur as a 'Great Soldier' as Pictured in Books by Willoughby and Frazier Hunt; MacArthur as Strategist," Dictations, RERC, Box 73, pp. 126–34.

2. "G-2 Estimate of Enemy Situation with Respect to 'Landgrabber,'" 16 January 1944, Quentin L. Lander Papers, USAMHI; "G-2 Estimate of the Enemy Situation to Accompany 'Reno IV': Outline Plan for Operations of the South West Pacific Area to Reoccupy the Southern Philippines," 20 January 1944, Lander Papers, USAMHI, pp. 16, 21–22.

3. Interview with Bonner F. Fellers, 26 June 1971, 1971 Interviews, James Collection, DMMA, RG 49, Box 2, p. 4.

4. Roger Olaf Egeberg, *The General: MacArthur and the Man He Called Doc* (New York: Hippocrene Books, 1983), pp. 45–46; George C. Kenney, *General Kenney Reports: A Personal History of the Pacific War* (New York: Duell, Sloan, and Pearce, 1949), p. 369; Frazier Hunt, *The Untold Story of Douglas MacArthur* (New York: Devin-Adair, 1954), p. 325.

5. Egeberg, *The General*, pp. 45–46.

6. Fellers Interview, p. 4.

7. Kenney, *General Kenney Reports*, p. 369.

8. Charles Willoughby, *Reports of General MacArthur: Japanese Operations in the Southwest Pacific Area*, vol. 2, part 1 (Washington, D.C.: Government Printing Office, 1966), p. 142.

9. Walter Krueger, *From Down Under to Nippon* (Washington, D.C.: Combat Forces Press, 1953), p. 58.

10. Ibid.; Willoughby, *MacArthur's Reports*, p. 142; Charles A. Willoughby and John Chamberlain, *MacArthur: 1941–1951* (New York: McGraw-Hill, 1954), pp. 174–75.

11. Wesley Frank Craven and James Lea Cate, eds., *The Army Air Forces in World War II: The Pacific*, vol. 4: *Guadalcanal to Saipan: August 1942 to July 1944* (Chicago: University of Chicago Press, 1950), p. 575.

12. Robert Ross Smith, *Approach to the Philippines* (Washington, D.C.: Government Printing Office, 1953), pp. 97–98; Samuel Eliot Morison, *History of United States Naval Operations in World War II*, vol. 8: *New Guinea and the Marianas, March 1944–August 1944* (Boston: Little, Brown, 1953), p. 67.

13. Willoughby and Chamberlain, *MacArthur*, p. 183; Willoughby, *MacArthur's Reports*, pp. 248–49, 263.

14. Willoughby, *MacArthur's Reports*, p. 263.

15. Kenney, *General Kenney Reports*, pp. 372–74; Matsutaro Yamaguchi's order, Bulletin 1046, 3 March 1944 order, WTSJD, p. 1.

16. Kenney, *General Kenney Reports*, pp. 372–73.

17. Morison, *New Guinea and the Marianas*, p. 66; Kenney, *General Kenney Reports*, p. 384; Willoughby and Chamberlain, *MacArthur*, p. 181.

18. Bulletin 1126, 11–24 March 1944 intelligence file, WTSJD, p. 6; Willoughby, *MacArthur's Reports*, p. 264.

19. Willoughby to Assistant Chief of Staff, G-3, "G-2 Estimates of Enemy Situation," 7 March 1944, Lander Papers, USAMHI.

20. Although the Japanese killed off a patrol on 25 March, they did not believe that the reconnaissance heralded an imminent attack. See Colonel Ishizu, Bulletin 1051, 4 April 1944 report, WTSJD, p. 10; Bulletin 1074, 31 March to 16 April 1944 intelligence file, WTSJD, p. 18.

21. "G-2 Estimates of Enemy Situation," 28 March 1944, Lander Papers, USAMHI.

22. "G-2 Estimates of Enemy Situation," 22 March 1944, Lander papers, USAMHI.

23. "MIS Daily Summary #761," 21/22 April 1944, DMMA, RG 3, Box 33, Appendix, pp. i–ii.

24. "MIS Daily Summary #734," 25/26 March 1944, DMMA, RG 3, Box 33, p. 4.

25. "MIS Daily Summary #742," 2/3 April 1944, DMMA, RG 3, Box 33, Appendix, p. ii.

26. Smith, *Approach*, p. 23.

27. Ibid., p. 21.

28. Craven and Cate, *Guadalcanal to Saipan*, p. 582.

29. "41st Infantry Division," Fellers Papers, DMMA, RG 44, Folder 5. See also Decker Interview, Decker Papers, USAMHI, Interview 2, p. 40.

30. "24th Infantry Division," Fellers Papers, DMMA, RG 44, Folder 5.

31. Willoughby Interview, 30 July 1971, 1971 Interviews, James Collection, DMMA, RG 49, Box 4, pp. 11–12.

32. For an account of this, see D. Clayton James, *The Years of MacArthur*, vol. 2 (Boston: Houghton Mifflin, 1975), pp. 274–77.

33. Daniel E. Barbey, *MacArthur's Amphibious Navy: Seventh Amphibious Force Operations, 1943–1945* (Annapolis: United States Naval Institute, 1969), pp. 27, 170; Riegelman, *Caves*, pp. 171–72.

34. An accusatory MacArthur often said to Eichelberger, "You are a good friend of George Catlett Marshall!" Eichelberger, "General Marshall, 1938 et al.," Dictations, RERC, Box 73, pp. 142–52. As Barbey later put it, "There was no place in the Southwest Pacific for two glamorous officers." See Barbey, *MacArthur's Amphibious Navy*, p. 27.

35. Barbey, *MacArthur's Amphibious Navy,* pp. 27, 170.

36. Marshall to MacArthur, 25 August 1943, Correspondence with the War Department, DMMA, RG 4, Box 17, Folder 1; MacArthur to Marshall, 26 August 1943, Correspondence with the War Department, DMMA, RG 4, Box 17, Folder 1.

37. Eichelberger, "Some Thoughts about Sutherland and Krueger," Dictations, RERC, Box 73, pp. 570–77; Robert L. Eichelberger, *Dear Miss Em: General Eichelberger's War in the Pacific, 1942–1945,* edited by Jay Luvaas (Westport, Connecticut: Greenwood Press, 1972), pp. 83, 97–98; Eichelberger, "Thoughts on Military Intelligence," Dictations, RERC, Box 73, pp. 515–24.

38. Eichelberger, "Some Thoughts about Sutherland and Krueger," pp. 570–77.

39. See Willoughby Interview, pp. 11–12.

40. Eddleman, Eddleman's Comments, KP, Box 40, pp. 3–4.

41. Robert L. Eichelberger, *Our Jungle Road to Tokyo* (New York: Viking Press, 1950), p. 102.

42. Ibid.; Eichelberger, "Debunks MacArthur," pp. 126–34; Riegelman, *Caves,* p. 89.

43. Fellers Interview, p. 4; Hunt, *Untold Story,* pp. 325–26; Kenney, *General Kenney Reports,* pp. 376–77.

44. Kenney, *General Kenney Reports,* pp. 376–77. Despite this confidence, MacArthur still wanted Nimitz's carriers, which, unlike Kenney's AAF, could provide *close* air support. He also wanted Nimitz's forces to neutralize Japanese air power to the west, writing to Nimitz earlier that Hollandia "will have been partially neutralized by land based air but nothing to westward can be reached." See SWPA to POA, 14 March 1944, Correspondence with the Navy, DMMA, RG 4, Box 10, Folder 5.

45. Area Army commander Kumaichi Teramoto, Enemy Publications 268, 12 February 1944, WTSJD, p. 27.

46. "MIS Daily Summary #706," 26/27 February 1944, DMMA, RG 3, Box 32, pp. 3–4.

47. Craven and Cate, *Guadalcanal to Saipan,* pp. 579–80, 587.

48. Kenney, *General Kenney Reports,* pp. 373–74.

49. Craven and Cate, *Guadalcanal to Saipan,* pp. 594–95. On 31 March, one Japanese diarist counted 100 destroyed Japanese planes on one airfield alone. See Bulletin 1115, 7 February to 23 April 1944 diary entries, WTSJD, p. C.

50. "Aircraft Operation Report," 29/30 March 1944, Sutherland Papers, DMMA, RG 30, Box 11.

51. "Aircraft Operation Report," 30/31 March 1944, Sutherland papers, DMMA, RG 30, Box 11, pp. 2–3.

52. Bulletin 1109, 27 March 1944 ordinance officer's report, WTSJD, pp. 1–10; Yamanaka, Bulletin 1114, 12 March 1944 letter, WTSJD, p. 1.

53. Craven and Cate, *Guadalcanal to Saipan,* pp. 594–95.

54. "MIS Daily Summary #742," 2/3 April 1944, DMMA, RG 3, Box 33, Appendix, p. iii.

55. Craven and Cate, *Guadalcanal to Saipan,* p. 598. There were nonbattle casualties, the worst of which was a 16 April mission to nearby Aitape that ran into heavy clouds on its way home; thirty-seven pilots were lost as a result.

56. Kenney, "Air Operations in the Southwest Pacific, 1944," *Army and Navy Journal,* 82(15):76.

57. A 24 April 1944 Navy communiqué announcing the Hollandia operation said, "At Hollandia, 67 planes were destroyed on the ground," which implies, but does not say outright, that naval air power was responsible for their destruction. See CINCPAC Press Release 372, 24 April 1944, in U.S. Navy, *Navy Department Communiques 301 to 600 and Pacific Fleet Communiques March 6, 1943, to May 24, 1945* (Washington, D.C.: Government Printing Office, 1945), pp. 141–42.

58. Barbey, *MacArthur's Amphibious Navy,* p. 167; Major General Hugh P. Casey, *Engineers of the Southwest Pacific, 1941–1945,* vol. 4: *Amphibian Engineer Operations* (Washington, D.C.: Government Printing Office, 1959), p. 68.

59. Riegelman, *Caves,* p. 101; Hollis T. Peacock, Reminiscences, Hollis T. Peacock Papers, USAMHI; W. N. Swan, *Spearheads of Invasion: An Account of the Seven Major Invasions Carried out by the Allies in the South-west Pacific Area during the Second World War, as Seen from a Royal Australian Naval Landing Ship Infantry* (London: Angus and Robertson, 1953), p. 82.

60. William F. Heavey, *Down Ramp!: The Story of the Army's Amphibian Engineers* (Washington, D.C.: Infantry Journal Press, 1947), p. 115; Major General Hugh J. Casey, *Engineers of the Southwest Pacific, 1941–1945,* vol. 1: *Reports of Operations* (Washington, D.C.: Government Printing Office, 1947), p. 158.

61. Smith, *Approach,* p. 48; Casey, *Amphibian Engineer Operations,* p. 259; Eichelberger, *Jungle Road,* p. 108; Eichelberger to Krueger, 18 March 1944, KP, Box 9, No. 48; Eichelberger to Krueger, 22 March 1944, KP, Box 9, No. 48.

62. Barbey, *MacArthur's Amphibious Navy,* p. 169.

63. Eichelberger, *Jungle Road,* p. 107.

64. Egeberg, *The General,* p. 53; Jack Turcott, *St. Louis Post-Dispatch,* 24 April 1944.

65. Eichelberger, *Jungle Road,* p. 107.

66. "24th Division History of the Hollandia Operation," Military Papers, RERC, Box 34, p. 60.

67. Turcott, *St. Louis Post-Dispatch,* 24 April 1944.

68. Barbey, *MacArthur's Amphibious Navy,* p. 173; Eichelberger, "Debunks MacArthur," pp. 126–34; Eichelberger, *Jungle Road,* p. 107.

69. Weldon E. (Dusty) Rhoades, *Flying MacArthur to Victory* (College Station: Texas A&M University Press, 1987), p. 220.

70. Peacock, Reminiscences, p. 3.

71. Casey, *Amphibian Engineer Operations,* p. 274. See also Riegelman, *Caves,* p. 104.

72. Eichelberger, *Jungle Road,* p. 109.

73. Eichelberger, 23 April 1944, 1944 Diaries, RERC, Box 1.

74. Robert Shaplen, *Newsweek,* 8 May 1944, pp. 23–25.

75. Lloyd E. Day, "Report on Reckless Operation," Lloyd E. Day Papers, USAMHI, p. 3; Asahel Bush, *St. Louis Post-Dispatch,* 25 April 1944; Swan, *Spearheads,* p. 86.

76. Day, "Report on Reckless Operation," p. 3; Bush, *St. Louis Post-Dispatch,* 25 April 1944.

77. Swan, *Spearheads,* p. 89.

78. Frank L. Kluckhohn, *New York Times,* 25 April 1944; Charles Pearson, *Yank,* 26 May 1944, 2(49):5.

79. Krueger, *From Down Under,* p. 66.

80. Interview with Jack C. Fuson, Jack C. Fuson Papers, USAMHI, pp. 50–51.

81. Casey, *Amphibian Engineer Operations,* pp. 292–93.

82. *History of the Second Engineer Special Brigade* (Harrisburg, Pennsylvania: Telegraph Press, 1946), p. 77.

83. Paul Wendell, Lewis H. Clark, Paul Westerfield, et al., "Soldiers and Policemen," Paul Westerfield Papers, USAMHI, p. 1.

84. Shaplen, *Newsweek,* 8 May 1944, pp. 23–25.

85. *Second Engineer Special Brigade,* p. 77; Paul Westerfield, "532nd Engineer Boat and Shore Regiment: The Hollandia Fire and Lake Sentani," Paul Westerfield Papers, USAMHI, pp. 1–3.

86. *Second Engineer Special Brigade,* p. 77.

87. Riegelman, *Caves,* p. 110.

88. Sy M. Kahn, *Between Tedium and Terror: A Soldier's World War II Diary, 1943–1945* (Chicago: University of Illinois Press, 1993), pp. 113–14.

89. *Second Engineer Special Brigade,* p. 77.

90. The 163rd RCT's Aitape saga is taken primarily from "Operations Report, Aitape (Persecution) Operations, 163rd Infantry Regiment, 41st Infantry Division," WNRC, RG 407, Box 10634, pp. 2–4.

91. "Allied Air Forces Intelligence Summary #192," 5 April 1944, Sutherland Papers, DMMA, RG 30, Boxes 28–40, p. 21.

92. Krueger, *From Down Under,* pp. 59–61; "MIS Daily Summary #755," 15/16 April 1944, DMMA, RG 3, Box 33, p. 3.

93. Spencer Davis, *St. Louis Post-Dispatch,* 24 April 1944.

94. Ibid.

95. Krueger, *From Down Under,* pp. 69–70.

96. Davis, *St. Louis Post-Dispatch,* 24 April 1944.

97. Jens Doe to Westerfield, 6 September 1969, Westerfield Papers, USAMHI.

98. Krueger, *From Down Under,* p. 70.

99. Karl C. Dod, *The Corps of Engineers: The War against Japan* (Washington, D.C.: Government Printing Office, 1966), p. 533.

100. Willoughby, *MacArthur's Reports,* p. 266.

101. Akio Kawamistsu, Bulletin 1195, 26 May 1944 diary entry, WTSJD, p. 2. For a moving account of the plight of the individual Japanese soldier in New Guinea, see Ogawa Masatsugu, "The 'Green Desert' of New Guinea," in Haruko Taya Cook and Theodore F. Cook, *Japan at War: An Oral History* (New York: New Press, 1992), pp. 267–75.

102. "24th Division History of Hollandia Operation," Military Papers, RERC, Box 34, p. 82.

103. Eichelberger, *Jungle Road,* pp. 109–10.

104. "24th Division History of Hollandia Operation," p. 74.

105. Major General Hugh J. Casey, *Engineers of the Southwest Pacific, 1941–1945,* vol. 7: *Engineer Supply* (Washington, D.C.: Government Printing Office, 1947), p. 123.

106. William J. Verbeck, *The Story of a Regiment in Action,* n.p., DMMA, p. 10b.

107. Eichelberger, *Dear Miss Em*, p. 107.

108. "24th Division History of Hollandia Operation," p. 94.

109. Eichelberger, *Jungle Road*, p. 113.

110. Ibid., pp. 115–16; Eichelberger, *Dear Miss Em*, pp. 108–9; Riegelman, *Caves*, p. 114.

111. Riegelman, *Caves*, p. 123.

112. Carl R. Thien, *Pacific Odyssey: Whistling past the Foxholes*, n.p., Carl R. Thien Papers, USAMHI, pp. 47–50; Assistant Adjutant General Peter Calza of I Corps to 6th Army, 2 May 1944, Personal, KP, Box 9, No. 48; Day, "Report on Reckless Operation," p. 3; Eichelberger, *Dear Miss Em*, pp. 110, 112.

113. Riegelman, *Caves*, pp. 157–58.

114. Casey, *Engineer Supply*, p. 123.

115. Eichelberger, 18 May 1944, 1944 Diaries, RERC, Box 1; Kahn, *Tedium and Terror*, pp. 124–30.

116. Morison, *New Guinea and the Marianas*, p. 92; Craven and Cate, *Guadalcanal to Saipan*, pp. 608–9.

117. Krueger, "Krueger's Comments on *Approach to the Philippines*," Personal, KP, Box 12, No. 70, p. 4; Dod, *Corps*, p. 532; John H. Dudley and William G. Staggs, "Engineer Troops on Airdrome Construction," *Military Engineer*, October 1945, 37(387).

118. Craven and Cate, *Guadalcanal to Saipan*, pp. 608–11.

119. Dod, *Corps*, p. 534.

120. Eddleman, Eddleman's Comments, KP, Box 40, p. 5.

121. Eichelberger, *Dear Miss Em*, p. 117; Eichelberger, 28 May 1944, 1944 Diaries, RERC, Box 1.

122. Paul P. Rogers, *The Bitter Years: MacArthur and Sutherland* (New York: Praeger, 1991), p. 89.

123. Ibid., p. 149.

124. Rhoades, *Flying MacArthur*, pp. 262–64.

125. Rogers, *Bitter Years*, p. 163.

126. Willoughby and Chamberlain, *MacArthur*, pp. 183–84.

127. Egeberg, *The General*, p. 44.

128. Robert W. Coakley and Richard M. Leighton, *Global Logistics and Strategy, 1943–1945* (Washington, D.C.: Government Printing Office, 1986), p. 465.

129. Willoughby, *MacArthur's Reports*, pp. 146–47.

5. Combat and Survival in a Hostile Environment

1. William Hardy, "My Overseas Service in World War Two," William Hardy Papers, USAMHI, pp. 1–2; E. M. Flanagan, Jr., *The Angels: A History of the 11th Airborne Division* (Navato, California: Presidio Press, 1989), pp. 73–75; George Sharpe, *Brothers beyond Blood: A Battalion Surgeon in the South Pacific* (Austin, Texas: Diamond Books, 1989), p. 13.

2. Sy M. Kahn, *Between Tedium and Terror: A Soldier's World War II Diary, 1943–1945* (Chicago: University of Illinois Press, 1993), pp. 5–9; Sharpe, *Brothers*, pp. 7–8.

3. Division Public Relations Section, *The 6th Infantry Division in World War II, 1939–1945* (Nashville: Battery Press, 1983), p. 39.

4. Weldon E. (Dusty) Rhoades, *Flying MacArthur to Victory* (College Station: Texas A&M University Press, 1987), p. 209.

5. Palmer Interview, ASOOH, pp. 325–26.

6. Ibid., p. 343.

7. Interview with Cecil C. Helena, Cecil C. Helena Papers, USAMHI, p. 22.

8. Krueger himself acknowledged and complained about this fact. See Krueger to Major General J. L. Frink, 20 August 1944, Decker Papers, USAMHI, No. 52, pp. 1–2.

9. Ibid., pp. 25–27; Flanagan, *Angels*, p. 80.

10. Walter Krueger, *From Down Under to Nippon* (Washington, D.C.: Combat Forces Press, 1953), p. 133; Thomas Kinkaid, *The Reminiscences of Thomas Cassin Kinkaid* (New York: Columbia University, Oral History Research Office, 1961), p. 277.

11. Anthony Arthur, *Bushmasters: America's Jungle Warriors of World War II* (New York: St. Martin's Press, 1987), p. 169.

12. Kahn, *Tedium and Terror*, p. 67; Daniel E. Barbey, *MacArthur's Amphibious Navy: Seventh Amphibious Force Operations, 1943–1945* (Annapolis: United States Naval Institute, 1969), p. 136.

13. Krueger to MacArthur, 13 March 1944, KP, Box 9, No. 54; MacArthur to Krueger, 11 April 1944, KP, Box 9, No. 54.

14. Elliott R. Thorpe, *East Wind, Rain: The Intimate Account of an Intelligence Officer in the Pacific, 1939–49* (Boston: Gambit, 1969), pp. 101–2. Eichelberger, for instance, frequently used thinly veiled references about future operations in his letters to his wife.

15. No one bothered to tell the censors about radar, so they permitted enlisted men to send home sketches of the device before high command caught on to the problem. See ibid., p. 101.

16. Ibid., pp. 102–4.

17. Krueger, *From Down Under*, p. 77.

18. Ibid., p. 135.

19. Oliver P. Newman, "Notes on U.S. Army Actions in Southwest Pacific up to and Including the Papua and Biak Campaigns (Draft Copy)," Newman Papers, USAMHI, p. 8.

20. Krueger, *From Down Under*, p. 136.

21. Harold Riegelman, *The Caves of Biak* (New York: Dial Press, 1955), pp. 172–73.

22. For figures, see Mattie E. Treadwell, *The Women's Army Corps* (Washington, D.C.: Government Printing Office, 1954), pp. 217–23.

23. Barbey, *MacArthur's Amphibious Navy*, pp. 142, 230; Krueger, *From Down Under*, p. 136.

24. Arthur, *Bushmasters*, p. 72; Charles E. Bennett, "Coconuts and Combat Too," USAMHI, pp. 62–63, 68–69; Major General Hugh J. Casey, *Engineers of the Southwest Pacific, 1941–1945*, vol. 2: *Organization, Troops and Training* (Washington, D.C.: Government Printing Office, 1953), pp. 106–8.

25. Casey, *Organization, Troops, and Training*, p. 108.

26. For a good description of the lives and crews of Liberty ships, see John Gorley Bunker, *Liberty Ships: The Ugly Ducklings of World War II* (Annapolis: Naval Institute Press, 1972), pp. 19–38.

27. Ibid., p. 140.

28. Ibid., p. 143.

29. Ibid., p. 161.

30. Barbey, *MacArthur's Amphibious Navy,* pp. 134–35.

31. Ibid., pp. 135–36, 138–40.

32. Robert J. Bulkley, Jr., *At Close Quarters: PT Boats in the United States Navy* (Washington, D.C.: Naval History Division, 1962), p. 241.

33. This emphasis is seen clearly in the Army's *Infantry in Battle* (Washington, D.C.: Infantry Journal, 1939).

34. Jonathan M. House, *Toward Combined Arms Warfare: A Survey of 20th-Century Tactics, Doctrine, and Organization* (Leavenworth, Kansas: Combined Studies Institute, 1984), pp. 73, 105–7.

35. For excellent books on the GI's war and his weapons in the South Pacific, see Eric Bergerud, *Touched with Fire: The Land War in the South Pacific* (New York: Viking Press, 1996); and Geoffrey Perret, *There's a War to Be Won: The United States Army in World War II* (New York: Random House, 1991).

36. Quoted in John Ellis, *The Sharp End: The Fighting Man in World War II* (New York: Scribner's, 1981), p. 111.

37. Eichelberger, for one, compared the situation to the Wild West practice of circling the wagons. See Robert L. Eichelberger, *Dear Miss Em: General Eichelberger's War in the Pacific, 1942–1945,* edited by Jay Luvaas (Westport, Connecticut: Greenwood Press, 1972), p. 137.

38. Quoted in Ellis, *Sharp End,* p. 79.

39. Riegelman, *Caves,* pp. 68–70.

40. Bergerud, *Touched with Fire,* pp. 368–75.

41. For a good discussion of this, see ibid., pp. 405–15. See also Arthur, *Bushmasters,* p. 165.

42. Ellis, *Sharp End,* p. 89.

43. Ibid., pp. 169, 178–79.

44. Bergerud, *Touched with Fire,* pp. 377–80.

45. Edward O. Logan, *The Enveloping Maneuver of the 124th Infantry Regiment East of the Driniumor River, Aitape, New Guinea, 31 July–10 August 1944* (St. Augustine, Florida: State Arsenal, 1988), pp. 30–31.

46. Bergerud, *Touched with Fire,* p. 287.

47. Edward Jerome Callahan, "Remembering War," Edward Jerome Callahan Papers, USAMHI, p. 24.

48. Bergerud, *Touched with Fire,* pp. 332–37.

49. Interview with William H. Gill, William H. Gill Papers, USAMHI, Tape 6, p. 11.

50. Harry E. Maule, ed., *A Book of War Letters* (New York: Random House, 1943), p. 217.

51. George C. Kenney, *General Kenney Reports: A Personal History of the Pacific War* (New York: Duell, Sloan, and Pearce, 1949), pp. 400–401; Thorpe, *East Wind,* p. 143.

52. "Data on Malaria Incidence in US Army Forces in SWPA," 1 June 1944, Correspondence with the War Department, DMMA, RG 4, Box 17, Folder 1.

53. Courtney Whitney, *MacArthur: His Rendezvous with History* (New York: Knopf, 1964), pp. 113–14.

54. Some rumor mills said that atabrine caused sterility, others impotence. See William C. Chase, *Front Line General* (Houston: Pacesetter Press, 1975), p. 43; Helena Interview, Helena Papers, USAMHI, pp. 24–25.

55. Krueger, *From Down Under,* p. 134; Eichelberger, *Dear Miss Em,* p. 149.

56. "Data on Malaria Incidence in US Army Forces in SWPA," 1 June 1944, Correspondence with the War Department, DMMA, RG 4, Box 17, Folder 1.

57. "MIS Daily Summary #824," 23/24 June 1944, DMMA, RG 3, Box 34, p. 4; "MIS Daily Summary #842," 11/12 July 1944, DMMA, RG 3, Box 35, p. 4.

58. Jules Archer, *Jungle Fighters: A GI Correspondent's Experiences in the New Guinea Campaign* (New York: Julian Messner, 1985), p. 175.

6. Wakde-Sarmi: Whoever Heard of Lone Tree Hill?

1. In the end, some 3000 Hollandia survivors managed to make it to Wakde-Sarmi. See Charles Willoughby, *Reports of General MacArthur: Japanese Operations in the Southwest Pacific Area,* vol. 2, part 1 (Washington, D.C.: Government Printing Office, 1966), p. 277.

2. Only 9000 men of the 32nd Division made it to Halmahera. The 35th Division arrived more intact and was deployed at Manokwari. United States Army, Military Intelligence Division, *Disposition and Movement of Japanese Ground Forces, 1941–1945* (Washington, D.C.: War Department, 1945), part 17, p. 11.

3. Robert Ross Smith, *Approach to the Philippines* (Washington, D.C.: Government Printing Office, 1953), p. 232.

4. Bulletin 1228, 24 April 1944 diary entry, WTSJD, p. 9.

5. Willoughby, *MacArthur's Reports,* p. 150; Walter Krueger, *From Down Under to Nippon* (Washington, D.C.: Combat Forces Press, 1953), p. 79.

6. Krueger, *From Down Under,* p. 79.

7. Ibid., p. 81.

8. George C. Kenney, *General Kenney Reports: A Personal History of the Pacific War* (New York: Duell, Sloan, and Pearce, 1949), pp. 394–96.

9. Major General Hugh P. Casey, *Engineers of the Southwest Pacific, 1941–1945,* vol. 4: *Amphibian Engineer Operations* (Washington, D.C.: Government Printing Office, 1959), p. 337.

10. Wesley Frank Craven and James Lea Cate, eds., *The Army Air Forces in World War II: The Pacific,* vol. 4: *Guadalcanal to Saipan: August 1942 to July 1944* (Chicago: University of Chicago Press, 1950), p. 620.

11. Kenney, *General Kenney Reports,* pp. 395–96.

12. Ibid., pp. 395–97.

13. Major General Hugh J. Casey, *Engineers of the Southwest Pacific, 1941–1945,* vol. 1: *Reports of Operations* (Washington, D.C.: Government Printing Office, 1947), p. 173.

14. Daniel E. Barbey, *MacArthur's Amphibious Navy: Seventh Amphibious Force Operations, 1943–1945* (Annapolis: United States Naval Institute, 1969), p. 166.

15. Smith, *Approach,* pp. 210–12.

16. 6th Army Headquarters, 25 February 1945, "Wakde-Sarmi Operation," KP, Box 24, p. 15.

17. Karl C. Dod, *The Corps of Engineers: The War against Japan* (Washington, D.C.: Government Printing Office, 1966), p. 535; "Allied Airforces Intelligence Summary #207," 13 May 1944, Sutherland Papers, DMMA, RG 30, Box 28–40, p. 21.

18. Edward J. Drea, *MacArthur's Ultra: Codebreaking and the War Against Japan, 1942–1945* (Lawrence: University Press of Kansas, 1992), p. 120.

19. "MIS Daily Summary #784," 14/15 May 1944, DMMA, RG 3, Box 34, Appendix, p. i.

20. "MIS Daily Summary #779," 9/10 May 1944, DMMA, RG 3, Box 34, p. 3.

21. "MIS Daily Summary #761," 21/22 April, DMMA, RG 3, Box 33, p. 5.

22. "MIS Daily Summary #767," 27/28 April 1944, DMMA, RG 3, Box 33, p. 4.

23. Krueger, *From Down Under*, p. 81.

24. "MIS Daily Summary #768," 28/29 April 1944, DMMA, RG 3, Box 33, p. 4.

25. "MIS Daily Summary #775," 5/6 May 1944, DMMA, RG 3, Box 34, p. 3.

26. "MIS Daily Summary #774," 4/5 May 1944, DMMA, RG 3, Box 34, p. 3.

27. "MIS Daily Summary #779," 9/10 May 1944, DMMA, RG 3, Box 34, p. 3.

28. "MIS Daily Summary #780," 10/11 May 1944, DMMA, RG 3, Box 34, pp. 2–3; "MIS Daily Summary #783," 13/14 May 1944, DMMA, RG 3, Box 34, p. 3.

29. Bulletin 1225, 21 March 1944 diary entry, WTSJD, p. 21.

30. "MIS Daily Summary #770," 30 April/1 May 1944, DMMA, RG 3, Box 33, p. 3. Indeed, one Japanese soldier at Sarmi wrote after Nimitz's pre-Reckless air assault, ""SARMI, WAKDE and SAWAR furiously attacked and the skies were filled with black smoke. SARMI Div HQ was the objective and it was bombed and strafed. WAKDE Airfield was bombed and put out of commission, while every airplane was destroyed. SAWAR Airfield was also raided and the airplanes were destroyed. The AMERICAN air force has definite air superiority." See Bulletin 1228, 21 June 1944, WTSJD, p. 8.

31. Kenney, *General Kenney Reports*, p. 397; "MIS Daily Summary #782," 12/13 May 1944, DMMA, RG 3, Box 34, p. 3.

32. Krueger, *From Down Under*, p. 81.

33. Major General Hugh J. Casey, *Engineers of the Southwest Pacific, 1941–1945*, vol. 8: *Critique* (Washington, D.C.: Government Printing Office, 1959), pp. 177–78; Westerfield and Bob Burns, "Bob Burns' Story of Toem-Wakde," Westerfield Papers, USAMHI, p. 1.

34. Dod, *Corps*, p. 535.

35. Westerfield and Burns, "Bob Burns' Story of Toem-Wakde"; Westerfield and Nathan J. Sonnenfeld, "Wine and Water on Wakde," Westerfield Papers, USAMHI, p. 1.

36. *History of the Second Engineer Special Brigade* (Harrisburg, Pennsylvania: Telegraph Press, 1946), p. 84.

37. "MIS Daily Summary #768," 28/29 April 1944, DMMA, RG 3, Box 33, p. 2.

38. Barbey, *MacArthur's Amphibious Navy*, p. 166; "MIS Daily Summary #779," 9/10 May 1944, DMMA, RG 3, Box 34, p. 3.

39. "MIS Daily Summary #786," 16/17 May 1944, DMMA, RG 3, Box 34, p. 2.

40. Westerfield, William C. Davidson, and Raymond H. Wilcopolski, "First Wave on Wakde Beach," Westerfield Papers, USAMHI, p. 1; Westerfield and Burns, "Bob Burns' Story of Toem-Wakde," pp. 1–2; William F. Heavey, *Down Ramp!:*

The Story of the Army's Amphibian Engineers (Washington, D.C.: Infantry Journal Press, 1947), p. 117.

41. Robert L. Eichelberger, *Our Jungle Road to Tokyo* (New York: Viking Press, 1950), p. 137.

42. William F. McCartney, *The Jungleers: A History of the 41st Infantry Division* (Washington, D.C.: Infantry Journal Press, 1948), p. 94.

43. "Operations Report, Toem-Wakde Operation, Tornado Task Force, 163rd Infantry Regiment, 41st Infantry Division Journal," WNRC, RG 407, Box 10634, p. 2.

44. *Second Engineer Special Brigade*, pp. 84–86; William F. Heavey, "Amphibian Engineers in Action," *Military Engineer*, July 1945, 38(237):256.

45. McCartney, *Jungleers*, p. 97; Casey, *Amphibian Engineer Operations*, pp. 346–47.

46. The attack on Wakde is recorded in "Operations Report, Toem-Wakde Operation, Tornado Task Force, 163rd Infantry Regiment, 41st Infantry Division," pp. 2–3.

47. Westerfield and Ralph Marrow, "Battle of Waterless Wakde," Westerfield Papers, USAMHI, pp. 1–2.

48. Limited Distribution Interrogation Report 13, n.d., WTSJD, p. 1.

49. Westerfield and Sonnenfeld, "Wine and Water on Wakde," pp. 1–2.

50. Casey, *Critique*, p. 178.

51. Westerfield and Marrow, "Battle of Waterless Wakde," p. 2; Casey, *Amphibian Engineer Operations*, p. 346.

52. Heavey, "Amphibian Engineers in Action," p. 256; Samuel Eliot Morison, *History of United States Naval Operations in World War II*, vol. 8: *New Guinea and the Marianas, March 1944–August 1944* (Boston: Little, Brown, 1953), p. 100.

53. McCartney, *Jungleers*, p. 97. Casey puts the number at four of five. See Casey, *Critique*, p. 178.

54. Quoted in Barbey, *MacArthur's Amphibious Navy*, p. 193.

55. Westerfield and Burns, "Bob Burns' Story at Toem-Wakde," pp. 3–4.

56. Westerfield and Sonnenfeld, "Wine and Water on Wakde," pp. 3–4.

57. *New York Times*, 22 May 1944.

58. McCartney, *Jungleers*, p. 98.

59. Westerfield and Marrow, "Battle of Waterless Wakde," pp. 5–6; Westerfield, Davidson, and Wilcopolski, "First Wave on Wakde Beach," pp. 4–6.

60. Craven and Cate, *Guadalcanal to Saipan*, p. 629.

61. "MIS Daily Summary #790," 20/21 May 1944, DMMA, RG 3, Box 34, p. 3.

62. Even so, Kenney said he required four or five airfields in the region to bring his 5th and 13th AAFs fully into action. See Kenney, *General Kenney Reports*, p. 394.

63. 6th Army Headquarters, "Wakde-Biak Operation," 25 February 1945, KP, Box 24, p. 29.

64. "SWPA Communiqué #770," 19 May 1944, SWPA Press Releases, DMMA, RG 3, Box 3.

65. Harold Braun, USAMHI, Questionnaire, Harold Braun Papers, USAMHI; Braun, Personal letter, 19 March 1994, Braun Papers, USAMHI.

66. Eddleman Interview, 24 August 1985, KP, Box 40, p. 2; Decker Interview, Decker Papers, USAMHI, Interview 2, p. 10.

67. Palmer Interview, ASOOH, pp. 100–101, 338.

68. MacArthur to Krueger, 18 April 1944, Correspondence with 6th Army, Sutherland Papers, DMMA, RG 30, Box 1, Folder 7.

69. Krueger's comments on *Approach to the Philippines,* Personal Correspondence, KP, Box 12, No. 70, pp. 4–5; Smith, *Approach,* pp. 237–38.

70. Krueger's comments on *Approach to the Philippines,* pp. 4–5.

71. "MIS Daily Summary #793," 23/24 May 1944, DMMA, RG 3, Box 34, p. 3.

72. "MIS Daily Summary #794," 24/25 May 1944, DMMA, RG 3, Box 34, p. 3.

73. "MIS Daily Summary #796," 26/27 May 1944, DMMA, RG 3, Box 34, pp. 4–5.

74. Anthony Arthur, *Bushmasters: America's Jungle Warriors of World War II* (New York: St. Martin's Press, 1987), p. 2.

75. The 158th RCT's Lone Tree Hill ordeal is detailed in "158th RCT, Operations Report, Sarmi-Wakde Campaign," WNRC, RG 407, Box 21182, pp. 3–6.

76. Lone Tree Hill's description is found in ibid., p. 5; "Tornado Task Force (Wakde-Sarmi), History of the Tornado Task Force," WNRC, RG 407, Box 1563, p. 3.

77. "158th RCT, Operations Report, Sarmi-Wakde Campaign," pp. 5–6.

78. Patrick, "Historical Report of Operations, Wakde-Sarmi, Tornado Task Force," WNRC, RG 407, Box 1563, pp. 2–3.

79. Arthur, *Bushmasters,* pp. 122–23.

80. Patrick to Krueger, 3 June 1944, Decker Papers, USAMHI, No. 55, pp. 3–4.

81. "158th RCT, Operations Report, Sarmi-Wakde Campaign," p. 6. Patrick, however, later told Krueger that the withdrawal was not executed very well, but he may have been trying to justify Herndon's relief to his boss. See Patrick to Krueger, 3 June 1944, pp. 3–4.

82. Patrick to Krueger, 3 June 1944, pp. 3–4.

83. Arthur, *Bushmasters,* pp. 126–27. Patrick later claimed to Krueger that none of Herndon's subordinates thought the situation on the Snaky was that serious, but this contradicts statements these men made to Herndon. See Patrick to Krueger, 3 June 1944, pp. 3–4.

84. Arthur, *Bushmasters,* p. 127.

85. Patrick to Krueger, 3 June 1944, pp. 1–3.

86. Krueger, *From Down Under,* p. 89.

87. Ibid.

88. Patrick to Krueger, 3 June 1944, pp. 1–3.

89. Ibid., pp. 3–4; Patrick, "Historical Report of Operations, Wakde-Sarmi, Tornado Task Force," p. 4.

90. Krueger, *From Down Under,* p. 90.

91. Ibid., p. 89.

92. Palmer Interview, ASOOH, pp. 329–30.

93. Arthur, *Bushmasters,* p. 157.

94. Krueger to MacArthur, 2 July 1944, Decker Papers, USAMHI, No. 46; Eichelberger to his wife, 5 August 1944, Correspondence, RERC, Box 9; Palmer Interview, ASOOH, pp. 323–24, 334, 338.

95. Sibert to Krueger, 17 June 1944, KP, Krueger Correspondence, Box 7, No. 43; Krueger, *From Down Under,* p. 90.

96. Krueger to Sibert, 19 June 1944, Krueger Correspondence, KP, Box 7, No. 43.

97. Sibert to Krueger, 17 June 1944; Smith, *Approach,* p. 264.

98. "Tornado Task Force (Wakde-Sarmi), History of the Tornado Task Force," p. 1.

99. "MIS Daily Summary #810," 9/10 June 1944, DMMA, RG 3, Box 34, p. 3.

100. "MIS Daily Summary #811," 10/11 June 1944, DMMA, RG 3, Box 34, p. 3; "MIS Daily Summary #820," 19/20 June 1944, DMMA, RG 3, Box 34, p. 3.

101. The details of the 6th Division's Lone Tree Hill battle are taken from "Historical Report: 'The Battle of Lone Tree Hill,'" WNRC, RG 407, Box 7010, pp. 1–4.

102. The story of these subsidiary operations is found in "Tornado Task Force (Wakde-Sarmi), History of the Tornado Task Force," pp. 9–10.

103. Palmer Interview, pp. 327–28.

104. Ibid.

105. Ibid., p. 326.

106. Captain Walter Karig, Lieutenant Commander Russell L. Harris, and Lieutenant Commander Frank A. Manson, *Battle Report: The End of an Empire,* vol. 4 (New York: Rinehart, 1948), p. 204.

107. Douglas MacArthur, *Reminiscences* (New York: McGraw-Hill, 1964), p. 193.

108. Smith, *Approach,* pp. 278–79; Courtney Whitney, *MacArthur: His Rendezvous with History* (New York: Knopf, 1964), p. 111; Willoughby, *MacArthur's Reports,* p. 156; Krueger, *From Down Under,* pp. 91–92; 6th Army Headquarters, 25 February 1945, "Wakde-Biak Operation," pp. 72–73.

109. "Monthly Summary of Operations for the Month of August 1945," DMMA, RG 3, Box 166. Smith, however, places American losses from 17 May to 1 September at 400 killed and 1500 wounded. See Smith, *Approach,* pp. 278–79.

7. Biak: A Belated and Unhappy Victory

1. George C. Kenney, *General Kenney Reports: A Personal History of the Pacific War* (New York: Duell, Sloan, and Pearce, 1949), p. 399.

2. Major General Hugh J. Casey, *Engineers of the Southwest Pacific, 1941–1945,* vol. 8: *Critique* (Washington, D.C.: Government Printing Office, 1959), p. 190; Major General Hugh P. Casey, *Engineers of the Southwest Pacific, 1941–1945,* vol. 4: *Amphibian Engineer Operations* (Washington, D.C.: Government Printing Office, 1959), pp. 360–61.

3. William F. Heavey, "Amphibian Engineers in Action," *Military Engineer,* July 1945, 38(237):257; "Operations Report for the 162nd Infantry Regiment, 41st Infantry Division, Hurricane (Biak) Task Force," WNRC, RG 407, Box 10628, p. 1.

4. Newman, "Notes on US Army Actions in the Southwest Pacific in World War Two up to and including the Papua and Biak Campaigns (Draft Copy)," Newman Papers, USAMHI, p. 6.

5. Heavey, "Amphibian Engineers in Action," p. 257.

6. Rusell Stroup, "Notes of Former Captain Rusell Stroup," Military Papers, RERC, Box 68; Westerfield, Hargis, Counts, and Schatzman, "Mine Platoon at Biak," Westerfield Papers, USAMHI, p. 1.

7. Daniel E. Barbey, *MacArthur's Amphibious Navy: Seventh Amphibious Force Operations, 1943–1945* (Annapolis: United States Naval Institute, 1969), pp. 195–99.

8. "GHQ Communiqué #780," 28 May 1944, SWPA Press Releases, DMMA, RG 3, Box 3.

9. Asahel Bush, *St. Louis Post-Dispatch,* 28 May 1944.

10. Bulletin 1395, April 1944, WTSJD, pp. 11–15; Samuel Eliot Morison, *History of United States Naval Operations in World War II,* vol. 8: *New Guinea and the Marianas, March 1944–August 1944* (Boston: Little, Brown, 1953), p. 107.

11. Morison, *New Guinea and the Marianas,* p. 107.

12. MacArthur to Marshall, 25 May 1944, Correspondence with the War Department, DMMA, RG 4, Box 16; Charles A. Willoughby and John Chamberlain, *MacArthur: 1941–1951* (New York: McGraw-Hill, 1954), p. 188.

13. Barbey, *MacArthur's Amphibious Navy,* p. 186.

14. "G-2 Estimates of Enemy Situation," 11 May 1944, Lander Papers, USAMHI, pp. 2–3.

15. Edward J. Drea, *MacArthur's Ultra: Codebreaking and the War against Japan, 1942–1945* (Lawrence: University Press of Kansas, 1992), p. 135.

16. Walter Krueger, *From Down Under to Nippon* (Washington, D.C.: Combat Forces Press, 1953), p. 83.

17. "MIS Daily Summary #791," 21/22 May 1944, DMMA, RG 3, Box 34, p. 3.

18. "MIS Daily Summary #797," 27/28 May 1944, DMMA, RG 3, Box 34, p. 4.

19. "MIS Daily Summary #791," p. 3; Krueger, *From Down Under,* p. 82.

20. "Operations Report for the 162nd Infantry Regiment, 41st Infantry Division, Hurricane (Biak) Task Force," p. 2.

21. Robert Ross Smith, *Approach to the Philippines* (Washington, D.C.: Government Printing Office, 1953), pp. 294–96.

22. The 162nd RCT's ordeal is related in "Operations Report for the 162nd Infantry Regiment, 41st Infantry Division, Hurricane (Biak) Task Force," pp. 2–5.

23. Spencer Davis, *St. Louis Post-Dispatch,* 31 May 1944.

24. Westerfield and Charles F. Brockman, "First Two Days in Parai Defile," Westerfield Papers, USAMHI, pp. 2–3.

25. Spencer Davis, *New York Times,* 1 June 1944.

26. Davis, *St. Louis Post-Dispatch,* 31 May 1944.

27. Robert L. Eichelberger, *Our Jungle Road to Tokyo* (New York: Viking Press, 1950), p. 136.

28. Krueger, *From Down Under,* p. 95.

29. Davis, 12 June 1944, *Australia Newsweek,* in Military Papers, RERC, Box 33.

30. Newman, "Notes on US Army Actions in the Southwest Pacific in World War Two up to and including the Papua and Biak Campaigns (Draft Copy)," p. 7.

31. Krueger, *From Down Under,* p. 95.

32. Matome Ugaki, *Fading Victory: The Diary of Admiral Matome Ugaki* (Pittsburgh: University of Pittsburgh, 1991), p. 366.

33. Lieutenant Commander T.E.L. McCabe to Willoughby, 13 May 1944, Sutherland Papers, DMMA, RG 30, Box 5.

34. Willoughby to MacArthur, 13 May 1944, Sutherland Papers, DMMA, RG 30, Box 5.

35. "MIS Daily Summary #787," 27/28 May 1944, DMMA, RG 3, Box 34, p. 4.

36. "MIS Daily Summary #803," 2/3 June 1944, DMMA, RG 3, Box 34, pp. 4–5; Limited Distributions Translations 4, 23 May 1944 translation of an 8 March 1944 message, WTSJD, pp. 1–2.

37. "MIS Daily Summary #804," 3/4 June 1944, DMMA, RG 3, Box 34, p. 4.

38. Morison, *New Guinea and the Marianas*, pp. 94, 122–23; "Narrative of the Hurricane Task Force Operations," WNRC, RG 407, Box 10528, pp. 4–5.

39. Ugaki, *Fading Victory*, pp. 385–86.

40. Craven and Cate state that the Japanese destroyed six American planes and damaged another eighty; 6th Army headquarters put the figure at nine destroyed and ninety-three damaged, and Barbey simply said that two thirds of Wakde's arsenal was put out of action. Kenney, not surprisingly, glosses over the issue. See Wesley Frank Craven and James Lea Cate, eds., *The Army Air Forces in World War II: The Pacific*, vol. 4: *Guadalcanal to Saipan: August 1942 to July 1944* (Chicago: University of Chicago Press, 1950), p. 630; 6th Army Headquarters, "Wakde Biak Operation," 25 February 1945, KP, Box 24, p. 42; Barbey, *MacArthur's Amphibious Navy*, p. 202.

41. "MIS Daily Summary #807," 6/7 June 1944, DMMA, RG 3, Box 34, p. 3.

42. Charles Willoughby, *Reports of General MacArthur: Japanese Operations in the Southwest Pacific Area*, vol. 2, part 1 (Washington, D.C.: Government Printing Office, 1966), p. 291.

43. Ibid.

44. "MIS Daily Summary #811," 10/11 June 1944, DMMA, RG 3, Box 34, p. 3.

45. This is Barbey's opinion. See Barbey, *MacArthur's Amphibious Navy*, p. 203.

46. Krueger, *From Down Under*, p. 97.

47. Karl C. Dod, *The Corps of Engineers: The War against Japan* (Washington, D.C.: Government Printing Office, 1966), p. 539; Smith, *Approach*, pp. 340–41.

48. Smith, *Approach*, pp. 340–41.

49. Ibid., pp. 326–27.

50. Newman, "Notes on the US Army in the Southwest Pacific in World War Two up to and including the Papua and Biak Campaigns," p. 7.

51. Ibid.

52. Ibid., p. 8.

53. Ibid., p. 7.

54. Ibid.

55. The 162nd RCT's Parai Defile experience is taken from "Operations Report for the 162nd Infantry Regiment, 41st Infantry Division, Hurricane (Biak) Task Force," pp. 6–7.

56. Westerfield and Ralph Marlow, "Probing Ibdi Pocket," Westerfield Papers, USAMHI, p. 6.

57. The attack on the Mokmer ridges is related in "Operations Report for the 162nd Infantry Regiment, 41st Infantry Division, Hurricane (Biak) Task Force,"

pp. 8–9; Newman, "Notes on the US Army in the Southwest Pacific in World War Two up to and including the Papua and Biak Campaigns," pp. 8–9.

58. Westerfield and Louis Botta, "Parai Defile through Death Ridge," Westerfield Papers, USAMHI, pp. 4–5.

59. Marshall to MacArthur, 9 June 1944, Official Correspondence, DMMA, RG 3, Box 1.

60. Eichelberger, Memo to Milton Kaye, Military Papers, RERC, Box 68, p. 5.

61. MacArthur to Krueger, 5 June 1944, Correspondence with 6th Army, DMMA, RG 4, Box 14, Folder 3.

62. Krueger to MacArthur, 5 June 1944, Correspondence with 6th Army, DMMA, RG 4, Box 14, Folder 3.

63. Krueger to MacArthur, 8 June 1944, Correspondence with 6th Army, DMMA, RG 4, Box 14, Folder 3.

64. Krueger, *From Down Under,* pp. 95–97.

65. Ibid., p. 99; Decker Interview, Decker Papers, USAMHI, Interview 2, pp. 22–23.

66. Krueger, Comments on *Approach to the Philippines,* Personal Papers, KP, Box 12, No. 70, pp. 6–8.

67. Ibid.

68. See, for instance, Bulletin 1365, 7, 17 June 1944, WTSJD, pp. 14–15, 20.

69. Krueger, *From Down Under,* pp. 99–101.

70. Ibid., p. 101.

71. Krueger, Comments on *Approach to the Philippines,* pp. 6–8.

72. MacArthur to Krueger, 14 June 1944, Correspondence with 6th Army, DMMA, RG 4, Box 14, Folder 3; Krueger, *From Down Under,* p. 101.

73. Krueger to MacArthur, 14 June 1944.

74. Krueger, *From Down Under,* p. 101; Krueger, Comments on *Approach to the Philippines,* pp. 6–8.

75. Harold Riegelman, *The Caves of Biak* (New York: Dial Press, 1955), p. 136.

76. Robert L. Eichelberger, *Dear Miss Em: General Eichelberger's War in the Pacific, 1942–1945,* edited by Jay Luvaas (Westport, Connecticut: Greenwood Press, 1972), p. 120.

77. Byers Interview, 24 June 1971, 1971 Interviews, James Collection, DMMA, RG 49, Box 2, pp. 16–17.

78. Ibid., p. 17.

79. Eichelberger, *Dear Miss Em,* p. 120.

80. Eichelberger, "RLE's Orders to Take I Corps to Biak," Dictations, RERC, Box 73, pp. 405–9.

81. Eichelberger, *Jungle Road,* p. 144.

82. Eichelberger, *Dear Miss Em,* p. 120.

83. Krueger to Fuller, 5 June 1944, "41st Division Journal," WNRC, RG 407, Box 10528, p. 35.

84. Krueger to Fuller, 11 June 1944, "41st Division Journal," WNRC, RG 407, Box 10528, p. 56.

85. Eichelberger, *Dear Miss Em,* pp. 128–30; Krueger to MacArthur, 16 June 1944, Correspondence with 6th Army, DMMA, RG 4, Box 14, Folder 3.

86. Byers Interview, pp. 17–18.

87. Ibid.

88. Eichelberger, *Dear Miss Em,* pp. 128–30; Byers Interview, p. 18. Eichelberger later claimed that Fuller was drunk. See Eichelberger, "Fellers, also Krueger," Dictations, RERC, Box 74, pp. 756–62.

89. Collins Interview, Collins Papers, USAMHI, Interview 2, pp. 33–34.

90. Riegelman, *Caves,* pp. 138–39.

91. Eichelberger, "Krueger Criticizes General Fuller," Dictations, RERC, Box 73, pp. 405–9.

92. Eichelberger, "Memo of Interview with General MacArthur," 13 September 1944, RERC, Box 9.

93. Eddleman Interview, Eddleman Papers, USAMHI, Interview 2, p. 19; Decker Interview, pp. 22–23.

94. Swing Interview, 26 August 1971, 1971 Interviews, James Collection, DMMA, RG 49, Box 4, p. 28.

95. Eichelberger, *Dear Miss Em,* p. 130.

96. Krueger to Eichelberger, 17 June 1944, Military Papers, RERC, Box 33.

97. Eichelberger, "Debunks MacArthur as a 'Great Soldier' as Pictured in Books by Willoughby and Frazier Hunt; MacArthur as Strategist," Dictations, RERC, Box 73, pp. 126–34.

98. Eichelberger to Krueger, 17 June 1944, Military Papers, RERC, Box 33.

99. Eichelberger to his wife, 17 June 1944, Personal Correspondence, RERC.

100. Eichelberger, *Jungle Road,* p. 154.

101. Eichelberger, "RLE First Hears that He Is to Command the 8th Army," Dictations, RERC, Box 73, pp. 405–9.

102. Eichelberger, "Debunks MacArthur," pp. 290–302.

103. Eichelberger, *Dear Miss Em,* pp. 132–33, 142.

104. Eichelberger, 16–17 June 1944, Military Papers, RERC, Box 33; Eichelberger, 15–16 June 1944, 1944 Diaries, RERC, Box 1.

105. Eichelberger, *Dear Miss Em,* pp. 132–33.

106. Ibid., p. 129.

107. Ibid., p. 135.

108. "History of the Biak Operation, 15–27 June 1944," WNRC, RG 407, Box 1571, pp. 6–7; "Hurricane Task Force (Biak), G-2 Message File (Folder 2)," WNRC, RG 407, Box 1571; Eichelberger, *Jungle Road,* p. 146.

109. Eichelberger, *Jungle Road,* p. 146.

110. Eichelberger's offensive is related in "History of the Biak Operation, 15–27 June 1944," pp. 6–12.

111. Eichelberger, 20 June 1944, 1944 Diaries, RERC, Box 1.

112. For a good explanation of this process, see Riegelman, *Caves,* pp. 145–54.

113. Ibid., p. 154.

114. Eichelberger, *Dear Miss Em,* pp. 140–42.

115. Eichelberger, "Some Thoughts about Sutherland and Krueger," Dictations, RERC, Box 73, pp. 570–77. Eddleman, however, denied that Krueger either hated Eichelberger or opposed the formation of the 8th Army. He also warned against putting too much stock in Eichelberger's views on Krueger: "To rate General Krueger on the basis of General Eichelberger's letters to his wife is like asking Satan to prepare an Efficiency Report on Jesus Christ." See Eddleman to William Leary, 13 August 1985, KP, Box 40, p. 2; Eddleman, Eddleman's Comments, KP, Box 40, p. 1.

116. GHQ, "Summary of Operations for the Month of July 1944," DMMA, RG 3, Box 166.

117. Dod, *Corps,* p. 539.

118. Major General Hugh J. Casey, *Engineers of the Southwest Pacific, 1941–1945,* vol. 6: *Airfield and Base Development* (Washington, D.C.: Government Printing Office, 1951), p. 257. The problem with Biak lumber, however, was that the shrapnel had to be removed.

119. Craven and Cate, *Guadalcanal to Saipan,* pp. 645–56.

120. Kenney, *General Kenney Reports,* pp. 400–401; Krueger, *From Down Under,* p. 103.

121. There are discrepancies over American losses. Morison puts them at 483 killed, 2361 wounded, and 3500 cases of illness. Smith states that the American lost around 400 killed and 2000 wounded, 150 injured, and 7234 sick. GHQ, however, said that SWPA lost on Biak 554 killed, 2653 wounded, and 54 missing. See Morison, *New Guinea and the Marianas,* p. 133; Smith, *Approach,* pp. 392–93; GHQ, "Summary of Operations for the Month of September 1944," DMMA, RG 3, Box 166.

122. 6th Army Headquarters, "Wakde-Biak Operation," 25 February 1945, KP, Box 24, pp. 63–64.

123. Courtney Whitney, *MacArthur: His Rendezvous with History* (New York: Knopf, 1964), p. 112.

124. Patrick to Krueger, 3 June 1944, Decker Papers, USAMHI, No. 55, p. 4.

125. Columbia Broadcasting System, *From Pearl Harbor into Tokyo: The Story as Told by War Correspondents on the Air* (New York: Columbia Broadcasting System, 1945), p. 169.

126. See, for instance, Willoughby and Chamberlain, *MacArthur,* p. 189; Krueger, *From Down Under,* p. 104; Douglas MacArthur, *Reminiscences* (New York: McGraw-Hill, 1964), p. 193.

8. Noemfoor: Moving Closer to the Target

1. George C. Kenney, *General Kenney Reports: A Personal History of the Pacific War* (New York: Duell, Sloan, and Pearce, 1949), p. 404.

2. Daniel E. Barbey, *MacArthur's Amphibious Navy: Seventh Amphibious Force Operations, 1943–1945* (Annapolis: United States Naval Institute, 1969), p. 205.

3. Bulletin 1365, 7, 17 June 1944, WTSJD, pp. 14–15, 20.

4. MacArthur to Marshall, 29 June 1944, Correspondence with the War Department, DMMA, RG 4, Box 17, Folder 1.

5. Shimizu reported on 1 June 1944: "According to air reconnaissance reports, it appears that the enemy is anticipating a landing at NOEMFOOR Is." Shimizu, Bulletin No. 1360, 1 June 1944 message, WTSJD, p. 4. He reaffirmed this in late June. See Shimizu, Bulletin 1328, late June 1944 message, WTSJD, p. 18.

6. Walter Krueger, *From Down Under to Nippon* (Washington, D.C.: Combat Forces Press, 1953), p. 108.

7. Robert Ross Smith, *Approach to the Philippines* (Washington, D.C.: Government Printing Office, 1953), p. 400.

8. Krueger, "Report of the Tabletennis Operation," WNRC, RG 407, Box 1508, p. 9.

9. Barbey, *MacArthur's Amphibious Navy*, p. 210.

10. "Allied Airforces Intelligence Summary #194," 29 March 1944, Sutherland Papers, DMMA, RG 30, Boxes 28–40, pp. 20–21; "Allied Airforces Intelligence Summary #212," 31 May 1944, Sutherland Papers, DMMA, RG 30, Boxes 28–40, p.17; "Allied Airforces Intelligence Summary #218," 21 June 1944, Sutherland Papers, DMMA, RG 30, Boxes 28–40, p. 27.

11. Edward J. Drea, *MacArthur's Ultra: Codebreaking and the War Against Japan, 1942–1945* (Lawrence: University Press of Kansas, 1992), pp. 141–42; "MIS Daily Summary #820," 19/20 June 1944, DMMA, RG 3, Box 34, p. 3.

12. Krueger, *From Down Under*, pp. 107–8; Krueger, "Report of the Tabletennis Operation," p. 8.

13. Smith, *Approach*, p. 398.

14. Krueger, *From Down Under*, p. 108.

15. Ibid.; Barbey, *MacArthur's Amphibious Navy*, pp. 205–7.

16. Krueger, *From Down Under*, p. 108–9; Krueger, "Report of the Tabletennis Operation," p. 8.

17. Anthony Arthur, *Bushmasters: America's Jungle Warriors of World War II* (New York: St. Martin's Press, 1987), p. 151.

18. Quoted in Wesley Frank Craven and James Lea Cate, eds., *The Army Air Forces in World War II: The Pacific, vol. 4: Guadalcanal to Saipan: August 1942 to July 1944* (Chicago: University of Chicago Press, 1950), pp. 653–56.

19. Ibid., pp. 656–57.

20. "Summary of Operations for the Month of July 1944," DMMA, RG 3, Box 166.

21. Major General Hugh J. Casey, *Engineers of the Southwest Pacific, 1941–1945*, vol. 1: *Reports of Operations* (Washington, D.C.: Government Printing Office, 1947), p. 182.

22. *History of the Second Engineer Special Brigade* (Harrisburg, Pennsylvania: Telegraph Press, 1946), p. 95.

23. Samuel Eliot Morison, *History of United States Naval Operations in World War II*, vol. 8: *New Guinea and the Marianas, March 1944–August 1944* (Boston: Little, Brown, 1953), p. 138.

24. "Unit History, 158th Infantry Regiment," WNRC, RG 407, Box 21182, pp. 1–2.

25. The exact number the Japanese prisoner gave varies from 3500 to 7000. See "MIS Daily Summary #833," 2/3 July 1944, DMMA, RG 3, Box 35, p. 3; Krueger, *From Down Under*, pp. 110–11; Krueger, "Report of the Tabletennis Operation," p. 10.

26. "Operational History of the Tabletennis (Noemfoor Island) Operation," WNRC, RG 407, Box 1508, p. 7.

27. Much of this incident is derived from Krueger, "Report of the Tabletennis Operation," pp. 7–10; "Alamo Force, Operation 'I,' Tabletennis (Noemfoor Island) Operation, G-3 Journal #6 and 7," WNRC, RG 407, Box 1511.

28. "MIS Daily Summary #833," 2/3 July 1944, DMMA, RG 3, Box 35, p. 3.

29. Krueger, *From Down Under,* pp. 110–11; "Operational History of the Tabletennis (Noemfoor Island) Operation," p. 7.

30. Fellers, "503rd Parachute Infantry Regiment," Fellers Papers, DMMA, RG 44, Folder 5; Palmer Interview, ASOOH, p. 335.

31. Callahan, "Remembering War," Callahan Papers, USAMHI, p. 23.

32. Krueger, "Report of the Tabletennis Operation," pp. 10–11; Krueger, *From Down Under,* p. 111; Bennett M. Guthrie, *Three Winds of Death: The Saga of the 503rd Parachute Regimental Combat Team in the South Pacific* (Chicago: Adams Press, 1985), p. 84.

33. Amazingly enough, in his memoirs Kenney wrote about the airdrop, "It was a good job and nicely executed, but unnecessary, as things turned out." He was right about the latter statement, but certainly not about the former. See Kenney, *General Kenney Reports,* p. 408.

34. See, for instance, Braun, Questionnaire, Braun Papers, USAMHI. Some in the 503rd, for their part, felt that their unit was discriminated against in the allocation of weapons and equipment. One referred to the 503rd as, "the bastard regiment of the Cyclone Task Force." See Guthrie, *Three Winds,* p. 87.

35. Paul Shoemaker, "Oriental Obliteration," *Infantry Journal,* March 1945, pp. 30–32; Arthur, *Bushmasters,* pp. 161–65; "Unit History, 158th Infantry Regiment," WNRC, RG 407, Box 21182, p. 3.

36. Rhoades, who visited the island, said that the rumor was that there were two swords. See Weldon E. (Dusty) Rhoades, *Flying MacArthur to Victory* (College Station: Texas A&M University Press, 1987), p. 278; Arthur, *Bushmasters,* p. 171; Guthrie, *Three Winds,* p. 93.

37. Arthur, *Bushmasters,* p. 166; Callahan, "Remembering War," p. 24.

38. Karl C. Dod, *The Corps of Engineers: The War against Japan* (Washington, D.C.: Government Printing Office, 1966), p. 563; Craven and Cate, *Guadalcanal to Saipan,* p. 660.

39. Major General Hugh J. Casey, *Engineers of the Southwest Pacific, 1941–1945,* vol. 8: *Critique* (Washington, D.C.: Government Printing Office, 1959), p. 202.

40. Callahan, "Remembering War," p. 27.

41. Craven and Cate, *Guadalcanal to Saipan,* pp. 660–61.

42. Krueger, "Report of the Tabletennis Operation," p. 9. GHQ, however, put American losses at the end of September at 85 killed, 545 wounded, and 19 missing. See GHQ, "Summary of Operations for the Month of September 1944."

9. Driniumor River:
A Strategically Worthless Operation?

1. Charles A. Willoughby and John Chamberlain, *MacArthur: 1941–1951* (New York: McGraw-Hill, 1954), p. 190.

2. Millard G. Gray, "The Aitape Operation," *Military Review,* July 1951, vol. 31, p. 60; Edward O. Logan, *The Enveloping Maneuver of the 124th Infantry Reg-*

iment East of the Driniumor River, Aitape, New Guinea, 31 July–10 August 1944 (St. Augustine, Florida: State Arsenal, 1988), p. 46.

3. In mid-June General Hisaichi Terauchi, commander of the Southern Army and both Adachi's and Anami's superior, told Adachi that his mission was solely to protect eastern New Guinea. Even so, Adachi decided to continue his attack. See Charles Willoughby, *Reports of General MacArthur: Japanese Operations in the Southwest Pacific Area,* vol. 2, part 1 (Washington, D.C.: Government Printing Office, 1966), p. 299.

4. Ibid.

5. Walter Krueger, *From Down Under to Nippon* (Washington, D.C.: Combat Forces Press, 1953), pp. 69–70.

6. "32nd Infantry Division," Fellers Papers, DMMA, RG 44, Folder 5.

7. William H. Gill, as told to Edward Jaquelin Smith, *Always a Commander: The Reminiscences of Major General William H. Gill* (Colorado Springs: Colorado College, 1974), p. 56.

8. Gill Interview, Gill Papers, USAMHI, Tape 5, pp. 19–20.

9. The story of these skirmishes can be found in "Operations Report, Aitape Operation, 32nd Infantry Division," WNRC, RG 407, Box 9020, pp. 5–9.

10. Quoted in Edward J. Drea, *MacArthur's Ultra: Codebreaking and the War against Japan, 1942–1945* (Lawrence: University Press of Kansas, 1992), p. 144.

11. "MIS Daily Summary #789," 19/20 May 1944, DMMA, RG 3, Box 34, p. 3.

12. "MIS Daily Summary #790," 20/21 May 1944, DMMA, RG 3, Box 34, p. 4.

13. "MIS Daily Summary #792," 22/23 May 1944, DMMA, RG 3, Box 34, p. 3.

14. "MIS Daily Summary #786," 26/27 May 1944, DMMA, RG 3, Box 34, p. 3.

15. "Summary of Operations for the Month of May 1944," DMMA, RG 3, Box 165.

16. Logan, *Enveloping Maneuver,* p. 3.

17. "MIS Daily Summary #810," 9/10 June 1944, DMMA, RG 3, Box 34, p. 4.

18. "MIS Daily Summary #815," 14/15 June 1944, DMMA, RG 3, Box 34, p. 3.

19. "MIS Daily Summary #821," 20/21 June 1944, DMMA, RG 3, Box 34, pp. 3–4.

20. "MIS Daily Summary #832," 1/2 July 1944, DMMA, RG 3, Box 35, p. 3.

21. "MIS Daily Summary #839," 8/9 July 1944, DMMA, RG 3, Box 34, p. 4.

22. Marshall to MacArthur, 11 June 1944, Correspondence with the War Department, DMMA, RG 4, Box 17, Folder 1, p. 11.

23. Krueger, *From Down Under,* p. 71.

24. Ibid., pp. 71–72; Interview with Charles P. Hall, Smith's interviews for *Approach to the Philippines,* USAMHI, p. 1; Gill, *Always a Commander,* p. 60.

25. Krueger, *From Down Under,* pp. 71–72; Gray, "Aitape," p. 51.

26. Edward J. Drea, *Defending the Driniumor: Covering Force Operations in New Guinea, 1944* (Leavenworth, Kansas: Combat Studies Institute, 1984), pp. 48–50.

27. Krueger, *From Down Under,* p. 71.

28. Logan, *Enveloping Maneuver,* p. 6.

29. U.S. Army, 31st Division, *History of the 31st Infantry Division: In Training and Combat, 1940–1945* (Baton Rouge: Army and Navy, n.d.), p. 19.

30. Marshall to MacArthur, 18 January 1944, Correspondence with the War Department, DMMA, RG 4, Box 16, Folder 5; MacArthur to Marshall, 29 January 1944, Correspondence with the War Department, DMMA, RG 4, Box 16, Folder 5.

31. Gill Interview, Tape 6, pp. 6, 8.

32. Gill, *Always a Commander*, p. 59.

33. Krueger, *From Down Under*, pp. 71–72; Krueger, Comments on *Approach to the Philippines*, KP, Box 12, No. 70, p.3; Gray, "Aitape," pp. 51–52; Gill Interview, Tape 6, p. 1.

34. Gray, "Aitape," p. 52; U.S. Army, XI Corps, *History of XI Corps, 15 June 1942–15 March 1946*, p. 13.

35. Gray, "Aitape," p. 52; Krueger, *From Down Under*, p. 72.

36. Gill, *Always a Commander*, p. 61; Hall to Krueger, 10 July 1944, Decker Papers, USAMHI, No. 66, p. 1.

37. Hall to Krueger, 10 July 1944, p. 1.

38. Gray, "Aitape," p. 53.

39. Krueger, *From Down Under*, p. 72.

40. Gray, "Aitape," p. 58.

41. Logan, *Enveloping Maneuver*, pp. 9–10.

42. See Stuart F. Yeo to his father, 2–3 July 1944, Stuart F. Yeo Papers, USAMHI.

43. Gill, *Always a Commander*, p. 61.

44. Hall Interview, Smith's interviews for *Approach to the Philippines*, p. 2; Hall to Krueger, 8 July 1944, Decker Papers, USAMHI, No. 65, pp. 1–2.

45. "Operations Report, Aitape Operation, 32nd Infantry Division," WNRC, RG 407, Box 9020, p. 3. In his memoirs, however, Krueger stated that the reconnaissance-in-force was Hall's idea, even though the official record, as well as Hall's own testimony, said otherwise. See Krueger, *From Down Under*, p. 72.

46. Hall Interview, p. 5.

47. Gill, *Always a Commander*, p. 60.

48. Ibid., pp. 56, 58; Gill Interview, Tape 5, p. 19.

49. Gill Interview, Tape 6, pp. 2–3; "Operations Report, Aitape Operation, 32nd Infantry Division," pp. 4–5.

50. Gill, *Always a Commander*, p. 60.

51. H. W. Blakeley, *The 32d Infantry Division in World War Two* (Madison: Combat Forces Press, 1957), p. 160; Hall Interview, p. 2.

52. Gill, *Always a Commander*, p. 60.

53. Hall Interview, p. 5.

54. Details of the attack are found in "Operations Report, Aitape Operation, 32nd Infantry Division," p. 4; "Journal and File, 128th Infantry Regiment, 32nd Infantry Division, Aitape Campaign," WNRC, RG 407, Box 9282.

55. Gray, "Aitape," p. 54.

56. Blakeley, *32nd Infantry*, p. 161; Robert Ross Smith, *Approach to the Philippines* (Washington, D.C.: Government Printing Office, 1953), p. 155.

57. Hall Interview, p. 5.

58. Gill, *Always a Commander*, p. 61.

59. Gill Interview, Tape 6, p. 6.

60. Interview with Julian W. Cunningham, Smith's interviews for *Approach to the Philippines*, p. 2.

61. See Robert L. Eichelberger, *Our Jungle Road to Tokyo* (New York: Viking Press, 1950), p. 23.

62. Gill claimed that Martin, while brilliant, was "fairly delicate." Cunningham later agreed that Martin was too timid and pessimistic. Krueger, for his part, said Martin was relieved because he did not have a big enough staff to conduct the battle, but Gill did. Despite this apparent lack of confidence in his abilities, Martin was eventually promoted to major general and went on to ably command the 31st Division under Eichelberger in the southern Philippines. See Cunningham Interview, p. 5; Krueger, Comments on *Approach to the Philippines*, p. 3; Gill, *Always a Commander*, p. 62.

63. "MIS Daily Summary #842," 11/12 July 1944, DMMA, RG 3, Box 35, pp. 2–3.

64. "MIS Daily Summary #843," 12/13 July 1944, DMMA, RG 35, Box 35, pp. 3–4.

65. Hall Interview, p. 4.

66. Hall to Krueger, 16 July 1944, Decker Papers, USAMHI, No. 63, p. 3; *History of XI Corps*, p. 17.

67. Gray, "Aitape," p. 50.

68. Hall to Krueger, 16 July 1944, pp. 1–2.

69. Hall Interview, p. 3.

70. Gray, "Aitape," p. 58.

71. Logan, *Enveloping Maneuver*, pp. 16, 37–38; Yeo, Yeo Papers, USAMHI, p. 10; *History of XI Corps*, p. 20; Gray, "Aitape," p. 60.

72. Gill, *Always a Commander*, p. 65.

73. Bulletin 1398, late July 1944, WTSJD, p. 12.

74. "MIS Daily Summary #847," 16/17 July 1944, DMMA, RG 3, Box 35, p. 3.

75. "MIS Daily Summary #852," 21/22 July 1944, DMMA, RG 3, Box 35, p. 2.

76. Details of the fighting around Afua are related in "Historical Report, 112th Cav RCT," WNRC, RG 407, Box 18082, pp. 7–14.

77. Hall to Krueger, 24 July 1944, Decker Papers, USAMHI, No. 63, p. 1.

78. Interview with Harmon Lamar Boland, Harmon Lamar Boland Papers, USAMHI, p. 11.

79. Cunningham Interview, p. 3.

80. Cunningham to Gill and Hall, 30 July 1944, Decker Papers, USAMHI, No. 69, pp. 1–2; Smith, *Approach*, p. 179.

81. Cunningham Interview, p. 2; Gill, *Always a Commander*, p. 59; "Operations Report, Aitape Operation, 32nd Infantry Division," p. 8.

82. Hall to Krueger, 30 July 1944, Decker Papers, USAMHI, No. 69, pp. 1–5.

83. Hall to Krueger, 28 July 1944, Decker Papers, USAMHI, No. 68, pp. 1–3.

84. Hall to Krueger, 24 July 1944, p. 2.

85. Hall Interview, p. 1.

86. Hall to Krueger, 16 July 1944, pp. 2–3.

87. Hall to Krueger, 24 July 1944, p. 2; Hall to Krueger, 28 July 1944, pp. 1–3.

88. Hall Interview, p. 1.

89. Hall to Krueger, 24 July 1944, p. 1.

90. Hall Interview, pp. 2–3.

91. Lieutenant Colonel George D. Williams, "Historical Record of the 3rd Battalion, 124th Infantry Regimental Combat Team," in Florida Department of Mili-

tary Affairs, *Unit War Reports: 3rd Battalion 124th Infantry Regiment, 1944–1945*, Special Archives Publication No. 8 (St. Augustine, Florida: State Arsenal, 1985), p. 6.

92. Hall to Krueger, 28 July 1944, pp. 1–3.

93. Logan, *Enveloping Maneuver*, p. 22.

94. Ibid., p. 15.

95. Ibid., pp. 35–37.

96. Ibid., p. 32.

97. GHQ, "Summary of Operations for the Month of August 1944," DMMA, RG 3, Box 166. Smith puts the loss at fifty killed and eighty wounded. See Smith, *Approach*, p. 200.

98. *History of the 31st Division*, p. 149.

99. GHQ, "Summary of Operations for the Month of August 1944."

10. Sansapor-Mar and Morotai: Mopping Up the Campaign

1. JPS 243, "Operations in the New Guinea-Bismarck Archipelago-Admiralty Islands Area, Subsequent to Cartwheel," 5 August 1943, RJCS, p. 21; GHQ, "G-2 Estimate of the Enemy Situation for 'Reno II,'" 31 July 1943, Sutherland Papers, DMMA, RG 30, Box 43, p. 5.

2. Karl C. Dod, *The Corps of Engineers: The War against Japan* (Washington, D.C.: Government Printing Office, 1966), p. 563; Robert Ross Smith, *Approach to the Philippines* (Washington, D.C.: Government Printing Office, 1953), pp. 425–27.

3. "MIS Daily Summary #842," 11/12 July 1944, DMMA, RG 3, Box 36, p. 5. Willoughby's figures remained pretty steady throughout July.

4. Douglas MacArthur, *Reminiscences* (New York: McGraw-Hill, 1964), p. 195; MacArthur to Marshall, 22 July 1944, Correspondence with the War Department, DMMA, RG 4, Box 15, Folder 5.

5. GHQ, "Considerations Affecting the Occupation of Suitable Airfield Sites in the Vogelkop," 24 June 1944, DMMA, RG 3, pp. 1–3.

6. Walter Krueger, *From Down Under to Nippon* (Washington, D.C.: Combat Forces Press, 1953), p. 117.

7. Ibid.

8. Wesley Frank Craven and James Lea Cate, eds., *The Army Air Forces in World War II: The Pacific*, vol. 4: *Guadalcanal to Saipan: August 1942 to July 1944* (Chicago: University of Chicago Press, 1950), p. 662.

9. Ibid., p. 663.

10. Krueger, *From Down Under*, p. 117.

11. Charles Pearson, *Yank*, 25 August 1944, 3(10):10.

12. Major General Hugh J. Casey, *Engineers of the Southwest Pacific, 1941–1945*, vol. 8: *Critique* (Washington, D.C.: Government Printing Office, 1959), p. 207.

13. Robert L. Eichelberger, *Our Jungle Road to Tokyo* (New York: Viking Press, 1950), p. 161.

14. Division Public Relations Section, *The 6th Infantry Division in World War II, 1939–1945* (Nashville: Battery Press, 1983), pp. 57–58; George Sharpe, *Brothers beyond Blood: A Battalion Surgeon in the South Pacific* (Austin, Texas: Diamond Books, 1989), p. 73.

15. Palmer Interview, ASOOH, pp. 334, 338.

16. "MIS Daily Summary #436," 5/6 August 1944, DMMA, RG 3, Box 35, p. 4.

17. Major General Hugh P. Casey, *Engineers of the Southwest Pacific, 1941–1945,* vol. 4: *Amphibian Engineer Operations* (Washington, D.C.: Government Printing Office, 1959), pp. 411–12. See also Robert J. Bulkley, Jr., *At Close Quarters: PT Boats in the United States Navy* (Washington, D.C.: Naval History Division, 1962), p. 254.

18. GHQ, "Summary of Operations for the Month of September 1944," DMMA, RG 3, Box 166. Smith put the losses at fourteen killed, thirty-five wounded, and nine injured. Morison claimed thirty-four killed and eighty-five wounded. See Smith, *Approach,* p. 445; Samuel Eliot Morison, *History of United States Naval Operations in World War II,* vol. 8: *New Guinea and the Marianas, March 1944–August 1944* (Boston: Little, Brown, 1953), p. 144.

19. Weldon E. (Dusty) Rhoades, *Flying MacArthur to Victory* (College Station: Texas A&M University Press, 1987), p. 250.

20. "G-2 Estimate of Enemy Situation to Accompany 'Reno V,'" 15 June 1944, Lander Papers, USAMHI, p. ii.

21. "MIS Daily Summary #898," 5/6 September 1944, DMMA, RG 3, Box 36, p. 4.

22. Daniel E. Barbey, *MacArthur's Amphibious Navy: Seventh Amphibious Force Operations, 1943–1945* (Annapolis: United States Naval Institute, 1969), p. 225.

23. Krueger, *From Down Under,* p. 125.

24. "MIS Daily Summary #906," 14/15 September 1944, DMMA, RG 3, Box 36, pp. 3–4.

25. Krueger, *From Down Under,* p. 127.

26. Ibid., pp. 126–27.

27. Asahel Bush, *St. Louis Post-Dispatch,* 16 September 1944.

28. U.S. Army, XI Corps, *History of XI Corps, 15 June 1942–15 March 1946,* p. 27.

29. Casey, *Amphibian Engineer Operations,* pp. 431–32.

30. Ibid., p. 426.

31. Robert Shaplen, *Newsweek,* 25 September 1944.

32. Roger Olaf Egeberg, *The General: MacArthur and the Man He Called Doc* (New York: Hippocrene Books, 1983), p. 54.

33. Barbey, *MacArthur's Amphibious Navy,* p. 227.

34. For an excellent and detailed explanation of the JCS's decision to strike Luzon instead of Formosa, see Robert Ross Smith, "Luzon versus Formosa (1944)," in United States Office of Military History, *Command Decisions* (New York: Harcourt, Brace, 1959), pp. 358–73.

35. Barbey, *MacArthur's Amphibious Navy,* p. 227.

36. Rhoades, *Flying MacArthur,* p. 283.

37. Frank L. Kluckhohn, *New York Times,* 15 September 1944.

38. Casey, *Amphibian Engineer Operations,* p. 427.

39. Ibid., pp. 432–34.

40. Spencer Davis, *St. Louis Post-Dispatch,* 16 September 1944.

41. "MIS Daily Summary #907," 15/16 September 1944, DMMA, RG 3, Box 36, p. 4.

42. Krueger, *From Down Under,* pp. 126, 129.

43. Smith, *Approach,* p. 492.

44. Wesley Frank Craven and James Lea Cate, eds., *The Army Air Forces in World War II,* vol. 5: *The Pacific: Matterhorn to Nagasaki, June 1944 to August 1945* (Chicago: University of Chicago Press, 1953), p. 315; US Army, 31st Division, *History of the 31st Division: In Training and Combat, 1940–1945* (Baton Rouge: Army and Navy, n.d.), p. 68.

45. Smith, *Approach,* p. 489; Craven and Cate, *Matterhorn to Nagasaki,* p. 312.

Conclusions

1. Roger Olaf Egeberg, *The General: MacArthur and the Man He Called Doc* (New York: Hippocrene Books, 1983), p. 69.

2. Ernest J. King and Walter Muir Whitehill, *Fleet Admiral King: A Naval Record* (New York: Norton, 1952), pp. 383–89.

3. Douglas MacArthur, *Reminiscences* (New York: McGraw-Hill, 1964), pp. 165–66.

4. "Air Operations in the Southwest Pacific," *Army and Navy Journal,* 1944, 82(15):78; George C. Kenney, *General Kenney Reports: A Personal History of the Pacific War* (New York: Duell, Sloan, and Pearce, 1949), p. 397.

5. Both Kinkaid and Barbey's chief planner, Captain Bern Anderson, testified to this. See Thomas Kinkaid, *The Reminiscences of Thomas Cassin Kinkaid* (New York: Columbia University, Oral History Research Office, 1961), p. 259; and Samuel Eliot Morison, *History of United States Naval Operations in World War II,* vol. 6: *Breaking the Bismarcks Barrier, 22 July 1942–1 May 1944* (Boston: Little, Brown, 1950), pp. 15, 48.

6. MacArthur, *Reminiscences,* p. 169.

7. Riegelman, who served under Eichelberger and Swift, later wrote, "Krueger was ruthless when it came to relieving commanders who did not deliver on Krueger's schedule." It was not Krueger's schedule, however, but MacArthur's. See Harold Riegelman, *The Caves of Biak* (New York: Dial Press, 1955), p. 137.

8. Charles A. Willoughby and John Chamberlain, *MacArthur: 1941–1951* (New York: McGraw-Hill, 1954), pp. 204–6.

9. MacArthur, *Reminiscences,* p. 166; Willoughby and Chamberlain, *MacArthur,* p. 208.

10. MacArthur, *Reminiscences,* p. 166.

11. Joseph C. Goulden, *Korea: The Untold Story of the War* (New York: McGraw-Hill, 1982), p. 91.

12. For a much harsher evaluation of Krueger, see Geoffrey Perret, *There's a War to Be Won: The United States Army in World War II* (New York: Random House, 1991), pp. 258–59, 261–62, 595.

BIBLIOGRAPHY

Archival Work

Robert L. Eichelberger Research Collection, Duke University, North Carolina
Walter Krueger papers, United States Military Academy, West Point, New York
Douglas MacArthur Memorial Archives, Norfolk, Virginia
United States Army Military History Institute, Carlisle, Pennsylvania
    Papers of Charles E. Bennett, Hamar Lamar Boland, Harold Braun, Edward
    Jerome Callahan, Stephen J. Chamberlin, James F. Collins, Joseph P. Cribbins,
    Lloyd E. Day, George Decker, Clyde Eddleman, Jack C. Fuson, William M. Gill,
    John Edwin Grose, William Hardy, Cecil C. Helena, Park A. Hodak, Frederic T.
    Kielsgard, Salvadore Lamagna, Quentin S. Lander, Richard J. Marshall, Aubrey
    S. Newman, Oliver P. Newman, Hollis L. Peacock, Carl Thien, Charles V. Trent,
    Arthur G. Trudeau, Paul Westerfield, Stuart F. Yeo, and Joseph Zimmer.
National Archives and Records Administration, Washington National Records
    Center, Suitland, Maryland

Published Primary Documents

Congressional Information Services. *Wartime Translations of Seized Japanese Documents: Allied Translator and Interpretation Section Reports, 1942–1946.* Bethesda, 1988.

University Publications of America. *Armed Forces Oral Histories, Army Senior Officer Oral Histories.* Frederick, Maryland: University Publications of America, 1989.

———. *Record of the Joint Chiefs of Staff, Part 1.* Frederick, Maryland: University Publications of America, n.d.

First-hand Accounts

Columbia Broadcasting System. *From Pearl Harbor into Tokyo: The Story as Told by War Correspondents on the Air.* New York: Columbia Broadcasting System, 1945.

Curtiss, Mina, ed. *Letters Home.* Boston: Little, Brown, 1944.

Eichelberger, Robert L. *Dear Miss Em: General Eichelberger's War in the Pacific, 1942–1945.* Edited by Jay Luvaas. Westport, Connecticut: Greenwood Press, 1972.

Florida Department of Military Affairs. *Unit War Reports: 3rd Battalion 124th Infantry Regiment, 1944–1945.* Special Archives Publication No. 8. St. Augustine, Florida: State Arsenal, 1985.

Gray, Lieutenant Colonel Millard G. "The Aitape Operation." *Military Review,* July 1951, 31:44–62.

Kahn, Sy M. *Between Tedium and Terror: A Soldier's World War II Diary, 1943–1945.* Chicago: University of Illinois Press, 1993.

Logan, Major Edward O. *The Enveloping Maneuver of the 124th Infantry Regiment East of the Driniumor River, Aitape, New Guinea, 31 July–10 August 1944.* St. Augustine, Florida: State Arsenal, 1988.

MacArthur, Douglas. *A Soldier Speaks: Public Papers and Speeches of General of the Army Douglas MacArthur.* New York: Praeger, 1965.

Maule, Harry E., ed. *A Book of War Letters.* New York: Random House, 1943.

Shoemaker, Paul S. "Oriental Obliteration." *Infantry Journal,* March 1945, pp. 30–32.

Ugaki, Matome. *Fading Victory: The Diary of Admiral Matome Ugaki.* Pittsburgh: University of Pittsburgh Press, 1991.

United States Army Air Forces. *Report of the Commanding General of the Army Air Forces to the Secretary of War.* Washington, D.C.: Government Printing Office, 1945.

United States Navy Department. *Navy Department Communiques 301 to 600 and Pacific Fleet Communiques, March 6, 1943, to May 24, 1945.* Washington, D.C.: Government Printing Office, 1945.

Memoirs

Archer, Jules. *Jungle Fighters: A GI Correspondent's Experiences in the New Guinea Campaign.* New York: Julian Messner, 1985.

Arnold, H. H. *Global Mission.* New York: Harper, 1949.

Barbey, Daniel E. *MacArthur's Amphibious Navy: Seventh Amphibious Force Operations, 1943–1945.* Annapolis: United States Naval Institute, 1969.

Boeman, John. *Morotai: A Memoir of War.* Garden City, New York: Doubleday, 1981.

Chase, William C. *Front Line General.* Houston: Pacesetter Press, 1975.

Coffman, Edward and Paul H. Hass, eds. "With MacArthur in the Pacific: A Memoir by Philip F. La Follette." *Wisconsin Magazine of History,* 1980–81, 64(2): 82–106.

Dunn, William J. "MacArthur's Mansion and Other Myths." *Army Magazine,* March 1973, 23:39–44.

Egeberg, Roger Olaf. *The General: MacArthur and the Man He Called Doc.* New York: Hippocrene Books, 1983.

Eichelberger, Robert L. *Our Jungle Road to Tokyo.* New York: Viking Press, 1950.

Gill, William H., as told to Edward Jaquelin Smith. *Always a Commander: The Reminiscences of Major General William H. Gill.* Colorado Springs: Colorado College, 1974.

Guthrie, Bennett M. *Three Winds of Death: The Saga of the 503rd Parachute Regimental Combat Team in the South Pacific.* Chicago: Adams Press, 1985.

Huff, Sid, with Joe Alex Morris. *My Fifteen Years with General MacArthur.* New York: Paperback Library, 1964.

Kenney, George C. *General Kenney Reports: A Personal History of the Pacific War.* New York: Duell, Sloan, and Pearce, 1949.

———. *The MacArthur I Know.* New York: Duell, Sloan, and Pearce, 1951.

King, Ernest J. and Walter Muir Whitehill. *Fleet Admiral King: A Naval Record.* New York: Norton, 1952.

Kinkaid, Thomas. *The Reminiscences of Thomas Cassin Kinkaid.* New York: Columbia University, Oral History Research Office, 1961.

Krueger, Walter. *From Down Under to Nippon.* Washington, D.C.: Combat Forces Press, 1953.

Leahy, William D. *I Was There: A Personal Story of the Chief of Staff to Presidents Roosevelt and Truman Based on His Notes and Diaries at the Time.* New York: McGraw-Hill, 1950.

MacArthur, Douglas. *Reminiscences.* New York: McGraw-Hill, 1964.

Niles, Gibson. *The Operations of the Alamo Scouts.* Fort Benning, Georgia: General Subject Section, Academic Department, The Infantry School, 1948.

Parnell, N. M. "Reminiscences of a Radio Operator." *American Aviation Historical Society,* Winter 1987, 32(4):254–65.

Rhoades, Weldon E. (Dusty). *Flying MacArthur to Victory.* College Station: Texas A&M University Press, 1987.

Riegelman, Harold. *The Caves of Biak.* New York: Dial Press, 1955.

Rogers, Paul P. *The Bitter Years: MacArthur and Sutherland.* New York: Praeger, 1991.

Sharpe, George. *Brothers Beyond Blood: A Battalion Surgeon in the South Pacific.* Austin, Texas: Diamond Books, 1989.

Swan, W. N. *Spearheads of Invasion: An Account of the Seven Major Invasions Carried out by the Allies in the South-west Pacific Area during the Second World War, as Seen from a Royal Australian Naval Landing Ship Infantry.* London: Angus and Robertson, 1953.

Thien, Carl R. *Pacific Island Odyssey: Whistling Past the Foxholes,* 1992.

Thorpe, Elliott R. *East Wind, Rain: The Intimate Account of an Intelligence Officer in the Pacific, 1939–49.* Boston: Gambit, 1969.

The War Reports of General of the Army George C. Marshall, General of the Army H. H. Arnold, and Fleet Admiral Ernest J. King. New York: Lippincott, 1947.

Wedemeyer, General Albert C. *Wedemeyer Reports!* New York: Holt, 1958.

Whitney, Courtney. *MacArthur: His Rendezvous with History.* New York: Knopf, 1964.

Willoughby, Charles A. and John Chamberlain. *MacArthur: 1941–1951.* New York: McGraw-Hill, 1954.

Official Histories

Bulkley, Captain Robert J. *At Close Quarters: PT Boats in the United States Navy.* Washington, D.C.: Naval History Division, 1962.

Bykofsky, Joseph and Harold Larson. *The Transportation Corps: Operations Overseas.* Washington, D.C.: Government Printing Office, 1957.

Casey, Major General Hugh J. *Engineers of the Southwest Pacific, 1941–1945,* 8 vols. Washington, D.C.: Government Printing Office, 1947–1959.

Coakley, Robert W. and Richard M. Leighton. *Global Logistics and Strategy, 1943–1945.* Washington, D.C.: Government Printing Office, 1986.

Craven, Wesley Frank and James Lea Cate, eds. *The Army Air Forces in World War II: The Pacific,* vol. 4: *Guadalcanal to Saipan, August 1942 to July 1944,* Chicago: University of Chicago Press, 1950.

———. *The Army Air Forces in World War II: The Pacific,* vol. 5: *Matterhorn to Nagasaki, June 1944 to August 1945.* Chicago: University of Chicago Press, 1953.

Dod, Karl C. *The Corps of Engineers: The War against Japan.* Washington, D.C.: Office of the Chief of Military History, Government Printing Office, 1966.

Karig, Captain Walter, Lieutenant Commander Russell L. Harris, and Lieutenant Commander Frank A. Manson. *Battle Report: The End of an Empire,* vol. 4. New York: Rinehart, 1948.

Matloff, Maurice. *Strategic Planning for Coalition Warfare: 1943–1944.* Washington, D.C.: Government Printing Office, 1959.

Mayo, Lida. *The Ordinance Department: On Beachhead and Battlefront.* Washington, D.C.: Government Printing Office, 1991.

Miller, John, Jr. *Cartwheel: The Reduction of Rabaul.* Washington, D.C.: Government Printing Office, 1959.

Morison, Samuel Eliot. *History of United States Naval Operations in World War II,* vol. 6: *Breaking the Bismarcks Barrier, 22 July 1942–1 May 1944.* Boston: Little, Brown, 1950.

———. *History of United States Naval Operations in World War II,* vol. 12: *Leyte, June 1944–January 1945.* Boston: Little, Brown, 1966.

———. *History of United States Naval Operations in World War II,* vol. 8: *New Guinea and the Marianas, March 1944–August 1944.* Boston: Little, Brown, 1953.

Morton, Louis. *United States Army in World War II: The War in the Pacific: Strategy and Command: The First Two Years.* Washington, D.C.: Government Printing Office, 1962.

Smith, Robert Ross. *Approach to the Philippines.* Washington, D.C.: Government Printing Office, 1953.

Treadwell, Mattie E. *The Women's Army Corps.* Washington, D.C.: Government Printing Office, 1954.

United States Army. Historical Division. *The Admiralties: Operations of the 1st Cavalry Division.* Washington D.C.: Government Printing Office: 1945.

———. *The Sixth Army in Action: A Photo History, January 1943–June 1945.* Kyoto, Japan: 8th Information and Historical Service, 1945.

United States Army. Military Intelligence Division. *Disposition and Movement of Japanese Ground Forces, 1941–1945.* Washington, D.C.: War Department, 1945.

United States Army. Office of Military History. *Command Decisions.* New York: Harcourt, Brace, 1959.

Willoughby, Charles A. *Reports of General MacArthur: The Campaigns of MacArthur in the Pacific.* Vol. 1. Washington, D.C.: Government Printing Office, 1966.

————. *Reports of General MacArthur: Japanese Operations in the Southwest Pacific Area.* Vol. 2, part 1. Washington, D.C.: Government Printing Office, 1966.

Williams, Mary H. *Chronology: 1941–1945.* Washington, D.C.: Government Printing Office, 1960.

Secondary Sources

Ambrose, Stephen E. "MacArthur: The Man and the Legend." *American History Illustrated,* January 1968, 11(9):5–12, 49–53.

Archer, Jules. *Front-Line General: Douglas MacArthur.* New York: Julian Messner, 1963.

Barnes, G. M. *Weapons of World War II.* New York: Van Nostrand, 1947.

Bergerud, Eric. *Touched with Fire: The Land War in the South Pacific.* New York: Viking, 1996.

Blair, Clay, Jr. *Silent Victory: The U.S. Submarine War against Japan.* New York: Lippincott, 1975.

Breuer, William B. *Devil Boats: The PT War against Japan.* Novato, California: Presidio Press, 1987.

Briggs, Philip J. "General MacArthur and the Presidential Election of 1944." *Presidential Studies Quarterly,* 1992, 22(1):31–46.

Bunker, John Gorley. *Liberty Ships: The Ugly Ducklings of World War II.* Annapolis: Naval Institute Press, 1972.

Calvocoressi, Peter and Guy Wint. *Total War: Causes and Courses of the Second World War.* London: Penguin, 1972.

Chwialkowski, Paul. *In Caesar's Shadow: The Life of General Robert Eichelberger.* Westport, Connecticut: Greenwood Press, 1993.

Collier, Basil. *The War in the Far East, 1941–1945.* London: Heinemann, 1969.

Cook, Charles O., Jr. "The Pacific Command Divided: The 'Most Unexplainable' Decision." *US Naval Institute Proceedings,* September 1978, 104(4):55–61.

————. "The Strange Case of Rainbow–5." *US Naval Institute Proceedings,* August 1978, 104(8):67–73.

Cook, Haruko Taya and Theodore F. Cook. *Japan at War: An Oral History.* New York: New Press, 1992.

Coox, Alvin D. *Nomonhan: Japan against Russia, 1939.* Stanford: Stanford University Press, 1985.

Costello, John. *The Pacific War.* New York: Atlantic Communications, Inc., 1981.

Day, David. *Reluctant Nation: Australia and the Allied Defeat of Japan 1942–45.* Oxford: Oxford University Press, 1992.

Deutsch, Harold C. "Clients of Ultra: American Captains." *Parameters,* 1985, 15(2):55–62.

Dower, John W. *War without Mercy: Race and Power in the Pacific War.* New York: Pantheon Books, 1986.

Drea, Edward J. *Defending the Driniumor: Covering Force Operations in New Guinea, 1944.* Leavenworth, Kansas: Combat Studies Institute, 1984.

————. *MacArthur's Ultra: Codebreaking and the War against Japan, 1942–1945.* Lawrence: University Press of Kansas, 1992.

————. "Ultra Intelligence and General Douglas MacArthur's Leap to Hollandia, January–April 1944." *Intelligence and National Security,* April 1990, 5(2):323–49.

Dull, Paul S. *A Battle History of the Imperial Japanese Navy (1941–1945).* Annapolis: Naval Institute Press, 1978.

Ellis, John. *Brute Force: Allied Strategy and Tactics in the Second World War.* New York: Viking Press, 1990.

————. *The Sharp End: The Fighting Man in World War II.* New York: Scribners, 1981.

English, John A. *On Infantry.* New York: Praeger, 1984.

Forbes, Joseph. "General Douglas MacArthur and the Implementation of American and Australian Civilian Policy Decisions in 1944 and 1945." *Military Affairs,* 1985, 49(1):1–4.

Goldstein, David M. "Ennis C. Whitehead: Aerospace Commander and Pioneer." Ph.D. diss., University of Denver, 1970.

Goulden, Joseph C. *Korea: The Untold Story of the War.* New York: McGraw-Hill, 1982.

Greenfield, Kent Roberts. *American Strategy in World War II: A Reconsideration.* Baltimore: The Johns Hopkins Press, 1963.

Harries, Meirion and Susie. *Soldiers of the Sun: The Rise and Fall of the Imperial Japanese Army.* New York: Random House, 1991.

Hayashi, Saburo, with Alvin D. Coox. *Kogun: The Japanese Army in the Pacific.* Quantico, Virginia: Marine Corps Association, 1959.

Hayes, Grace Person. *The History of the Joint Chiefs of Staff in World War II: The War against Japan.* Annapolis: Naval Institute Press, 1982.

Holzimmer, Kevin C. "Walter Krueger, Douglas MacArthur, and the Pacific War: The Wakde-Sarmi Campaign as a Case Study." *Journal of Military History,* October 1995, 59:661–85.

Horner, D. M. *High Command: Australia and Allied Strategy, 1939–1945.* Canberra: Allen & Unwin, 1982.

House, Jonathan M. *Toward Combined Arms Warfare: A Survey of 20th-Century Tactics, Doctrine, and Organization.* Leavenworth, Kansas: Combat Studies Institute, 1984.

Hoyt, Edwin P. *How They Won the War in the Pacific: Nimitz and His Admirals.* New York: Weybright and Talley, 1970.

————. *Japan's War: The Great Pacific Conflict, 1853 to 1952.* New York: McGraw-Hill, 1986.

Hunt, Frazier. *The Untold Story of Douglas MacArthur.* New York: Devin-Adair, 1954.

Infantry in Battle. Washington, D.C.: Infantry Journal, 1939.

James, D. Clayton. "MacArthur's Lapses from an Envelopment Strategy in 1945." *Parameters,* 1980, 10(2):26–32.

————. *The Years of MacArthur.* 2 vols. Boston: Houghton Mifflin, 1970, 1975.

Keegan, John. *The Second World War.* New York: Viking Press, 1990.

Kennedy, Paul. *The Rise and Fall of the Great Powers: Economic Change and Military Conflict from 1500 to 2000.* New York: Vintage, 1987.

Lawless, Major Roger E. "The Biak Operation." *Military Review,* June 1953, 33:48–62.

Leary, William, M., ed. *We Shall Return!: MacArthur's Commanders and the Defeat of Japan, 1942–1945.* Lexington: University Press of Kentucky, 1988.

Liddell Hart, B. H. *History of the Second World War.* New York: Putnam's, 1971.

Luszki, Walter A. *A Rape of Justice: MacArthur and the New Guinea Hangings.* New York: Madison Books, 1991.

Manchester, William. *American Caesar: Douglas MacArthur, 1880–1964.* Boston: Little, Brown, 1978.

Mayo, Lida. *Bloody Buna.* Garden City, New York: Doubleday, 1974.

Miller, Edward S. *War Plan Orange: The U.S. Strategy to Defeat Japan, 1897–1945.* Annapolis: Naval Institute Press, 1991.

Perret, Geoffrey. *There's a War to Be Won: The United States Army in World War II.* New York: Random House, 1991.

Petillo, Carol Moris. *Douglas MacArthur: The Philippine Years.* Bloomington: Indiana University Press, 1981.

Pogue, Forrest C. *George C. Marshall: Ordeal and Hope, 1939–1942.* New York: Viking Press, 1966.

———. *George C. Marshall: Organizer of Victory, 1943–1945.* New York: Viking Press, 1973.

Pokrass, Gregory S. "The Red Arrow Division in New Guinea." *Milwaukee County Historical Society,* 1983, 6(3):83–91.

Potter, E. B. *Nimitz.* Annapolis: Naval Institute Press, 1976.

Reynolds, Clark G. "Admiral Ernest J. King and the Strategy for Victory in the Pacific." *Naval War College Review,* Winter 1976, 28(3):57–64.

———. "MacArthur as a Maritime Strategist." *Naval War College Review,* March–April 1980, 33:79–102.

Sachton, Frank J. "Southwest Pacific Alamo Scouts." *Armored Cavalry Journal,* January–February 1947, 56:55–56.

Schaller, Michael. *Douglas MacArthur: The Far Eastern General.* New York: Oxford University Press, 1989.

Shortal, John F. *Forged by Fire: General Robert L. Eichelberger and the Pacific War.* Columbia: University of South Carolina Press, 1987.

———. "Hollandia: A Training Victory." *Military Review,* 1986, 66(5):40–48.

———. "MacArthur's Fireman: Robert L. Eichelberger." *Parameters,* 1986, 16(3):58–67.

Spector, Ronald. *Eagle against the Sun: The American War with Japan.* New York: Free Press, 1985.

Steinberg, Rafael. *Island Fighting.* Alexandria, Virginia: Time-Life Books, 1978.

———. *Return to the Philippines.* Alexandria, Virginia: Time-Life Books, 1980.

Stouffer, Samuel A., Arthur A. Lumsdaine, et al. *The American Soldier: Combat and Its Aftermath,* vol. 2. New York: Wiley, 1965.

Sufrin, Mark. "'Take Buna or Don't Come Back Alive.'" *American History Illustrated,* November 1970, 5(7):4–10, 43–47.

van Creveld, Martin. *Fighting Power: German and U.S. Army Performance, 1939–1945.* Westport, Connecticut: Greenwood Press, 1982.

van der Vat, Dan. *The Pacific Campaign: World War II The U.S.–Japanese Naval War, 1941–1945.* New York: Simon and Schuster, 1991.

Wallace, Robert. *The Italian Campaign.* Alexandria, Virginia: Time-Life Books, 1981.

Weigley, Russell F. *The American Way of War: A History of United States Military Strategy and Policy.* Bloomington: Indiana University Press, 1977.

Weinberg, Gerhard L. *A World at Arms: A Global History of World War II.* Cambridge: Cambridge University Press, 1994.

Weller, Jac. *Weapons and Tactics: Hastings to Berlin.* London: Nicholas Vane, 1966.

Wheeler, Gerald E. *Kinkaid of the Seventh Fleet: A Biography of Admiral Thomas C. Kinkaid.* Washington, D.C.: Naval Historical Center, 1995.

Willmott, H. P. *Empires in the Balance: Japanese and Allied Pacific Strategies to April 1942.* Annapolis: Naval Institute Press, 1982.

Unit Histories

Arthur, Anthony. *Bushmasters: America's Jungle Warriors of World War II.* New York: St. Martin's Press, 1987.

Blakeley, H. W. *The 32d Infantry Division in World War Two.* Madison: Combat Forces Press, 1957.

Division Public Relations Section. *The 6th Infantry Division in World War II, 1939–1945.* Nashville: Battery Press, 1983.

Flanagan, E. M., Jr. *The Angels: A History of the 11th Airborne Division.* Navato, California: Presidio Press, 1989.

Heavey, Brigadier General William F. *Down Ramp!: The Story of the Army Amphibian Engineers.* Washington, D.C.: Infantry Journal Press, 1947.

History of the Second Engineer Special Brigade. Harrisburg, Pennsylvania: Telegraph Press, 1946.

Lancaster, Roy. *The Story of the Bushmasters.* Detroit: Lancaster, n.d.

McCartney, William F. *The Jungleers: A History of the 41st Infantry Division.* Washington, D.C.: Infantry Journal Press, 1948.

United States Army. XI Corps. *History of XI Corps, 15 June 1942–15 March 1946.*

United States Army. 31st Division. *History of the 31st Infantry Division: In Training and Combat, 1940–1945.* Baton Rouge: Army and Navy Publishing Co., nd.

United States Army. The 33d Infantry Division Historical Committee. *The Golden Cross: A History of the 33d Infantry Division in World War II.* Washington, D.C.: Infantry Journal Press, 1948.

United States Army. Far East Command. *18th Army Operations.* Vol. 1. Washington, D.C.: Office of the Chief of Military History, 1957.

Verbeck, William J. *The Story of a Regiment in Action.*

Wright, Bertram C. *The 1st Cavalry Division in World War II.* Tokyo: Tappan, 1947.

Zimmer, Joseph E. *The History of the 43d Infantry Division, 1941–1945.* Baton Rouge: Army and Navy, n.d.

INDEX